Genetic Translation Studies

Bloomsbury Advances in Translation Series

Series Editor:
Jeremy Munday, Centre for Translation Studies, University of Leeds, UK

Bloomsbury Advances in Translation publishes cutting-edge research in the field of translation studies. This field has grown in importance in the modern, globalized world, with international translation between languages a daily occurrence. Research into the practices, processes and theory of translation is essential and this series aims to showcase the best in international academic and professional output.

A full list of titles in the series can be found at:
www.bloomsbury.com/series/bloomsbury-advances-in-translation

Related titles in the series include:

Celebrity Translation in British Theatre
Robert Stock

Collaborative Translation
Edited by Anthony Cordingley and Céline Frigau Manning

Intercultural Crisis Communication
Edited by Federico M. Federici and Christophe Declercq

Retranslation
Sharon Deane-Cox

Sociologies of Poetry Translation
Edited by Jacob Blakesley

Telling the Story of Translation
Judith Woodsworth

The Pragmatic Translator
Massimiliano Morini

Translating in Town
Edited by Lieven D'hulst and Kaisa Koskinen

Translation, Adaptation and Transformation
Edited by Laurence Raw

Translation Solutions for Many Languages
Anthony Pym

What Is Cultural Translation?
Sarah Maitland

Genetic Translation Studies

*Conflict and Collaboration
in Liminal Spaces*

Edited by
Ariadne Nunes, Joana Moura and Marta Pacheco Pinto

BLOOMSBURY ACADEMIC
LONDON • NEW YORK • OXFORD • NEW DELHI • SYDNEY

BLOOMSBURY ACADEMIC
Bloomsbury Publishing Plc
50 Bedford Square, London, WC1B 3DP, UK
1385 Broadway, New York, NY 10018, USA
29 Earlsfort Terrace, Dublin 2, Ireland

BLOOMSBURY, BLOOMSBURY ACADEMIC and the Diana logo
are trademarks of Bloomsbury Publishing Plc

First published in Great Britain 2021
This paperback edition published in 2022

Copyright © Ariadne Nunes, Joana Moura, Marta Pacheco Pinto
and Contributors, 2021

Ariadne Nunes, Joana Moura and Marta Pacheco Pinto have asserted their
right under the Copyright, Designs and Patents Act, 1988, to be identified as Editors of this work.

For legal purposes the Acknowledgements on p. xiii constitute
an extension of this copyright page.

Cover design by Rebecca Heselton
Cover image: Illustration © Abstract vector by freepik (www.freepik.com)

All rights reserved. No part of this publication may be reproduced or transmitted in any form or
by any means, electronic or mechanical, including photocopying, recording, or any information
storage or retrieval system, without prior permission in writing from the publishers.

Bloomsbury Publishing Plc does not have any control over, or responsibility for, any third-party
websites referred to or in this book. All internet addresses given in this book were correct at the
time of going to press. The author and publisher regret any inconvenience caused if addresses
have changed or sites have
ceased to exist, but can accept no responsibility for any such changes.

A catalogue record for this book is available from the British Library.

Library of Congress Cataloging-in-Publication Data
Names: Nunes, Ariadne, editor. | Moura, Joana, editor. | Pinto, Marta Pacheco, editor.
Title: Genetic translation studies : conflict and collaboration in liminal spaces / edited by Ariadne
Nunes, Joana Moura and Marta Pacheco Pinto.
Description: London, UK ; New York, NY : Bloomsbury Academic, [2020] | Series: Bloomsbury
advances in translation | Includes bibliographical references and index. | Identifiers: LCCN
2020023029 (print) | LCCN 2020023030 (ebook) | ISBN 9781350146815 (hardback) | ISBN
9781350146822 (ebook) | ISBN 9781350146839 (epub)
Subjects: LCSH: Translating and interpreting. | Translating and interpreting–Methodology. |
Literature–Translations–History and criticism.
Classification: LCC P306 .G4377 2020 (print) | LCC P306 (ebook) | DDC 418/.02–dc23
LC record available at https://lccn.loc.gov/2020023029
LC ebook record available at https://lccn.loc.gov/2020023030

ISBN:	HB:	978-1-3501-4681-5
	PB:	978-1-3502-1300-5
	ePDF:	978-1-3501-4682-2
	eBook:	978-1-3501-4683-9

Series: Bloomsbury Advances in Translation

Typeset by Integra Software Services Pvt. Ltd.

To find out more about our authors and books visit www.bloomsbury.com
and sign up for our newsletters.

Contents

List of figures and tables	vii
Notes on contributors	ix
Acknowledgements	xiii

1 What is genetic translation studies good for?
   Ariadne Nunes, Joana Moura and Marta Pacheco Pinto — 1

Part 1 Genetic approaches to translation and collaboration

2 Latency, inference, interaction: Notes towards a blurry picture of translation genetics in Portugal *João Dionísio* — 27

3 Unveiling the creative process of collaborative translation: *Chronicle* by Robert Fitzgerald and Saint-John Perse *Esa Christine Hartmann* — 43

4 Czesław Miłosz's genetic dossier in the Polish translations of 'Negro spirituals' *Ewa Kołodziejczyk* — 55

5 The genesis of a compilative translation and its *de facto* source text *Laura Ivaska* — 71

6 Allographic translation, self-translation and alloglottic rewriting: Towards a digital edition of poetry by Pedro Homem de Mello *Elsa Pereira* — 89

Part 2 Translators' stories and testimonies

7 The body in letters: Peter Handke as translator of René Char *Joana Moura* — 109

8 On the bodily dimension of translators and translating *Barbara Ivančić and Alexandra L. Zepter* — 123

9 The translator's view of translation: Analysis of testimonies published in the Portuguese journal *Colóquio Letras* (1980–2000) *Dominique Faria* — 135

10 Mapping context through epitext: Gregory Rabassa's writings and his translations of Lobo Antunes's works *Marisa Mourinha* — 147

Part 3 Translators at work

11 The Coindreau archives: A translator at work *Patrick Hersant* 163
12 Authorship and (self-)translation in academic writing: Towards a genetic approach *Karen Bennett* 179
13 Camilo Castelo Branco, author and translator *Carlota Pimenta* 197
14 Vasconcelos Abreu's *O Panchatantra*: An unpublished and unfinished translation *Marta Pacheco Pinto and Ariadne Nunes* 213
15 Coda 233

Index 235

List of figures and tables

Figures

2.1	Biblioteca Nacional de Portugal, Esp. E 3, 67–67r	33
3.1	Manuscript of Robert Fitzgerald, *Chronicle*, page 1 (1960)	46
6.1	Published allographic translations (Portuguese to French) of Pedro Homem de Mello's poetry	90
6.2	Published allographic translations (Portuguese to English) of Pedro Homem de Mello's poetry	91
6.3	Draft allographic translations (Portuguese to English), later published in *Lusitanian Lyrics* (Hawkins 1941a)	92
6.4	A side-by-side comparison of the manuscript (HTS, Hawkins's letter to Mello), on the left, and the final translation (Hawkins 1941a: 24), on the right, using Juxta collation software	92
6.5	Generic model of the ongoing edition	93
6.6	Pedro Homem de Mello's self-translation and alloglottic rewriting	94
6.7	A side-by-side comparison of the Portuguese and French typescripts of 'Canção à ausente', in BNP, E14, box 9 (folder 2)	95
6.8	A side-by-side comparison of the Portuguese and French typescripts of 'Sonata', in BNP, E14, box 9 (folder 2)	96
6.9	Editorial model of the ongoing project	98
6.10	Document witnesses of the poem 'Canção verde'	99
6.11	Encoded apparatus for line 33 of witness O (French version) and line 34 of witness P (French version), using the location-referenced method	100
6.12	Encoding an allographic translation, within the element <note>	100
6.13	Display of witnesses N, O and P in the VM's interface	101
6.14	Display of an allographic translation (encoded as <note>), in the VM's interface	101
11.1	IMEC, Michel Gresset collection, Maurice-Edgar Coindreau subcollection (hereafter cited as CND), box 3, Translations 1952–57, 'La Maison d'haleine' by William Goyen, typescript, fol. 1	165
11.2	IMEC, CND 3, Translations 1952–57, 'La Maison d'haleine' by William Goyen, manuscript, fol. 1	166

11.3	IMEC, CND 4, Translations 1959–67, 'La Sagesse dans le sang' by Flannery O'Connor, manuscript, fols. 2–3	168
11.4	IMEC, CND 2, Translations 1927–48, 'Des Souris et des hommes' by John Steinbeck, typescript, fol. 2	170
11.5	IMEC, CND 2, Translations 1927–48, 'Des Souris et des hommes' by John Steinbeck, typescript, fol. 1	171
11.6	IMEC, CND 3, Translation 1952–57, 'La Harpe d'herbes' by Truman Capote, typescript, fol. 12	171
11.7	IMEC, CND 2, Translations 1927–48, 'Terre tragique' by Erskine Caldwell, typescript, fol. 202	172
11.8	IMEC, CND 2, Translations 1927–48, 'Un Pauvre type' by Erskine Caldwell, typescript, fol. 55	173
11.9	IMEC, CND 3, Translations 1952–57, 'La Harpe d'herbes' by Truman Capote, typescript, fol. 41	173
11.10	IMEC, CND 5, Translations 1969–78, 'Les Confessions de Nat Turner' by William Styron, typescript, fol. 177	174
13.1	Correction in the upper interlinear space	202
13.2	Analytical difference	203
13.3	Correction made before the beginning of the next writing stage	209
14.1	The title page of Vasconcelos Abreu's *Panchatantra* (volume A)	217
14.2	The title page of the source edition used in volume B	220
14.3	The title page of the source edition used in volume A	222

Tables

2.1	Reconstruction of the composition of *Leal Conselheiro*, chapter 99	31
2.2	D. Duarte, *Leal Conselheiro*, conclusion of chapter 98 and beginning of chapter 99	32
2.3	Transcription of Alfred Austin's 'Now do I know that Love is blind, for I' and Alberto Caeiro's 'Agora que sinto amor'	34
2.4	Passages from the English, French and Portuguese translations of Evgenéa Iaroslavskaïa's text	37
14.1	Volumes A and B: the translation of the Introduction's last sentence	218
14.2	Volumes A and B: A comparison of the handwritten drafts of the Introduction to *Panchatantra*	218
14.3	Sebastião Rodolfo Dalgado's statements on translation	225

Notes on contributors

Karen Bennett lectures in translation and academic writing at the Nova University in Lisbon. She has an MA and PhD in Translation Studies from the University of Lisbon, and researches the translation and transmission of knowledge (among other things) with the Centre for English, Translation and Anglo-Portuguese Studies (CETAPS) and University of Lisbon Centre for English Studies (ULICES/CEAUL). She has published three books, numerous articles and book chapters, and has recently co-edited a special issue of *The Translator* with Rita Queiroz de Barros on the subject of international English and translation.

João Dionísio is Associate Professor at the School of Arts and Humanities, University of Lisbon, and researcher at the Centre of Linguistics, University of Lisbon. He edited several volumes of the critical edition series of Fernando Pessoa's works. At present, he is finishing a book on the role played by translation on the genesis of the literary oeuvre by M. S. Lourenço, a Portuguese modern writer and philosopher.

Dominique Faria lectures at the University of the Azores and is a member of the Centre for Comparative Studies of the University of Lisbon. She is the coordinator of the Department of Languages, Literatures and Cultures, the director of the Master's degree in Translation and the director of the PhD course on Island Literatures and Cultures. She is also the Vice-President of the Portuguese Association of French Studies. Her main research interests include cultural translation, contemporary French and francophone literature and island studies. She has published in journals such as *Équivalences* and *Trans. Revista de Traductologia*, and has recently co-edited *Littérature de langue française à l'épreuve de la traduction en Péninsule Ibérique* (Manuscrit, 2017).

Esa Christine Hartmann (PhD) is Associate Professor of German and French at the University of Strasbourg, and associated member of the research group *Multilingualism, Translation, Creation* of the Institut des textes et manuscrits modernes (ITEM/CNRS, Paris), as well as member of the research group *European Multilingualism* of the laboratory LiLPa at the University of Strasbourg. Her publications in genetic translation studies analyse the collaborative translation process of Saint-John Perse and his translators, and include *Au miroir de la traduction: avant-texte, intratexte, paratexte* (co-edited with Patrick Hersant, Archives Contemporaines, 2019), as well as *Les Manuscrits de Saint-John Perse. Pour une poétique vivante* (L'Harmattan, 2007).

Patrick Hersant is Associate Professor at Paris 8 University, teaching literature and translation studies, and a researcher at the Institut des textes et manuscrits modernes

(ITEM/CNRS, Paris). His current research interests include author–translator collaborations and the genetics of translation, notably through the study of translator's drafts and correspondences. He recently edited *Traduire avec l'auteur* (Sorbonne Université Presses, 2019); *Au miroir de la traduction: avant-texte, intratexte, paratexte* (co-edited with Esa Hartmann, Archives Contemporaines, 2019); and Coleridge, *Kubla Khan* (Presses Universitaires de Bordeaux, 2016). As a translator, he has published French versions of Philip Sidney, R. L. Stevenson, Edward Lear, F. Scott Fitzgerald, Seamus Heaney and Hannah Sullivan.

Barbara Ivančić is Associate Professor at the University of Bologna, teaching German Language and Translation. Her main research interests include the notion of embodiment related to language and translation (*Manuale del traduttore*, Milano: Editrice Bibliografica, 2016) as well as the collaboration between authors and translators ('Dialogue between Translators and Authors. The Example of Claudio Magris', in C. Buffagni, B. Garzelli and S. Zanotti (eds), *The Translator as Author. New Perspectives on Literary Translation*, Münster: Lit Verlag, 2011). She translates literary texts and essays from German and Croatian into Italian. She was awarded the Ladislao Mittner Prize 2018 in Translation Science.

Laura Ivaska is a doctoral candidate at the Department of English at the University of Turku, Finland. She holds an MA in Italian Translation Studies (University of Turku) and an MA in International Studies (University of Washington, USA). Her research interests include indirect translation, the use of several source texts and the intersection of translation studies and textual studies.

Ewa Kołodziejczyk earned her MA in the Polish Studies at the Jagiellonian University in Krakow and in Translation from the Institute of Applied Linguistics at the University of Warsaw. She received her PhD in 2005, and her habilitation in 2016. Her doctoral dissertation on the avant-garde interwar poetry was published as *Czechowicz – Beauty, at Most. His Poetical Outlook against the Background of Literary Modernism* (2006). Her recent book *The American Postwar Years of Czesław Miłosz* (2015) was awarded The Professor Tadeusz Kotarbiński Prize. She works in the Department of Contemporary Literature Documentation.

Joana Moura holds a BA in German/English from King's College London (2008), an MA (2011) and a PhD (2017) in Comparative Literature from SUNY Stony Brook. She is currently an Invited Assistant Professor at the Catholic University in Lisbon where she teaches languages and translation (English/German) and academic writing. She also collaborates in the research project *Moving Bodies: Circulations, Narratives and Archives in Translation* at the Centre for Comparative Studies, University of Lisbon. Her main research interests lie in the fields of translation studies and comparative literature, focusing on fictional representations of translators in literature and film and on genetic translation studies.

Marisa Mourinha holds a BA in Philosophy and a post-graduate degree in Comparative Literature from the School of Arts and Humanities of the University of Lisbon, and is now a doctoral candidate in the Comparative Studies programme at the same institution, with a project on the translations of António Lobo Antunes. She collaborates in the research project *Moving Bodies: Circulations, Narratives and Archives in Translation* at the Centre for Comparative Studies of the University of Lisbon. Her main areas of interest are translation studies, contemporary poetry and film studies.

Ariadne Nunes (PhD in Comparative Studies 2014) is a research fellow at IELT – Institute of Literature and Tradition Studies, Nova University of Lisbon, with a post-doctoral project on Machado de Assis' last novels. She collaborated on the critical edition of *Crónica de D. João I* – part I, by Fernão Lopes (IN-CM, 2017), and co-edited *Relance da Alma Japonesa*, by Wenceslau de Moraes, with Marta Pacheco Pinto (IN-CM, 2015), and *Coração, Cabeça e Estômago*, by Camilo Castelo Branco, with Cristina Sobral (IN-CM, 2019). Her main research interests include textual criticism, medieval literature and Brazilian literature.

Elsa Pereira is a research fellow at the Centre of Linguistics, School of Arts and Humanities, University of Lisbon, working on a genetic–critical edition of poetry by Pedro Homem de Mello (1904–84), funded by the Portuguese Foundation for Science and Technology (FCT/DL 57/2016/CP1443/CT0033). She graduated from the University of Porto, where she completed BA, MA and PhD in Romance Literatures and Cultures. Her main publications include a critical edition of the works of Jorge da Câmara (d. 1649), published by Martin Meidenbauer, and a critical–genetic edition of the works of João Penha (1839–1919), published by CITCEM. Her main research interests are in the area of Portuguese literature, with a main focus on textual studies, scholarly editing and digital humanities.

Carlota Pimenta holds a PhD in Textual Criticism (2017) and an MA in Romance Studies/Portuguese Literature (2009) awarded by the School of Arts and Humanities of the University of Lisbon. She is currently an Invited Assistant Professor at the Catholic University in Lisbon where she teaches Portuguese as a foreign language. She is also a member of the research projects *Critical and Genetic Edition of Camilo Castelo Branco* and *'Os Degraus do Parnaso', by M. S. Lourenço: Edition of the Manuscripts* in the Centre of Linguistics of the University of Lisbon. She co-edited *Novelas do Minho*, by Camilo Castelo Branco, with Ivo Castro (IN-CM, 2017), and collaborated on the critical edition of *Crónica de D. João I* – part I, by Fernão Lopes (IN-CM, 2017). Her main research interests include textual criticism, genetic criticism and Portuguese literature.

Marta Pacheco Pinto (PhD in Translation History, 2013) is a research fellow at the Centre for Comparative Studies, University of Lisbon, with a post-doctoral project that seeks to build an annotated bibliography of published translations from Japanese into Portuguese (1543–2014). As member of the Centre for Comparative Studies, she coordinates two research projects: *Moving Bodies: Circulations, Narratives, and Archives in Translation* and *Texts and Contexts of Portuguese Orientalism – International Congresses of Orientalists (1873–1973)* (PTDC/CPC-CMP/0398/2014). She has published in peer-reviewed journals, such as *Perspectives*, the *Journal of Lusophone Studies*, *mTm* or the *Journal of World Languages*, and has (co-)edited several books. Her research interests range from the history of translation in Portugal in connection with Portuguese Orientalism to genetic translation studies. She also teaches in the international doctoral programme in Comparative Studies at the University of Lisbon.

Alexandra L. Zepter (PhD) teaches Linguistics, German Language and Didactics at the University of Cologne. She received her PhD in Linguistics at Rutgers University (United States) and previously studied Dance and Choreography at Folkwang University under the direction of Pina Bausch. Her main research interests include the connection of language (learning), cognition and the bodily dimension (*Sprache und Körper. Vom Gewinn der Sinnlichkeit für Sprachdidaktik und Sprachtheorie*, Peter Lang, 2013), especially in the context of teaching and learning German in heterogeneous and multilingual classrooms (e.g. *TextBewegung. Sprach- und Bewegungsaufgaben entwickeln, erproben und evaluieren*, together with Kirsten Schindler, Peter Lang, 2017).

Acknowledgements

The editors would like to thank Jeremy Munday, for having encouraged us to collaborate with Bloomsbury in the Advances in Translation series, as well as the anonymous peer reviewers for their invaluable feedback on this volume. A special thanks is also due to the reviewers who kindly accepted to take part in this project by commenting on our contributors' works.

Special thanks are also due to João Ferreira Duarte and João Dionísio for their comments and revision to the volume's Introduction. Last but not least, the editors are grateful to Andrew Wardell and Becky Holland for their editorial support.

1

What is genetic translation studies good for?

Ariadne Nunes
Institute of Literature and Tradition Studies, Nova University of Lisbon
Joana Moura
Catholic University of Portugal/
Centre for Comparative Studies, University of Lisbon
Marta Pacheco Pinto
Centre for Comparative Studies, University of Lisbon

When in one of the founding handbooks to translation studies Gideon Toury discussed Avraham Shlonsky's 1946 Hebrew translation of Hamlet's monologue 'To Be or Not to Be', he set out by claiming that his aim was to provide 'an account of the successive revisions made by one translator while working on one textual segment of considerable independence … to uncover the *constraints* to which that translator subjected himself as he went along and the way he manoeuvred among them' (1995: 193; emphasis in the original). Based on the analysis of those successive revisions and constraints, Toury's objective 'in the tentative reconstruction of a translation process' (1995: 193) was ultimately to determine the 'modernist norms' governing it. Toury did so by building hypotheses based on a deductive comparison of the textual materials stored in the Shlonsky Archive, namely from the collation of a manuscript (the first draft) and a typescript (possibly produced on the basis of a cleaner, interim copy of the manuscript) with autograph revisions by the translator. Toury then went on to complement his analysis with the study of two final *versions*, one which was staged and the published book version. The descriptive translation studies (DTS) scholar sought to reconceive the translation process in a way that bears clear affinities with the reconstruction of the writing process pursued by geneticists.

The reading strategy and methodological approach followed by Toury show that genetic criticism and translation studies have more in common than one would expect at first, with genetic criticism occupying notwithstanding a shadowy presence in translation research. The aim of this book is to give visibility to this encounter by making the case for genetic translation studies (GTS). This chapter charts GTS as a relational concept that seeks to go beyond the textual surface level by defying in particular the commonly accepted notions of translation as a stable, finished text and the translator as a surrogate author.

An unexpected intersection? The genetic dossier of translation(s) and translator(s)

When outlining the compositional history of the Hebrew translation of Hamlet's monologue, Toury was careful to describe the different stages of his archaeological method, which started off with the reordering and classification of the materials collected from archival research. Although Toury does not name this procedure, in genetic criticism this reordering of textual evidence corresponds to the 'genetic dossier' working phase (Grésillon 1994: 242). As Toury's case study illustrates and as reinforced by the chapters in this volume, by gathering data for empirical research, the genetic dossier can help the translation studies researcher disclose the intricacies of the translator's – and other translational agents' – working method.

Typically, a genetic dossier includes the writer's *avant-textes*, either endogenetic (drafts, manuscripts, typescripts, proofs) or exogenetic (personal papers, private library that may offer handwritten marginalia for study, letters, interviews, for instance, containing verbal data that, though external to the text, was appropriated to become part of it [e.g. de Biasi 1996: 43–4]).[1] The dossier is diachronically organized in order to show the evolving phases of the writing process, of which the published text may be considered just a phase. This process may continue even after the publication of the text with its reeditions, (re)translations and different forms of reception (the so-called *post-textes*)[2] (Cordingley and Montini 2015: 2) that can also be included in the genetic dossier, although this has not been the focus of genetic criticism.

In fact, with reference to an author's genetic dossier, Pierre-Marc de Biasi contends that this post-textual phase has nothing to do with genetic criticism and the genetic perspective, rather pertaining to 'the criticism of the reception and history of the book' (1996: 42). The same issue has been addressed by other scholars, including Elsa Pereira in the present volume, who considers otherwise. Faced with a wide range of interlinguistic materials, from allographic translations to self-translations and authorial witnesses, Pereira suggests developing an appropriate editorial design that allows for assembling these materials together in a digital archive. One of the premises on which the present book capitalizes is precisely that post-textual documentation can belong to the exogenesis, as seems to be implied in Dirk Van Hulle's mapping of macro- and microgenesis (2016: 47 and 49).

In this vein, the very 'criticism of the reception and history of the book' becomes a key component of any translator's or translation's genetic dossier. This genetic dossier necessarily includes materials from the translator's workshop ranging from translator's drafts, manuscripts or corrected proofs (see Dionísio, Hartmann, Kołodziejczyk, Ivaska, Pereira, Hersant, Pimenta, Pinto and Nunes in this volume) to a translator's memoir, (auto)biography or interviews (see Ivančić and Zepter, Faria and Mourinha), any reviews of the text to be translated that may have been collected or used by the translator, or any translations in another language. The latter constitute the afterlives of a text beyond its first printing, each possibly contributing to renewed textual variation. Indeed, the genetic dossier of the source text may also be incorporated into the genetic dossier of translation(s). Since editors, revisers of literary translations and publishing houses all have a say in the production of translations by conforming them to their own marketing strategies, editor's and reviser's drafts, as well as publisher's records and publishing contracts, are all part of the genetic translation dossier.

Therefore, in GTS, *post-textes* relating to both the source text(s) and the translation may have to do with genetic criticism. While Anthony Cordingley and Céline Frigau Manning in reasserting the emergence of GTS add that '[t]he methods of textual genetics ... generally accoun[t] for collaboration when it becomes manifest (material) in the genesis of a translation' (2017: 11), *post-textes* can unveil non-manifest collaborative or conflictual networks and other non-manifest relations (such as intertextuality)[3] that may have contributed to fashioning the textual object; in such cases the *post-textes* pertain to the genetic perspective.

What is more, an author can always go back to the work demised and hone it on the basis of its translation. Samuel Beckett is a well-known example of this retrospective practice; Dirk Van Hulle (2015: 46–8) quotes his *Happy Days/Oh les beaux jours* to illustrate a process in which the (French) translation participates in the remaking of the (English) genesis. Moreover, an author can call for a new translation. A striking example of this is the English retranslation of Orhan Pamuk's *The Black Book*. As Eker Roditakis (2018) has demonstrated, its first translation came out in 1994 by the hand of Güneli Gün and was followed by a retranslation in 2006 by Maureen Freely. It was Pamuk himself who commissioned Freely for the task in view of the negative criticism and harsh reviews Gün's translation had received both in the United Kingdom and the United States. The scholar concludes that 'the decision for retranslation was not taken *entirely* due to target system dynamics, but interference from the source system' (2018; emphasis in the original) – or, if you will, interference from the genesis.

Back in 1995 Toury acted as a geneticist when surveying what he termed 'the translator's "laboratory"', in which he included materials relating only to the translator's workshop – in other words, the translator's dossier. He further stated that 'it is not too difficult to tease apart the layers comprising each version and put them in their correct order, which is a *precondition* for any justification of observations in terms of a reconstructed translation process' (1995: 196; emphasis added). Genetic criticism has from the outset relied on this same precondition and can help both translation practitioners and researchers go beyond things taken for granted. Similarly, the chapters gathered in this volume show that the genetic dossier is the product of an empirical-inquisitive methodology central to GTS, for it helps organize and set the corpus for analysis.

At the crossroads of translation studies and genetic criticism

In 2015, Anthony Cordingley and Chiara Montini announced a genetic turn in translation studies with their special issue of *Linguistica Antverpiensia*. In their introduction, they specifically coined this new field of research located at the intersection between translation studies and genetic criticism as 'genetic translation studies'. Its object, these authors claim, 'is the textual evidence of the activity of translation rather than the translating subject', thus focusing on the practices of the 'working translator and the evolution, or genesis, of the translated text by studying translators' manuscripts, drafts and other working documents' (2015: 1).

The new field promotes an understanding of the text as a 'work in progress' rather than a 'finished work' (Cordingley and Montini 2015: 3), that is, as a process rather than a product. Serenella Zanotti and Rosa Maria Bollettieri make this point in their definition of genetic criticism: 'Differently from textual criticism, manuscript genetics does not aim to reconstruct one particular state of the text, but rather the process by which the text came into being' (2015: 128). GTS, as a hybrid between descriptive translation studies and genetic criticism, is, we add, ultimately about piecing together a response to the 'how' question (how a text was translated) and searching for transparency in deconstructing agency in authorial or translatorial writing. In this twofold movement, the translating subject eventually crops up as an object of research within GTS, hence, we argue, becomes inextricable from it.

Using works by James Joyce and Samuel Beckett, Van Hulle has identified five contact zones between translation studies and genetic criticism, with which the contributors to this volume engage: 'genesis as part of translation; translation of the genesis; genesis of the translation; translation as part of the genesis; and finally, the genesis of the untranslatable' (2015: 40). For Van Hulle, the purpose of this productive interaction, which he explores in terms of binary combinations, is to 'enhance a form of textual awareness' (2015: 40) that is pragmatically beneficial for practitioners in translation and genetic criticism alike. On the one hand, it can help translators find solutions for their translation task by going back to the genesis (genesis as part of translation) or, conversely, it is the translation that can lead geneticists to identify and possibly better understand questions pertaining to the complex genesis of the source text (translation of the genesis). On the other, unfolding the complex genesis of the translation and chronologically arranging the order of the extant versions can compel the examination of the genetic dossier of the source text (genesis of the translation), just as self-translators can rewrite the genesis on the basis of their own translations (translation as part of the genesis).

Van Hulle's last example, which is illustrated in connection with Beckett's self-proclaimed untranslatability of *Worstward Ho* (1983), brings us back to our earlier discussion of de Biasi's claim that the post-textual phase does not concern genetic criticism. For according to Van Hulle, GTS rests upon reconsidering how translation complicates the seemingly stable difference between endogenesis and epigenesis in genetic criticism by putting it in terms of a difference 'not in kind but in degree':

> Although the 'endogenesis' is supposed to take place 'inside' the private sphere of the author's workspace, it is never entirely immune to outside elements, such as 'exogenetic' sources or suggestions by partners, friends, editors, correctors and publishers. (2015: 50)

The focus on degree rather than on kind to explain the difference between these two levels of analysis shows that 'the nexus between translation and genesis turns out to be a bidirectional interaction' (Van Hulle 2015: 51) rather than 'a unidirectional link between two fields of research (genetic criticism applied to translation)' (2015: 40).

These fields, genetic criticism and translation studies, emerged as disciplines in their own right in the 1970s. In spite of having their roots in a text-based scholarship, they do not often dialogue with each other. Perhaps this liminal dialogue lies in the fact that, unlike translation studies scholars (and translators themselves) who move across linguistic and cultural boundaries, geneticists have tended until recently to operate within one language and culture system.

Indeed, to state the obvious, genetic criticism and translation studies deal with questions of *auctoritas*, authority and authorship, albeit the difference in status that each has traditionally ascribed to the figures of author and translator, respectively, and consequently to the writing production of each of them. Perhaps less evidently, the act itself of transcribing a text, an early stage of genetic criticism, can be construed as a mode of translation (Robinson 2013: 121). Although Peter Robinson does recognize interpretation as integral to both transcription and translation, other views posit the translation metaphor as anchored in an age-old conception of translation as just imitation, copy or reproduction of the original *auctoritas*, with no room for creativity, a concern raised in Pimenta's chapter in this volume.

The history of literary translation is no way short of examples supporting the antithetical view between author and translator. Arguments privileging untranslatability often evoke an author's or a work's unmatched aura of originality and creativity. Literalness, for instance, is perhaps the oldest law of translation, having been prevalent during the Renaissance (Hermans 1997) or the Romantic period in respect for the authorial genius. When the first Bible translations into vernacular languages emerged, they were seen with discomfort and suspicion by the religious authorities, for profaning the sacred word. In the same vein, when Erasmus published the first edition of the Greek New Testament, which was accompanied by a Latin translation, the variants it incorporated in relation to the Vulgate 'caused much furor' (Hendel 2015: 11). The edition questioned the authority of the biblical text, allowing anyone – and not just the Church – to interpret the Scriptures. Theologians were, however, quick to contest that 'philological knowledge was unnecessary, since God has preserved the original texts and translations intact' (Hendel 2015: 13). Yet, no original writing of the New Testament has survived the two-thousand-year span of time until Erasmus's edition, so determining its archetypal text was a way of making it known, thereby justifying Erasmus's edition.[4]

Textual scholarship, whose traditional goal has been to restore the absent authorial text, was not indifferent to the Romantic prizing of originality. The Romantic overvalue of authorship drove scholars to the concern over preserving authorial documentation as an object of interest, either under the material form of personal collections and libraries or under the textual form of critical editions. By contrast, when in the 1960s and 1970s structuralist theories claimed the study of the text proper, disparaging the author or authorial intention, genetic criticism rose as a method that places the focus on the writer instead of the author, the writing (process) instead of the text (product) (de Biasi 2011: 11). In this vein, the work developed by Louis Hay and his team of German and French scholars on the Heine's manuscripts acquired by the

French National Library in 1966 was pioneer in adopting a genetic approach to texts (Deppman, Ferrer and Groden 2004: 7).

Studying manuscripts and archival material has supported a textual analysis that leaves aside context or authorial considerations. Since the genetic critical approach to manuscripts does not intend to discover their original meaning – that is, the authorial intention – but instead to underscore the creative writing process and its historicity, it challenges the idea of authorial genius and of writing as the result of a divine-like inspiration. Epiphanic myths as that of the modernist poet Fernando Pessoa's 'triumphal day', the day when his heteronyms spontaneously came to life (8 March 1914),[5] are denied by the genetic dossier, which displays the process of literary creation as an act of continuous labour, revision and rewriting (Castro 1990: 92–3).

Embodied in particular by the French school epitomized by Hay (1979), Grésillon (1994) and de Biasi (2011), genetic criticism has brought in the need to consider the different versions of a text, hence defying the notion of *ne varietur* and the teleological stability of sense. Similarly, translation studies have shown that translations are not inferior to, or second-order representations of, the so-called original, and have struggled to free its agents from this gloomy picture. It is as if we were before a symmetrical picture: whereas genetic critics have been interested in prizing what comes before the published text, translation studies scholars have been more focused on prizing what comes after.[6]

The underlying difference in symbolic capital setting original and translation apart has prompted criticism of the translator's invisibility, as has been most famously posited by Lawrence Venuti. In *The Translator's Invisibility*, he contends that, historically, the production and reception of translations, especially in anglophone cultures, have been plagued by the age-old illusion that a translation should be as fluent and transparent as possible when it reaches the receiving language and culture. As Venuti notes, translation practice and theory in the West have accordingly cultivated the ethos that 'the translation is not in fact a translation, but the original' (1995: 1). Venuti's call to pay attention to the translator figure and to escape what he designates the historically dominant regime of fluency when evaluating and producing translations brings in the need to study the translator's agency while considering the other agents that take part in the process of translation. The focus is then not only on translation as product but also as *process*.

The emphasis on agency was, and continues to be, particularly important for translation studies and has culminated in Andrew Chesterman's advocacy for the subfield of translator studies (2009: 13). The scholar anchors his theory in translation sociology for it having paved the way for the emergence of a translational agent-centred model of studies. Chesterman subdivides translation sociology into the sociology of translations, the sociology of translators and the sociology of translating, with genetic approaches having a more visible contribution to the last two branches. A genetic perspective may help map out translator's networks and disclose a translator's discourse, reflection and attitudes towards his or her work, all the while contributing to 'the study of the phases of the translation event: translation practices and working procedures, quality control procedures and the revision process, co-operation in team translation, multiple drafting, relations with other agents including the client, and the like' (Chesterman 2009: 17). This translator-oriented standpoint has led other prominent scholars to develop methodologies that investigate the intricacies of the translator's creative process by incorporating the translator's biography in the study of translation, the so-called microhistories of translation and translators (e.g. Adamo 2006; Munday 2014; Wakabayashi 2018).

Focusing on an archive-based approach to translation and its relevance to an agent-oriented history of translation, Jeremy Munday, among others, has emphasized the need to study translators' drafts as records of their creativity and to privilege translators' personal papers, including correspondence and other relevant documentation, as part of 'a microhistory of translation and translators' (2014).[7] The 'microhistory' concept combines a translator- and process-oriented approach to translation that inevitably summons the genetic perspective and has the potential to revise translation historiography by bringing to the fore unacknowledged or marginalized actors and correcting 'biases in the selection and presentation of material, in the gaps in our knowledge and in forms of overtly mediated testimonies' (Munday 2014: 77). Censorship translation studies, which constitute Munday's point of departure in his plea for microhistories of translation, are yet another example of how genetic criticism has infused into translation studies and translation history in particular. Not only do they delve into *avant-* or *post-textes*, but they always involve the collection and analysis of censorship files, which include censors' reports, the identification of problematic content submitted for evaluation, and examination of censors' advice and textual intervention (cuts or additions). This methodological procedure pertains to genetic criticism.

As descriptive-oriented scholarships, both genetic criticism and translation studies tend to rely on comparison and inference as important stages of the (re)constructive process. Sergio Romanelli has clearly stated this when he claimed that '[b]oth make use of an inductive research methodology' (2015: 90). Beyond methodological affinities, both resort to lexicon and metaphors whose overlap becomes more salient when intersecting both fields. The metaphors and figurative language more commonly used by the contributors in this volume can be mapped into five main categories: (a) metaphors of genesis, such as 'birth', 'gestation' (of the translation process) and 'generation' (Hartmann), (b) metaphors of materiality, such as 'amendments' (Kołodziejczyk; Ivaska; Pimenta), 'embodiment' (Moura; Ivančić and Zepter), 'mark(s)' (Bennett) or 'materialize' and 'incorporate' (Kołodziejczyk; Moura; Bennett); (c) metaphors evoking the idea of detective work, such as 'clue(s)' (Ivaska; Pinto and Nunes), 'trace' or 'tracing' (Dionísio; Hartmann; Ivaska; Pereira; Moura; Faria; Hersant; Bennett; Pimenta), 'witness(es)' (Dionísio; Kołodziejczyk; Pereira; Hersant; Pimenta), 'investigating' (Moura; Bennett); (d) metaphors referring to trustworthiness, such as 'testimony' (Faria; Mourinha; Pinto and Nunes); (e) figurative language evoking the notions of 'dialogue' (Hartmann; Pereira; Moura; Pinto and Nunes), 'intimacy' (Moura), 'coulisse(s)' (Hartmann) and 'collaboration' (Dionísio; Hartmann; Ivaska; Pereira; Moura; Faria; Mourinha; Bennett). These metaphors and phrases highlight the interdisciplinary nature of a fresh field of inquiry that is still creating its own lexicon and filling in existing gaps. As Susantha Goonatilake recalled back in the 1990s, metaphors 'cross disciplinary boundaries', 'provide new insights and act as probes' (1998: 250).

Our volume refines a lexical field that is common to researchers who are reaching out either to genetic criticism in their research on translation and translators or to translation studies in their genetic criticism studies. In this sense, GTS already has its own object of study, but is making its way in terms of stabilizing research methods, lexicon or metalanguage.

In spite of sharing the same epistemological paradigms, genetic scholars have been, in Cordingley and Montini's words, 'slow to adapt their methodology to the translated text', only considering that translators working documents were 'worthy objects of study' when the translator 'had acquired independent "symbolic power" in the cultural field' (2015: 6). Such an acquisition of symbolic power applies more visibly to authors who are translators themselves, either of the works of others (take, for example, Portuguese writers Fernando Pessoa and José Saramago, or Joan Maragall, Gertrude Stein, Bernard Shaw and Murakami Haruki) or of their own works, as in self-translation (Oscar Wilde, Samuel Beckett, Vladimir Nabokov, Peter Handke are among the most well known). In these cases of symbolic power, or *auctoritas*, translators more often than not have their names nominatively identified on book covers, seemingly teaming up as coauthors.

As a matter of fact, and as pointed out by Karen Bennett herein, self-translation was one of the starting points for the rise of genetic criticism's interest in translation scholarship, for, let us not forget, as Julio-César Santoyo rightly emphasizes, 'from the point of view of the *auctoritas* (auctor-itas), the self-translated text *is* a second original' (2013: 28; emphasis in the original). Furthermore, translators themselves are reticent to preserve material traces of their work, a fact that adds to the 'slowness' of the genetic movement towards translation studies (Hersant 2017: 98).

Whereas genetic critics have, albeit reluctantly, found support in translation studies to make sense of a different kind of textual object, translation scholars have tended to overlook the explicit engagement with genetic scholarship. 'Genetic criticism' has been absent as a keyword, 'translation research term' (Pym 2011), theoretical framework or research methodology, future challenge, or even index subject from the main books of reference in DTS, in particular dictionaries (e.g. Shuttleworth and Cowie 1997) and handbooks (e.g. Gambier and van Doorslaer 2010; Millán and Bartrina 2013; D'hulst and Gambier 2018). Quite significantly, the *Routledge Encyclopedia of Translation Studies* has just released its third edition (in October 2019), and it includes for the first time an entry on 'genetic criticism' by the hand of Anthony Cordingley. The winds of paradigm shift are blowing.

Until recently most publications on the new field of GTS have, however, departed from genetic criticism, which seems to have been more eager to dialogue with translation studies than the other way around. At least three journals on textual scholarship have published thematic issues on translation: in 2011, Brazilian scholars Claudia Amigo Pina and Mônica Gama co-edited an issue of the Portuguese-language journal *Manuscrítica. Revista de Crítica Genética* with a special section on translation; in 2012, Dirk Van Hulle, Wout Dillen and Caroline Macé co-edited *Text beyond Borders: Multilingualism and Textual Scholarship* in *Variants* (the official journal of the European Society for Textual Scholarship); and in 2014, Fabienne Durant-Bogaert was responsible for the thirty-eighth issue of the journal *GENESIS*.

Revue internationale de critique génétique on *Traduire*. Bilingual writers and self-translators stand out as the main focus of study by GTS[8] and research groups such as the Institut des textes et manuscrits modernes in Paris (ITEM), the Voice in Translation project at the University of Oslo, or the Núcleo de Estudo de Processos Criativos at Universidade Federal de Santa Catarina, in Brazil, have certainly played an important role in shaping this field. The present volume joins this broader move and makes translation studies get out of their comfort zone and dialogue with textual scholarship.

Conflict and collaboration in liminal spaces

The idea for this book arose from the international conference *Unexpected Intersections: Translation Studies and Genetic Criticism*, which was held in Lisbon in 2017 under the aegis of the Centre for Comparative Studies of the University of Lisbon and within the activities of its research project *MOV. Moving Bodies: Circulations, Narratives and Archives in Translation*. The book presents itself as a more mature forum for discussing what Alexandra Lopes has called the 'liminal space of translation … the text outside/inside the text which discusses the text' (2012: 130), that is to say, a liminal space of creation whose materiality lies in the texts produced by literary agents – authors, translators, revisers, editors, publishers, and so on.

The concept of 'liminal spaces' is employed in our book's subtitle in a twofold sense that yet converges into the unacknowledged importance of genetic criticism for literary translation studies. It brings in the idea of a discursive space in-between disciplines, of a passing through genetic criticism to explore translational research questions. Furthermore, the 'liminal space' metaphor allows us to foreground the materiality of texts as exposed in the traces left behind by the agents responsible for creating a translation. The study of *avant-textes*, epitexts and peritexts, usually referred to as liminal spaces for lying outside the main body of text and producing meanings that can result from multiple agencies apart from the author's and the translator's, has been considered ancillary to the study of the stable text. Our claim is that both the 'inside' (translation proper) and the 'outside' (*avant-* and *post-textes*) benefit from being studied on a par and on a complementary basis; together they create a new space of inquiry, which constitutes our locus of analysis.

As this volume makes the case for, GTS is particularly operative in providing access to the backstage of literary production by unlocking processes of authorial/translatorial interaction, which can either be of conflict or collaboration (or both), not only between author and translator and between multi-translators (online translation communities have been playing an important role on this matter),[9] but also of collaboration between author, editor and translator, translator and reviser, translator and proofreader, translator and reader and so on.

Beckett can once again be taken as a quick example here. American translator Richard Seaver, who rendered into English 'La Fin', anecdotally tells of Beckett's collaboration in his translation of this short story. After Seaver mailed Beckett the first draft of his translation, they agreed to meet in a bar to go over it together:

Beckett studies first the English, then the French, then back and forth another time … shaking his head. My heart, to coin a phrase, sank. Clearly my rendition was inadequate. But I was wrong; it was the *original* that displeased him. 'You can't translate that', he said, referring to a passage further along, 'it makes no sense.' … On we went, phrase by phrase, Beckett praising my translation as a prelude to shaping it to what he really wanted, reworking here a word, there an entire sentence, chipping away, tightening, shortening, always finding not only *le mot juste* but the phrase *juste* as well, exchanging the ordinary for the poetic, until the prose sang. (Seaver 2006: 105; emphases in the original)

Seaver draws the picture of a peculiar collaborative effort in which the author finds himself in conflict with his own original writing once he is confronted with his text in a different idiom. Therefore, going back to the genesis – that is, the source text of the translation – can lead to a productive conflict in the collaborative creation of a translation, and even ultimately challenge the status of source text by turning it into an unfinished text.

It is important to note that academic publications dealing with collaborative translation have been on the rise, in which textual genetics is shown to be an effective reading strategy to expose collaboration in translation. Cordingley and Manning's collection on *Collaborative Translation: From the Renaissance to the Digital Age* (2017) is one fine example thereof. In this regard, Munday emphasizes the relevance of collecting and analysing '[m]ultiple drafts, often with handwritten corrections at different stages of production, and related correspondence between translator, author and editor' to clarify their 'decisions and their motivation at different stages and shed light on cognitive translation processes at work' (2014: 72). Joanna Trzeciak Huss, in her entry on 'Collaborative Translation' to *The Routledge Handbook of Literary Translation*, convincingly argues that GTS can secure the sociological link between studies of collaborative translation and literature:

Studies of collaborative translation need to find ways for sociological analysis to make contact with literary analysis. Perhaps this will be accomplished through hybridisation of existing theories, such as actor-network theory with Skopostheorie, or genetic translation studies (Cordingley and Montini 2015) with generative criticism (Baker 1986), such that studying the genesis of literary translations can help pull the fig leaf off of the printed page to reveal the choices that give rise to the aesthetic contours of the text. (2018: 461)

Referring to GTS rather as a theory, Huss corroborates that collaborative translation, literary translation and subsequently literary history are the areas in which it can have a more valuable contribution.

Edited by Jansen and Wegener, the two-volume *Authorial and Editorial Voices in Translation* (2013) was pioneer in drawing attention to the role of intervening subjects that are usually rendered invisible in the translation process, namely editors, literary revisers and publishing houses. We hasten to note that literary revisers, copy editors and typesetters as well tend to be the poor relation of the literary publishing market, but equally partake in the translator's working context and can shape, to different extents, the final textual product.

Under the unifying concept of 'multiple translatorship', the recently published *Textual and Contextual Voices of Translation* (2017) carries on the work initiated in the previous volumes and resets translation as an inherently multiple voiced activity in its genesis, thus giving visibility to agencies other than the translator that are implied in the translation event and have the power to comment on or influence a translation. This book goes a step further by including readers themselves as agents who shape the translation process. It additionally highlights, on the one hand, the role of literary critics in fashioning a text's reception, hence acting as literary and 'translational norms' gatekeepers who can constrain, for instance, retranslations (as in fact the Pamuk example above illustrates) and republishings at large, and, on the other, the relevance of '[i]nterpretative communities (Fish 1980) and readers' individual characteristics, social backgrounds, and cultural and literary repertoires' (Alvstad et al. 2017: 9). The mention to translational norms cannot go unnoticed, in that GTS may be the key to bridge the gap between praxis (performance) and cognition (competence) (e.g. Sapiro 2014: 91). The translator's or translation's genetic dossier is one of the means of accessing the translator's workshop and bridging that gap, a point that Romanelli has made when emphasizing the need to 'understand the translation process from within' (2015: 102).

On this issue of 'understanding from within', a writer's bilingualism or polyglotism opens suspicion as to his or her writing praxis. Self-translation, indirect translation, even pseudo-translation or pseudo-original, are all (re)writing processes that have shaped literary history worldwide and in which GTS can have a say, either in helping to trace these textual phenomena, or in identifying the voices, hands and collaborative relationships that are often elided in these processes.

As pointed out, self-translation has been increasingly concentrating the attention of translation studies scholars (e.g. Hokenson and Munson 2006; Cordingley 2013) and is herein addressed by Elsa Pereira in the case of a Portuguese contemporary poet–translator and by Karen Bennett in relation to academic writing practices. Among other sources, both rely on Rainier Grutman, who argues that working manuscripts allow in such cases to 'better assess the exact nature of the role played by the author of the original, to better grasp the meaning(s) upon which the transfer has taken place and to reestablish the order of the writing of the versions in the different languages' (2016: 128).

As early as 2008 Van Hulle had lifted the veil on this much desired intersection between self-translation and genetic criticism in his *Manuscript Genetics: Joyce's Know-how, Beckett's Nohow*. The role of the digital should not be downplayed in this intersection, as supported by the Samuel Beckett Digital Manuscript Project.[10] Directed by Van Hulle and Mark Nixon, this project reunites digitally the manuscripts of Beckett's works, bringing together digital facsimiles of documents, adding transcriptions of Beckett's manuscripts and allowing for the comparison of bilingual and genetic versions, as well as for the analysis of the textual genesis of his works. As a product of globalization and scientific policies towards research data provision, the digital archive provides ready access to textual materials, paving the way for all-out research opportunities, which will undoubtedly dictate the future of GTS.

Along with self-translation, indirect translation has also been garnering recent scholarly interest, benefitting from GTS particularly in its search for the genesis and hidden ancillary instruments to the translation process, and has furthermore stimulated researchers to look into translators' archives in the search for clues about this usually covert practice (e.g. Ivaska and Paloposki 2017). Alexandra Assis Rosa, Hanna Pięta and Rita Bueno Maia welcome the opening up of genetic criticism to the translated text and go as far as to claim that the study of indirect translation 'is probably the area, within TS, more closely linked with the traditional practices of close reading as literary criticism or the Spanish *filología* or the renewed area of genetic criticism' (2017: 125). Laura Ivaska's chapter in the present volume is quite revealing in addressing the advantages of the genetic dossier to identify the source text of an indirect translation that occasionally resorts to direct translation.

The often-quoted *Thousand and One Nights*, which has been a source for countless indirect translations at least in the Western world since Galland's famous translation (1704–11), has likewise offered itself as a terrain for cross-examining annotated manuscripts, close reading and extratextual materials, specifically diaries and documents resulting from archival research, some actually providing access to unmaterial, non-existent *avant-textes*. This is, for example, the subject matter of *Marvellous Thieves. Secret Authors of the Arabian Nights* (2017). In seeking to expose unacknowledged collaborative networks at the genesis of a French and a handful of English-language translations of the Arabic collection, Paulo Horta's aim is to 'uncover the storytellers, the treasure hunters, the booksellers, the translators, the poets, and the local linguists who made their own contributions to the creation of this most famous of story collections' (2017: 3). Throughout the essay the scholar borrows methodological approaches and discussions from genetic criticism without claiming to do so. We cannot help mentioning Horta's hypothesis that the orphan tales inhabiting Galland's translation were told to him by a Syrian traveller and storyteller at the service of another French countryman: 'They [the orphan tales] did not require translation. Diyab could narrate his stories in French, and Galland was able to record them in this language' (Horta 2017: 29). In this sense, and even if the orphan tales were a creation of Galland himself, they can be equated with pseudo-translation. Archival research has been shown time and again to play a crucial role in identifying 'pseudo' textual phenomena, either pseudo-translations or pseudo-originals.

Pseudo-translation has by far been given more attention in translation scholarship in comparison to pseudo-originality.[11] Perhaps this is so because the former kind of textual manifestation has visibly contributed to the progress of literary history – from Montesquieu's *Lettres persanes* (1721) to MacPherson's *Ossian* (1761), or the self-help books Berthe Dangennes published throughout the 1910s as French translations of recently discovered Japanese manuscripts under the fictitious authorship of philosopher Yoritomo Tashi, not to mention detective or crime fiction that developed as a genre across several European literatures via pseudo-translation. More obviously, pseudo-translation is a text that seeks to function and be accepted as a translation, while a pseudo-original seeks to go unnoticed as a translation, and it goes without saying that the frontier between pseudo-originality and plagiarism is very dim. GTS makes these textual phenomena *go noticed* and helps destabilize or complexify these categories.

As succinctly shown, and as the chapters in this volume reinforce, GTS has a promising future, all the more now with the growing importance of archives and libraries as sites of material and cultural memory, as well as with technological progress. The tendency to preserve all the materials involved in the production of a given cultural artefact – be it a book, a play, a song, a film, an exhibition – has not only enriched archives but also made their contents more and more attractive for study. Although genetic criticism has been particularly fruitful in the field of literary translation, research on other areas of translatorial activity that rely on successful creative strategies, such as audiovisual translation, may also benefit from it.

This concern with applying genetic criticism to other media, which tend to be multi-actor and involve multi-stage production, has been illustrated by Zanotti (2014). She provides a 'hands-on' genetic approach to the Italian dubbing process of the American film *Young Frankenstein* (1974) by analysing typescripts of the dialogue adapter and identifying the different types of intervention by the dubbing director that resulted in extensive rewriting of the script during the recording phase. Another significant move in this direction has also been made by Luis Pérez-González (2017: 30–1), who explicitly names genetic criticism as a new methodology in the study of amateur subtitling agency. The chapters in this volume do not provide any case study in audiovisual translation, yet the research questions posed and methodologies followed herein may be easily adjusted not only to audiovisual translation but also to intersemiotic genres in translation, such as children's literature, comics, manga or graphic novels.

Technological advancements, and with them the digital turn, have made accessible new objects of study and innovated the ways in which these new objects may be handled. The increasing digitization projects of authors' and translators' archives and their provision on the World Wide Web have certainly revolutionized researchers' access to information. The potentialities of the hypertext have expanded the formats for research organization or presentation, such as the side-by-side display of multiple texts, translated and non-translated, thus making it possible to virtually recreate a writer's writing process. Whereas in this book Joana Moura makes use of the documentation stored in an author's digital archive, that of Peter Handke,[12] Elsa Pereira addresses more straightforwardly the advantages of digitally editing translations.

The current age of digital reproduction offers endless possibilities of 'computerized dematerialization' (Jenny 2000: 212) of archival documentation. Let us not forget that the perishable condition of paper may result in the 'imminent destruction' (2000: 212) of manuscripts, typescripts and all the other material in the archive. In this sense, Laurent Jenny further underlines what seems to be an anecdotal contribution of technology to subvert 'the opposition between the original [the traditional object of study of genetic criticism] and the copy, between the materiality and the immateriality of the archive' (2000: 212–13); in other words, technology itself reproduces the object of study and turns it into another copy. Yet, this reproductive structure does not supersede the need of direct observation when carrying out the bibliographic or codicological description or edition of a manuscript or printed (ancient) books.

Certainly gone are the days when the print medium was exclusive for the production, circulation and reception of literature. Digital editions, on their part, are simultaneously text-centric and document-centric (Rebhein and Gabler 2013: 4); this is a vantage point for editing self-translations in which all the existing versions/witnesses may be relevant to both the establishment of the critical text and the analysis of the writing process. Additionally, with reference to genetic editions, the digital environment enables the reader to see all the layers of the text under construction, 'from blank page to fully written text' (Robinson 2013: 110). On this matter, it would be a challenge for the editor whether or not to include materials pertaining to the epigenesis, translations in particular, in the genetic dossier. Via the digital, the editor can also add and interrelate annotations and commentaries to the documents. For instance, by identifying intertextual relationships and cross-referencing them with the author's literary production, the hypertextual condition of a digital archive enables 'map[ping] the complex relationship between writing and reading' (Sichani 2015: 15). Though complex, the digital medium responds easily to readers' or the editor's requests in that editions can be updated on demand. These potentialities confirm Gabler's argument that 'the editing of manuscripts ... belongs exclusively in the digital medium, as it can only there be exercised comprehensively' (2010: 52; see also Sichani 2015: 3). The more sophisticated level on which technology may improve editions is by promoting collaborative editions, where the users of the digital archives or editions may not only read and compare transcriptions, documents or editions but also actively intervene in their display. The *Book of Disquiet* digital archive[13] is a good illustration thereof, in that users can create virtual editions of the *Book*, which was left unfinished by the poet Fernando Pessoa.

On this volume

Genetic Translation Studies: Conflict and Collaboration in Liminal Spaces is divided into three parts: 'Genetic Approaches to Translation and Collaboration', 'Translators' Stories and Testimonies' and 'Translators at Work'.

The opening part of the volume begins with a chapter written from the perspective of a textual scholar based in Portugal. João Dionísio enquires into the existence of the field of GTS in Portugal through the conceptual lens of 'latency', 'inference' and 'interaction'. Dionísio acknowledges overlaps of interest between genetic criticism and translation studies, notwithstanding what he calls 'the [present] lack of a self-aware interpretive community that mostly accounts for the latency of genetic translation studies in Portugal'. To challenge the boundaries of genetic criticism and illustrate those overlaps, Dionísio provocatively examines three disparate examples. He first discusses a late medieval text on translation by reigning King Duarte, this being in the volume the only example of a pre-nineteenth-century testimony, then moves on to interrogate the influence of translation in the writing production of Portuguese modernist poet Fernando Pessoa. As Dionísio himself states, these examples frame translation as part of the genesis, whereas his last example, that of the Portuguese translation of the autobiographical account by the Russian anarchist Evgenéa Iaroslavskaïa, frames the genesis as part of translation. This variety of materials allows Dionísio to look at ethical issues and other constraints editors face when dealing with translations, and to ultimately argue for a model of collaboration based on 'a balanced consideration of individual agency and contextual voices'.

Esa Christine Hartmann contributes to GTS by applying the concept of 'closelaboration' to the genesis of collaborative translation between 'peer poets'. Her chapter studies the English translation of the prose poem *Chronicle* of Saint-John Perse (1887–1975) by the American poet, critic and translator Robert Fitzgerald (1910–85). Hartmann seizes on the back-and-forth correspondence between author and translator, the translation manuscript heavily annotated by the poet himself, and the translator's 'Questions and Proposed Revisions' document with corrections and comments by Perse. By cross-examining this *avant*-textual documentation under a threefold approach (genetic, semantic and poetic), Hartmann argues for the importance of etymology, musicality and rhythm in Saint-John Perse's poetics.

Genetic analysis can also help disclose political agendas in translation, as Ewa Kołodziejczyk shows in her chapter, which examines the genesis of the Polish translations of fourteen 'Negro spirituals' produced in 1948 by Czesław Miłosz (1911–2004) while serving as a secretary to the Polish People's Republic Embassy in Washington, DC. Kołodziejczyk contends that the translations' genetic dossier unveils the author's political opposition and resistance to the Soviet domination in Poland after the Second World War. Before proceeding with a close reading of the archival material, Kołodziejczyk explores what she proposes to call the author's empirical dossier, that is, his encounter in the 1940s with African American culture that is approached on three levels: the socio-economic, the political and the cultural-artistic. The empirical dossier, which is more revealing about authorial motivation and background, is used to complement and clarify the comparative analysis of the textual evidence, namely source texts, handwritten drafts, typescripts and published versions. By adding Miłosz's practice of drawriting to the translator's genetic dossier, Kołodziejczyk discusses it as an integral part of his creative process, for 'covering manuscripts of his poems with little drawings, blackening space around an emerging verse with ink, which illustrates a strong bodily engagement in his intensive mental work'. Altogether the empirical and the genetic dossiers substantiate Miłosz's resistance to the Communist regime and his cry for universal freedom.

Laura Ivaska's study illustrates another translator's microhistory by focusing on a special case of collaborative practice, that of compilative translation, when a text is fashioned on several source texts, including translations into other languages and the so-called original. Relying on recent scholarship on indirect translation and borrowing methodological and theoretical notions from textual criticism, she examines the genetic dossier of the Finnish translation of Greek novelist Nikos Kazantzakis's *Veljesvina* (1967), which was translated by Kyllikki Villa. Ivaska combines the analysis of the translator's papers and correspondence with the textual comparison of the different source texts (the French and English translations and the original Greek) to conclude that the translator constructed her own *de facto* source text. Cautious of indirect translation, the Finnish translator is shown to have operated as a textual critic by having followed the *best-text method*, which questions the notions of original – and source text for that matter – as something fixed.

A different kind of compilative work is put forward by Elsa Pereira, whose chapter presents an ongoing project of digital genetic edition, therefore providing an important contribution to GTS and digital scholarly editing. Pereira follows a computational approach to a variety of interlingual materials related to the process of poetic creation by Portuguese writer Pedro Homem de Mello (1904–84). Those materials include translations of his poetry by others – special attention is given to his collaboration and friendship with his English translator, Arnold C. Hawkins – as well as self-translations that underwent substantial, recreative rewriting. Pereira discusses first the theoretical implications of incorporating these materials and how to do so in a genetic–critical edition; then she introduces her editorial model before demonstrating step by step the functionalities of the software she is using, as well as the Text Encoding Initiative (TEI-P5 standard) in combination with the open-source interface of the Versioning Machine, which enables the simultaneous display of multiple versions of the same text. This chapter responds directly to the technological appeal of genetic criticism when applied to translated texts.

In the first chapter of the second section, Joana Moura reflects on Peter Handke's conception of translation as a bodily experience in examining Handke's genetic dossier of his translations of René Char's poetry, which is part of Handke's collection at the Austrian National Library Literary Archive. This chapter explicitly engages with the notion of 'corporeality' by identifying traces of it through a close reading of the correspondence (letters, postcards and photographs) between Handke and Char at the time of Handke's German translation of a selection of poems from Char's *Le Nu perdu*, entitled *Rückkehr stromauf* (1984). Moura's argument is that the translator–author epistolary dialogue materializes a physical, sensorial and emotional bond that Handke used as translational resources. Reading the bodily experience of translation as an affective reaction to a source text and to an authorial agency illustrates a type of collaboration that, as Moura suggests, can be best described as phenomenological.

The second chapter carries on the discussion around translators' bodily experiences of translation by creating awareness of translators' bodies based on the examination of specific exogenetic tools: translators' biographies. Barbara Ivančić and Alexandra L. Zepter explore these mediated testimonies as 'the lived experience of translation', which provide insight not only into translators' life trajectories but also into particular translation processes, translators' strategies and personal conceptions about translation. The authors set the framework for reading these testimonies through the lens of embodiment theories, extending the notion of 'embodiment', that is, the claim that human cognition and the human body form a functional unit together, to the genesis of translation. The chapter draws on four translators' self-representations as depicted in their biographies (Swetlana Geier, Susanna Basso, Laura Bocci and Franco Nasi), pointing out the central role of the 'body' as both a motional and emotional experience in such representations. By the same token, the translation act gets a corporeal dimension, here investigated in relation to the corporeal dimensions of language itself. Some examples are put forward to illustrate differences in an individual's mental processing of concepts, which obviously leaves traces in his or her translated texts, thereby influencing the genesis of translation.

The two following chapters deal with translators' competence and performance as an insight into their 'black box' through the analysis of similar extratextual materials. Both chapters offer fertile theoretical ground for future genetic studies anchored in post-textual documentation, for retrospectively enlightening the genesis of translation practices. Departing from a sociologically oriented standpoint, Dominique Faria discusses translators' views about translating Portuguese literature by reviewing first-hand testimonies published in the Portuguese literary journal *Colóquio Letras* from 1980 to 2000 as 'a retrospective account of the translation process'. She argues that during the 1980s and 1990s this academic journal testified to the growth of discourses attributing an important role to translation and translators in spreading Portuguese literature abroad, although the discipline of translation studies was then still underdeveloped and ill-represented in Portugal.

In order to explain this somewhat contradictory picture, Faria examines eight translators' position-takings on translation so as to disclose personal conceptions about translation, practitioners' translational praxis and affective responses to translating. The results point towards a tendency for these translators, who were principally based outside Portugal and some were connected to the academy, to conceive of the translation process as a triangular relationship involving mostly translator, text and reader. Although translators tend to subsume themselves into the authors' creativity and assume an invisible position, the fact is that the journal, by giving voice to these agents, improved translation's status in Portugal.

In line with Faria's preference for exogenetic material and a sociologically informed framework, Marisa Mourinha focuses on Gregory Rabassa's statements about translation and on some writings on his translational performance, namely reviews and academic studies. Rabassa's own articles and memoir are used to analyse his theorization of translation and simultaneously serve as a counterpoint to discuss Rabassa's translation of Portuguese-language writer António Lobo Antunes into English. Despite advocating that translation is a collaborative work, Rabassa came across Lobo Antunes's resistance to talk about the translation of his novels.

Based on this translator's epitexts, Mourinha dwells into several covert contact zones between translation and genetic criticism with regard to Rabassa's translations of Lobo Antunes's novels. For instance, she examines the genesis as part of the translational peritext, when referring to the choice of the American publisher Grove Press to recover via a literal translation the original title that had, however, to be discarded for the publication of Portuguese novel *As Naus* due to copyright issues. Other contact zones include the genesis of Lobo Antunes's English translations that *post-textes* show to have been at a given moment supplemented by the then wife of the writer and to be indebted to the translator's personal erudite, higher language style. The genesis of non-translation of specific items is also addressed in some of those translated novels, which, as Mourinha points out, is indicative of a foreignizing strategy – a source-culture-oriented decision that is common in contexts where the source language gathers more prestige or literary capital than the target language, which is not the case under scrutiny.

Patrick Hersant opens the third and last section of the volume with a chapter examining textual evidence of the creative process of a renowned French translator of American English novelists who worked for Gallimard publishing house, Maurice Coindreau (1892–1990). Based on the research conducted at the Maurice Coindreau archives preserved at the Institut mémoires de l'édition contemporaine (IMEC), Hersant follows a genetic approach to a sample of drafts to identify the various stages of Coindreau's translation process and infer about his translatorship, which Hersant refers to as Coindreau's translative poetics and literary style. Hersant proposes a source–draft(s)–target comparative analysis of several examples drawn from the translator's repertoire, including authors such as William Goyen, Flannery O'Connor, John Steinbeck, Truman Capote, William Styron, John Dos Passos and Erskine Caldwell. The examples offer a wide coverage of Coindreau's creative process, which involved extensive improvement of his translations towards target-language fluency and correctness, moreover, allowing for the discussion of lexical accuracy, syntagmatic reorganization and language register (sociolect translation). Altogether, these elements foreground his evolution as a translator.

The second chapter continues along the lines of translatorial writing, namely authorial motivation and erasure of third-party agencies by turning to the phenomenon of self-translation in academic writing. Taking the Portuguese academy as a case study, Karen Bennett combines insights from an earlier survey-based study of hers with reflections on the epistemological and ethical consequences of the manifold forms of self-translation in academic writing. Bennett explores the advantages of making use of genetic criticism to unveil scholars' unacknowledged reliance on translators, revisers and proofreaders, as well as study the intricate process of writing and (self-)translating academic texts. She contends that the widespread and, to a large extent, mandatory practice of translation in academic circles has resulted in the Portuguese academic discourse mimicking the dominant English language academic text, and proposes the concept of 'epistemological translation' to describe a shift between academic writing paradigms, irrespective of involving texts to be translated or texts directly written in English. Anthony Pym's 'interculture' is used in this sense to designate 'a space that contains elements of at least two linguistic and epistemological cultures', a workshop-like zone that highlights the complex interactions taking place behind the translation/production of academic texts, which Bennett encapsulates under Verena Jung's notion of 'intertext'.

The two closing chapters bring in case studies of philological praxis by early- and late-nineteenth-century figures of Portuguese literary and intellectual life; they differently explore an individual's authorial or scientific competence against translational performance. Prolific novelist Camilo Castelo Branco (1825–90) is the selected object of study in Carlota Pimenta's chapter. Departing from a geneticist's perspective, Pimenta takes issue with the novelist's translation practice and scrutinizes the genesis of the only existing translation manuscript by Camilo, that of *História de Gabriel Malagrida*, the Portuguese translation of the Jesuit priest Paul Mury's 1865 French novel.

Pimenta discusses Camilo's writing process as a translator based on his amendments to the translated text, which are formally examined in terms of their chronological and quantitative occurrence, distribution and scope. The latter consists in what Pimenta refers to as amplitude, a category of genetic analysis relating to the textual distance between amendments that can elucidate on the time lag between writing and rewriting. This kind of 'correction'-tracking research, which leads Pimenta to infer about Camilo's predominant practice of direct reading-translating, is contrasted with the writer's practices as a literary author. In addressing the genesis of the translation vis-à-vis the genesis of other Camilian originals, Pimenta concludes that the speed of writing and the number of corrections are closely linked to the writer's creative freedom. When translating, Camilo Castelo Branco evinces a spontaneous and fast speed of writing, making fewer amendments to the text than he would were he involved in his own creative writing; Pimenta builds therefore, and perhaps not unexpectedly, an image of Camilo as more confident as a translator and more hesitant as an author. At least one question remains hovering in the background: whether Camilo was more demanding with his own creative writing and incautious with regard to translating, for let us not forget that Camilo lived off his writing production and translation was then commonly viewed as a second-rate activity.

The last chapter, written jointly by Marta Pacheco Pinto and Ariadne Nunes, revisits philological scholarship to write the genetic history of an incomplete manuscript and ultimately map the presence of Sanskrit literature in fin-de-siècle Portugal. It examines the genesis of a two-volume handwritten translation of the Indian classic *Panchatantra* by orientalist–translator Guilherme de Vasconcelos Abreu (1842–1907). Left unfinished and unpublished, the existing volumes provide evidence of the Sanskritist's translation methodology, which is shown to comply with the expected scientific paradigm of literalness, as well as clues as to his abandoning of the translation project. As suggested, this abandoning seems to rely on a kind of epistemological conflict regarding the function and purpose of the translation. The analysis of the handwritten drafts allows the scholars to question the more general role played by orientalist translation not only in Vasconcelos Abreu's body of work as both a Sanskritist and a Sanskrit instructor in nineteenth-century Portugal, but also on the latent state of the discipline of Sanskrit studies in Portugal. The study of the genesis is combined with the discussion of exogenetic materials, by which Pinto and Nunes highlight intertextual networks exposing the Sanskritist's sources and scientific allegiances that contributed to shaping his scholarship and that of those who succeeded him.

Altogether, the contributors to this volume enquire into the potential benefits arising from the multiple intersections and exchanges between translation studies and genetic criticism by claiming, either explicitly or implicitly, the existence of a new subarea of research, that of GTS.

In 1995, Gideon Toury closed his chapter 'A Translation Comes into Being. Hamlet's Monologue in Hebrew' arguing that 'it is much too early to draw too general conclusions from a research method which is still in swaddling clothes' (1995: 205). In 2020, we end this introduction arguing that GTS is a new methodological and epistemological ground that is slowly making its entrance as a research field in the landscape of translation studies, and is certainly here to stay and thrive.

Notes

1. The terms 'endogenesis' and 'exogenesis' were for the first time coined by Raymonde Debray-Genette (1979), 'Genèse et poétique: le cas Flaubert', in *Essais de critique génétique*, 21–67, Paris: Flammarion.
2. See the 'posttext (stage)' entry of the *Lexicon of Scholarly Editing* at http://uahost.uantwerpen.be/lse/index.php/lexicon/posttext-stage/ (accessed 11 October 2019).
3. See the case study provided in Tsivia Frank-Wygoda's working paper 'Intertextuality, Hermeneutics and Textual Genetics: Edmond Jabès' *The Book of Questions*' (2016).
4. See Gerry Andersen on the 'Ancient New Testament Manuscripts: The Greek Editions': https://www.valleybible.net/AdultEducation/ClassNotes/Manuscripts/GreekEditions.pdf (accessed 8 October 2019).
5. This is described in a letter from Pessoa to his friend and literary critic Casais Monteiro (1908–72) as a moment of trance, during which he wrote around 30 poems of *Guardador de Rebanhos* (The Keeper of Sheep), by heteronym Alberto Caeiro, the six-poem *Chuva Oblíqua* (Oblique Rain), by Fernando Pessoa himself, and *Ode Triunfal* (Triumphal Ode), by heteronym Álvaro de Campos, in addition to creating Ricardo Reis (see letter to Adolfo Casais Monteiro, 13 January 1935, at https://www.casafernandopessoa.pt/pt/fernando-pessoa/textos/heteronimia [accessed 30 August 2019]).
6. We kindly thank João Dionísio for pointing this out during his review of this chapter.
7. A similar concept is operated in genetic criticism: the micro-level analytics, which seeks to make sense of detailed variation from version to version, is proposed by de Biasi (2011: 221–50) when reading the incipit of Flaubert's *La Légende de Saint Julien l'hospitalier* (1875).
8. It is also noteworthy that poetry has been the genre that has attracted more attention to debate genetic translation issues, as ultimately confirmed by Munday's coedition of *Poetry Translation: Agents, Actors, Networks, Contexts* (2016), which privileges a sociology-oriented approach to poetic creation.
9. Take for example the well-known online collaborative translation platform of Murakami Haruki's European translators (Zielinska-Elliott and Kaminka 2017: 167–91) or Günter Grass's famous translation seminars, when the writer was available for a few days to discuss with his translators the main issues posed by his work (Letawe 2017: 130–44).
10. See https://www.beckettarchive.org/ (accessed 31 August 2019).
11. See, for example, Dionísio Martinez Soler's '*Lembranças e Deslembranças*: A Case Study on Pseudo-Originals' (2006). Although it is not based on the analysis of genetic material, this study is a case in point in revealing the presence of a pseudo-original in a bilingual poetry edition to conceal self-translation.
12. See https://handkeonline.onb.ac.at (accessed 28 August 2019).
13. See https://ldod.uc.pt (accessed 28 August 2019).

References

Adamo, Sergia (2006), 'Microhistory of Translation', in Georges L. Bastin and Paul F. Bandia (eds), *Charting the Future of Translator History*, 81–100, Ottawa: University of Ottawa Press.

Alvstad, Cecilia, Annjo Greenall, Hanne Jansen and Kristiina Taivalkoski-Shilov (eds) (2017), 'Introduction: Textual and Contextual Voices of Translation', in *Textual and Contextual Voices of Translation*, 3–17, Amsterdam and Philadelphia: John Benjamins.

Baker, Peter (1986), *Modern Poetic Practice*, New York, Bern and Frankfurt am Main: Peter Lang.

Castro, Ivo (1990), 'O manuscrito do Guardador', in *Editar Pessoa*, 91–102, Lisboa: Imprensa Nacional–Casa da Moeda.

Chesterman, Andrew (2009), 'The Name and Nature of Translator Studies', *Hermes – Journal of Language and Communication Studies*, 42: 13–22.

Cordingley, Anthony (2013), *Self-Translation: Brokering Originality in Hybrid Culture*, London and New York: Bloomsbury.

Cordingley, Anthony and Céline Frigau Manning (eds) (2017), *Collaborative Translation: From the Renaissance to the Digital Age*, London and New York: Bloomsbury.

Cordingley, Anthony and Chiara Montini (2015), 'Genetic Translation Studies: An Emerging Discipline', *Linguistica Antverpiensia. New Series: Themes in Translation Studies*, 14: 1–18.

De Biasi, Pierre-Marc (1996), 'What Is a Literary Draft? Toward a Functional Typology of Genetic Documentation', trans. Ingrid Wassenaar, *Yale French Studies*, 89: 26–58.

De Biasi, Pierre-Marc (2011), *Génétique des textes*, Paris: CNRS éditions.

Debray-Genette, Raymonde (1979), 'Genèse et poétique: le cas Flaubert', in *Essais de critique génétique*, 21–67, Paris: Flammarion.

Deppman, Jed, Daniel Ferrer and Michael Groden (2004), 'Introduction: A Genesis of French Genetic Criticism', in Jed Deppman, Daniel Ferrer and Michael Groden (eds), *Genetic Criticism: Texts and Avant-Textes*, 1–16, Philadelphia: University of Pennsylvania Press.

D'hulst, Lieven and Yves Gambier (2018), *A History of Modern Translation Knowledge: Sources, Concepts, Effects*, Amsterdam and Philadelphia: John Benjamins.

Dionísio Martinez Soler (2006), '*Lembranças e Deslembranças*: A Case Study on Pseudo-Originals', in João Ferreira Duarte, Alexandra Assis Rosa and Teresa Seruya (eds), *Translation Studies at the Interface of Disciplines*, 185–96, Amsterdam and Philadelphia: John Benjamins.

Eker Roditakis, Arzu (2018), 'Reviewers as Readers with Power: What a Case of Retranslation Says about Author, Translator and Reader Dynamics', *Mémoires du livre/Studies in Book Culture*, 9 (1). Available online: https://doi.org/10.7202/1043124ar (accessed 22 August 2019).

Fish, Stanley (1980), *Is There a Text in This Class? The Authority of Interpretive Communities*, Cambridge: Harvard University Press.

Frank-Wygoda, Tsivia (2016), 'Intertextuality, Hermeneutics and Textual Genetics: Edmond Jabès' *The Book of Questions*', *European Forum at the Hebrew University, Working Paper*, 152: https://ef.huji.ac.il/sites/default/files/europe/files/frank-wygoda_for_web.pdf (accessed 11 October 2019).

Gabler, Walter (2010), 'Theorizing the Digital Scholarly Edition', *Literature Compass*, 7 (2): 43–56.

Gambier, Yves and Luc van Doorslaer (eds) (2010), *Handbook of Translation Studies*, vol. 1, Amsterdam and Philadelphia: John Benjamins.

Goonatilake, Susantha (1998), *Toward a Global Science: Mining Civilizational Knowledge*, Bloomington and Indianapolis: Indiana University Press.

Grésillon, Almuth (1994), *Éléments de critique génétique*, Paris: Presses Universitaires de France.

Grutman, Rainier (2016), 'Manuscrits, traduction et autotraduction', in Chiara Montini (ed.), *Traduire. Genèse du choix*, 115–28, Paris: Éditions des Archives Contemporaines.

Hay, Louis (ed.) (1979), *Les Essais de critique génétique*, Paris: Flammarion.

Hendel, Ronald (2015), 'The Untimeliness of Biblical Philology', *Philology*, 1 (1): 9–28. Available online: https://www.ingentaconnect.com/content/plg/phil/2015/00000001/00000001/art00002 (accessed 27 August 2019).

Hermans, Theo (1997), 'The Task of the Translator in the European Renaissance: Explorations in a Discursive Field', in Susan Bassnett (ed.), *Translating Literature. Essays and Studies*, 14–40, Cambridge: D.S. Brewer.

Hersant, Patrick (2017), 'Author–Translator Collaborations: A Typological Survey', in Anthony Cordingley and Céline Frigau Manning (eds), *Collaborative Translation. From the Renaissance to the Digital Age*, 91–110, London and New York: Bloomsbury.

Hokenson, Jan W. and Marcella Munson (2006), *The Bilingual Text: History and Theory of Literary Self-Translation*, London and New York: Routledge.

Horta, Paulo Lemos (2017), *Marvellous Thieves. Secret Authors of the Arabian Nights*, Cambridge, MA, and London: Harvard University Press.

Huss, Joanna Trzeciak (2018), 'Collaborative Translation', in Kelly Washbourne and Ben Van Wyke (eds), *The Routledge Handbook of Literary Translation*, 448–67, London and New York: Routledge.

Ivaska, Laura and Outi Paloposki (2017), 'Attitudes towards Indirect Translation in Finland and Translators' Strategies: Compilative and Collaborative Translation', *Translation Studies*, 11 (1): 33–46.

Jansen, Hanne and Anna Wegener (eds) (2013), *Authorial and Editorial Voices in Translation*, Montreal: Éditions québécoises de l'oeuvre.

Jenny, Laurent (2000), 'Genetic Criticism and Its Myths', *Yale French Studies. 50 Years of Yale French Studies: A Commemorative Anthology. Part 2: 1980-1998*, 97: 198–214.

Letawe, Céline (2017), 'Günter Grass and His Translators: From a Collaborative Dynamic to an Apparatus of Control?', in Anthony Cordingley and Célina Frigau Manning (eds), *Collaborative Translation. From the Renaissance to the Digital Age*, 130–44, London and New York: Bloomsbury.

Lopes, Alexandra (2012), 'Under the Sign of Janus: Reflections on Authorship as Liminality in Translated Literature', *Revista Anglo Saxonica*, III (3): 129–56.

Millán, Carmen and Francesca Bartrina (2013), *The Routledge Handbook of Translation Studies*, London and New York: Routledge.

Munday, Jeremy (2014), 'Using Primary Sources to Produce a Microhistory of Translation and Translators: Theoretical and Methodological Concerns', *Translator: Studies in Intercultural Communication*, 20 (1): 64–80.

Munday, Jeremy and Jacob Blakesley (eds) (2016), *Translation and Literature*, special issue *Poetry Translation: Agents, Actors, Networks, Contexts*, 26.

Pérez-González, Luis (2017), 'Investigating Digitally Born Amateur Subtitling Agencies in the Context of Popular Culture', in David Orrego-Carmona and Yvonne Lee (eds), *Non-Professional Subtitling*, 15–36, Newcastle upon Tyne: Cambridge Scholars Publishing.

Pym, Anthony (2011), 'Translation Research Terms: A Tentative Glossary for Moments of Perplexity and Dispute', in Anthony Pym (ed.), *Translation Research Projects 3*, 75–99, Tarragona: Intercultural Studies Group.

Rebhein, Malte and Walter Gable (2013), 'On Reading Environments for Genetic Editions', *Scholarly and Research Communication*, 4 (3): 1–21.

Robinson, Peter (2013), 'Towards a Theory of Digital Editions', *Variants*, 10: 105–31.

Romanelli, Sergio (2015), 'Manuscripts and Translations: Spaces for Creation', *Linguistica Antverpiensia, New Series: Themes in Translation Studies*, 14: 87–104.

Rosa, Alexandra Assis, Hanna Pięta and Rita Bueno Maia (2017), 'Theoretical, Methodological and Terminological Issues Regarding Indirect Translation: An Overview', *Translation Studies*, 10 (2): 113–32, DOI: 10.1080/14781700.2017.1285247.

Santoyo, Julio-César (2013), 'On Mirrors, Dynamics and Self-Translations', in Anthony Cordingley (ed.), *Self-Translation. Brokering Originality in Hybrid Culture*, 27–38, London and New York: Bloomsbury.

Sapiro, Gisèle (2014), 'The Sociology of Translation', in Susan Bermann and Catherine Porter (eds), *A Companion to Translation Studies*, 82–94, West Sussex: Wiley Blackwell.

Seaver, Richard (2006), 'Richard Seaver on Translating Beckett', in James Knowlson and Elizabeth Knowlson (eds), *Beckett Remembering, Remembering Beckett. Uncollected Interviews with Samuel Beckett and Memories of Those Who Knew Him*, 100–7, London and New York: Bloomsbury.

Shuttleworth, Mark and Moira Cowie (1997), *Dictionary of Translation Studies*, Kinderhook: St. Jerome Publishing.

Sichani, Anna-Maria (2015), 'Literary Drafts, Genetic Criticism and Computational Technology. The Beckett Digital Manuscript Project', in Dirk Van Hulle, Shane Weller and Vincent Neyt (eds), *The Beckett Digital Manuscript Project*, https://ride.i-d-e.de/issues/issue-5/beckettarchive/?hilite (accessed 28 August 2019).

Toury, Gideon (1995), *Descriptive Translation Studies and Beyond*, Amsterdam and Philadelphia: John Benjamins.

Van Hulle, Dirk (2015), 'Translation and Genetic Criticism: Genetic and Editorial Approaches to the "Untranslatable" in Joyce and Beckett', *Linguistica Antverpiensia, New Series: Themes in Translation Studies*, 14: 40–53.

Van Hulle, Dirk (2016), 'Modelling a Digital Scholarly Edition for Genetic Criticism: A Rapprochement', *Variants*, 12–13: 34–56.

Venuti, Lawrence (1995), *The Translator's Invisibility. A History of Translation*, London and New York: Routledge.

Wakabayashi, Judy (2018), 'Microhistory', in Lieven D'hulst and Yves Gambier (eds), *A History of Modern Translation Knowledge: Sources, Concepts, Effects*, 251–4, Amsterdam and Philadelphia: John Benjamins.

Zanotti, Serenella (2014), 'Translation and Transcreation in the Dubbing Process: A Genetic Approach', *Cultus: The Journal of Intercultural Mediation and Communication*, 7: 107–32.

Zanotti, Serenella and Rosa Maria Bollettieri (2015), 'Exploring the Backstage of Translations: A Study of Translated-Related Manuscripts in the Anthony Burgess Archives', *Linguistica Antverpiensia: Themes in Translation Studies*, 14: 127–48.

Zielinska-Elliott, Anna and Ika Kaminka (2017), 'Online Multilingual Collaboration: Haruki Murakami's European Translators', in Anthony Cordingley and Céline Frigau Manning (eds), *Collaborative Translation. From the Renaissance to the Digital Age*, 167–91, London and New York: Bloomsbury.

Part One

Genetic approaches to translation and collaboration

2

Latency, inference, interaction: Notes towards a blurry picture of translation genetics in Portugal

João Dionísio
Centre of Linguistics, University of Lisbon

Preliminary remarks

In the introduction to the volume of *Linguistica Antverpiensia* focused on genetic translation studies, not only do Anthony Cordingley and Chiara Montini present the contents of this special issue, they also claim that this is an emerging discipline. The contributions to the volume have to do with case studies and perspectives on a broad international scale, suggesting that such emergence is polygenetic. Because, excepting for a passing reference in the introduction to the Luso-Spanish couple José Saramago and Pilar del Rio as an example of a merger of the lives of authors and translators (Cordingley and Montini 2015: 14), there is no article regarding Portuguese authors or translators in the issue, it may be pertinent to set out by making a brief reference to a few signs pointing to the possibility of emerging genetic translation studies in the Portuguese context. These signs are meant to be illustrative and the following notes are made from the perspective of a textual scholar (not of a translation studies scholar).

In order to delimit the range of activities to be taken into account, I will bear in mind the practical scope of the field according to Cordingley and Montini: 'Genetic translation studies focuses ... on the transformations of the translated text during the process of its composition' (2015: 1). Taking this into consideration, it is useful to observe that the mostly scattered traces of genetic translation studies in Portugal appear in different formats, namely: (1) analyses of the making of some translations as well as genetic editions of translations (Fischer 2012; Firmino 2013: 54–9); (2) apparatuses of critical editions dealing with translations that, while usually conveying information on transmission variants, may also provide data referring to their composition stages (Anastácio 1998: ii, xxv, xxxi–xxxv *et passim*); (3) public displays of genetic materials, including documents witnessing preliminary stages of translations, as was the case of the

---

I am grateful to Nonna Pinto for having given me access to information regarding her translation of Evgenéa Iaroslavskaïa's narrative. I would also like to express gratitude to Serviço de Arquivo da Casa de Mateus (Vila Real). Figure 1 is reproduced with the permission of the National Library of Portugal.

exhibition at the National Library of Portugal to celebrate the twenty-fifth anniversary of the Portuguese Contemporary Culture Archive (Duarte and Oliveira 2007); and (4) initiatives such as 'Poetas em Mateus', a series of collaborative translation seminars promoted by the Casa de Mateus Foundation that gathered poets and translators and resulted in a final public reading of the source poems and their translations, as well as in a series of books produced by the publishing house Quetzal.

One of the major challenges faced by scholars who are interested in the genesis of translations is the scarcity of available materials. A case in point can be unfortunately illustrated by the fact that the Archive of the Casa de Mateus Foundation does not keep video or audio recordings of its working sessions or even of public readings. As a consequence, the 'Poetas em Mateus' initiative is known by its end result, that is, the printed and distributed translation as product, rather than by the process that led up to it. This notwithstanding, it must be acknowledged that, even when there is material evidence of the translation process, not much work has been done in Portugal to shed light on what can be extracted from working documents. In this respect, it is telling that, to the best of my knowledge, almost none of the documents presented at the 2007 exhibition at the National Library of Portugal have attracted attention from the point of view of translation genetics. However, more than the absence of records or the timid exploration of some interesting documents, it is, I would argue, the lack of a self-aware interpretive community that mostly accounts for the latency of genetic translation studies in Portugal. Additionally, and speaking from a position grounded in textual scholarship, the general verdict made by Cordingley and Montini also applies to the Portuguese context, for the examples I have presented above show that most of the genetic translation research has been directed to the reinforcement of 'canonical authors or persons of historical interest for the very reason that only these person's translation papers were collected' (Cordingley and Montini 2015: 7). Not wishing to downplay the relevance of canonical authors and persons of historical interest for translation genetics, what follows is a reflection upon the possibility of broadening the object of study usually ascribed to genetic criticism. I seek to do this by addressing chronologic, typological and agency factors in the delimitation of the object of study. According to a recent conceptual divide (Alvstad and Rosa 2015; Alvstad, Greenall, Jansen and Taivalkoski-Shilov 2017: 3, 5), the first part of this chapter is developed under the aegis of textual voices (i.e. voices found within the translated texts); the second is approached in tune with the recognition of the impact of contextual voices (i.e. voices of those agents who somehow influence the textual voices). In other words, given the multidirectional links between translation and genetic criticism, the first part deals with translation as part of the genesis, whereas the second part focuses on the genesis as part of translation (Van Hulle 2015).

Inference

Genetic criticism has played a foundational role in the study of text as process, against the long-lasting and still prevailing view of text as product. As such it fought against the idea of literary creation in the guise of Romantic revelation, according to which the author would be a vehicle to inspiration, and instead called attention to the documented labour of the writer. Meanwhile, a number of factors have understandably led genetic critics to favour one stage of the process, the stage more closely linked with *ab initio* or, as it were, unrestrained writing, to the detriment of other stages. The semantic scope of the word 'genesis' has allowed for this preference: the programmatic term 'genesis' is frequently associated with the first book of the Bible, which *includes* the narration of the creation of the world. Accordingly, is one supposed to focus on this inaugural moment (following the King James Bible version, 'In the beginning God created the heaven and the earth') or include the other episodes narrated in this book? Is one supposed to ascribe more importance to the creation or bear in mind that the making of the world is but one of the various topics tackled in the book of the Genesis? These may sound like synecdoche questions and the answers to them, while taking on many shapes, point to a difficult balance between inclusive theories and selective practices.

Whereas genetic critics rightly affirm that the published or finished text is nothing more than a state in the process of textualization, one should perhaps point out that it is no less a state for that reason. In this sense, I agree with Pierre-Marc de Biasi when he includes the published text in the table referring to the Typology of Genetic Documentation, that is, the 'stages, phases and operational functions which enable the ordering of different types of manuscript according to their location and status in the process of production of a work' (de Biasi 1996: 34–5). Later on, de Biasi seems to eschew the inclusion of the stage of the published text in the continuum of textual becoming when he concludes that the work scheme he puts forth is 'applicable to the analysis of a literary project, whether completed or unfinished, that has never been published' (1996: 37). A similar grain of ambiguity can be found vis-à-vis the status of the draft. On one occasion the draft is said to be only a 'moment of this process', but on another it is claimed that genetic criticism has placed the rough draft at the 'center of its investigations' (1996: 29). The grounds for such a standpoint are, of course, understandable: ages of technical constraints, ignorance and biased views have been directly or indirectly responsible for the undervaluation, if not destruction, of uncountable preliminary documents of our written heritage. Therefore, a reappraisal of the status of these documents came hand in hand (i) with a sense of urgency to study them out of, as it were, compensation, and also (ii) with the accompanying devaluation of the published text, which has been viewed as a *memento* against teleology. However, in my view, neither the sense of urgency nor the attack on teleology justifies that the study of the process be limited to 'documents to be seen over the period that extends from the end of the first third of the nineteenth century to the 1980s' (de Biasi 1996: 49), meaning, up to our days or even be limited to autographic documents.

It is pertinent to revisit this topic considering what looks like a reassessment of the published text, as shown by a recent issue of *GENESIS*, centred on the question of post publication (see Mahrer 2017), and seeking to view research objects and objectives separately. What identifies a field of study as such is not so much the objects as the objectives served by a given type of observation and critical discourse. That is why the following remark by Pierre-Marc de Biasi is of crucial importance:

> The *avant-texte* does not therefore mean the material manuscripts ..., but rather the critical discourse by which the geneticist, having established the objective results of their analysis (transcriptions, relative dating, classification, etc.), reads them as successive moments of a process. (1996: 38)

As a consequence, the cornerstone in this activity is arguably the inference behind critical discourse and following observation, that is, the reasoning enabling the critic to make an informed conjecture on successive moments of a process and to offer an interpretation of the process itself. Let us go back to our reference definition: 'Genetic translation studies focuses ... on the transformations of the translated text during the process of its composition' (Cordingley and Montini 2015: 1). In order to deal with these transformations, I would argue that it is not mandatory to work with an autographic tradition or *corpus*.

Two different examples will be summoned here in my effort to demonstrate this.

The first is a chapter of a medieval moral treatise concluded in the 1430s by Duarte, king of Portugal (1391–1438). This treatise, titled *Leal Conselheiro* (Loyal Councillor), has reached us in its full form through a manuscript kept at the National Library of France. In a late copy of a private notebook held by King Duarte, one finds versions of essays that would be later included as chapters in *Leal Conselheiro*. One such chapter contains the rules that the reader is invited to keep in mind in order to translate well from Latin into Portuguese, followed by a few examples. In the first part of the chapter the core matter is then a set of general translation rules that also appear as an independent text in the notebook. My conjecture is that King Duarte, aware of the vagueness of these rules and seeking an ideal of clearness, decided to illustrate them. The first example was obtained through a convenient extraction of another originally independent text from the notebook: hence he inserted his Portuguese translation of the *Juste Judex* Latin piece, a prayer possibly designed 'for protection against the malice of his enemies' (Askins 2007: 252).

Later on, King Duarte did perhaps realize that using this verse as an example for the translation rules he put forth would not be enough and, for the sake of completeness, he concluded the chapter with another example, that of a literal translation in prose, drawn from a passage by one of his favourite authors, the Church Father John Cassian. The source text is taken from book 6, on the spirit of fornication, of Cassian's *The Institutes of the Cenobia and the Remedies for the Eight Principal Vices*: it is a comparison between the diet followed by those who fight in athletic games and the abstinence put into practice by some monks, the so-called athletes of Christ. Such a textual choice is in agreement with King Duarte's interest in virtues and sins, something that is clearly signalled in different sections of his moral treatise. Finally, I imagine that the first example (the prayer) was articulated with the set of rules, the second (Cassian's extract) with the first example, and a general and short introduction was appended at the beginning. Extant evidence may lead us to imagine a three-stage process of composition (Table 2.1):

Table 2.1 Reconstruction of the composition of *Leal Conselheiro*, chapter 99.

Stage 3	*Leal Conselheiro*, chapter 99		
Stage 2	Introduction		
Stage 1	General rules	Translation of *Juste Judex*	Translation of Cassianus's *De institutis Coenobiorum* (book 6, extract)

I am well aware that this is a rather schematic proposal of a reconstruction, based on the identification of specific features of the chapter components (doctrine followed by examples; in turn, examples selected according to the representation of basic textual types – verse, prose). It is not possible to determine anything about either the chronologic sequence of stage 1 (the author may have first drafted any of the examples and only afterwards thought of the rules or the other way around) or about stage 2 (he may have composed the introduction first and then articulated the different components, or vice versa). However, one can infer that a composition process based on addition was at play, as a vestige of this operation is still visible in the Paris codex: the short introduction appears before the chapter rubric, a misplacement that probably mirrors the document witness which served as model for the transcription (Table 2.2).

At this stage, it is important to note that neither the codex transmitting the moral treatise nor the late copy of the private notebook is autographic. But the fact that both are copies does not rule out the possibility of us basing our critical discourse on them, once we have laid out the tangible results of our analysis (transcriptions, relative dating, classification, etc.), which enable us to read them as different moments of a process. We are thus led by inference to the impression of being before a 'textual amalgam'. Similar to what happens in the writing of other chapters, in which King Duarte 'assimilated numerous passages from other texts', here he gives the idea of being willing to 'go down to posterity as a scissors and paste man'. King Duarte's writing method is thus 'expansive in nature' and, because he 'incorporated several source texts into his own work', one may call this method a 'Montagetechnik' (Van Hulle 2004: 156–7). In these few last remarks, I have been shamelessly plundering the words of Dirk Van Hulle on the writing of three major twentieth-century novels: James Joyce's *Finnegans Wake*, Thomas Mann's *Doktor Faustus* and Proust's *Recherche*. In this particular case I would like to argue that the possibility of describing the writing process of medieval and modern texts alike through the same critical vocabulary points to the existence of some common ground as far as the objective of genetic scholarship is concerned. In other words, the fact that some literary works are preserved in autographs is not a necessary prerequisite for the analysis of the writing process; likewise, the fact that some literary works are not preserved in autographs should not hinder us from reflecting on their writing process.

Let us now turn to a modern text, exclusively transmitted by autograph documentation. It is a poem by Fernando Pessoa (1888–1935) bearing the *incipit* 'Agora que sinto amor' (Now that I feel love)[1] and ascribed to one of his major heteronyms, Alberto Caeiro (for a consideration of this poem against the backdrop of Pessoa's bilingualism, see Dionísio 2018). Although up until now only one document witness

Table 2.2 D. Duarte, *Leal Conselheiro*, conclusion of chapter 98 and beginning of chapter 99.[2]

Line	Text
6	Esto me parece que deue seer mostra
7	do a poucas e certas pessoas ca
8	sse o vyrem os que som fora de tal pro
9	posito e pratica mais querram pras
10	mar e contradizerme que filhar dello pera
11	senhor ou amygos proveitosa ensinança.
12	Por que muytos que som leterados nom sabem
13	treladar bem de latym em lynguagem penssey
14	escrever estes auysamentos pera ello ne
15	cessarios. Capitullo LRix da manei
16	ra pera bem tornar algũa leitura em
17	nossa lynguagem
18	Prymeiro conhecer bem a ssentença
19	do que ha de tornar e poella inteiramente
20	nom mudando acrescentando nem
21	mynguando algũa cousa do que
22	esta scripto O ssegundo que nom
23	ponha pallauras latinadas nem doutra

Source: Bibliothèque Nationale de France, Portugais 5, fol. 93r.
The three lines preceding the rubric and the first line taken by the rubric, here highlighted in grey, contain the misplaced introduction to chapter 99.

of 'Agora que sinto amor' has been located (Figure 2.1), it displays three major writing stages: it was first typed with blue ribbon; afterwards with red ribbon; then the sheet was removed from the machine and Pessoa finally revised it with two types of black ink (Pessoa 2015, ed. Castro: 255–62).

As to the deleted segment immediately before the poem,[3] it is a Portuguese sentence roughly synonymous with the following sentence, in English and in brackets. The latter sentence turns out to be the concluding line of a sonnet, 'Love's Blindness', by the Victorian poet Alfred Austin (Caeiro 2001, ed. Martins and Zenith: 214), a poem that was included in the anthology *Sonnets of This Century*, with a critical introduction on the sonnet by William Sharp, possibly printed in 1902. Fernando Pessoa must have bought a copy of this edition sometime between 1902 and 1905 (Pittella 2017: 278), having annotated line 14 of Austin's poem as 'the only good thing here' (Pittella 2017: 336, 340) – one does not know whether this assessment was penned as a reader or according to the perspective of an author who frequently drew on other writers.

I would like to argue that the poem by Pessoa stems from Austin's sonnet (Table 2.3), and in order to prove my point, it is useful to note that the English text is

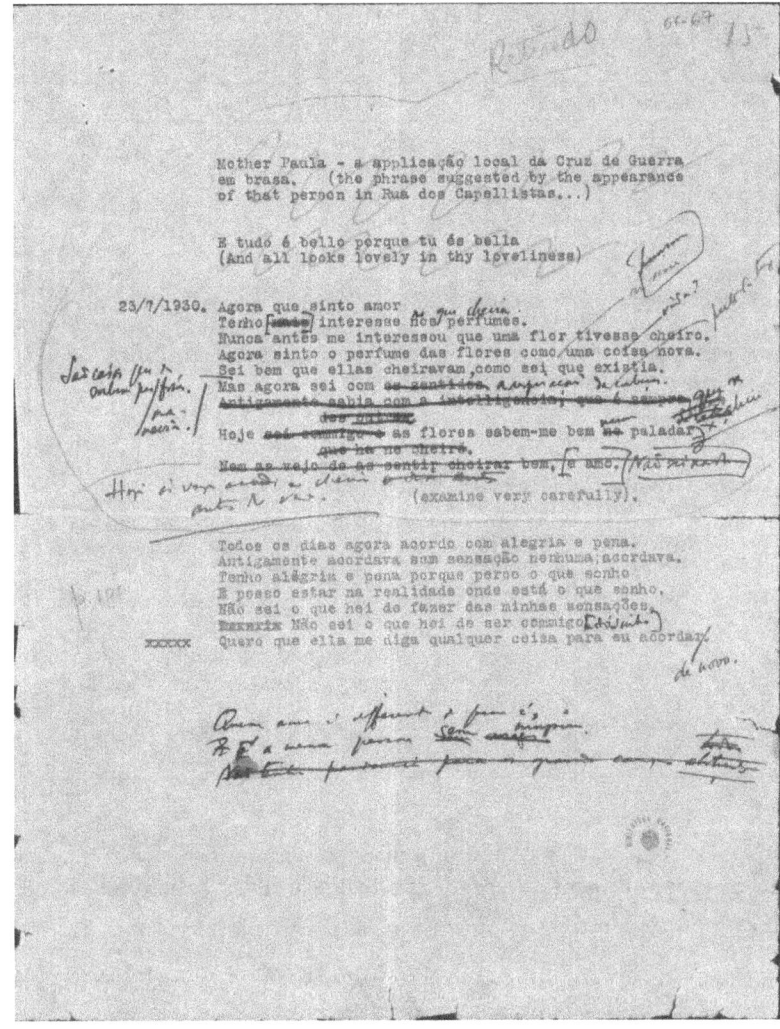

Figure 2.1 Biblioteca Nacional de Portugal, Esp. E 3, 67–67r.

made up of two sections: one, in which the absence of the love object is said to erase beauty from the world; the second, in which everything looks beautiful due to the love object's presence. Pessoa reshapes this poem into a text about the discovery of sensations in the present in contrast to the past, which is said to have been deprived of those sensations. Among other common features, Caeiro's text explores and amplifies the time markers referring to the present that appear at the beginning of the English sonnet ('*Now* do I know …'), reproducing the adverb at the beginning of line 1 ('*Agora* que sinto amor'), 4 ('*Agora* sinto o perfume das flores como se visse uma coisa nova'), 7 ('Mas *agora* sei com a respiração da parte de traz da cabeça') and 10 ('Todos os dias *agora* acordo com alegria e pena') (Pessoa, ed. Castro 2015: 70). The adverbial

Table 2.3 Transcription of Alfred Austin's 'Now do I know that Love is blind, for I' and Alberto Caeiro's 'Agora que sinto amor'.

Alfred Austin	Fernando Pessoa and Alberto Caeiro
Now do I know that Love is blind, for I	Agora que sinto amor
Can see no beauty on this beauteous earth,	Tenho interesse no que cheira
No life, no light, no hopefulness, no mirth,	Nunca antes me interessou que uma flor tivesse cheiro.
Pleasure nor purpose, when thou art not nigh.	Agora sinto o perfume das flores como se visse uma coisa nova.
Thy absence exiles sunshine from the sky,	Sei bem que ellas cheiravam, como sei que existia.
Seres Spring's maturity, checks Summer's birth,	São coisas que se sabem por maneira.
Leaves linnet's pipe as sad as plover's cry,	Mas agora sei com a respiração da parte de traz da cabeça.
And makes me in abundance find but dearth.	Hoje as flores sabem-me bem num paladar que se cheira.
But when thy feet flutter the dark, and thou	Hoje ás vezes acordo e cheiro antes de ver.
With orient eyes dawnest on my distress,	
Suddenly sings a bird on every bough,	Todos os dias agora acordo com alegria e pena.
The heavens expand, the earth grows less and less,	Antigamente acordava sem sensação nenhuma; acordava.
The ground is buoyant as the ether now,	Tenho alegria e pena porque perco o que sonho.
And all looks lovely in thy loveliness.	
	E posso estar na realidade onde está o que sonho.
	Não sei o que hei de fazer das minhas sensações,
	Não sei o que hei de fazer sósinho.
	Quero que ella me diga qualquer coisa para eu acordar de novo.

repetition, by underscoring present time markers, suggests that Austin's text, beyond the interest explicitly generated by the concluding line, may have worked for Pessoa as a poetic trigger.

This process seems to have gone through four stages: (1) reading the poem by Austin in an anthology; (2) evaluating the poem and writing down a literary assessment: 'the only good thing here'; (3) translating 'the only good thing' into Portuguese; (4) writing a new poem in Portuguese that is reminiscent of the structure (but not the content) of the Victorian sonnet. The first three phases are clearly source-oriented, unlike the fourth phase. The last stage emerges more clearly as part of the process if one recalls Psssoa's position on translation as a means to correct a previously extant text (Patrício 2012: 307–14). Furthermore, the last stage seems close to what de Biasi calls 'sifting'. I use 'sifting' here in the sense of an 'endogenetic framing mechanism' (de Biasi 1996: 47), which selects out of all the observable features of a textual entity-specific elements to be appropriated. Once these elements are removed from their source situation, the original context disappears, and the elements become available to be re-textualized into an endogenetic situation, more unstable at the beginning of the process, and gradually turning more fixed as time goes by. We can only imagine how Pessoa's poem underwent this process, but the ingredients seem to be lexical data (love, knowledge, sense of olfaction) subordinated to the newness of present experience.

In the two cases I have just briefly discussed, the text by King Duarte and the poem attributed to Alberto Caeiro, I have tried to show that both of them, regardless of the autographic or apographic status of the extant document witnesses, can only be interpreted by means of inference. For instance, the type of changes introduced in the first general text on translation by King Duarte is plausibly ascribed to him on the grounds that a scribe would not have had that type of responsibility, a strong hypothesis reinforced by the fact that compiling is one of the writing techniques Duarte frequently uses, and by the presence of the grammatical first person as probably referring to the author. In the second case, we have before us a line by Alfred Austin and its translation, while no trace of it emerges in the following poem by Caeiro. However, after one reads the whole poem by Austin it is fair to assume that, besides some lexical coincidence, an importation of the textual structure is apparent, translated, if you will, into the design of the Portuguese poem. Such a realization is only viable through inductive inference: no trace of Austin's line and its translation emerges *verbatim* in the subsequent poem assigned to Caeiro, and a structure based on the contrast presence/absence is too trivial to account for a specific nexus between the two texts. But, if one takes into consideration Pessoa's assessment of the English poem, the co-presence of the Portuguese poem and what looks like a triggering double sentence (in Portuguese and English) in the very same document, and, additionally, Pessoa's notion of translation as correction, then it is plausible to argue that a link exists between the two texts.

Consequently, a common trace in old and modern document witnesses, as well as in autographic and apographic materials, is their elliptical nature for even if a large *dossier génétique* has been kept, it only represents a rather small part of the whole making process leading from a mental project to a self-contained work (see Grésillon 1994: 141–75; for a coincident position in the quarters of translation studies, see Toury 1995: 185).

Interaction

In the second section, I would like to touch upon the way a genetic perspective on translation work enables a refinement of our perception of how translators cooperate with other agents during the translation process (Cordingley and Montini 2015: 4). By realizing that a considerable number of people contribute to shape the translation as we know it in its published version, the Romantic vision of authorial power becomes faulty if we equate it with unlimited autonomy on the part of the individual translator. In this respect, while *critique génétique* struck a blow to the Romantic perspective by bringing to the foreground archive documents more dependent upon hard work than on revelation, translation genetics may have pushed this move a step further by acknowledging how different types of constraints affect the translator's work (Jansen and Wegener 2013; Cordingley and Montini 2015: 2; Solum 2017).[4] Out of all the topics touched upon by Cordingley and Montini, I will briefly discuss the understanding of translation 'as a multitasked, interactive process', underscoring the chain of intervening agents who work for the publishing house or are marginal to it, as well as historical, economic and institutional factors (Cordingley and Montini 2015: 9–10, 13).

Against this backdrop, I will focus on the Portuguese translation of a biographical narrative written by the Russian anarchist Evgenéa Iaroslavskaïa which has come out in 2017. Born in 1902, into a well-off family of Jewish intellectuals, the author came to idealize poverty in her childhood, which set the basis for her viewpoint of the outcast as someone heroic (Shapovalov 2001: 19). After the imprisonment of her husband, Alexander Iaroslavsky, Evgenéa Iaroslavskaïa was detained several times for theft and afterwards condemned to exile in Siberia. Having broken free from prison, she made plans to help her husband escape, but was rearrested and sentenced to three years of forced labour at the Solovetskii camps. Following her husband's execution in December 1930, she made a public protest and attacked the camp commander. As a consequence, Evgenéa Iaroslavskaïa was taken to an isolation camp, sentenced to death and executed on 16 June 1931. Her autobiography was written in prison and kept in her case file (Shapovalov 2001: 24).

The narrative of her life is singly transmitted by a handwritten document unearthed by Irina Fligué at the KGB archives in St Petersburg in 1996 (Shapovalov 2001: xi; Fligué 2017: 149). Curiously, this narrative was first published in 2001 in English in *Remembering the Darkness: Women in Soviet Prisons*, edited and translated by Veronica Shapovalov; and only in 2008 was it published in Russian in a special issue of the journal *Zvezda*. In 2017 Les Éditions du Seuil had it published in French and afterwards in the same year the publishing house Guerra & Paz issued it for the Portuguese market.

The nature of the document that conveys this narrative, written in difficult confinement circumstances and presenting some writing mistakes, makes evident that there is an editorial issue to be approached before or as the text is translated. It is Evgenéa Iaroslavskaïa herself who declares that during her school years she was not good at spelling: 'My weakest subject was spelling – and up to now I have not learnt to spell correctly, without mistakes' (ed. Shapovalov 2001: 27). Under these conditions, is the translator supposed to preserve the misspellings for the sake of preserving an aura of authenticity? A possible decision would be to find somewhat equivalent misspellings in the target language (for instance, in the Portuguese version, one could think of spelling deviations, such as 'óragãos de investigação', 'caixote do lexo', 'Lenigrado'). Or should he or she signal them by *sic* within brackets thereby indicating an exact quote of a spelling error or even comment upon it in footnotes? Or alternatively, are these mistakes to be silently corrected?

In the twenty-phase scheme of the translation process that I had access to, because of the courtesy of the Portugese translator, Nonna Pinto, the design of the strategy to approach these mistakes was made early on, with the cooperation of both the editor Irina Fligué and the Portuguese publisher. As it happens, not only the Portuguese translation but already the English and French versions dealt with such evidence of dysgraphia in the very same way: the dysgraphic mistakes were silently corrected.

In other instances, however, the three translations did not follow the same route. Veronica Shapovalov, who made the English translation, is clear as to the extent of her editorial intervention, stating that the manuscript was edited in Russian before the translation was made. Editing includes here deletions that were introduced to 'avoid repetitions, inconsistencies, and digressions irrelevant to the main narrative' (2001: xi). And she adds: 'It was my goal in editing to carry through the intention of each narrative by preserving as much as possible the authors' unique voices, perceptions, attitudes, and motivations, while eliminating infelicities of style and grammar common to impromptu speech and writing' (2001: xi). She also felt constrained to make 'the difficult choice of deleting sections that did not have direct bearing on the main themes of the collection: resistance to the totalitarian system, everyday life in women's barracks, and problems unique to women' (2001: xi). As Shapovalov's book is an anthology, she seems to have applied the anthology principle to the shaping of the text prior to the translation work. The outcome of this strict selection seems to be a discursive standardization with surgical deletions. The following (Table 2.4) are examples of such an orientation (highlighted are the phrases which are absent from the English translation).

The title, on the other hand, is a different matter. In spite of its visibility and the function of identification it performs, when translated, the title is occasionally subject to remarkable variation, namely when it designates a text which was previously unknown to the translation target audience. In contrast to such title variation, often assignable to options made by the translator, the French and the Portuguese translators decided to give the same title to the narrative by Evgenéa Iaroslavskaïa. Or did they? To make an appropriate interpretation of the shared title, it is necessary to observe the addendum to the agreement made between the Russian editor of the document, Irina Fligué, and the French publishing house. There it is stated that, as far as term and

Table 2.4 Passages from the English, French and Portuguese translations of Evgenéa Iaroslavskaïa's text.

Shapovalov translation	Kislov translation	Pinto translation
to be the daughter of a laundress, (26)	comme la fille de la lavandière de notre cour (20)	tal como a filha de uma lavadeira do nosso prédio (21)
A patriotic passion for everything German, especially for literature and language. The German landscapes used to fill my heart with tenderness. (26)	... un sentiment patriotique ... pour tout ce qui est allemand. La littérature allemande, la langue allemande, les paysages d'Allemagne, le Rhin allemand me remplissent d'attendrissement encore aujourd'hui. (21)	... patriotismo relativamente a tudo o que é alemão. A literatura alemã, a língua alemã, as paisagens da Alemanha, o Reno alemão – ainda me enchem de comoção (22)
Literature, art, and good food interested me immensely more than the most aesthetic rags. (26)	les sujets culturels, comme par exemple l'art et la littérature, et même la gastronomie, m'intéressaient et m'intéressent toujours beaucoup plus que les plus esthétiques [*illisible*] chiffons. (22)	não só os interesses culturais, como literatura e arte, mas também um bom prato me interessavam e interessam muito mais do que a mais bela vestimenta. (23)

territory of use are concerned, the agreement will take effect for all languages, except Russian, and in all countries. This means, for instance, that, as long as the agreement is valid, the text written by Evgenéa Iaroslavskaïa-Markon is bound to be titled *Révoltée*. It was within the scope of this agreement that the Portuguese publishing house Guerra & Paz obtained permission to have this work translated and to publish it in Portugal. Accordingly, the Portuguese version came out with the title *Revoltada*.

Laterally to the legal framework, there is, nevertheless, at least one good alternative: the title page of the French edition immediately before the beginning of the narrative bears the title 'Mon autobiographie' (Iaroslavskaïa-Markon 2017: 1), the text being explicitly referred to under this noun in two passages (Iaroslavskaïa-Markon 2017: 17 and 61, 'cette autobiographie') and in another as 'ma "biographie"' (Iaroslavskaïa-Markon 2017: 84), while in the English version the narrative is always mentioned as 'autobiography' (ed. Shapovalov 2001: 15, 40, 48). Besides, among several additional texts following the account in the French edition, there is one, the 'Ordonnance de renvoi', that mentions it as 'l'autobiographie de IAROSLAVSKAÏA, rédigée par elle personnellement' (ed. Shapovalov 2001: 59; Iaroslavskaïa-Markon 2017: 133); in fact, the top of the first page of the manuscript bears the title, 'Mon autobiographie', which, according to Irina Fligué, would not be altogether correct because of its pleonastic overtones.

Olivier Rolin, a prominent writer who is published by Éditions du Seuil, is the author of the preface to the French edition. There he also refers to the 'autobiography' (Rolin 2017: 9), but in the one footnote of the preface that he wrote for the French edition, he claims responsibility for the title of the book:

> Irina Fligué's postface informs us about the conditions under which Evguénia Iaroslavskaïa wrote the autobiographical account, which obviously did not bear a title. It was I who gave it that of *Révoltée*, which I did not consider to betray its author. I could have also named it *Rebelle*. (Rolin 2017: 14)[5]

No doubt that *Révoltée* or even *Rebelle* is less bland and more commercially appealing than *Autobiography*. Rolin agrees then with Veronica Shapovalov, who says that Evgenéa Iaroslavskaïa 'was a rebel purely for the sake of rebellion' (2001: 19). Therefore, whereas the English version transmits the title *My Autobiography* (ed. Shapovalov 2001: 25), the Portuguese translation, because it depends on the French idea of text, had to adopt *Revoltada*. The Portuguese translator, who, as it happens, is not competent in French, had consequently no say as far as the title is concerned because, even before the translation work started, the title of the narrative was already in place, alien to the author's, the editor's or the translator's views on the text.

Closing remarks

To conclude, instead of endorsing or disputing one of the main contentions of Cordingley and Montini's article, namely that a new field of research, 'genetic translation studies', was born in the past decade (2015: 1), it is perhaps more important to acknowledge that there is a significant area of common interest shared by genetic critics and translation scholars.

Following the introduction and the two parts of the present chapter, the tentative conclusion is that, mainly due to the lack of a self-aware interpretive community, translation genetics is, for the time being, a latent discipline in Portugal. It remains to be seen whether, as a discipline, it will bloom, either as a result of the effects produced by conferences focusing on shared ground by *critique génétique* and translation studies or else through the strengthening of the interest on the genetics of translation in strong academic communities such as the one centred on Pessoa studies.

As to the discussion of its object and objectives, I have tried to argue that a less restricted view of what is currently deemed a valid research object in the traditional quarters of genetic criticism is welcome. In other words, to my mind, a research object does not have to fulfil requirements as to the date of production of the documents under analysis and/or its autographic status. The fact that this is not a mandatory condition becomes more conspicuous when one works on a contemporary research object and realizes that there is not an absolutely autonomous agency, but a network of interacting and negotiating subjects, as in the case of the translation of Evgenéa Iaroslavskaïa's text. In other words, as the individual archival document circulates from hand to hand (of the editor, publisher, lawyer, fellow writer, translator), the textualization process is shaped by different agencies. Again, Cordingley and Montini call attention to this when they point out that we have been witnessing a departure from an inherited model of writing as individual authorship for one constructed around a plurality of actors and processes (Cordingley and Montini 2015: 13). In this regard, as so often happens, there is the risk of going from one extreme to the other; that is, for the sake of demystifying Romantic models of agency, one may fall in the trap of a symmetrically unrealistic model of flat collaboration. To fight off this risk, it would be advantageous to explore an approach based on a balanced consideration of individual agency and contextual voices.

Notes

1   Unless otherwise noted, all translations are mine.
2   The text is transcribed according to a semi-diplomatic protocol, the abbreviations having been developed. Other textual features (namely orthography and split words at the end of the line) were kept.
3   There are two segments before the lines attributed to Alberto Caeiro. Both of them, located on the upper part of the page, were typed and afterwards crossed out with a pencil. The first segment may refer to Paola Frassinetti (1809–82), the foundress of Congregation St Dorothea who was beatified by Pope Pius XI on 8 June 1930 (note that the poem by Caeiro is dated 23 July 1930, that is, a month and a half after the beatification. Paola Frassinetti was also the subject of a book Pessoa held in his library: (1926), *Paula Frassinetti, Fundadora da Congregação das Irmãs de Santa Doroteia. Notas biográficas*, Lisboa: Escola Tipográfica das Oficinas de S. José. Available online: http://bibliotecaparticular.casafernandopessoa. pt/9-55 (accessed 31 October 2019). So far it has not been possible to establish a connection between this first segment and what follows, apart from a possible shared date of typing.

4   In the field of genetic criticism, a similar role has been played by theatre genetics (see, for example, Grésillon et al. 2010). In turn, the constraints mentioned above are crucial ingredients to the sociological perspective on the production and circulation of texts. But, whereas the sociological approach to editing, grounded in contributions by D. F. McKenzie and Jerome McGann, among others, has become a relevant perspective within Anglo-American textual scholarship, French book history and *critique génétique* can perhaps benefit from closer collaboration.
5   Editors' translation *(Editors' note)*.

References

Alvstad, Cecilia and Alexandra Assis Rosa (2015), 'Voice in Retranslation: An Overview and Some Trends', special issue of *Target*, 27 (1): 3–24.

Alvstad, Cecilia, Annjo K. Greenall, Hanne Jansen and Kristiina Taivalkoski-Shilov (eds) (2017), 'Introduction: Textual and Contextual Voices of Translation', in *Textual and Contextual Voices of Translation*, 3–17, Amsterdam and Philadelphia: John Benjamins.

Anastácio, Vanda (1998), *Visões de Glória (uma Introdução à Poesia de Pêro de Andrade Caminha)*, Lisboa: FCG – JNICT.

Askins, Arthur L.-F. (2007), 'Notes on Three Prayers in Late 15th Century Portuguese (the *Oração da Empardeada*, the *Oração de S. Leão, Papa*, and the *Justo Juiz*): Text History and Inquisitorial Interdictions', *Península, Revista de Estudos Ibéricos*, 4: 235–66. Available online: http://ler.letras.up.pt/uploads/ficheiros/4206.pdf (accessed 3 October 2018).

Caeiro, Alberto (2001), *Poesia*, Fernando Cabral Martins and Richard Zenith (eds), Lisboa: Assírio & Alvim.

Cordingley, Anthony and Chiara Montini (2015), 'Genetic Translation Studies: An Emerging Discipline', *Linguistica Antverpiensia, New Series: Themes in Translation Studies*, 14: 1–18.

De Biasi, Pierre-Marc (1996), 'What Is a Literary Draft? Toward a Functional Typology of Genetic Documentation', trans. Ingrid Wassenaar, *Yale French Studies*, 89: 26–58.

Dionísio, João (2018), 'Remarques sur la création plurilingue chez Fernando Pessoa', *GENESIS (Manuscrits-Recherche-Invention)*, 46: 93–102. Available online: https://journals.openedition.org/genesis/2858 (accessed 19 September 2019).

Duarte, D. (2008–), *Leal Conselheiro*, electronic edition, Madison: University of Wisconsin and Universidade de Lisboa (Centro de Linguística and Faculdade de Letras). Available online: http://digital.library.wisc.edu/1711.dl/IbrAmerTxt.LealConselheiro (accessed 3 October 2018).

Duarte, Luiz Fagundes and António Braz de Oliveira (eds) (2007), *As Mãos da Escrita. 25.º Aniversário do Arquivo de Cultura Portuguesa Contemporânea*, Lisboa: Biblioteca Nacional de Portugal.

Firmino, Jessica Fontes (2013), 'A Génese de uma Tradução de Camilo Castelo Branco: *História de Gabriel Malagrida*', MA diss., School of Arts and Humanities of the University of Lisbon, Lisboa. Available online: http://repositorio.ul.pt/bitstream/10451/10142/1/ulfl148004_tm.pdf (accessed 3 October 2018).

Fischer, Claudia J. (2012), 'Auto-Tradução e Experimentação Interlinguística na Génese d'"O Marinheiro" de Fernando Pessoa', *Pessoa Plural*, I (Spring): 1–69. Available online: https://www.brown.edu/Departments/Portuguese_Brazilian_Studies/ejph/pessoaplural/Issue1/PDF/I1A01.pdf (accessed 3 October 2018).

Fligué, Irina (2017), 'Postface – "Je jure de venger par le verbe et par le sang"', in Evguénia Iaroslavskaïa-Markon, *Révoltée*, trans. Valéry Kislov, 147–74, Paris: Seuil.

Grésillon, Almuth (1994), *Éléments de critique génétique. Lire les manuscrits modernes*, Paris: Presses Universitaires de France.

Grésillon, Almuth, Marie-Madeleine Mervant-Roux and Dominique Budor (2010), *Genèses théâtrales*, Paris: CNRS Editions.

Iaroslavskaia-Markon, Evgénia (2017), *Revoltada*, trans. Nonna Pinto, pref. Olivier Rolin, postf. Irina Fligué, Lisboa: Guerra & Paz.

Iaroslavskaïa-Markon, Evguénia (2017), *Révoltée*, trans. Valéry Kislov, pref. Olivier Rolin, post. Irina Fligué, Paris: Seuil.

Jansen, Hanne and Anna Wegener (2013), 'Multiple Translationship', in Hanne Jansen and Anna Wegener (eds), *Authorial and Editorial Voices in Translation, 1: Collaborative Relationships between Authors, Translators and Performers*, 1–35, Montréal: Éditions québécoises de l'oeuvre.

Mahrer, Rudolf (ed.) (2017), 'Après le texte. De la réécriture après publication', *GENESIS. Revue internationale de critique génétique*, 44. Available online: https://journals.openedition.org/genesis/1579 (accessed 3 October 2018).

Patrício, Rita (2012), *Episódios. Da Teorização Estética em Fernando Pessoa*, Vila Nova de Famalicão: Húmus and Centro de Estudos Humanísticos, Universidade do Minho.

Pessoa, Fernando (2015), *Poemas de Alberto Caeiro*, ed. Ivo Castro, Lisboa: Imprensa Nacional–Casa da Moeda.

Pittella, Carlos (2017), 'Sonnet 101 with Prof. Pessoa. Fernando Pessoa's Marginalia on an Anthology of 19th-Century English Sonnets', *Pessoa Plural*, 11 (Spring): 277–375. Available online: https://www.brown.edu/Departments/Portuguese_Brazilian_Studies/ejph/pessoaplural/Issue11/PDF/I11A14.pdf (accessed 3 October 2018).

Rolin, Olivier (2017), 'Avant propos', in Evguénia Iaroslavskaïa-Markon, *Révoltée*, trans. Valéry Kislov, 7–14, Paris: Seuil.

Shapovalov, Veronica (ed. and trans.) (2001), *Remembering the Darkness. Women in Soviet Prisons*, Lanham: Rowman & Littlefield.

Solum, Kristina (2017), 'Translators, Editors, Publishers, and Critics: Multiple Translatorship in the Public Sphere', in Cecilia Alvstad, Annjo K. Greenall, Hanne Jansen and Kristiina Taivalkoski-Shilov (eds), *Textual and Contextual Voices of Translation*, 39–60, Amsterdam and Philadelphia: John Benjamins.

Toury, Gideon (1995), *Descriptive Translation Studies and Beyond*, Amsterdam and Philadelphia: John Benjamins.

Van Hulle, Dirk (2004), *Textual Awareness. A Genetic Study of Late Manuscripts by Joyce, Proust, and Mann*, Ann Arbor: The University of Michigan Press.

Van Hulle, Dirk (2015), 'Translation and Genetic Criticism: Genetic and Editorial Approaches to the "Untranslatable" in Joyce and Beckett', *Linguistica Antverpiensia, New Series: Themes in Translation Studies*, 14: 40–53.

3

Unveiling the creative process of collaborative translation: *Chronicle* by Robert Fitzgerald and Saint-John Perse

Esa Christine Hartmann
*University of Strasbourg/Institut des textes et manuscrits modernes –
ITEM/CNRS, Paris*

Introduction

The creative process that gives birth to a literary translation often remains secret for a long time. Unveiling the creative process of collaborative translation therefore means gaining a deeper insight into the fascinating coulisses of a translator's work, and, more specifically, of the translation process emerging from the manuscripts. In fact, 'the working documents of the translator conserve the traces of their translation process, i.e. the inscription of the various stages of his working experience. … These documents are situated in the coulisses of the translator's laboratory' (Passos 2014: 69),[1] inviting the reader to investigate the creative process of translation, which we define as the coming into being of the translation with all its thematic, stylistic, rhythmical and ideological aspects. Like the author's manuscript of the original text, the translator's draft shows the different stages of textual and translingual gestation, and represents an interesting object of research and analysis for genetic translation studies.[2] The purpose of this new scientific approach is to analyse the practices of the 'working translator and the evolution, or *genesis*, of the translated text by studying translators' manuscripts, drafts and other working documents' (Cordingley and Montini 2015: 1; emphasis added).

Considering the English translations of Saint-John Perse's poetic work,[3] the analysis of the translators' manuscripts, which are conserved in the Saint-John Perse Foundation in Aix-en-Provence (France), sheds light on the genetic process of collaborative translation. This study aims to explore the sinuous gestation of the collaborative translation process that gave birth to the English version of Saint-John Perse's poem *Chronique* (1960) by the American poet, critic and translator Robert Fitzgerald (1910–85). While Fitzgerald's manuscript shows Saint-John Perse's corrections and variants, the collaborative translation process can also be traced, thanks to an interesting correspondence between the two poets, including a list of questions and answers about difficult passages.

Marrying both the melody of a hymn and an epopee, the poem *Chronique* celebrates the cosmic advent of the 'Great Age' and exalts the crowning of human destiny on the threshold of a mythical space and an archaic time. The aesthetical simplicity of its sublime style suggests the greatness of the 'Great Age'; the poetic images evoke the symbolic dimension of the divine. Accordingly, *Chronique* invites a solemn and almost hieratic translation that creates a mimetic rhythm: the long, quiet verses embody the cosmic breathing of the 'Great Age' that represents the mythical background of the poem. In its spiritual quest for the divine, the advent of the 'Great Age' conveys a highly symbolic language, detached from concrete and material references and enriched by mythological, archetypal and etymological allusions that develop a dense metaphorical network within the poem. In his suggestions and corrections, Saint-John Perse constantly seeks to recreate these poetical principles.

Analysing the English translation of *Chronique* from a genetic standpoint hence allows us to follow the sinuous gestation of the translation process, as well as the semantic and phonetic laws that govern the poet's choices. In fact, Saint-John Perse's variants point out the conservation of original etymologies in the English translation, the creation of new alliterations and assonances in the English text and the importance of rhythmic equation and semantic correspondence. We can also make good semantic use of the poet's variants that reveal an unexpected interpretative key, since Saint-John Perse's self-translation process uncovers the underpinnings of his poetics, both in the French text and in the English translation.

The first part of this study follows a *genetic approach*, tracing the different stages of the collaborative translation process. The second part presents a *semantic analysis* of the different variants, leading to the clarification of the difficult metaphors in the French poem. The *poetic approach* in the third part of this study aims to elaborate a poetics of *Chronicle* as a collaborative translation that unites the work of two poets.

Examining the genesis of a collaborative translation

In 1960, *Chronique* was translated into English by Robert Fitzgerald and published in 1961 in the Bollingen Series by Pantheon Books (New York), when Saint-John Perse had returned to France from his exile in Washington. After T. S. Eliot, Denis Devlin, Hugh Chisholm and Wallace Fowlie, Robert Fitzgerald, an eminent translator of the Greek classics, was the fifth translator of Saint-John Perse's poetic work. Similar to his lifelong relationship with the famous poet T. S. Eliot, Saint-John Perse undertook a rich literary exchange with Robert Fitzgerald, author of *Poems* (1935), *A Wreath of the Sea* (1944) and *In the Rose of Time* (1956). Bearing the classical echo of Keats and Shelley, Robert Fitzgerald's poetry was influenced by the sublime style that the poet also displayed in his translations of the Greek Tragedians, which allowed him to unite a great many predispositions to understand Saint-John Perse's mythical rhetoric and to reproduce it in his mother tongue (Levillain 1987: 211). Equality of status and similarity of style thus represent two main conditions in favour of the poets' teamwork and the success of their collaborative translation. As Saint-John Perse acknowledges in his letter to Robert Fitzgerald, he chiefly relies on Fitzgerald's poetic sense and sensibility to cope with the difficulties of his text:

I am of course at your entire disposition to enlighten and assist you in writing on all matters you would need to elucidate concerning the interpretation of my text. I am aware of the high risk of being mistaken. However, you are a poet and this means a lot; it is actually the most important quality in these circumstances. (6 May 1960, Saint-John Perse Foundation)

As Robert Fitzgerald confesses in his letter to Jackson Matthews, who was employed by the Bollingen Series and to whom Fitzgerald sent the first draft of his translation, he used all the intertextual resources at hand to understand Saint-John Perse's text. However, the poet's help remains capital for the elucidation of metaphorical details:

I am not content with it, but I've used every resource I could think of, including Eliot's *Anabase* and a copy of Fowlie's *Amers* ... Au secours! What are villages of horn? And so on ... The exaltation of the poem is painful, magnificent, but there are always those hard, irreducible details. The poet will help, I know, but I don't want to thrust a version at him until you have passed on it. It must be in English. I find that some of Fowlie's is not.[4] (letter to J. Matthews, 12 July 1960, Bollingen Archive, Library of Congress)

Spanning the various stages of the writing process from which this collaborative translation progressively emerges, the two manuscripts conserved at the Foundation – Robert Fitzgerald's manuscript 'Chronicle' bearing the variants and corrections of Saint-John Perse, as well as his 'Questions and Proposed Revisions (31 October 1960)'[5] – reveal a captivating complementarity. In fact, between June and December 1960, the first edition of the translation was sent to Matthews for a first review; a second edition by Fitzgerald was then sent to Saint-John Perse, who annotated Fitzgerald's manuscript according to his poetic art. His revisions were accompanied by the following words:

In order to respond to this concern [the immediate concern of respecting the text] and to help you grasp the meaning of this poem, I dare send your manuscript back to you, overcharged by corrections in red ink.[6] Of course, these corrections engage you only in the points where they reveal a true misinterpretation. They are less numerous. The other corrections only try for the most part to bring you closer to the meaning in its details. Other corrections again express the simple formal concern for harmony, movement or rhythm to the ear. Finally, in some points, the text itself is corrected, conforming to the edition published by Gallimard.

It is not necessary to tell you that this literal, gradual assistance to make the reading of my text as clear as possible implies my respect for your full artistic freedom – the freedom of a poet and writer to judge by himself in his language what is imposed by taste in matters of adaptation, transposition or recreation. My mastery of the English language is far too poor for my red-ink-corrections to pretend to more than enlighten or guide you in the form of mere indications. You do not have to take them literally as formal suggestions. This would deprive me, as a poet, of your art of translating. (12 October 1960, Saint-John Perse Foundation)

This letter not only expresses the polite justifications of the author's interference in the work of his translator, but shows a statement of his representation of literary translation, which is perceived in its most creative and artistic form that legitimates poetic licence as an 'adaptation, transposition or recreation'. Despite his desire for control (Anokhina 2016; Sperti 2016), Saint-John Perse seems to count on Fitzgerald's 'art of translating'. Nevertheless, Saint-John Perse's corrections reveal his preference for conserving the mythological images that arise from the imaginary background of the original poem, his endeavour of recreating the particular rhythm

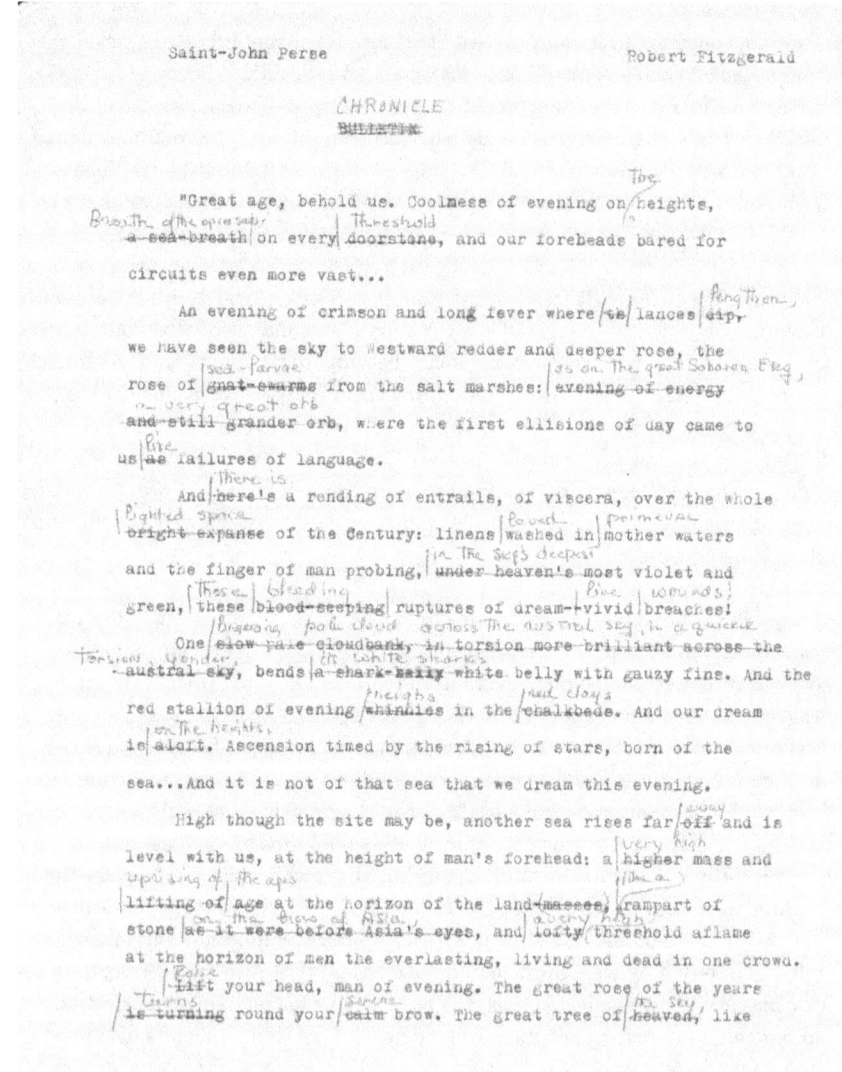

Figure 3.1 Manuscript of Robert Fitzgerald, *Chronicle*, page 1 (1960).

of its very long, breathing verses, and his penchant for metaphors that convey both a material and a symbolic meaning.

Once Fitzgerald had received the poet's suggestions in red ink (Figure 3.1), he reworked his text and questioned some of Saint-John Perse's suggestions in his 'Questions and Proposed Revisions'. This document shows a highly interesting hermeneutic dialogue between author and translator that illuminates the reading of Saint-John Perse's poem *Chronique*. Validating many of Fitzgerald's revisions, Saint-John Perse explains some difficult metaphors that remained obscure. The revision of the translation thus reveals a critical consciousness of the text: from the author–translator correspondence emerges a history of reception.

Analysing the semantics of translation variants

A great number of Saint-John Perse's variants tend to establish the exact image at the origin of a metaphor, which relates to a concrete biological or geological referent that acquires a symbolic meaning in the poem. For instance, the colour of 'insects of the salt marsh', which would be the literal translation of the French 'insects des marais salants', represents an enigma for the translator:

French text: 'nous avons vu le ciel en Ouest plus rouge et rose, du rose *d'insectes des marais salants* …' (Saint-John Perse 1972: 289)

Fitzgerald's translation: 'we have seen the sky to Westward redder and deeper rose, the rose of *gnat-swarms* from the salt marshes' (manuscript, p. 1)

Saint-John Perse's variant: 'we have seen the sky to Westward redder and deeper rose, the rose of *sea-larvae* from the salt marshes' (manuscript, p. 1)

Fitzgerald's question: 'First, I question "sea-larvae" for "insects". Larvae are not yet winged, but the sky is red with flying things' ('Questions and Proposed Revisions', p. 1)

Fitzgerald's proposed revision: '…we have seen the sky to Westward redder and deeper rose, the rose of *sea-midges* from the salt marshes' ('Questions and Proposed Revisions', p. 1)

Fitzgerald's comment: 'Now it has come to me that *"sea-larvae" are pink, like shrimps*, and I understand much more of the passage' (letter to Saint-John Perse, 4 November 1960, Saint-John Perse Foundation)

Saint-John Perse's answer: 'Yes, I had accepted your transposition, but the French text meant indeed the *"larvae" of aquatic insects*, such as the *minuscule molluscs of floating plankton*, which sometimes and under certain conditions adopt a *pink colour*, like in the extreme phases of decantation of the salt marshes' (letter to R. Fitzgerald, 7 November 1960, Saint-John Perse Foundation)

In fact, Saint-John Perse's explanation reproduces an expression that appears in the original manuscript of the French text, where we read the following variants in the margin: 'aux senteurs de//terre rouge/rousse//*d'algues rousses*/sèches' (manuscript *Chronique* 1, p. 1). According to the poet's imaginary chain of associations, the *pink algae* ('*algues rousses*') of the manuscript of the French text give birth to the pink 'sea-larvae', the pink 'molluscs of floating plankton' (letter to Fitzgerald) in his explanation for the English translation. Consequently, Saint-John Perse's creative memory motivates his corrections on the English manuscript.

A geological example can be added to this biological case. Fitzgerald encounters the enigmatic word 'erg' in the immediately following sentence:

French text: 'soir de grand erg, et très grand orbe' (Saint-John Perse 1972: 289)

Fitzgerald's translation: 'evening of energy and still grander orb' (manuscript, p. 1)

Saint-John Perse's variant: 'as on the great Saharan Erg, a very great orb' (manuscript, p. 1)

Fitzgerald's question: 'I do not understand *soir de grand erg* in the French nor "as on the great Saharan Erg" in the English, and I do not understand how the former is rendered by the latter. The word "erg" is not capitalized in the French and seems to bear its technical sense as an electrical unit of work done: to capitalize it and qualify it as "Saharan" makes it seem, instead, a place-name, but one that in English has trivial punning overtones from its similarity in English pronunciation to "Ur". This ugly (ergly) effect is very far from the beauty of the French parallel phrasing and voweling, *erg* and *orbe*. ... Fourth, *orb* in English is now generally used for sun, moon, or planet, and almost never for *orbis terrarum*, but *très grand orbe* seems to refer to the earth' ('Questions and Proposed Revisions', pp. 1–2)

Fitzgerald's revision: '... evening of pure charge, and pure grand globe' ('Questions and Proposed Revisions', p. 2)

Saint-John Perse's correction: 'evening of vast Saharan space and ever widening sky' ('Questions and Proposed Revisions', p. 2)

Evidently, Fitzgerald was not familiar with the semantic plurality of the word 'erg', which may refer to a unit of energy ('an electrical unit of work done'), but also designates in Arabic a dune of the Saharan desert, a geological reality that had integrated the French lexical treasure due to the French colonies in North Africa. Although Fitzgerald elegantly translates it as 'evening of energy', Saint-John Perse wishes to recreate the visual analogy between the sand dune of the desert (erg) and the cosmic roundness of the globe (orb), both images corresponding to the disc of the lowering sun at the horizon ('an evening of crimson and long fever'). Unfortunately, the sound of the word 'erg' in English does not allude to the grandeur of the evoked scene and its sacred character, Fitzgerald fearing an 'ugly/ergly' effect. Saint-John Perse proposes 'vast

Saharan space', an archaic space that invites and celebrates the advent of the 'Great Age' of the poem.

Accordingly, one of the key metaphors that represents the 'Great Age' of *Chronicle* is the image of the sunset. The lowering sunrays that fall on the 'lighted space of the Century' certainly gain a cosmic signification in light of the mythical space that symbolizes human destiny. How might this metaphorical image of the sunset be translated?

French text: 'Un soir de rouge et longue fièvre *où s'abaissent les lances*' (OC, p. 389)

Fitzgerald's translation: 'An evening of crimson and long fever *where the lances dip*' (manuscript, p. 1)

Saint-John Perse's variant: 'An evening of crimson and long fever *where lances lengthen*' (manuscript, p. 1)

Fitzgerald's question: 'If this contains an image of lowering sunrays, could it be kept more fully in English perhaps this way:'
Revision: 'An evening of crimson and long fever *where lances incline and lengthen...* or ... *where lances are sloping far...*' ('Questions and Proposed Revisions', p. 1)

Saint-John Perse's answer: 'yes' and underlines 'An evening of crimson and long fever *where lances incline and lengthen*' ('Questions and Proposed Revisions', p. 1)

The warlike metaphor of the 'lances' evokes the inclining sunrays. Curiously, Saint-John Perse chooses the verb 'to lengthen' for the French 's'abaisser' (to deepen). This choice may be motivated by the poetic desire for creating an alliteration in [l], the sonority of which suggests the lengthening of the sunrays: *lances lengthen*.

The dialogue between author and translator thus reflects the reception of the French text by the translator, but also a semantic reading of the English version by the author. Saint-John Perse's explanation of difficult passages often reveals the original imaginary association chain, from which the metaphorical network of the poem emerges.

From collaborative translation to the poetics of *Chronicle*

In this sense, Fitzgerald's questions and Saint-John Perse's answers and explanations reveal the principal aspects of the imaginary universe of the poem *Chronique*, but also its poetics. The first correction we perceive on Fitzgerald's manuscript refers to the title of the poem. *Chronique* is first translated into 'Bulletin' by Fitzgerald; yet, Saint-John Perse prefers the English word 'Chronicle', which conserves the same Latin etymology. This preference reveals the deeper meaning of the title *Chronique* that evokes the mythical and sacred dimension of the archaic time and space evoked in this poem. On the contrary, the concreteness of the word 'Bulletin' does not accomplish such an association with transcendence by failing to evoke the sublime voice of the 'Great Age'.

The greatest part of Saint-John Perse's variants and corrections meets the same concern of tone, style and rhythm. For instance, Saint-John Perse proposes 'threshold' instead of 'doorstone' for *seuils*, in order to evoke the spiritual passage between immanence and transcendence. Similarly, he prefers 'over the whole lighted space of the Century' to Fitzgerald's 'over the whole bright expanse of the Century' for *sur toute l'aire illuminée du Siècle*, in this way assimilating the geological space to a mythical area – the scene of the antique amphitheatre, where the Century performs its destiny. This archaic image is also conveyed by the cosmic, mythical and historical shape of the 'rampart of stone on the brow of Asia', which Saint-John Perse suggests for *rampart de pierre au front d'Asie* and which invites us to think of the Trojan walls, replacing the version proposed by Fitzgerald, 'rampart of stone as it were before Asia's eyes'.

This archaic dimension of representation is stylistically reproduced by the use of the same Latin etymology in the English translation. Therefore, Saint-John Perse suggests 'linens *laved* in primeval waters' instead of 'linens *washed* in mother waters' for *linges lavés dans les eaux mères*. Moreover, this translingual association between the French 'lavés' and the English 'laved' allows conserving the alliteration in [l]: *linges lavés/linens laved*. The present image reminds the reader of a sacred ritual, the archaic value of which and the idea of origin conveyed by it being reinforced by Saint-John Perse's variant 'primeval waters' instead of 'mother waters' for *eaux mères*. However, in his letter to Fitzgerald, Saint-John Perse, who fears an archaism, questions his etymological choice: '(page 9, strophe 3) "*laved*", for *washed*, is it not too archaic or literary? Please judge yourself, otherwise than by the ear' (7 November 1960, Saint-John Perse Foundation).

The sublime style of *Chronique/Chronicle* is particularly conveyed in this last example, where Saint-John Perse's second correction unconsciously adopts the sacred tone and language of the King James Bible, a rhetorical model that had previously inspired T. S. Eliot for his translation of Saint-John Perse's poem *Anabase* (Levillain 1987: 317).

> French text: 'Mais Dieu se tait dans *le quantième*' (Saint-John Perse 1972: 391)
>
> Fitzgerald's translation: 'But God is silent in *the nth degree*' (manuscript, p. 2)
>
> Saint-John Perse's correction: 'But God is silent in *his chronicle*' (manuscript, p. 2)
>
> Fitzgerald's note: 'I wish it were possible to render this more closely. Perhaps: But God is silent *on the nth day*.'
>
> Saint-John Perse's variant: *But God does not dwell in the date or day.*
>
> Saint-John Perse's note: 'The nth day, like in French "la n^{th} puissance", seems to imply "the highest, the ultimate, the last day, something like the Judgement Day". "Silent on" would thus be equivocal. The idea is that God does not exist, does not reveal himself in such fraction of time, in such hour of the day or of the year' ('Questions and Proposed Revisions', p. 3)

Saint-John Perse's second proposition, 'But God does not dwell/in the date or day', shows the ritual rhythm of the iambic pentameter (5/5) which is emphasized in this verse by a quadruple alliteration in [d] – d*oes*/d*well*/d*ate*/d*ay*. At the same time, Saint-John Perse's wording echoes the sacred tone of the biblical text, which is aesthetically and semantically conveyed by the pantheistic presence of the unrevealed 'God'.

Saint-John Perse's variants highlight the importance of musical rhythm. For instance, the poet favours words that create a hieratic rhythm produced by numerous alliterations, as in the following passage:

French text: 'Et dans l'embrasement d'un soir aux senteurs d'algue sèche' (Saint-John Perse 1972: 390)

Fitzgerald's translation: 'And in the conflagration of an evening odorous with dry algae' (manuscript, p. 2)

Saint-John Perse's variant: 'And in the fiery glow of an evening fragrant with dry algae' (manuscript, p. 2)

Saint-John Perse's proposition does not significantly alter the meaning of Fitzgerald's translation, but it creates an alliteration in [f] – *f*iery/o*f*/*f*ragrant, as well as an assonance in [ai] – *fi*ery/*dry*. The tone and the harmony of these poetic lines, together with its musical rhythm, create the stylistic scenery of the 'Great Age' and bear the secret meaning of the poem.

Conclusion

Be it through the harmonization of tone, rhythm and lexis emphasizing the sublime, the creation of alliterations and assonances evoking the grandeur of the 'Great Age', the preference for a symbolic language enriched by mythological and archetypal allusions or the conservation of the original etymologies in the English translation, Saint-John Perse's participation in the English translation of *Chronique* certainly unveils the keystones of its poetics.

Underlining the hermeneutic aspect of this collaborative translation, the dialogue between author and translator enlightens the reading of the original poem and enriches its reception with a new authorial interpretation, which often clarifies the meaning of difficult metaphors. Seen from a genetic standpoint, however, Saint-John Perse's suggestions and revisions in English perform a translingual recreation of the initial text, a secondary creation mirroring the genesis of the oeuvre premiere. In this sense, the collaborative translation process must be considered as a true creative process that accomplishes the passage between two languages and two cultures.

This *closelaboration*[7] of *Chronicle* by the two poets Robert Fitzgerald and Saint-John Perse, who we have observed working together on the nascent English text and sharing the experience of creative translation, seems to transform the usual question of authorship and authority into the equality and complementarity of a real 'peer review process':

I ask you, very sincerely, to never consider any suggestion as imperative, or as something which could limit your free final appreciation: the appreciation of an artist (writer and poet) responsible for and only judge of the artistic transposition into the English language. (Saint-John Perse to Robert Fitzgerald, 11 March 1964, Saint-John Perse Foundation)

It has been a delight for me to see in what perfect English you have touched and clarified my version where it remained – and sometimes sadly – inadequate. It is in every way stronger and better for your hand. (Robert Fitzgerald to Saint-John Perse, 4 May 1964, Saint-John Perse Foundation)

Made in the context of their next collaborative translation adventure for the creation of *Birds* (*Oiseaux*, 1965), the statements of the two poet–translators – although remaining under a slight suspicion of polite flattery – seem to express a relationship of mutual respect and consideration that facilitates the *closelaboration* activity as a dynamic translingual exchange between peer poets.

Notes

1. Unless otherwise noted, all translations are mine.
2. Genetic translation studies were first explored, illustrated and conceptualized in the following publications: Marie-Hélène Paret Passos (2011), *Da Crítica Genética à Tradução Literária: uma interdisciplinaridade*, Vinhedo: Horizonte; and Sergio Romanelli (2013), *Gênese do Processo Tradutorio*, Vinhedo: Horizonte.
3. Saint-John Perse (Alexis Leger) was a French poet and diplomat (1887–1975), who was awarded the Nobel Prize in Literature in 1960. For an integral and exhaustive analysis of Saint-John Perse's manuscripts and poetics, see Esa Christine Hartmann (2007), *Les Manuscrits de Saint-John Perse. Pour une poétique vivante*, Paris: L'Harmattan.
4. Wallace Fowlie's translation *Seamarks* (1957) of the poem *Amers* (1956) was intensely corrected by Saint-John Perse under the influence of a parallel translation by John Marshall. Fowlie complained of the numerous corrections by the poet. See Hartmann (2018).
5. For the transcription of this document, see Hartmann (2007: 485–6).
6. Saint-John Perse's corrections were written on Fitzgerald's manuscript by his wife Dorothy Leger, with the exception of the correction of the title 'Bulletin' into 'Chronicle', which shows the handwriting of the poet himself.
7. The Cuban writer Guillermo Cabrera Infante calls closelaboration this intimate relationship between author and translator, who elaborate together the nascent text of the translation (Levine 1991: xiii).

References

Anokhina, Olga (2016), 'Vladimir Nabokov and His Translators: Collaboration or Translation under Duress?', in Anthony Cordingley and Céline Frigau Manning (eds), *Collaborative Translation: From the Renaissance to the Digital Age*, 111–29, London and New York: Bloomsbury.

Cordingley, Anthony and Céline Frigau Manning (eds) (2016), *Collaborative Translation: From the Renaissance to the Digital Age*, London and New York: Bloomsbury.
Cordingley, Anthony and Chiara Montini (2015), 'Genetic Translation Studies: An Emerging Discipline', *Linguistica Antverpiensia, New Series: Themes in Translation Studies*, 14: 1–18.
Durand-Bogaert, Fabienne (ed.) (2014), *Traduire*, special issue of *GENESIS. Revue internationale de critique génétique*, 38 (14).
Fitzgerald, Robert (1930), *Chronicle*, manuscript (first stage) for the English translation of *Chronique*, Saint-John Perse Foundation. Typescript of 14 pages. With corrections in red ink by Dorothy Leger. Correction of the title '[Bulletin] Chronicle' by Saint-John Perse.
Fitzgerald, Robert (1930), Letter to Saint-John Perse, 4 November, Saint-John Perse Foundation.
Fitzgerald, Robert (1960), 'For the English Translation of *Chronique*. Questions and Proposed Revisions', 31 October, Saint-John Perse Foundation. Typescript, 4 pages. With corrections and comments in black ink by Saint-John Perse.
Hartmann, Esa Christine (2007), *Les Manuscrits de Saint-John Perse. Pour une poétique vivante*, Paris: L'Harmattan.
Hartmann, Esa Christine (2018), 'Discovering the Coulisses of Artistic Collaboration: A Genetic Reading of the English Translation of Saint-John Perse's Poem *Amers*', *Ilha do Desterro. A Journal of English Language, Literature in English and Cultural Studies*, 76 (2): 153–64.
Levillain, Henriette (1987), *Sur deux versants. La création chez Saint-John Perse d'après les versions anglaises de son œuvre poétique*, Paris: Corti.
Levine, Suzanne Jill (1991), *The Subversive Scribe. Translating Latin American Fiction*, Saint-Paul: Graywolf Press.
Montini, Chiara (ed.) (2016), *Traduire. Genèse du choix*, Paris: Éditions des archives contemporaines.
Munday, Jeremy (2014), 'Using Primary Sources to Produce a Microhistory of Translation and Translators: Theoretical and Methodological Concerns', *Translator: Studies in Intercultural Communication*, 20 (1): 64–80.
Paret-Passos, Marie-Hélène (2011), *Da Crítica Genética à Tradução Literária: uma interdisciplinaridade*, Vinhedo: Horizonte.
Paret-Passos, Marie-Hélène (2014), 'De *Finnegans Wake* à *Finnicius Revém*. Approche génétique des cahiers de travail d'un traducteur', *GENESIS. Revue internationale de critique génétique*, 38 (14): 69–83.
Saint-John Perse (1930), Letter to Robert Fitzgerald, 7 November, Saint-John Perse Foundation.
Saint-John Perse (1961), *Chronicle*, trans. Robert Fitzgerald, New York: Pantheon Books, Bollingen Series (bilingual edition).
Saint-John Perse (1972), *Œuvres complètes*, Paris: Gallimard.
Sperti, Valeria (2016), 'La traduction littéraire collaborative entre privilège auctorial et contrôle traductif', in Alessandra Ferraro and Rainier Grutman (eds), *L'Autotraduction littéraire. Perspectives théoriques*, 169–88, Paris: Classiques Garnier.

4

Czesław Miłosz's genetic dossier in the Polish translations of 'Negro spirituals'

Ewa Kołodziejczyk
Institute of Literary Research, Polish Academy of Sciences, Warsaw

Introduction

Czesław Miłosz's post-war translations of 'Negro spirituals', the very first translations of these songs into Polish, did not appear in Communist Poland by chance. This chapter dwells on the genetic dossier of these translations to demonstrate the poet's political motivations both in his published arrangement of the songs into a cycle and in the ways particular utterances were paraphrased in Polish.

Miłosz's encounter with African American culture explains why he took an interest in 'Negro spirituals'. The first part of this chapter reveals his observation of the post-war American political scene, where racism still played a role, and suggests his interest in the socio-economic status of the African American minority. Additionally, it reveals him as a visitor of art exhibitions, where he saw African American paintings and sculpture, and as a reader and critic of African American literature. His particular individual experience informs his empirical dossier and precedes his endeavours as a translator.

Second, this chapter explores Miłosz's translation process. As Katarzyna Jakubiak rightly argues, the selection of songs was deliberate, so it could indirectly express a craving for political freedom, whereas directly uttering such a want was not possible in Poland, where all publications were censored. The second part of the chapter compares the source texts, draft manuscripts and typescripts to unveil the translator's political practices of re-writing and putting translations into a meaningful order. Also, this section depicts his 'drawriting' and doodles as an integral part of the creative process. The close reading of draft manuscripts and typescripts reveals Miłosz's hidden intentions of using 'Negro spirituals' as an Aesopian voice in the unofficial debate of Polish intellectuals concerning the political situation of the time. The concurrent study of the empirical prehistory and the genetic dossier of these translations fully demonstrate that Miłosz's literary gestures had political intent and contributed to the intellectual resistance against Communism.

Czesław Miłosz's encounter with African American culture in the 1940s

Czesław Miłosz was born in the village of Szetejnie in 1911 and raised in Vilnius, both of which were then part of the former territory of Poland, and are in present-day Lithuania. His family belonged to the large Polish-speaking population in that multicultural, multiethnic and multireligious border region (Franaszek 2017: 13–49). Such a rich family and community background may have fostered Miłosz's perception of the complex post-war American culture. Later he confessed:

> I inherited not only the distant past but also the past that was on the cusp of turning into the present moment: Bleriot's flight over the English Channel, ordinary people's Fords in America, cubism and the first abstract paintings, Max Linder's films, the Japanese War of 1905. (Miłosz 2001: 28)

Once the Second World War had ended, Miłosz tried to make a life for himself and was part of the diplomatic corps of Communist Poland's post-war government. He became one of the numerous writers who fled the country with diplomatic passports hoping they could enjoy more artistic freedom far from the Communist regime. In 1946, he found himself appointed cultural attaché to the Consulate General of the Polish People's Republic in New York City. A year later, he received a promotion to the post of second secretary to the Embassy of the Polish People's Republic in Washington, DC.

Paradoxically, the political custom afforded to diplomats allowed Miłosz to remain more independent outside of the Communist state: he had access to Western culture and immersed himself into reading books and periodicals that were either not translated or censored or inaccessible in Poland. He became a member of the intellectual milieu in New York City, partaking in the anti-Stalinist editorial boards of *politics* and *Partisan Review*. He met acclaimed international poets and scientists, including Albert Einstein. He travelled around the United States where he participated in conferences and cultural events. This independence allowed him to internationalize his mind (Miłosz 2007: 549).

Moving to France in 1950, he then served at the Polish embassy in Paris. In 1951, he defected and was granted political asylum in France. He remained in the Paris area until 1960, serving afterwards as professor of Slavic languages and literature at the University of California, Berkeley. In 1980, he was awarded the Nobel Prize for Literature. Having lived in exile for fifty years, he moved from the United States to Krakow in 2001, and died there in 2004.

In pre-war Poland, Miłosz's encounter with African American culture was fairly typical for an Eastern European intellectual, whose thorough education included a history of the American Civil War. To simplify, it was shaped – on the one hand – by the Polish translation of Harriet Beecher-Stowe's famous anti-slavery novel *Uncle Tom's Cabin*, Fennimore Cooper's and Jack London's novels that were part of a reading canon for young boys from the intelligentsia, and – on the other – by the growing number of Walt Whitman's poetry translations into Polish. It should be noted that all of the above enumerated authors were white, not black. Only during his initial stay in the United States did Miłosz first get acquainted with authentic black culture. His encounter with African American heritage took place on at least three different, yet overlapping, levels: socio-economic, political and cultural. Whereas the first level involves direct and unmediated relationships, the following two are based on various kinds of representations, specifically books, media broadcast and visual arts. Miłosz's journalism and essays from this time evoke most of these representations and form an exogenetic background of his translations of 'Negro spirituals'. The way Miłosz perceived his experience with African American culture on the above-mentioned levels shall be examined in the following three sections.

Socio-economic level

In spite of racial segregation, Miłosz interacted with African Americans on a regular basis. He showed interest in the socio-economic conditions in which their culture developed. In his diplomatic reports for the Ministry of Foreign Affairs and journalistic work published in the Polish press, he raised the problem of racism in the United States. Yet, whereas journalists in Poland used racism as a convenient means to criticize America, Miłosz impartially described the standards of living in a multiracial society. He discussed the relationship between race and social standing. Privately, his family was helped by African American domestic helpers and nannies. In contrast to white Americans, he called blacks 'the only living human beings in the United States' (Miłosz 2007: 427).[1] He commented more broadly:

> [T]he only living people ... are the Black and the Native Americans, if we take people as groups and not as individuals. It is the lowest, poorest, the most underprivileged group. Mexicans, masses of whom live at Polish peasants' living standards, or worse, are alive – they feel, love, create art, fill exhibition halls with crowds: and the great Mexican leftist political painters draw their energy from them. (Miłosz 2007: 428)

As they remained the lowest social stratum in American society, in his view they were faithful to non-commercial values, and, as the poet emphasized, they retained 'a sense of tragic' inscribed in their individual and collective fates. Miłosz, who was bitterly confronting his war trauma with the prevailing American historical worldview, immediately sensed solidarity with black Americans. Moreover, the diplomat living in Manhattan quickly noticed areas of New York City inhabited both by Slavic immigrants and African American citizens. In his journalistic pieces published in the Polish press under the pseudonym 'Jan M. Nowak', he mentioned numerous fights between white and black people that, in fact, were conflicts between Poles and black New Yorkers sharing the same neighbourhoods (Nowak 1947b: 9). The crucial difference between these groups was that Poles, as whites, could climb the American social ladder with greater ease. While white immigrants could integrate in the American melting pot, their black neighbours could not, merely because they were black. However, he emphasized that 'the living standards of the black population, very low by American standards, are higher than those of the Polish population today' (Nowak 1947b).

Political level

As a voracious observer of the American political scene, Miłosz critically commented on appalling incidents of discriminatory acts against African Americans. In his series 'Living in the U.S.A.', authored under the pseudonym 'Jan M. Nowak', he described instances of segregation in public transport; regrettable legacies of Ku-Klux-Klan in the organization of the Columbians; disgraceful acts of the Mississippi Senator, Theodore Bilbo, who was accused of inciting violence against black citizens wanting to vote in the South (Nowak 1947a: 7). Around 1947, however, the poet ceased to send his coverage of such incidents to Polish journals. After the Iron Curtain separated Eastern and Central Europe from the West, anti-American propaganda in Poland exploited such instances to undermine democracy's leading role in global politics. In one of his journalistic pieces he offers a critique of the manipulative depiction of African Americans in the post-war United States:

> In 'Kuźnica', in the issue from December, 10, 1946, on the front page, below a big title 'One of the four freedoms: freedom from fear' one may see photos of Ku-Klux-Klan and hanged Negroes ... it is puzzling that the journal uses sensational methods that in America are a monopoly of a certain type of daily press which could not be further away from intellectualism and it is steered clear with contempt by educated people. Presenting America as a country, where Negros are hanged is more less as precise as telling that in Poland everybody wears bowlers, because this headgear has been insofar in use by the owners of hackney carriages in Krakow. (Nowak 1947b: 9)

Prior to ceasing unwanted ties to Polish propagandists, Miłosz managed to review the book *Last of the Conquerors* by William Gardner Smith for the Polish audience that, after the Second World War, could not easily access American contemporary literature and lacked good literary translations. The novel presents the author's own experience as a soldier serving in the racially segregated army in the US-controlled zone of Germany after the Second World War. Smith reveals post-Nazi Germany, paradoxically, as being less racially prejudiced than the United States. His novel questions the silent post-war expectation that the model of American society should be followed and imitated in the contemporary world. Beneath this critique lurks the hidden truth that African Americans had not been yet liberated from sufferings under the Jim Crow system, neither at home nor in the military abroad. Miłosz inadvertently supports racism in his somewhat sarcastic summarization of the novel's plot, and concludes:

> The novel is not an outstanding achievement, it is hard to expect such an oeuvre from a twenty-year-old author anyway. It is valuable in its naivety and

truthfulness ... The book is full of bitterness and a sense of grievance. In America, they say it is far from words to deeds, and even that words serve as a security flapper better that their absence. Therefore the book had a good press and also came out in the 25 cent edition. (1949: 2)

This seeming racism in his journalism may be interpreted as an instance of self-censorship. While Miłosz did not avoid the topic of racial discrimination, he sometimes mitigated its problematic prevalence in America in his determination not to provide the Communists in Poland with any evidence against America. On the contrary, in describing contemporary African American art, he defused the arguments of those who based their judgements of the United States on racism (Kołodziejczyk 2011: 21).

Cultural-artistic level

Czesław Miłosz regularly visited museums and art galleries in New York City and Washington, DC. Among his greatest artistic discoveries was African American visual arts, with a special focus on Horace Pippin's and Jacob Lawrence's paintings and Richmond Barthé's sculpture. His review of an exhibit from the Museum of Modern Art depicts black artists along with Mexican and Chilean political activists, providing such an observation:

One group of artists strikes for their autonomy. These are black artists. May not my interest in them be attributed to chance or to some kind of postwar sensitivity, may not be ascribed either to passion for exoticism or to underestimation of their white counterparts. I simply visited an exhibition that I liked. This way all these dangerous generalizations about countries or nations often arise. (Miłosz 1947: 3)

In his descriptions of Pippin's and Lawrence's paintings, Miłosz deliberately focuses on their political and historic themes, such as the exploitation of slaves, the execution of John Brown or life in Harlem, to demonstrate that such artistic representations of sensitive topics might have found their place in public institutions irrespective of the racial problems the society was then experiencing. This may suggest that an internal debate about American history allows such topics, and it does not exclude its victims from artistic dialogue. Also, Miłosz emphasizes the biblical background of black artists' oeuvres, which corresponds to his own spiritual perception of African Americans, and additionally attributes their art a universal value. By 1947, Miłosz came across so-called 'black poets', and he immediately began translating their works into Polish. His selection of poets, to name a few, included Margaret Walker, Luis Palés Matos, Kenneth Everard Ingram, Bruce McM Wright, George Campbell, Jacques Roumain, Hugh Doston Carberry, Helen Johnson, Owen Dodson, Nicolas Guillèn and Ildefonso Pereda Valdes. Nowadays, such a selection makes it obvious he was ahead of his time and of the concept of 'the Black Atlantic' that emerged much later (Gilroy 1993). Not only did Miłosz's interest in post-war African American visual arts and poetry result in illuminating cultural otherness, it directed him to African American art history and political thought as exemplified in works by Gunnar Myrdal, W. E. B. Du Bois, Earl Browning, Alaine Locke, James A. Porter, Clair Drake and Horace R. Cayton. All of these circumstances and experiences significantly tinted the future translator's view of African American culture and formed his unique empirical and intellectual dossier. Such a material and non-material dossier preceded and determined his act of 'Negro spirituals' translation into Polish, and may well be seen as part of a translator's encyclopaedia as defined by Elżbieta Tabakowska (1999: 54). Tabakowska introduces a distinction between a translator's encyclopaedia and a translator's dictionary. In her view, a translator's encyclopaedia is in-depth knowledge of a source culture that allows establishing verbal equivalents of certain terms in a target language. In other words, it allows the creation of a translator's dictionary. Without such knowledge, an act of translation may never be successful. In this dynamic scheme, a translator's encyclopaedia and dictionary, which are strongly interconnected and interrelated realms, mutually determine and advance themselves.

The process of translation of 'Negro spirituals' as reflected in the genetic dossier

In 1948, Miłosz translated fourteen 'Negro spirituals': *Come Down, Moses*; *Where Shall I Be When the First Trumpet Sounds*; *I Know Moonrise*; *I Wish I Have Had an Eagle Wing*; *God's Goin' to Set This World on Fire*; *Joshua Fit the Battle of Jericho*; *Going to Pull My War-Clothes*; *'Tis Me, O Lord*; *Couldn't Hear Nobody Pray*; *Sometimes I am*; *Swing Low, Sweet Chariot*; *My Blood Ran Icy-Cold*; *Singing' Wid a Sword in My Han'*; and *Good News, the Chariot's Coming*. The compilation of selected songs comes from four main sources by W. E. B. Dubois, J. W. Johnson, J. A. Lomax and A. Lomax and C. Sandburg.[2] Miłosz's private library does not, however, include these books, so it is uncertain whether he owned his copies or used library collections. Only five out of fourteen of Miłosz's translations were selected for publication in the 1940s, despite the fact that the poet asked the editor-in-chief:

> I urge you, if you are willing to print it, to give it as it is rather than split it, as in such a case it probably loses its sense. If it didn't fit at all, delete one or two songs, at your discretion. And I ask of you, do not give any photos of Negros to ornament the page, the text explains itself clearly enough, and I don't want to use my work in this direction for any propaganda. I translated this, as Tadeusz Kassern was going to compose music for it, and I will use this for my anthology of poetry of various nations I am currently working on. (Miłosz 2007: 200)

Irrespective of the poet's request, the translations appeared in print in two batches.[3] The first one included only four songs: *Zejdź, Mojżeszu* (Come Down, Moses); *O, chciałbym mieć orle skrzydła* (I Wish I Have Had an Eagle Wing); *To ja, o Panie* (Tis Me, O Lord); *Kiedy złote trąby zagrają* (Where Shall I Be When the First Trumpet Sounds); and *Widzę, księżyc wschodzi* (I Know Moonrise). The latter included just one song *Jerycho* (Joshua Fit the Battle of Jericho). It was the very first ever publication of

'Negro spirituals' in Polish.[4] Dividing the translations into parts and excluding a large number of them, however, damaged the poet's original intentions of how to present the selected songs, so that they might tell an archetypal story of a slave, whose personal hope and belief in liberation led him to achieve inner freedom and strength. Miłosz furiously commented: 'Recently I was mad at "Nowiny Literackie" [Literary News] that killed my "Negro spirituals" by publishing an extensive preface along with two or three tiny poems. Perhaps these "Negro spirituals" do not turn on, as you say, in Polish, but the bigger batch gives a certain idea of an aura that called them into being, and that was my intention' (2007: 445).

Studying the body of Miłosz's 'spirituals' reveals the translator's clear political aspirations and practices. Katarzyna Jakubiak argues the purposeful selection of the songs: two of the 'spirituals' openly expressed a craving for freedom and two other included a motif of flight which the slaves immediately identified as a symbol of escape. Some of them voiced a promise of heaven interpreted analogously as a place free from racial prejudice, while others mentioned a moment of a family reunion, also read as an allusion to liberation of people deprived of contact with their relatives (Jakubiak 2011: 206). The song about Joshua's storming the wall of Jericho related to a ritual dance (*a ring shout*), and together constituted a performative act of forming an army and going to battle (Jakubiak 2011: 207). In other words, the selected 'Negro spirituals' used an Aesopian language of secret communication among slaves. The communication was veiled, however, by seemingly religious content of Christian prayers. Therefore, as the researcher rightly mentions, it was driven by the 'ethics of deception' (2011: 222). Jakubiak argues that the translations of 'Negro spirituals' served Miłosz as his own Aesopian language for critiquing the Communist regime in Poland, and she analyses the ways in which the poet used them to fulfil his concealed political purpose. First, she points to his selection of one particular 'spiritual's' version out of several available variants (e.g. *Going to Pull My War-Clothes*). Second, she emphasizes how well Miłosz recognized and used metaphors of freedom and resistance to convey his political message. Of particular value, her remarks on his compilation of several versions of one 'spiritual' into one translation (e.g. *God's Going to Set This World on Fire*) illustrate the blurred roles of the poet/author and the translator.

The archival record of Miłosz's 'Negro spirituals' provides even more examples of the translator's subversive practices. The major part of the translations' documentation may be found at the poet's archives at Beinecke Rare Book and Manuscript Library at Yale University in the collection 'Czesław Miłosz Papers GEN MSS 661', arranged in two folders (box 139, folder 2213–14). The folders include manuscripts of all translations as well as a foreword's manuscript and a typescript to append the collection in print. Moreover, three manuscripts of the English versions of 'Negro spirituals' copied by the poet are available: *Going to Pull My War-Clothes*; *Oh, I Wish I Have Had an Eagle Wing*; and *Dere's No Hiding Place Down Dere*. Interestingly, the very last 'spiritual' was not translated into Polish. Its content alluded, perhaps too obviously, to Miłosz's double-sword situation as an anti-regime poet hiding behind a diplomatic position, which could not serve as a place to hide for too long. Offering the song's translation for print would have been a suicidal misstep, yet the very act of privately copying the 'spiritual' may be interpreted in therapeutic categories and illustrates the poet's situation at the time. As his biographer explains: 'By the late 1940s, Miłosz was finding it difficult to conceal his feelings much longer. Poison-pen letters at the embassy were addressed to his superiors, and at the beginning of February 1950 the ministerial committee decided that Miłosz is an individual who ideologically is totally alien' (Franaszek 2017: 277). By this time the poet tried to align his diplomatic duties with his true views, to no avail.

The draft manuscripts are not numbered or dated within the folders, so the current order of the pages may be either random or added by the Beinecke archivists; therefore, it does not reflect an authentic order of the poet's work with the source texts. The National Library in Warsaw houses another part of the documentation under the title 'Tłumaczenia [Translations]. Vol. 2. Akc. 18492'. It includes a set of typescripts of translated 'Negro spirituals' arranged in a sequence the poet willed to keep in print. Moreover, the typescripts are incorporated into an anthology of poetry translations Miłosz intended to publish in Poland while he was in the United States in the 1940s. The working titles of the collection are either *Antologia afrykańska* (The African Anthology) or *Czarna teczka* (A Black Folder). Interestingly enough, the 'Negro spirituals' along with 'black poets' translations constitute an integral entity there. Even though the anthology has never come out as a separate book, such a rule of publishing the 'spirituals' together with 'black poets' prevailed in all Miłosz's later anthologies of poetry translations.

The papers deposited both in Poland and the United States form the translator's genetic dossier. De Biasi states that a genetic dossier may be defined 'as the whole body of known, classified, and transcribed manuscripts and documents connected with a text whose form has reached, in the opinion of its author, a state of completion or near completion. When fairly complete, the genetic documentation of a published work generally exhibits four main phases that I have entitled the precompositional, compositional, prepublication and publication phases' (1996: 31),[5] and it includes:

> [B]esides documentation gathered by the writer, a more or less diverse series of draft documents that bear witness to the evolution of the work: there are outlines [plans], scenarios [scénarios], sketches [ébauches], rough drafts [brouillons], edited clear copies [mise au net], a final manuscript [manuscrit définitif], corrections on proofs, etc. In sum, there is a whole history from which the work issues and whose aesthetic culmination it appears to be, but this history is sometimes so different from the definitive result that one must also see it in a dimension of the work. (de Biasi 2004: 38)

Miłosz's archival documentation of 'Negro spirituals' translations satisfies all conditions laid down in de Biasi's definition. Almuth Grésillon adds that the genetic dossier may also be 'a set constituted by written documents that can be attributed in the aftermath of a specific writing project, and it does not matter whether it has resulted in a published text or not' (1994: 109).

Interestingly, besides the translator's endeavours inscribed in a linguistic form, the genetic dossier exposes another activity accompanying the process of translation, namely the poet's practice of 'drawriting'. Miłosz had a habit of covering manuscripts of his poems with little drawings, blackening space around an emerging verse with ink, which illustrates a strong bodily engagement in his intensive mental work. As Bożena Shallcross argues: '[T]wo types of inscription reveal two different sides of creation: one tending to discipline and chisel the words, the other spontaneous, improving, seemingly whimsical, yet suggestive of an obsessive insistence on forging a fledgling poem' (2011: 61). The fact that this dual experience of drawing and handwriting is presented equally in his translation manuscripts provides some interesting insights into the poet's perception of his occupation as a translator. It turns out to have been an integral part of his oeuvre, no different than his own creative work, also indicated by the contents of his poetry volumes, frequently complemented by his poetry translations. In the case of 'Negro spirituals', Miłosz's doodles adorn his verbal creative process in a slightly different way than usual. Instead of the tiny flowers, stars or geometric figures he typically sketched, a pictorial frame of the translated songs consists of black and white heads with sullen grins on their faces in left profiles drawn in a way as if they were silent spectators of the translations' coming into being. Here, integrating images with words reveals a secret emotional aura in the translations. Miłosz invokes the vision of a battlefield, where the translation emerges and gradually develops to become an ultimate instrument of resistance against projected observers besieging it as if it were a fortress or military unit. Does this image allude to the original context of performing 'Negro spirituals', or does it anticipate a censorial response to the translations by the editors of *Nowiny Literackie* and their political supervisors? Even though answers to such questions remain speculative, Miłosz's visualization of the potential ways 'Negro spirituals' and his translations might have been received demonstrate his deep belief in the power of the poetic word.

Further study of the body of manuscripts and typescripts allows us to expand Katarzyna Jakubiak's list of political gestures concealed behind the translator's seemingly innocent practices. These additional elements are, respectively, (1) anthologizing the translated songs in a targeted order so they could tell a story of enslavement and gradual liberation, (2) omitting some stanzas or lines from the manuscript in the final typescript, (3) further re-writing of the translations (some typescripts are not a carbon script of the manuscripts, as some additional editing is frequently implemented) and using an old or vintage vocabulary so the translations could resemble and recall certain patterns of Polish poetry, which may be interpreted, on the one hand, as a form of domestication, and on the other, as appealing to the Romantic paradigm of Polish poetry engaged in political issues.

The collection of manuscripts does not reveal any logic in the sequence of translated 'Negro spirituals'. Unlike the set of printed songs that resembles an anthology, it seems random and determined only by the arbitrary sequence of the books the translator kept at hand at the very moment of his work. The collection of typescripts, however, unveils some additional meanings inscribed into the sequence of translations. The first two songs, *Jerycho* (Joshua Fit the Battle of Jericho), *Zejdź, Mojżeszu* (Come Down, Moses), allude to biblical symbols of evil incarnated in political realms of Jericho and Egypt. The four next songs that are grouped together: *Kiedy złote trąby zagrają* (Where Shall I Be When the First Trumpet Sounds), *Widzę księżyc wschodzi* (I Know Moonrise), *Czasem ja jestem* (Sometimes I Am) and *O, chciałbym ja mieć orle skrzydło* (I Wish I Have Had an Eagle Wing) include metaphors of flight – birds and celestial phenomena in the night depicting a speaking persona's craving for physical and spiritual freedom.

A scene of judgement, a visit to a cemetery after dark, a vision of a soul enjoying peace after death constitute an imagery of post-mortem liberation, positively valorized the plighted contrary to the current state of enslavement. The song *Bóg będzie ogniem spalać ten świat* (God's Goin' to Set This World on Fire) is a prophecy of godly punishment of sins, and equally of cowardice – expressed in metaphorical allusions with clear political undertones. The three following songs, *Niczyjej tutaj modlitwy nie słyszę* (Couldn't Hear Nobody Pray), *Moja krew stygnie* (My Blood Ran Icy-Cold) and *To ja, o Panie* (Tis Me, O Lord), talk about the hardships of a wanderer on the way to Kanaan. The way leads through spiritual 'waste land', an image which symbolizes people's solitude in their quest for fulfilment. The songs also express the speaking persona's longing for the mother figure, alluding to the poet's mother's recent demise. The four closing songs, *Dobra nowina, rydwan przybywa* (Good News, the Chariot's Coming), *Mój wojenny strój tutaj złożę* (Going to Pull My War-Clothes), *Leć niżej, słodki rydwanie* (Swing Low, Sweet Chariot) and *Śpiewając z mieczem w dłoni* (Singing' Wid a Sword in My Han'), feature more optimistic imagery including: the ending of the war, future abundances of inaccessible goods, family reunions, coming back home and singing with angels. The songs complement the collection with a mood of joy and reconciliation. Generally, the targeted order of the translations leads from an experience of spiritual fight to a final triumph of the liberated soul. In this way, the translator articulates his hope for political change and his encouragement for a 'catacomb' activity.

Miłosz's manuscript omissions and rewritings, further playing with the source texts, may be illustrated by comparison of a handwritten translation of *Good News, the Chariot's Coming* with its typescript. The differences are marked in italics.

The manuscript	**The typescript**
Dobra nowina, Rydwan przybywa!	Dobra nowina, Rydwan przybywa!
Dobra nowina, Rydwan przybywa!	Dobra nowina, Rydwan przybywa!
Dobra nowina, Rydwan przybywa!	Dobra nowina, Rydwan przybywa!
A ja nie chcę tutaj pozostać.	*A ja nie chcę już tutaj zostać.*
Jest długa biała suknia, wiem to, w Niebie.	Jest długa biała suknia, wiem to, w Niebie.
Jest długa biała suknia, wiem to, w Niebie.	Jest długa biała suknia, wiem to, w Niebie.
Jest długa biała suknia, wiem to, w Niebie.	Jest długa biała suknia, wiem to, w Niebie.
I na pewno zabierze mnie ze sobą.	*A ja nie chcę już tutaj zostać.*
Jest gwiaździsta korona, wiem to, w Niebie.	Jest gwiaździsta korona, wiem to, w Niebie.
Jest gwiaździsta korona, wiem to, w Niebie.	Jest gwiaździsta korona, wiem to, w Niebie.
Jest gwiaździsta korona, wiem to, w Niebie.	Jest gwiaździsta korona, wiem to, w Niebie
I na pewno zabierze mnie ze sobą.	*A ja nie chcę już tutaj zostać.*
Dobra nowina, Rydwan przybywa!	
Dobra nowina, Rydwan przybywa!	
Dobra nowina, Rydwan przybywa!	
I na pewno zabierze mnie ze sobą.	

Jest harfa złota, wiem to, w Niebie.	Jest złota harfa, wiem to, w Niebie.
Jest harfa złota, wiem to, w Niebie.	Jest złota harfa, wiem to, w Niebie.
Jest harfa złota, wiem to, w Niebie.	Jest złota harfa, wiem to, w Niebie.
I na pewno zabierze mnie ze sobą.	*A ja nie chcę już tutaj zostać.*
Są srebrne pantofle, wiem to, w Niebie.	*Pantofelki srebrne, wiem, są w Niebie.*
Są srebrne pantofle, wiem to, w Niebie.	*Pantofelki srebrne, wiem, są w Niebie.*
Są srebrne pantofle, wiem to, w Niebie.	*Pantofelki srebrne, wiem, są w Niebie.*
I na pewno zabierze mnie ze sobą.	*A ja nie chcę już tutaj zostać.*
Dobra nowina, Rydwan przybywa!	Dobra nowina, Rydwan przybywa!
Dobra nowina, Rydwan przybywa!	Dobra nowina, Rydwan przybywa!
Dobra nowina, Rydwan przybywa!	Dobra nowina, Rydwan przybywa!
I na pewno zabierze mnie ze sobą.	*A ja nie chcę już tutaj zostać!*

The crucial difference between the manuscript and the typescript comes down to omitting one refrain and replacing the last stanza of the refrain, 'I na pewno zabierze mnie ze sobą' (And surely it will take me along), with the translation, 'A ja nie chcę już tutaj zostać!' (And I do not want to stay here any longer!). Even though none of these translations are faithful to the stanza *And I don't want it leave me behind*, the one from the manuscript is more distant from the original. However, the introduced replacement may not intend to amend the translation so it could fully articulate the intentions of the source text. Rather, it may allude to Miłosz's hesitation as to whether he should have stayed in or left the United States. In 1948, the poet shared this dilemma in his correspondence with Alexander Janta-Połczyński. Also, the poet consulted with Albert Einstein about his future plans and even considered joining the Primavera, a community of Hutterites in Paraguay or England. As his biographer concludes: 'The young Polish writer felt that Einstein was not able to comprehend the scale of the physical and, in particular, the existential crisis he was going through. Einstein tried to tell Miłosz that the torment he was experiencing would not last long and that it would be better for him not to sever links with his homeland' (Franaszek 2017: 271). In addressing this severe crisis, Miłosz was only able to subtly suggest it in his poetry translations, so his literary audience in Poland might have been able to guess the hardships of his emigration and its associated political catch. Anthony Cordingley and Chiara Montini point out the fact that translators are often assumed to adopt a position or strategy to which they remain committed, whereas 'by studying the process of a translation's composition, one observes translators using different strategies at different moments in the composition of their translation' (2015: 4). The researchers argue that studying a translator's genetic dossier may unveil a different approach in a translator's first efforts to mirror the source text versus the later phases of a translation, where a translator gradually gains power over the source text and exercises a greater 'agency'. 'A translation that may have begun as highly source oriented may finally demonstrate greater freedom from its source and creativity', they conclude (Cordingley and Montini 2015: 4). This is exactly the case with Miłosz's translations of 'Negro spirituals', where the final version depends more on the poet's willingness to communicate his own situation than to emulate the source text's particular meanings.

In his translations, Miłosz must have faced a problem of linguistic insufficiency to reflect African American English in Polish. However, in the solution he adopted, he bypassed it and introduced a vocabulary and a word order that fitted best with his intentions as a translator. Namely, he did not use any of the Polish dialects that would have been irrelevant to the style of 'Negro spirituals'. Instead, he introduced phrases, masculine grammatical rhymes and a syntax pattern that would have imitated medieval Polish poetry and religious songs, especially laments and beggar's songs. As many of them survived in Polish oral folk culture, the employed genetic and linguistic patterns somehow related to the oral realm of 'Negro spirituals'. Again, a comparison of the manuscripts and typescripts illustrates more and more the consistent usage of these patterns in the respective songs. For instance, in *Zejdź, Mojżeszu* (Come Down, Moses), the phrase '*uciśniony* od *utrapień* wiela' (oppressed by numerous oppressions) resembles medieval poetry where this kind of word repetition was one of the most prevalent aesthetic devices. In *Moja krew stygnie* (My Blood Runs Icy-Cold), the phrase '*muszę już iść*' (I must go now) is replaced by a more vernacular '*pora już iść*' (It's time to go now). In *Niczyjej tutaj modlitwy nie słyszę* (Couldn't Hear Nobody Pray), a contemporary toponym 'Kanaan' was replaced by a more archaic 'Chanaan'. The additional amendments that were implemented in the typescripts illustrate both ways the poet polished the final versions and the ultimate modifications in the overall message of the translations. The medieval stylization of the translations has a strong subversive power. Among many deceptive statements, Communism averred that in a country run by the working class and peasantry, a society is classless, and therefore, all members of this so-called classless society are equal and free from class discrimination. Communism employed such a statement to rewrite European history as an argument against capitalist bourgeois and feudal societies. Miłosz's linguistically moving his translations to medieval times may suggest problems raised in the songs which refer to the feudal, not the contemporary, realm. The act of 'mediaevalizing' seemingly confirms Communist political assumptions based on opposing the progressive present and the backwards past, and it fits the political critique either of the present life circumstances of people under racism and/or capitalism. The stylization brings associations with religious traditions of medieval or folk Christian prayers as well. Miłosz states:

> The contribution of 'Negro spirituals' to the folk songs of all times and all nations has been enormous. Not only on account of their music, but also on account of their poetry. Among the many things that enable us to tell genuine poetry from the counterfeit sort, only this seems indisputable: the full blaze and power of the simplest words. At the opposite end stand the greyness and torpor of those very same words used in journalism, whether rhymed or not. For many thousands of years poetry was the plinth of magic rites, and in magic the word is not a description of things, it is the thing-in-itself or its delegate. (1946: 4)

Further, the translator's foreword to the selection of his 'Negro spirituals' emphasizes their link to Christianity. Yet by calling this Christianity 'catacomb', and equating these collective prayers as pretexts to political gatherings, the translator accentuates their circumspect and illegal aspect, and indeed provides his Polish readers with a camouflaged instruction of how to perform prohibited actions against the regime in oppressive circumstances. Along with his instructive foreword, the order of the translated 'spirituals' in print is an encrypted parable of the fate of an enslaved individual or a group. On the other hand, by stressing religious and folk context, the translator's foreword situates them in an unobvious and deceptive context. Such a subversive practice reinforces the political message that the translator intended to convey.

Conclusion

The present chapter sheds light on the deep connections between a translator's empirical and genetic dossier – connections inherent in Czesław Miłosz's translations of 'Negro spirituals'.

As far as his genetic dossier is concerned, Miłosz's particular verbal choices, as visualized in the archival documentation, suggest translations built less on syntagmatic fidelity and imitation than on thematic communication. As a translator, the poet used these texts in his sophisticated and veiled crusade against the Soviet-dominated system, a system in which cold war–style accusations of racism were common instruments used to denigrate the United States, and so the collective African American expression of longing for freedom would have been, ironically, warmly received. The vocabulary selected for the translation forms an Aesopian language of communication between the translator and his audience.

The comparative study of the translations' source texts, draft manuscripts, typescripts and published versions demonstrates a continuity that Jeremy Munday called a 'microhistory' of the translation (2014: 64–80). It bears witness to what the translator does with the source texts, yet it does not fully explain the translator's aims or motivations. Only expanding a textual, genetic dossier with an empirical dossier or, in Tabakowska's words, a translator's encyclopaedia, helps to understand why the poet selected given literary works for translation, and such expansion legitimizes certain practices he adopted in the whole process of translation. Miłosz's experience with African American cultural heritage, his interaction with African American people and his political observations of the ways African American minority fought for equal rights in the post-war multiracial society all preceded his translations. Only such preliminary competence allowed Miłosz to discover 'Negro spirituals' for himself and understand the potentials they had to form a universal message of liberty in other languages. Tabakowska concludes:

> Everybody interested in translation as a process or as a product agree that a translator's knowledge cannot be only the dictionary knowledge; it must be also

the broadest possible encyclopedic knowledge. Hence the advices and instructions given to young trainees of translation art: learn, read, watch TV, talk to people, go to theatre and exhibitions, closely track updates in women's fashion, collect old invitations and tickets etc. etc. The difficulty lays, as always, in inability to set the limits. Where does a dictionary become an encyclopedia, and semantic knowledge become a pragmatic one? How large should the dictionary be? How many volumes should the encyclopedia consist of? These are obviously absurd questions. (1999: 54)

Even though a translator's genetic dossier is limited to textual evidence, it often refers to non-material extensions that reflect various kinds of a translator's experiences. In the case of translators, all of their 'precompositional' skills, to use de Biasi's term (1996: 31), gild their genetic dossier, even if they may not be easily detected from their writings or other material evidence. Such a dossier may specify the aims of translations and selected strategies adopted in the performed work.

Notes

1. Unless otherwise noted, the English translations of Miłosz's writings are mine.
2. See Dubois (1903); Johnson (1925); John and Alan Lomax (1947); Sandburg (1927).
3. Respectively, in *Nowiny Literackie* (1948), no. 24, and *Odrodzenie* (1948), no. 12.
4. The poet would reprint nine of his 'Negro spirituals' in his later poetry volumes or his anthologies of poetry translations. Yet he consistently omitted the songs *Zejdź, Mojżeszu* (Come Down, Moses); *Moja krew stygnie* (My Blood Ran Icy-Cold); *Dobra Nowina, Rydwan przybywa* (Good News, the Chariot's Coming); *Śpiewając z mieczem w dłoni* (Singing' Wid a Sword in My Han').
5. See also Bellemin-Noël (1972: 15); Deppman, Ferrer and Groden (2004: 8).

References

Bellemin-Noël, Jean (1972), *Le Texte et l'avant-texte: les broullions d'un poème de Milosz*, Paris: Larousse.

Cordingley, Anthony and Chiara Montini (2015), 'Genetic Translation Studies: An Emerging Discipline', *Linguistica Antverpiensia, New Series: Themes in Translation Studies*, 14: 1–18.

De Biasi, Pierre-Marc (1996), 'What Is a Literary Draft? Toward a Functional Typology of Genetic Documentation', trans. Ingrid Wassenaar, *Yale French Studies*, 89: 26–58.

De Biasi, Pierre-Marc (2004), 'Toward a Science of Literature: Manuscript Analysis and the Genesis of the Work', in Jed Deppman, Daniel Ferrer and Michael Groden (eds), *Genetic Criticism: Texts and Avant-Textes*, 36–68, Philadelphia: University of Pennsylvania Press.

Deppman, Jed, Daniel Ferrer and Michael Groden (eds) (2004), *Genetic Criticism: Texts and Avant-Textes*, Philadelphia: University of Pennsylvania Press.

Dubois, William and Edward Burghardt (1903), *The Souls of the Black Folk*, New York: Dover Publications.
Franaszek, Andrzej (2017), *Miłosz. A Biography*, Cambridge, MA, and London: The Belknap Press of Harvard University Press.
Gilroy, Paul (1993), *The Black Atlantic. Modernity and Double Consciousness*, Cambridge, MA: Harvard University Press.
Grésillon, Almuth (1994), *Éléments de critique génétique. Lire les manuscrits modernes*, Paris: CNRS Editions.
Jakubiak, Katarzyna (2011), 'Translation's Deceit. Czesław Miłosz and "Negro Spirituals"', *'Przekładaniec' between Miłosz and Milosz*, 25: 199–220.
Johnson, James Weldon (1925), *The Book of American 'Negro Spirituals'*, New York: Viking Press.
Kołodziejczyk, Ewa (2011), 'Miłosz's American Alphabet', trans. Mikołaj Denderski, *'Przekładaniec' between Miłosz and Milosz*, 25: 7–25.
Lomax, John A. and Alan Lomax (1947), *Folk Song*, New York: Duell, Sloan and Pearce.
Miłosz, Czesław (1946), 'Negro Spirituals. Wstęp' ('Negro Spirituals'. A Foreword), trans. Mikołaj Denderski, *Nowiny Literackie*, 26: 4.
Miłosz, Czesław (1947), 'Abstrakcja i poszukiwania' (Abstraction and Exploration), *Odrodzenie*, 7: 3.
Miłosz, Czesław (1949), 'Dwie książki o wojnie' (Two Novels about War), *Odrodzenie*, 15: 1.
Miłosz, Czesław (1999), *Kontynenty* (Continents), Kraków: Wydawnictwo Literackie.
Miłosz, Czesław (2001), *Rodzinna Europa* (Native Realm), Kraków: Wydawnictwo Literackie.
Miłosz, Czesław (2007), *Zaraz po wojnie. Korespondencja z pisarzami 1945–1950* (After the War. Correspondence with Writers in the Years 1945–50), Kraków: Wydawnictwo Literackie.
Munday, Jeremy (2014), 'Using Primary Sources to Produce a Microhistory of Translation and Translators: Theoretical and Methodological Concerns', *Translator: Studies in Intercultural Communication*, 20 (1): 64–80.
Nowak M., Jan [Miłosz, Czesław] (1947a), 'Życie w USA' (Living in the U.S.A.), *Odrodzenie*, 1: 7.
Nowak M., Jan [Miłosz, Czesław] (1947b), 'Życie w USA' (Living in the U.S.A.), *Odrodzenie*, 7: 9.
Nowak M., Jan [Miłosz, Czesław] (1947c), 'Życie w USA' (Living in the U.S.A.), *Odrodzenie*, 9: 4.
Sandburg, Carl (1927), *The American Songbag*, New York: Hartcourt, Brace & Co.
Shallcross, Bożena (2011), 'Poeta i sygnatury' (The Poet and His Signatures), *Teksty Drugie*, 5: 53–61.
Tabakowska, Elżbieta (1999), *O przekładzie na przykładzie. Rozprawa tłumacza z Europą Normana Daviesa* (On Translation upon Quotation. The Translator's Dissertation with Europe by Norman Davies), int. Norman Davies, Kraków: Znak.

5

The genesis of a compilative translation and its *de facto* source text

Laura Ivaska
University of Turku

Introduction

Stereotypically, translation involves one source text and one target text (cf. Bistué 2013). However, a translation may also be compilative in nature, meaning that it 'makes use of several source texts' (Toury 2012: 100 n. 4). Although this practice has been identified, its dynamics have not gained much attention. Borrowing methodological and theoretical notions from textual scholarship, this chapter seeks to explain what translating compilatively means in practice; that is, how a translator makes use of several texts in different languages in the translation process. In addition, drawing evidence from translators' papers, the motivations behind the decision to make a compilative translation are discussed.

This chapter presents a case study of Kyllikki Villa's Finnish translation, *Veljesviha* (1967), of Nikos Kazantzakis's novel Οι αδερφοφάδες (1963), which – according to the title page information – is based on three texts: the French and the English translation (1965, translated by Pierre Aellig, and 1966, translated by Athena Gianakas Dallas, respectively) as well as the Greek original. The analysis of archival material and the comparison of the four language versions reveal that the Finnish translator applied the *best-text method* in her work. I borrow the concept of *best-text method* from textual criticism, in which it is understood as 'selecting a "best text" [from among various candidates] and altering it only at places that [seem] obviously erroneous' (Tanselle 1994: 1). As the analysis will show, in the case of *Veljesviha*, the translator's *best-text* was the French translation.

For the general reading public, *Veljesviha* is most likely just a translation of Οι αδερφοφάδες, but strictly speaking the text from which *Veljesviha* was translated is not a Greek version, nor is it a French or an English version; instead, Villa constructed the *de facto* source text of the Finnish translation through the comparison of the different language versions. Although this *de facto* source text (cf. Nickau's threefold source text in Kujamäki 1998: 258; Levý's 'prototype' in Jettmarová 2011: xx–xxi) remains out of our reach – perhaps it never even had a physical form – traces of it, or at least clues to understanding how the translator constructed it, can be found in the translator's papers and correspondence (Van Hulle 2015: 45; Shengyu 2018: 42), and further evidence can be gathered by collating the texts involved.

The analysis presented in this chapter offers insights into the genesis of the compilative translation and its *de facto* source text, demonstrating the active role of the translator in constructing her own source text instead of using a published text as the basis of her translation. As will be discussed in the concluding section, this way of constructing the *de facto* source text suggests that it is not enough to conceptualize the *source text* as equal to 'the original' – or to any other published text, for that matter. In fact, the way compilative translations are done challenges the idea that texts – including texts that could function as source texts – are fixed.

Compilative translation

Compilative translation, a term coined by Popovič (1978: 20 qtd. in Toury 2012: 100) and later redefined by Toury (2012: 167) as the instances in which 'several intermediate translations were used, into one language or several, alternately or together, or even a combination of the ultimate original and translation(s) thereof', is currently understood to be a subtype of *indirect translation*. Indirect translation, in turn, refers to translations that have as their source text 'a text (or texts) other than (only) the ultimate source text' (Ivaska and Paloposki 2018: 43 n. 1). Compilative translation can be seen to fall under the umbrella of indirect translation (Rosa, Pięta and Maia 2017: 115) because, when several source texts are involved, at least one of them is necessarily something other than the ultimate source text, or the 'original' text itself. An example of compilative translation can be found in the translation of biblical texts; for example, the first Finnish translation of the New Testament (1548) by Mikael Agricola is based on six versions of the text in four languages – Greek, Latin, German and Swedish (Itkonen-Kaila 1997).

Both indirect and compilative translations go by many names and definitions, which sometimes create terminological and conceptual confusion; for instance, *compilative translation* has also been referred to as *eclectic translation* (e.g. Ringmar 2007; Kittel 1991: 32; Pięta 2012).[1] The exact meaning of each term and the boundaries of the different ways in which indirect (and compilative) translations are done are yet to be determined. To facilitate the process, Rosa, Pięta and Maia propose that different types of indirectness could be identified based on

(a) the number and type of mediating texts involved in the process (one or more);

(b) the number of intervening languages (one or more) and their choice – involving the use of only one mediating language vs. the use of more than one mediating language and/or the ultimate SL (source language), one or more mediating language(s), and the ultimate TT (target language);

(c) the degree of indirectness (second-hand, third-hand …);

(d) the presentation of indirectness (either hidden or open); and
(e) the status of indirectness (which for research purposes can be either proven or only presumed). (2017: 119)

As for the translation under study in this chapter, the title page information suggests that (a) there are three texts and (b) three languages involved; (c) the degree of indirectness is of first/second grade; (d) the translation is openly indirect and compilative; and thus (e) the status of indirectness is proven and will be confirmed through the analysis that follows. The degree of indirectness, however, is difficult to define due to the compilative nature of the translation and the perhaps somewhat exceptional combination of texts involved: one of the mediating texts is in the ultimate source language (Greek), for which the second-handedness of the translation is questionable, but as the analysis below will demonstrate, the Greek text is not the translator's primary point of reference, which supports the categorization as a second-hand indirect/compilative translation.

When a text in the ultimate source language is being used in the making of a compilative translation, one might expect that the translators would use the strategy called *support translation*; that is, they would 'check *translations* into languages other than their own target language in order to see whether colleagues have found satisfactory solutions to certain problems' (Dollerup 2000: 23–4; emphasis added). This definition, however, does not apply to *Veljesviha* because one of the texts that the Finnish translator checks is not a translation, but rather a text in the ultimate source language (Greek). Furthermore, in Dollerup's definition, the checking of other translations is motivated by the attempt to find solutions to translating difficult passages; in the case of *Veljesviha*, however, the translator seems to consult several texts to identify and emend translation errors in her primary point of reference (the French translation) and to add (back) elements of Greek culture to the Finnish translation.[2]

The Finnish translation does not seem to correspond to any of the types of indirect translation identified by Washbourne (2013: 611–12), either; the closest is perhaps '[t]ranslation into L4 based on triangulations of L2 and L3 translations' except that in the case of *Veljesviha*, the L1 (Greek) is also involved. It seems to be precisely the (secondary) role of the ultimate source language that makes this translation different from those discussed in previous research. It is, nevertheless, necessary to find ways to identify and categorize different types of indirect (and compilative) translations. For a categorization based on the use of the source texts, Rosa, Pięta and Maia have proposed that the following features be observed:

(a) their language (ultimate ST vs. mediating text vs. ultimate TT); (b) their importance or role in the translation process (primary vs. secondary); and (c) the frequency of their use during the translation process (permanent vs. occasional use); and also [d] their intended receiver (public texts, i.e. for wider readership vs. private texts, designed for use by the translator only). (2017: 119–20)

In order to draw conclusions on the importance or role, as well as on the frequency of use of the individual texts involved in the making of a compilative translation, a textual analysis is needed; thus, I shall return to these categories in the concluding section.

The translator as textual critic: Translation based on many texts and the *best-text* method

Compilative translation implies that there are several versions of a work,[3] such as a novel, either in one language or several languages, and that more than one of them is involved in the making of a translation. However, whether a translation can actually have more than one source text depends on what is understood by *source text*. Unfortunately, definitions of source text are often vague, and in general the topic has not gained much attention in translation studies – perhaps due to the prevalence of the target text/culture paradigm (Baer 2017). The point of departure in this chapter is Toury's definition of translation as a text for which 'there is *another text*, in another language/culture, which has both chronological and logical priority over it' (2012: 29; emphasis added). This definition suggests that this an*other text* – the source text – is a singular entity.

In line with this, the making of a compilative translation can be seen to consist of first comparing the several texts involved in the process, which leads to the creation of a (source) text that never existed before (Greetham 1994: 334),[4] and then translating this text. For example, according to Shengyu (2018: 37), the English translation of the eighteenth-century Chinese novel *Hongloumeng* by David Hawkes is based on a source text that Hawkes created by collating the 1964 Renmin Wenxue Chubanshe edition with other Chinese editions. Shengyu (2018: 37–8) calls the result of the collation a *base text* or a *translator's lost copy*, in order to distinguish the other versions of the novel from the *de facto* source text of the English translation, which came into being as a result of the collation. This distinction is not trivial because the (base) text that Hawkes created is 'totally different from any of the previous existent editions' (Shengyu 2018: 37). This has implications for identifying the text with which the translation should be compared: judging the quality of a translation by comparing it with *a* text instead of comparing it with its *de facto* source text is misleading and bound to result in faulty conclusions (see e.g. Dedner 2012: 125–6; Toury 2012: 100–1). In addition, pinpointing the exact *de facto* source text may affect the categorization of the translation; for example, can a translation be considered a retranslation[5] if its source text is *de facto* different from that of the previous translation(s)?

When translators compare different versions of a novel and thus compile the *de facto* source text of their translation, they are operating in the field of textual scholarship, a group of disciplines – including textual criticism and genetic criticism – 'that deal with describing, transcribing, editing or annotating texts and physical documents' (Katajamäki and Lukin 2013: 8). Both textual and genetic criticism study the relationships between the different texts that reflect one work, and it can sometimes be difficult to discern between the two (Cordingley and Montini 2015: 3). In general, however, the latter is traditionally more focused on the pre-publication stage and the former on post-publication transformations (Van Hulle 2015: 50). Although many textual scholars seem to have been 'concerned only with establishing suitable methodologies *within* a given language, and have not normally devoted much attention to the problem of textual criticism *between* languages' (Greetham 1984: 133;

emphases in the original), genetic translation criticism has recently gained ground (see Cordingley and Montini 2015), and textual scholars have taken up to discuss translation (e.g. the 2012 number of *Variants*, the journal of the European Society for Textual Scholarship, was published under the theme *Texts beyond Borders: Multilingualism and Textual Scholarship*).

There is definitely much that the two share, and the theoretical framework provided by textual criticism regarding collation can, in fact, be applied to analysing and describing the genesis of a compilative translation. Namely, the way the *de facto* source texts of compilative translations are done is similar to how critical editions are made. Critical editions are the fruit of 'the comparative analysis of multiple texts' (McGann 1991: 50), and there are different approaches to making them. Greetham (1994: 311) identifies two distinct traditions that represent different approaches to critical editing: the Alexandrian analogy, in which one accumulates 'as much documentary evidence as possible' and then makes 'eclectic decisions based upon a sense of the "rightness" of each reading' – thus producing a text that suits the editor's own taste and intentions – and the Pergamanian anomaly, in which the goal is to choose a text that seems 'complete, consistent, and of good provenance, and to reproduce it faithfully', although this does not mean that the text would be produced as such – it will be edited in one way or another.[6] The *best-text method*[7] represents the latter approach. It refers to selecting 'a single document as authority for establishing a text' (Greetham 1994: 4), which is then amended 'only at places that [seem] obviously erroneous' (Tanselle 1994: 1). In textual criticism, the result of the collation could be published as such, but when it comes to compilative translation a further step is taken: the resulting text is translated.

Material and methods

The case study presented here is the Finnish translation, *Veljesviha* (1967), by Kyllikki Villa, of Nikos Kazantzakis's *Οι αδερφοφάδες* (1963). The title page information of the translation (Kazantzakis 1967, translated by Villa) states:

The Finnish translation is based on the following editions:
Les Frères ennemis, Meaux 1965 Οι αδελφοφάδες, Athens 1963
The Fratricides, New York 1966[8]

Before collating these language versions, I analyse archival material relating to the Finnish translation that consists of translator Kyllikki Villa's papers and correspondence.[9] The analysis is complemented with letters sent by Villa to her Greek contacts, Pandelis Prevelakis[10] and Eleni Kazantzakis.[11] More details about Villa's life and work are drawn from her published travel diary *Äidin lokikirja* (Mother's Logbook) (Villa and Villa 2013). As Munday (2013: 134) points out, materials found in translator archives offer 'an insight into decision-making' and the translation process in general, as they reveal 'some of the normally hidden traces of translatorial activity and are a real-time record of some of the translator's decision-making processes' (2013: 126).

Most importantly, though, archival material combined with methodology from textual scholarship can help to reconstruct the 'path of cumulative decisions [made during the creation or translation process] which previously could only be guessed at from a reading of the edited [or translated] text' (Romanelli 2015: 89). Unfortunately, no draft manuscripts of Villa's translation have been found to trace some of the transformations in more detail.

However, without any textual analysis of the translation and the texts involved in the translation process, the conclusions drawn from the archival material necessarily remain speculative. Thus, in the second part of the analysis I compare the four language versions (Finnish, French, English and Greek)[12] to corroborate and confirm the findings of the analysis of the archival material – namely, that Villa used the *best-text method* in constructing the *de facto* source text of the Finnish translation. The qualitative analysis is based on the first and the seventeenth chapters of the novel and provides evidence to support the claims that (1) the French served as Kyllikki Villa's *best-text* and (2) Villa made amendments based on the Greek and/or English language version.

The source text(s)/language(s) of a translated text – or rather, each passage, sentence or even word – can be detected by comparing the micro- and macro-textual features, such as 'translation errors, syntactic structures, loan words, [and] proper names (in the case of fictional writing)' (Rosa, Pięta and Maia 2017: 123–4), of the different language versions. For example, Solberg's analysis of omissions and certain lexical choices demonstrates that 'the Danish translation [of Simone de Beauvoir's *La jeune fille*, originally written in French] influenced both the Norwegian translation and the Swedish translation' (Solberg 2016: 91) and that 'the Norwegian translation is a second mediating text influencing the Swedish translation, in addition to the Danish text' (Solberg 2016: 92).

Analysis of the archival material

Kyllikki Villa bought the French translation of *Οι αδερφοφάδες* when travelling in Greece in the summer of 1966;[13] her published travel diary suggests that this happened in Athens on 5 August 1966 (Villa and Villa 2013: 98). In the diary she also writes on 20 August 1966 that she has finished reading *Les Frères ennemis* (Villa and Villa 2013: 107), which is, of course, the title of the French translation. This is also the title that appears in the translation contract for the Finnish translation of the novel,[14] which suggests that the French version was probably Villa's *best-text* against which she compared the other language versions. Also, considering that Villa first read the novel in French, it would make sense if she decided to base her work primarily on that version. Furthermore, Villa received the English and the Greek versions only about a month after the translation contract had been signed,[15] meaning that she might have already started translating from the French before receiving them, although she might have gone back to the already translated text to make changes if prompted by comparison with the English and/or Greek texts. In any case, Eleni Kazantzaki, the author's widow, sent Villa the two versions upon Villa's request. The translator justified the need for them by explaining that when she had been translating Pandelis Prevelakis's novel *Ο ήλιος του θανάτου* (1959; in Finnish *Ikuinen aurinko,* 1963) a couple of years earlier compilatively (from Danish, German and Greek; see Ivaska 2016), she checked some words from the Greek version with the help of a dictionary.[16]

Villa also asked E. Kazantzaki which of the two translations – the French or the English – was better,[17] suggesting that she was aware of the possibility of deviations accumulating when translating from a translation (Edström 1991), and she might have been actively trying to tone down this effect by choosing her *best-text* carefully. E. Kazantzaki informed Villa that the French translation was very loyal, whereas the English version had 'a big mistake' in the very beginning of the translation.[18] The fact that E. Kazantzaki praised the French translation, on the one hand, and signalled a problem in the English version, on the other, may have led Villa to use the French as the *best-text*. Furthermore, Villa's choice may have been influenced by the fact that she apparently did not have a high proficiency in English (see, e.g. Villa and Villa 2013: 230) or Greek (Villa and Villa 2013: 53); in fact, if Villa had known enough Greek, she would probably have preferred to translate directly from the Greek (see Ivaska and Paloposki 2018). Further evidence attesting to the compilative nature of the translation can be found in a grant application to the Finnish Ministry of Education. In the application – signed and dated after the deadline imposed in the translation contract for the Finnish translation[19] had passed – Villa explains that she translated the novel by comparing the French and the American to the Greek version.[20]

As discussed above, Villa's rationale for comparing several versions seems to have been to minimize the number of translation errors and to add (back) elements of Greek culture to the Finnish translation; the year after *Veljesviha* was published, Villa wrote about indirect translation in a newspaper article, and seemed to be of the opinion – based perhaps on the very experience of translating *Οι αδερφοφάδες* – that when translating indirectly, it might be a good idea to make a compilative translation, consulting the text in the language in which the text was first published:

> I know from my own experience that when comparing two translations one always exposes surprising, even unbelievable discrepancies (because every translator makes mistakes). In such cases it is good if one can, for example, try and read the original with the help of a dictionary or ask for help from someone who knows the language. (Villa 1968 qtd. in Ivaska and Paloposki 2018: 40; their translation)

Unfortunately, however, the archival material does not provide any precise evidence regarding the extent and manner in which Villa made use of the three texts or collaborated with someone who knows Greek. A small clue can, nevertheless, be found in a letter to Pandelis Prevelakis, in which Villa writes about translating *Οι αδερφοφάδες*:

> I have now 310 pages written but they have not yet been checked and corrected. In general, my way of working is quite fast, but in this case it is not, because I cannot stop the comparison with the American version and especially with the original work. Can you imagine that I truly can, very very slowly, read Greek! And there

are places where I could say to have translated directly from the original. Both translators have here and there shortened the text slightly; it also seems to me that the translations are very free. I would like to keep the Greek metaphors … there are some words or passages that I would like to check with you or Ms. K.[21]

Based on this letter, Villa did consult both the English and especially the Greek version, but sadly neither the correspondence nor other archival material reveals whether she checked some words and/or passages with either Prevelakis or Ms. K, who is presumably Eleni Kazantzaki. However, letters from a few years earlier when Villa was translating Prevelakis's *Ο ήλιος του θανάτου* reveal that she asked Prevelakis to explain some words and that she also received the author's explanations, although unfortunately the word lists themselves have not been located (see also Ivaska 2016).[22] Since the two had already established this kind of collaborative working method, perhaps they also made use of it in the Kazantzakis translation – Prevelakis had been a close friend of Kazantzakis and knew his works well, which explains why he would get involved in this translation project.

Textual comparison

To confirm that Villa's *best-text* was the French translation, the four language versions – Finnish, French, English and Greek – are compared. By simply glancing at how the texts are structured it is possible to tell that Villa's *de facto* source text was modelled following the French example. Namely, whereas the Greek original has 118 paragraphs in the first chapter and the English only 105, the French and the Finnish both have 131. Of these 131, the change of a paragraph in one corresponds with a new paragraph in the other in 129 cases; on one occasion there is a new paragraph starting in the Finnish but not in the French, and on one occasion the opposite happens. However, there is another layout difference suggesting the contrary: the French and the Greek versions are divided into three subchapters, signalled by a blank space between paragraphs, but the Finnish and the English translations lack this formatting choice. This may be due to different formatting norms, but it can also be interpreted to suggest that the Finnish translation does not slavishly follow the French example; the choice to omit the subchapters may have been inspired by the English example.

Below, three examples drawn from the first chapter of the novel that deal with additions, omissions and translation errors are given to confirm the role of the French as the *best-text*, and two further examples demonstrate that the English and/or Greek versions were used to make amendments to the *best-text*, which through this process was turned into the *de facto* source text of the Finnish translation. The passages are given in the four languages with an English approximate translation; the particular element(s) under analysis are in italics.

The use of the French version as the *best-text* is evident where a passage appears both in the Finnish and in the French but neither in the English nor in the Greek; in other words, there is an addition in the French version that has been carried on to the Finnish translation:

Finnish (p. 15):
Koko kylä kohotti kätensä ja vastasi *kuin kaiku* kovalla äänellä huutaen:
(The whole village rose its hands and replied *like an echo*, shouting in a loud voice:)

French (p. 19):
Levant les mains au ciel, tout le village lui *fit écho* dans un grand cri:
(Raising their hands to the sky, the whole village *echoed him* in a loud shout:)

English (p. 14):
The people raised their hands to the sky; they raised their voices loudly.

Greek (p. 18):
Σήκωσε ὁ λαὸς τὰ χέρια στὸν οὐρανό, σήκωσε βουὴ μεγάλη:
(The people raised their hands to the sky, a big clamor arose:)

As for omissions, when a passage appears in Greek and English but in neither French nor Finnish, we have reason to believe that Villa's *de facto* source text (and thus also the Finnish translation) was influenced by the French version:

Finnish (p. 19):
Tuli vastaan kyliä; mistään ei puuttunut pappia.
(Villages came to a village after another village; none lacked a priest.)

French (p. 24):
Les villages se succédaient; tous étaient pourvus de prêtre.
(Villages followed each other: they all had a priest.)

English (p. 18):
He passed through villages, *knocked on doors*, they all had their priests,

Greek (p. 22):
Περνοῦσε χωριά, *χτυποῦσε τὶς πόρτες*, ὅλα εἶχαν παπά,
(He was passing villages, *knocking on the doors*, all had a priest,)

Furthermore, a translation error that appears as identical in both the French and the Finnish versions suggests a genealogical relationship between the two through the mediation of the *de facto* source text:

Finnish (p. 24):
Olipa kerran luostari, jossa oli *neljäsataa* munkkia.
(Once upon a time, there was a monastery that had *four hundred* monks.)

French (p. 30):
Il était une fois un monastère qui comptait *quatre cents* moines.
(Once upon a time, there was a monastery that had *four hundred* monks.)

English (p. 22):
There was once a monastery that had *three hundred* monks,

Greek (p. 27):
Ἦταν μιὰ φορὰ ἕνα Μοναστήρι κι εἶχε *τρακόσιους* καλόγερους
(Once upon a time a monastery with *three hundred* monks)

The above are examples of instances where the influence of the French language version in the Finnish translation is undeniable; similar affinities can be found throughout the first chapter. Although the analysis has not been carried out in a quantitative manner – because more often than not it is impossible to pinpoint the exact text from which Villa drew[23] – the instances when the Finnish version is similar to the French seem to be more numerous than when it is similar to the English and/or the Greek. Corroborating this with the fact that the Finnish translation is divided into paragraphs similar to the French, it seems safe to conclude that the French version was Villa's *best-text*.

However, Villa claims to have also consulted the English and the Greek versions, and it is, in fact, possible to locate passages where the Finnish translation is similar to the English and/or the Greek versions and different from the French, signalling a departure from and amendments to the French *best-text* in those places. However, the English translation is very similar to the Greek version, and thus it is often impossible to tell which one of the two Villa consulted. For example, the following passage contains an omission in the French version – as compared with the Greek and the English versions – that has not been replicated in the Finnish:

Finnish (p. 12):
Vaimo ei luonut silmiään muihin miehiin kuin omaansa *eikä mies katsellut muuta naista kuin omaansa*; kaikki kulkivat Jumalan polkuja …
(A wife did not lay her eyes on men other than her own, *nor did a man look at women other than his own*; everybody walked God's paths …)

French (p. 15):
La femme ne levait pas les yeux sur un autre homme que le sien; tous suivaient les sentiers de Dieu …
(A woman did not look upon a man other than her own; everybody followed God's paths …)

English (p. 11):
Not one wife raised her eyes to look at another man, *not one husband raised his eyes to look at another woman*. Everyone followed the path of God,

Greek (p. 14):
γυναίκα δὲ σήκωνε τὰ μάτια της νὰ κοιτάξει ξένον ἄντρα, *ἄντρας δὲ σήκωνε τὰ μάτια να κοιτάξει ξένη γυναίκα*, ὅλοι ἀκλουθοῦσαν τὴ στράτα τοῦ Θεοῦ …
(Not one wife raised her eyes to look at a foreign man, *a husband did not lift his eyes to look at a foreign woman*, everyone followed God's path …)

Although it is not possible to tell whether Villa followed the English or the Greek version, it is very unlikely that she would have read only the French version and decided to add the exact meaning that appears in both the English and the Greek versions without being influenced by one or the other (or both). In other words, this passage proves that Villa did not simply use the French version as a source text but consulted the English and/or the Greek text as well.

An exception to not being able to tell whether Villa made an amendment following the example of the English or the Greek is provided by religious vocabulary, which seems to have its origin in the Greek version. In Greece, the Greek Orthodox Church is the predominant religion, but in Finland, as well as in France and the UK/United States – the countries where the versions Villa consulted have been published – it has a rather marginal status, and thus it seems unlikely that this vocabulary would have been introduced into the Finnish translation without the example of the Greek:

Finnish (p. 12):
kävivät *liturgiassa* sunnuntaisin, he toivat kirkkoon *prosforat*, valmistivat *kollyban* vainajille,
(they went to *the liturgy* on Sundays, they brought *prosforas* to the church, prepared *kollyba* for the dead)

French (p. 15):
ils allaient *à l'office* le dimanche, ils offraient *le pain bénit*, faisaient cuire *le blé* pour les morts,
(they went to *the service* on Sundays, they offered *the consecrated bread*, cooked *the wheat* for the dead)

English (p. 11):
they went *to church* every Sunday, brought *holy bread*, prepared *kolyva*,* [the word *kolyva* is in italics in the English, and followed by a footnote: 'Boiled and prepared wheat that is blessed and distributed at memorial services for the dead.']

Greek (p. 14):
πήγαιναν κάθε Κυριακὴ *στὴ λειτουργία*, ἔφερναν *πρόσφορα*, ἔκαναν *κόλλυβα*,
(every Sunday they went to *the liturgy*, they brought *consecrated breads*, they made *kollyba*)

Whereas in the English version people simply go *to church* and in the French they go 'to the service' (*à l'office*), in the Greek and the Finnish versions they go to a *liturgy* (*liturgiassa*; *στὴ λειτουργία*); if the Finnish translation was based on the French, *jumalanpalvelus* (worship) and *messu* (mass) would be more likely translations for the French *office* (service). Moreover, the English *church* could be translated simply as *kirkko* ('church'). Similarly, the use of the word *prosfora* in the Finnish instead of *pyhitetty leipä* or *pyhä leipä* ('consecrated bread' or 'holy bread,' as in the French [*pain bénit*] and the English [*holy bread*]) signals the influence from Greek. Thus, Villa either consulted the Greek version or was acquainted with Greek Orthodox religion and knew to use these specific religious terms to add some Greek Orthodox flavour to the Finnish text, which can be found in the Greek version but that in this passage lacks from the French and the English versions. Similarly, the (transliteration of the) word *kollyba[n]* seems to be influenced by the Greek version (*κόλλυβα*); first, the word is completely lacking from the French version and, second, in the English version, it has been transliterated in a more transcriptive way as *kolyva*.

To be able to conclude that Villa also consulted the English version, it would be necessary to locate passages in which the English and the Finnish are similar while deviating from the Greek and the French. As the first chapter provided no results supporting such a conclusion, I randomly chose another chapter from the latter half of the twenty-chapter novel for analysis: Chapter 17. Keeping in mind that a translator's strategy does not necessarily remain uniform throughout a translation, and with the archival material suggesting that Villa might not have had the English version at her disposal when she started translating the novel, I wanted the other analysed chapter to be from later in the book. Unfortunately, however, I was not able to locate any passages that would confirm the explicit use of the English version also because, as already mentioned, the English translation is, overall, very similar to the Greek version.

Discussion and conclusions

Returning to Rosa, Pięta and Maia's (2017: 119–20) suggestions for features to observe when categorizing source texts (see above), the following can be concluded about the texts involved in the creation of *Veljesviha* (and its *de facto* source text):

- French: a mediating text with a primary role and permanent use;
- English: a mediating text with a secondary role and occasional use (?);
- Greek: the ultimate source text with a secondary role and occasional use.

This way of using these two/three texts corresponds with the *best-text method*: the French text is clearly used as the primary point of reference (the *best-text*), whereas the other two texts have a secondary, occasional role, although the exact role of the English version remains unclear; perhaps Villa used it as a *support translation*. The status of the French as the *best-text* is evident in that the division of the text in the first chapter into paragraphs is almost identical in the Finnish translation (while also different from the Greek and the English). Furthermore, an omission, an addition and a translation error that occur in the French – as compared with the Greek and/or the English – that can also be found in the Finnish version suggest that they must stem from the French source. Thus, the French was Villa's *best-text* for constructing the *de facto* source text of her Finnish translation, and it is the *best* text upon which Villa could build the *de facto* source text as well, in the sense that between French, English and Greek, Villa knew French the best.

Villa's decision to use the French translation as the *best-text* may also be traced back to her having read the novel first in French and signing the translation contract on that basis. Furthermore, her limited proficiency in English and Greek as well as Eleni Kazantzaki's statement that the French translation is better than the English may also have played a role. The choice to compare several versions, however, seems to stem directly from Villa. Based on her (later) comments regarding the problems entailed in indirect translation, she seems to have chosen the compilative translation strategy to avoid repeating translation errors by forming a better idea of what the text says in Greek. By collating the French with the English and the Greek versions, Villa could emend omissions found in the French version, and by using Greek Orthodox vocabulary found in the Greek – but not in the French version – she could add a Greek flavour to the Finnish translation. In fact, the archival material regarding this specific translation suggests that Villa wanted to read the Greek version to keep – or rather, to reintroduce in her *de facto* source text and thus also in the Finnish translation – Greek metaphors; the use of culture-bound elements, in this case religious terminology, can be seen to serve a similar end.

The use of the *best-text* method thus enabled Villa to reintroduce some Greek flavour to the Finnish translation; had she simply translated from the French, she might not have realized that the French translator had replaced the Greek Orthodox terms with more generic vocabulary. Thus, compilative translating may enable counterbalancing some of the negative effects associated with indirect translation, which has been accused of being 'a major source of deviations' (Dollerup 2000: 23; see also Edström 1991: 12). Similarly, compilative translating seems capable of offsetting what Hadley (2017: 183) calls the *concatenation effect hypothesis* – that 'indirect translations exhibit a proclivity towards omitting cultural elements particular to their source cultures, and also towards downplaying the foreign origins of their source texts' (see also Kujamäki 2001: 50–1).

However, some of the omissions found in the French version have been carried over to the Finnish translation, suggesting that compilative translating is not a panacea. The transmission of omissions can be interpreted by looking at Villa's agency, or her 'willingness and ability to act' (Kinnunen and Koskinen 2010: 6). On the one hand, Villa's limited skills in English and Greek must have meant that collation was not an easy task; had there been a translation available in a language in which Villa had a higher proficiency, such as Swedish (e.g. Ivaska and Paloposki 2018: 42), the results of the collation might have been different. On the other hand, Villa may have deliberately refrained from making all the emendations that the collation of the language versions prompted. In any case, one thing regarding Villa's agency is certain: she did not settle with translating from one of the available versions of the novel but instead took an active role in shaping – or creating – the *de facto* source text of her translation through the collation.

In fact, this study shows that '[t]he genesis of a translation can be complex, sometimes even more complex than the genesis of the original text' (Van Hulle 2015: 44); in this case, it is made complex by the additional step of creating the *de facto* source text. Further research on the genesis of translations could help 'render visible certain complexities of the compositional process' (Cordingley and Montini 2015: 6), for example, by illuminating the bigger picture of the work that translators do before they even start translating (Shengyu 2018: 43). Although the scarcity of translators' archives poses a limitation to such studies, Munday suggests that research on translation processes could be complemented with the help of 'interviews and think-aloud protocols, corpus-based studies of texts and translator choices, and perhaps also keystroke logging and eye-tracking studies' (2013: 134). Hopefully, future studies exploiting methods such as these will shed more light not only on the genesis of translations in general but also on compilative translation practices, on the different kinds of collaboration that may be part of those processes (see e.g. Bistué 2013; Alvstad 2017; Cordingley and Manning 2017) and especially on the ways in which translators construct their *de facto* source texts. The study of these aspects will help draw a fuller picture of translations and translating.

Finally, compilative translation reveals aspects of the source text that deserve more attention than what can be given here.[24] First, indirect and compilative translations highlight the fact that a source text does not necessarily correspond to 'the original'; instead, at least one of the source texts of an indirect translation is itself a translation. Second, compilative translation has the potential to disrupt the 'kind of exclusive, binary and unidirectional relationship between source text and target text' (Delabastita 2008: 239), which is sometimes taken as a given in Western translation studies or to 'de-sacralize' the original (Baer 2017: 230). In the case of *Veljesviha*, for example, the mediating French and English translations are elevated to the status of a source text, and they even share this status simultaneously with the Greek ultimate source text itself. If, however, translation is understood to have *one* source text, then compilative translating must be understood to also entail the creation of a single-text *de facto* source text before any translating can actually occur. However, as these *de facto* source texts do not necessarily ever take any written form (Emmerich 2011; Shengyu 2018; see also Apter 2005), then, third, we must conclude that source texts can also exist in immaterial forms. In other words, source texts seem to be more fluid and flexible than one might expect, and it is peculiar how little attention the source text is attracting despite its central role in defining what translation – as well as translation studies – is all about.

Acknowledgements

I would like to thank the anonymous peer reviewers and the editors as well as Outi Paloposki and Martti Leiwo for their insightful feedback on this chapter. I would also like to thank the staff at the Prevelakis Archives at the University of Crete, the Kyllikki Villa Archives at Archives of the Finnish Literature Society and the Nikos Kazantzakis Museum Archive for their help with locating archival materials.

This research was made possible thanks to a research grant from Kone Foundation, a research trip to the Cretan archives by the Arvo Allonen memorial scholarship granted by Suomi-Kreikka-yhdistysten liitto.

Notes

1 For more discussion on terminology, see Rosa, Pięta and Maia (2017); Schultze (2014); Washbourne (2013); Ringmar (2007).
2 Similarly, Dollerup's definition excludes what Alvstad and Rosa label *compilative inter- and intralingual retranslation* and define as the 'use of the source text and of one or several previous translations into the *target* language' (2015: 17; emphasis added).

3   According to Shillingsburg, '[f]rom the receiver's perspective, a work is the imagined whole implied by all differing forms of a text that we conceive as representing a single literary creation' (1996: 43).
4   Dollerup makes the distinction between 'intermediary realisations [that] have been made for actual audiences' and 'cases where there are no genuine consumers of intermediate realisations' (2000: 17). The source text of a compilative translation that is constructed by collating several texts is more likely to fall into the latter category – it is the end product of the whole process, the translation that seems more likely to get published.
5   Retranslation is here understood as a 'second or later translation[s] of a *single source text* into the same target language' (Koskinen and Paloposki 2010: 294; emphasis added).
6   The other option to making a critical edition is to make *documentary* or *noncritical editions*, which refers to reproducing or republishing texts in forms in which they have already been published, for example, in the form of a facsimile or diplomatic edition (Tanselle 1994: 4).
7   The *best-text* method is sometimes also referred to as the *copy-text method* (see Tanselle 1994: 1), and Shengyu (2018: 37) uses the term *copy-text* to refer to the text that 'David Hawkes used for collating other Chinese versions' to the 1964 Renmin Wenxue Chubanshe edition.
8   Unless otherwise noted, all translations are mine. The name of the novel in Greek is misspelled in the Finnish translation; the spelling appearing in Greek editions is Οι αδερφοφάδες.
9   Kyllikki Villa Archives, Archives of the Finnish Literature Society, Helsinki, Finland.
10 Pandelis Prevelakis Archives, University of Crete, Rethymno, Greece.
11 Nikos Kazantzakis Museum Archive, Heraklion, Greece.
12 Unfortunately, I have been unable to locate a copy of the first Greek edition published in 1963, and thus the version used for the comparison is a second printing from 1965. The French translation used in the analysis lacks information on the printing date; the title page only states that the copyright is from 1965 and that the book was printed in France.
13 Letter from Kyllikki Villa to Eleni Kazantzaki, 17 November 1966; Nikos Kazantzakis Museum Archive.
14 Translation contract between Tammi publishing house and Kyllikki Villa, 19 October 1966; Kyllikki Villa Archives, Archives of the Finnish Literature Society.
15 Letter from Eleni Kazantzaki to Kyllikki Villa, 23 November 1966; Kyllikki Villa Archives, Archives of the Finnish Literature Society.
16 Letter from Kyllikki Villa to Eleni Kazantzaki, 17 November 1966; Nikos Kazantzakis Museum Archive.
17 See the previous note.
18 Letter from Eleni Kazantzaki to Kyllikki Villa, 23 November 1966; Kyllikki Villa Archives, Archives of the Finnish Literature Society.
19 Translation contract between Tammi publishing house and Kyllikki Villa, 19 October 1966; Kyllikki Villa Archives, Archives of the Finnish Literature Society.
20 Grant application to the Finnish Ministry of Education, 15 September 1967; Kyllikki Villa Archives, Archives of the Finnish Literature Society.
21 Letter from Kyllikki Villa to Pandelis Prevelakis, 10 February 1967; Pandelis Prevelakis Archives, University of Crete.

22   Letter from Kyllikki Villa to Pandelis Prevelakis, 18 September 1963; Pandelis Prevelakis Archives, University of Crete. Letter from Pandelis Prevelakis to Kyllikki Villa, 1 October 1963; Kyllikki Villa Archives, Archives of the Finnish Literature Society.
23   There are also passages where there is no difference between the four language versions, proving that a translation can accurately reflect the ultimate source text whether translated directly or indirectly. Similarly, there are passages where all the four are different, suggesting that change is inherent in translation – in fact, translation is all about changing the language.
24   The question of the source text is elaborated further in an unpublished article manuscript by Ivaska and Huuhtanen titled 'Beware the Source Text: Five (Re)translations of the Same Work, But from Different Source Texts'.

References

Alvstad, Cecilia (2017), 'Arguing for Indirect Translations in Twenty-First-Century Scandinavia', *Translation Studies*, 10 (2): 150–65.

Alvstad, Cecilia and Alexandra Assis Rosa (2015), 'Voice in Retranslation: An Overview and Some Trends', special issue of *Target*, 27 (1): 3–24.

Apter, Emily (2005), 'Translations with No Original: Scandals of Textual Reproduction', in Sandra Bermann and Michael Wood (eds), *Nation, Language, and the Ethics of Translation*, 159–74, Princeton: Princeton University Press.

Baer, Brian James (2017), 'De-sacralizing the Origin(al) and the Transnational Future of Translation Studies', *Perspectives*, 25 (2): 227–44.

Bassnett, Susan (1998), 'When Is a Translation Not a Translation?', in Susan Bassnett and André Lefevere (eds), *Constructing Cultures: Essays on Literary Translation*, 25–40, Clevedon: Multilingual Matters.

Bistué, Belén (2013), *Collaborative Translation and Multi-Version Texts in Early Modern Europe*, Farnham: Ashgate.

Cordingley, Anthony and Céline Frigau Manning (eds) (2017), *Collaborative Translation: From the Renaissance to the Digital Age*, London and New York: Bloomsbury.

Cordingley, Anthony and Chiara Montini (2015), 'Genetic Translation Studies: An Emerging Discipline', *Linguistica Antverpiensia, New Series: Themes in Translation Studies*, 14: 1–18.

Dedner, Burghard (2012), 'Intertextual Layers in Translations: Methods of Research and Editorial Presentation', *Variants*, 9: 115–31.

Delabastita, Dirk (2008), 'Status, Origin, Features: Translation and Beyond', in Anthony Pym, Miriam Shlesinger and Daniel Simeoni (eds), *Beyond Descriptive Translation Studies: Investigations in Homage to Gideon Toury*, 233–46, Amsterdam: John Benjamins.

Dollerup, Cay (2000), 'Relay and Support Translations', in Andrew Chesterman, Natividad Gallardo San Salvador and Yves Gambier (eds), *Translation in Context*, 7–26, Amsterdam: John Benjamins.

Edström, Bert (1991), 'The Transmitter Language Problem in Translations from Japanese into Swedish', *Babel*, 37 (1): 1–14.

Emmerich, Karen (2011), 'The Afterlives of C. P. Cavafy's Unfinished Poems', *Translation Studies*, 4 (2): 197–212.

Ferrer, Daniel (2016), 'Genetic Criticism with Textual Criticism: From Variant to Variation', *Variants*, 12-13: 57-64.
Greetham, D. C. (1984), 'Models for the Textual Transmission of Translation: The Case of John Trevisa', *Studies in Bibliography*, 37: 131-55.
Greetham, D. C. (1994), *Scholarly Editing: A Guide to Research*, New York: The Modern Language Association of America.
Hadley, James (2017), 'Indirect Translation and Discursive Identity: Proposing the Concatenation Effect Hypothesis', *Translation Studies*, 10 (2): 183-97.
Itkonen-Kaila, Marjan (1997), *Mikael Agricolan Uusi Testamentti ja sen erikieliset lähtötekstit* (Mikael Agricola's New Testament and Its Several Source Texts in Different Languages), Helsinki: SKS.
Ivaska, Laura (2016), 'Uncovering the Many Source Texts of Indirect Translations: Indirect Translations of Modern Greek Prose Literature into Finnish 1952-2004', poster presented at the 8th European Society for Translation Studies Congress, Aarhus, Denmark, 15-17 September.
Ivaska, Laura and Outi Paloposki (2018), 'Attitudes towards Indirect Translation in Finland and Translators' Strategies: Compilative and Collaborative Translation', *Translation Studies*, 11 (1): 33-46.
Jettmarová, Zuzana (2011), 'Editor's Introduction to the English Edition', in Jiří Levý, *The Art of Translation*, xv-xxvi, Amsterdam: John Benjamins.
Katajamäki, Sakari and Karina Lukin (2013), 'Textual Trails from Oral to Written Sources: An Introduction', *RMN* Newsletter, 7: 8-17.
Kazantzakis, Nikos ([1963] 1965), Οι αδερφοφάδες, δευτέρα έκδοση, Αθήναι: Εκδόσεις Ελ. Καζαντζάκη.
Kazantzakis, Nikos (1965), *Les Frères ennemis*, trans. Pierre Aellig, France: Librairie Plon.
Kazantzakis, Nikos ([1966] 1967), *The Fratricides*, trans. Athena Gianakas Dallas, Oxford: Bruno Cassirer.
Kazantzakis, Nikos (1967), *Veljesviha*, trans. Kyllikki Villa, Helsinki: Tammi.
Kinnunen, Tuija and Kaisa Koskinen (2010), 'Introduction', in Tuija Kinnunen and Kaisa Koskinen (eds), *Translators' Agency*, 4-9, Tampere Studies in Language, Translation and Culture, series B4, Tampere: Tampere University Press.
Kittel, Harald (1991), 'Vicissitudes of Mediation: The Case of Benjamin Franklin's Autobiography', in Harald Kittel and Armin Paul Frank (eds), *Interculturality and the Historical Study of Literary Translations*, 25-35, Berlin: Eric Schmidt.
Koskinen, Kaisa and Outi Paloposki (2010), 'Retranslation', in Yves Gambier and Luc van Doorslaer (eds), *Handbook of Translation Studies*, vol. 1, 294-8. Amsterdam: John Benjamins.
Kujamäki, Pekka (1998), *Deutsche Stimmen der* Sieben Brüder: *Ideologie, Poetik und Funktionen literarischer Übersetzung*, Frankfurt am Main: Peter Lang.
Kujamäki, Pekka (2001), 'Finnish Comet in German Skies: Translation, Retranslation and Norms', *Target*, 13 (1): 45-70.
McGann, Jerome (1991), *The Textual Condition*, Princeton: Princeton University Press.
Munday, Jeremy (2013), 'The Role of Archival and Manuscript Research in the Investigation of Translator Decision-Making', *Target*, 25 (1): 125-39.
Pięta, Hanna (2012), 'Patterns in (In)directness: An Exploratory Case Study in the External History of Portuguese Translations of Polish Literature (1855-2010)', *Target*, 24 (2): 310-37.
Reimer, Stephen R. ([1998] 2015), 'Manuscript Studies: Medieval and Early Modern'. Available online: https://sites.ualberta.ca/~sreimer/ms-course/course/editns.htm (accessed 30 November 2018).

Ringmar, Martin (2007), 'Roundabouts Routes: Some Remarks on Indirect Translations', in Francis Mus (ed.), *Selected Papers of the CETRA Research Seminar in Translation Studies 2006*, 1–17, Leuven: CETRA. Available online: https://www.arts.kuleuven.be/cetra/papers/files/ringmar.pdf (accessed 30 November 2018).

Romanelli, Sergio (2015), 'Manuscripts and Translations: Spaces for Creation', *Linguistica Antverpiensia, New Series: Themes in Translation Studies*, 14: 87–104.

Rosa, Alexandra Assis, Hanna Pięta and Rita Bueno Maia (2017), 'Theoretical, Methodological and Terminological Issues Regarding Indirect Translation: An Overview', *Translation Studies*, 10 (2): 113–32.

Schultze, Brigitte (2014), 'Historical and Systematical Aspects of Indirect Translation in the de Gruyter Handbuch Übersetzung – HSK. 26.1–3: Insight and Impulse to Further Research', *Zeitschrift für Slawistik*, 59 (4): 507–18.

Shengyu, Fan (2018), 'The Lost Translator's Copy: David Hawkes' Construction of a Base Text in Translating *Hongluomeng*', *Translation Review*, 10 (1): 37–64.

Shillingsburg, Peter L. (1996), *Scholarly Editing in the Computer Age: Theory and Practice*, 3rd edn, Ann Arbor: The University of Michigan Press.

Solberg, Ida Hove (2016), 'Finding the X Factor: Support Translation and the Case of *Le Deuxième sexe* in Scandinavia', in Turo Rautaoja, Kaisa Koskinen and Tamara Mikolič Južnič (eds), *New Horizons in Translation Research and Education*, vol. 4, 86–114, Joensuu: Publications of the University of Eastern Finland.

Tanselle, G. Thomas (1994), 'Editing without a Copy-Text', *Studies in Bibliography*, 47: 1–22.

Toury, Gideon (2012), *Descriptive Translation Studies and Beyond*, rev. ed., Amsterdam: John Benjamins.

Van Hulle, Dirk (2015), 'Translation and Genetic Criticism: Genetic and Editorial Approaches to the "Untranslatable" in Joyce and Beckett', *Linguistica Antverpiensia, New Series: Themes in Translation Studies*, 14: 40–53.

Villa, Kyllikki (1968), 'Balkanilaista proosaa ja kääntäjäin mietteitä' (Balkan Prose and Translator's Thoughts), *Maaseudun tulevaisuus*, 18 July.

Villa, Kyllikki and Saara Villa (2013), *Äidin lokikirja* (Mother's Logbook), Helsinki: Like.

Washbourne, Kelly (2013), 'Nonlinear Narratives: Paths of Indirect and Relay Translation', *Meta*, 58 (3): 607–25.

6

Allographic translation, self-translation and alloglottic rewriting: Towards a digital edition of poetry by Pedro Homem de Mello

Elsa Pereira
Centre of Linguistics, University of Lisbon

This chapter focuses on a series of interlingual materials related to the genetic dossier of twentieth-century Portuguese author Pedro Homem de Mello (1904–84), whose poetry is the object of an ongoing digital edition. In general terms, we may organize such documents into two main categories: a group of allographic translations (made by other people rather than the poet) and a series of authorial witnesses, ranging from self-translation to alloglottic rewriting, which involves a thorough reinvention of a text using a different language. We will, therefore, be referring to Umberto Eco's concept of 'intersystemic interpretation with marked variation in the substance' and focus on its main subtypes.[1]

The chapter starts by presenting examples of this form of textual variation and analysing their theoretical implications for a genetic–critical edition. It will then proceed to elaborate on the editorial approach adopted in the project and the use of the electronic medium to organize the digital archive.

Allographic translations

Starting with the first type of interlinguistic interpretation identified by Eco, we must note that Pedro Homem de Mello had several of his works translated into French and English, either by native speakers or by Portuguese writers living abroad. That was the case with the books related to his activity as an ethnographer[2] and also with some of his poetry, which was rendered in French by commission of several promoters of the Portuguese culture abroad (Figure 6.1).

The research leading to this article was developed at CLUL – Centre of Linguistics of the University of Lisbon and supported by a post-doc grant from FCT – Fundação para a Ciência e a Tecnologia (SFRH/BPD/92155/2013), through Portuguese and European funds. The author wishes to thank João Dionísio and Francisco Topa for their comments on earlier versions of this essay. Special thanks are also due to the owners of the documents mentioned in the article: Mariana Homem de Mello, Rita Homem de Mello, Helena Telles da Silva, and Biblioteca Nacional de Portugal.

Portuguese → French

- **'Chanson verte', by Armand Guibert** (translation of the poem 'Canção verde' [Mello 1951: 25–7]).
  Le Journal des poètes 9 (1952a): 9.
- **'La Maison brûlée', by Pierre Hourcade and Adolfo Casais Monteiro** (translation of the poem 'Casa queimada' [Mello 1951: 19–20]).
  Le Journal des poètes 9 (1952a): 9.
  (1971) Isabel Meyrelles (ed.), *Anthologie de la poésie portugaise du XIIe au XXe siècle*, 212–13, Paris: Gallimard.
- **'Remords', by Evelyne Kesteven** (translation of the poem 'Remorso' [Mello 1948: 26–8]).
  (1971) Isabel Meyrelles (ed.), *Anthologie de la poésie portugaise du XIIe au XXe siècle*, 211–12, Paris: Gallimard.
- **'Chanson verte', 'Hier', 'Divorce', 'Horizon', 'Extase', by Isabel Meyrelles** (translation of the poems 'Canção verde' [Mello 1951: 25–7], 'Véspera' [Mello 1954: 55–6], 'Divórcio' [Mello 1955: 15–16], 'Horizonte' [Mello 1957: 339], 'Extase' [Mello 1967: 78–9]).
  João Gaspar Simões (ed.), *Le Deuxième modernisme: la Génération de Presença: 1927–1940*, trans. Isabel Meyrelles. (Unpublished. BNP, E16, box 42/29)[3]

Figure 6.1 Published allographic translations (Portuguese to French) of Pedro Homem de Mello's poetry.

Besides these translations, there is also a collection of seventy-seven poems translated into English by Arnold Hawkins and released in book form, with a few sparse reprints in periodicals (Figure 6.2).

The English compilation was targeted at the British community in Porto (where the author and the translator lived and worked as lecturers)[4] and was favourably received by the critics. One of them praised the challenging nature of the translation in the following terms:

> This book ... is certainly a great novelty, daring, risky. ... Homem de Mello ... is perhaps the hardest of any of the contemporary Portuguese poets to translate. Firstly, his poems are classical rather than 'modernistic', which means to say that most of them are in Portuguese verse-forms which are unusual and exotic if reproduced with English words. ... Secondly, Homem de Mello is not only classicist in form, he is what is called a 'traditionalist poet'. ...
>
> He has his roots in the popular poetry of Portugal, ... in popular song, music, and dance. ...
>
> So the second pitfall in translating Homem de Mello was this: to keep the popular freshness of the original in a language whose poetical achievement is aristocratic. (Hawkins 1941b: 9)

Allographic Translation, Self-Translation and Alloglottic Rewriting 91

> Portuguese → English
>
> 'Abstraction', 'Alcácer-Quibir', 'Alentejo', 'Autumn', 'Beginning', 'Black Eyes', 'Blessing', 'Blue and Rose the Day Advances', 'Calvary', 'Canvas', 'Captivity', 'Caravel to Sea', 'Carmelites', 'Charneca', 'Chimera', 'Cloud', 'Concert', 'Confession', 'Counsel', 'Curse', 'Dance of the Hours', 'Darkness', 'Desert', 'Destiny', 'Echo', 'Epitome', 'Faith', 'Falling Star', 'Fatality', 'Fatherland', 'Flight (I see a balloon, a dozen, in the air)', 'Flight (The poet-musician seeks)', 'Grace', 'Gratitude', 'Hail!', 'Hapiness', 'Harmony', 'Illusion', 'Inspiration', 'Limbo', 'Lost Kiss', 'Lost Steps', 'Miracle', 'Narrow Pathway', 'Night', 'Noon', 'On the Land', 'Pines of Portugal', 'Prayer', 'Prophecy', 'Refuge', 'Renunciation', 'Revelation', 'Rock', 'Scene', 'Secret', 'Shadow', 'Silence', 'Song to an Absent Love', 'Spring', 'Spring in Autumn', 'Star', 'The Graveyards', 'The Moon', 'The Past', 'The Rivers', 'The Shades', 'The Spectres', 'Trees', 'Tritons', 'Truth', 'Water-Colour', 'Waves', 'Weep not the Dead', 'When the Wind Bent the Tall Willow Over', 'Words', 'Youth', by Arnold C. Hawkins
> [translation of poems from the books *Caravela ao Mar* (Mello 1934), *Jardins Suspensos* (Mello 1937) and *Segrêdo* (Mello 1939b)].
> In Arnold C. Hawkins (1941a), *Lusitanian Lyrics*, Porto: Lello & Irmão.
>
> **'Dance of the Hours', 'Scene', 'Truth', by Arnold C. Hawkins**
> [reprints from *Lusitanian Lyrics* (Hawkins 1941a)].
> In *The Anglo-Portuguese News*, 95 (1941a): 4; 98 (1941b): 6–7; 219 (1943): 4.

Figure 6.2 Published allographic translations (Portuguese to English) of Pedro Homem de Mello's poetry.

Although the name of the poet is absent from the book cover, and it is only on the title page that we find reference to the translation,[5] Hawkins (1941a: vii) states in the preface that 'this book is an adventure in friendship', referring to the close bond that existed between author and translator[6] and apparently suggesting that Pedro Homem de Mello was somehow involved in the process. This impression is also confirmed by the correspondence in the poet's private collection, which contains several intermediate versions that Hawkins sent for Mello's approval (Figure 6.3).

As we can see in the example provided in Figure 6.4, there are, indeed, some variants between those drafts and the published versions of the book.

However, it remains unclear if the poet has made any contributions to the final version, considering that he was fluent but not proficient in English and that his correspondence with Hawkins is entirely in French. Since we are not sure whether the author had any input, as often happens in authorized translations,[7] the question is whether we should include these materials in a digital critical–genetic edition of poetry by Pedro Homem de Mello.

Traditionally, allographic translations are not considered in a genetic edition, because they belong to what some textual critics call *derivative works*. As Elena

> Portuguese → English
>
> **'Silence', 'Canvas', 'Illusion', 'Harmony', 'Youth', 'Calvary', 'Miracle', 'Chimera', 'Fatality', 'The Moon', 'Blessing', by Arnold C. Hawkins** [drafts included in Arnold Hawkins's correspondence to Pedro Homem de Mello, dated from 1939 to 1947. These manuscripts are currently owned by one of the poet's daughters-in-law, Helena Telles da Silva].

Figure 6.3 Draft allographic translations (Portuguese to English), later published in *Lusitanian Lyrics* (Hawkins 1941a).

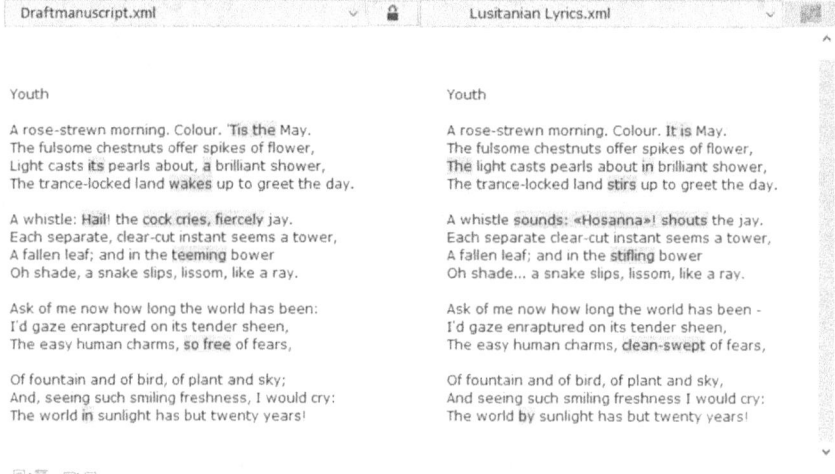

Figure 6.4 A side-by-side comparison of the manuscript (HTS, Hawkins's letter to Mello), on the left, and the final translation (Hawkins 1941a: 24), on the right, using Juxta collation software. The highlighted passages correspond to the variants.

Pierazzo (2015: 53) points out a different ontological status is involved in allographic translations, due to the presence of other types of authorship, and consequently, these documents are somehow independent of the source text from which they derive. Still, Dirk Van Hulle identified five different ways in which translations may inform the work of genetic scholars and possibly earn a place in the edition:

> [T]ranslation studies and genetic criticism inform each other in at least five different ways: genesis as part of translation; translation of the genesis; genesis of the translation; translation as part of the genesis; and finally the genesis of the untranslatable. (Van Hulle 2015: 40)[8]

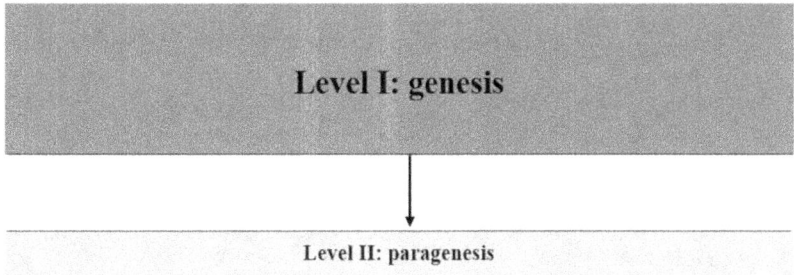

Figure 6.5 Generic model of the ongoing edition.

The challenge here would be to integrate the allographic materials into the editorial design, while preserving their independence from the author's documents. That kind of architecture requires a non-linear approach, organized on different levels.

For the ongoing project, we decided to make allographic translations available in a paragenetic device located in marginal notes (see below, part 3), while the body of the edition is reserved for the authorial genesis, assembling various types of document witnesses (Figure 6.5). This includes not only the manuscripts, typescripts and printed texts that Pedro Homem de Mello produced in his mother tongue, but also a few poems written in his second language, French,[9] and a group of unpublished exercises that fall into what Gérard Genette (1994: 202) calls *traductions auctoriales* (or self-translations).

Self-translation and alloglottic rewriting

In the poet's archive, owned by the Portuguese National Library, there is a folder (BNP, E14, box 9 [folder 2]) that stands out in the collection, due to the bilingual nature of the materials therein. It contains typescript copies of seventeen compositions that Pedro Homem de Mello published from 1933 to 1951, most of which explicitly mention the books to which they belong. Side by side with those fair copies of the Portuguese originals, the author placed in the folder one – sometimes two – French version(s) for each composition (Figure 6.6).

Manuscripts from earlier writing stages of the French versions did not survive, but some of these typescripts include autograph revisions that bring them closer to the status of a work in progress. Initially, they were destined to be published as translations in the bilingual booklet collection *Autour du Monde*, which the Parisian house Pierre Seghers organized between 1952 and 1970. This is suggested by a letter, dated 2 January 1952, where Alain Bosquet invited Pedro Homem de Mello to participate with selected poems translated into French.[10] The same information is confirmed by a news article from 24 May 1952 (Anonymous 1952b: 4), which refers to the forthcoming publication

> BNP, E14, box 9 (folder 2):
> - **'Refus'** (self-translation of the poem 'Recusa' from Mello 1951: 64–5);
> - 'Sonata' (from Mello 1947: 80) + **'Sonate'**;
> - 'Desencanto' (from Mello 1939b: 17–18) + **'Désenchantement'**;
> - **'Aquarelle'** (self-translation of the poem 'Aquarela' from Mello 1937: 86–7);
> - 'Peixe vermelho' (from Mello 1939b: 49–50) + **'Le poisson rouge'**;
> - 'Canção verde' (from Mello 1951: 25–7) + **'Chanson verte'** + **'Chanson verte'**;
> - 'Naufrágio' (from Mello 1940: 17–19) + **'Naufrage'** + **'Naufrage'**;
> - 'Infinito' (from Mello 1934: 117) + **'Infini'**;
> - 'O bailador de fandango' (from Mello 1942: 63–4) + **'Le danseur de fandango'**;
> - 'Vila verde' (from Mello 1947: 47–9) + **'Ville Verte'**;
> - 'Canção à ausente' (from Mello 1939b: 53–4) + **'Absence'**;
> - 'Barco vazio' (from Mello 1939b: 11–13) + **'Le bateau vide'**;
> - 'Pecado' (from Mello 1942: 21–3) + **'Péché'**;
> - 'Quando o vento dobrou todo o salgueiro' (from Mello 1939b: 61–2) + **'Quand le vent vient plier le saule vert'**;
> - 'Profecia' (from Mello 1937: 90–1) + **'Profécie'**;
> - 'Espanto' (from Mello 1951: 32–3) + **'Étonnement'**;
> - 'Herói morto' (from Mello 1945: 121) + **'Le héros mort'**.

Figure 6.6 Pedro Homem de Mello's self-translation and alloglottic rewriting.

in Paris of an anthology of poems translated by the author himself. For some reason, however, the volume never saw the light of day[11] and chances are that those self-translations eventually became a recreative exercise with new scribal purposes, as they involve reinventing the texts while rendering them into a different language.

In previous articles (Pereira 2017a, b), we have already observed that Homem de Mello often submitted his compositions to thorough rewriting processes, favouring structural variance and 'vertical revision' to make a 'different sort of work out of' previous texts (Tanselle 1990: 53). This procedure resulted in multiple different versions with extreme variation phenomena and could also be related to the writing habits of many authors from the modernist period, whose approach to revision shaped literary style at the beginning of the twentieth century. As Hanna Sullivan (2013: 16) pointed out, all the main techniques we recognize as modernist are intimately related to experimental acts of revision, which sometimes 'could be a way to defamiliarize circulating work and to make it new for the second time' (Sullivan 2013: 239).

There are many examples of this type of practice in Homem de Mello's poetry, and that also seems to happen in the unpublished French versions we are considering in this chapter. It is true that, despite substantial rhythmic variation,

Allographic Translation, Self-Translation and Alloglottic Rewriting 95

some compositions correspond partially to a more literal *metaphrastic translation*,[12] as happens in Figure 6.7 (where 'Absence' roughly follows 'Canção à ausente', published in the 1939 book *Segrêdo*).

However, many of the French typescripts included in BNP, E14, box 9 (folder 2) are very different from the respective Portuguese versions, and it is not only due to the apparent distance between languages and their syntactic rules or vocabulary. Indeed, they seem to correspond to Oustinoff's concept of *(re)creative self-translation*,[13] which entails a radical manipulation of the original, sometimes making it difficult to recognize similarities between the two texts. Let us compare, for example, 'Sonata' (copy from the 1947 book *Bodas Vermelhas*) with the contiguous French version in the author's typescripts.

Altogether, only the title and a few partial lines were literally preserved during the process of self-translation, but not all those words appear in the same position (Figure 6.8). The poem was thoroughly rewritten and shortened by one line, the rhythm and the strophic scheme were altered, and even the lyric message is not entirely coincident. So much so that we cannot but ask ourselves what kind of textual instances they are. Will they be a source and a target text of a translation, made by the same

BNP, E14, box 9 [folder 2] (copy from Mello 1939: 53-4).	BNP, E14, box 9 [folder 2]
CANÇÃO À AUSENTE	ABSENCE
Para te amar ensaiei os meus lábios… Deixei de pronunciar palavras duras. Para te amar ensaiei os meus lábios!	Oui. Rien que pour t'aimer j'ai amminci mes lèvres Car j'ai presque oublié les mots durs d'autrefois. Oui. Rien que pour t'aimer j'ai amminci mes lèvres…
Para tocar-te ensaiei os meus dedos… Banhei-os na àgua limpida das fontes. Para tocar-te ensaiei os meus dedos!	Oui. Rien que pour t'aimer j'ai rafraichi mes doigts En les berçant dans l'eau de la fontaine Oui. Rien que pour t'aimer j'ai raffraichi mes doigts
Para te ouvir ensaiei meus ouvidos! Pus-me a escutar as vozes do silênsio… Para te ouvir ensaiei meus ouvidos!	Oui. Rien que pour t'aimer j'ai fermé les oreilles À toute la chanson dont les forêts sont pleines Oui. Rien que pour t'aimer j'ai fermé les oreilles.
E a vida foi passando, foi passando… E à força de esperar a tua vinda De cada braço fiz mudo cipreste…	Ainsi Les nuits Après les jours passèrent…
A vida foi passando, foi passsando… E nunca mais vieste!	Et dans l'attente vaine Mes bras ont pris la forme des cyprès.
	Ainsi Les nuits Après les jours passèrent…
	Mais toi (toi! toi!) tu n'es venu jamais!

Figure 6.7 A side-by-side comparison of the Portuguese and French typescripts of 'Canção à ausente', in BNP, E14, box 9 (folder 2). The highlighted passages correspond to the matching text.

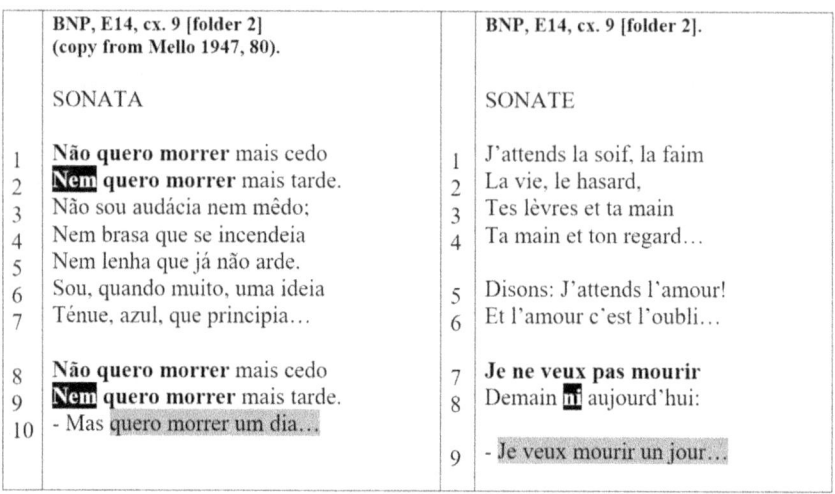

Figure 6.8 A side-by-side comparison of the Portuguese and French typescripts of 'Sonata', in BNP, E14, box 9 (folder 2). The highlighted passages correspond to the matching text: the passages with a light grey and a dark grey background are in linear correspondence, while the bold passages and the white text against a black background appear in a different position.

person? Are they two versions of a single poem, written in different languages? Or, on the contrary, are we dealing with two separate texts that share only a few matching words? María Recuenco had already asked similar questions and identified different theoretical positions regarding self-translations,[14] which we could associate to three main procedures in terms of editorial handling.

Some critics consider that, regardless of the distance between source and target texts, self-translation does not substantially differ from an allographic translation, as both establish a modelling relation with the original. This is true for Anton Popovič, who offered a straightforward definition: 'Due to its modelling relation to the original text, the autotranslation cannot be regarded as a variant of the original text, but as a true translation' (1976: 19). According to this understanding, the French script depends on the Portuguese text by way of a subaltern relation. Therefore, we should edit self-translations just like we did for the allographic translations in this project – that is, in a paragenetic device, adjacent to the main level of the edition.

For other experts, though, the interlingual exercise must be regarded as an extension of the writing process: '[O]ne has to examine them … in the light of the continuation of the writer's work in the source language and in the light of his former work in the target language' (Perry 1981: 181). The French witness would thus not be hierarchically dependent on the Portuguese instance (as happens in translations), but would constitute an alternate version of the same poem, within a circuitous creative process where all witnesses have the same status. Brian Fitch and Rainier Grutman belong to this second school of thought, according to which we would have to integrate the alloglottic witnesses in the author's writing chronology and present them on a par with the Portuguese versions of the poem:

What is, I feel, appropriate is to attribute equal status to both versions ... The fact of the matter is that both ... are alternative outcomes of the same textual productivity. ... The only difference is that the second versions also involve a shift of language-system. (Fitch 1985: 119)

The distinction between original and (self)translation therefore collapses, giving way to a more flexible terminology in which both texts can be referred to as 'variants' or 'versions' of comparable status. (Grutman 2009: 259)

For other authors, still, this is not a mere translation, nor a version of the same text, but a whole different poem; it is a new original with its own macrostructure:

[The author] passes, of course, from one language to another, but also, and above all, from one text to another: he creates a new textuality, a full textuality. (Bensimon 2002: 135)

[S]elf-translators ... may finally develop a new text with all the characteristics of a second original. (Santoyo 2004: 229)

Following this third hypothesis, favoured by Paul Bensimon and Julio-César Santoyo, among others, the Portuguese and the French texts should be presented as two independent poems in the author's *oeuvre*, despite their common ground.

While any one of the approaches described would be valid from a theoretical standpoint, the ongoing edition of poetry by Pedro Homem de Mello opted for the second possibility. The French authorial witnesses will be considered within the work's genesis (in contrast to the paragenetic framework of the allographic translations), and the contiguous placement of the documents in the author's folder suggests that they form a textual cluster with the Portuguese copies.[15] Therefore, they are to be considered versions of the same poem, regarded in terms of a '[l]arge-value hypertext or macrotext' (Rada 1991: 68), of which there is no primary instance.

In doing so, we refer to the idea of *work* as a collection of texts linked through variation (Shillingsburg 2004: 77) and to Siegfried Scheibe's concept of authorization, according to which all author's versions 'are of equal standing' (Scheibe 1995: 175). It means that, instead of a single base text, each poem will be presented as a series of individual versions that are assembled in one unit. That brings us to a new editorial paradigm, called *versioning* or *multiple texts* (Reiman 1987: 167–80), which is based on a heuristic display of textual *fluidities*, through the functional integration of text and apparatus.

By arguing in favour of this option, we face a practical problem, though, because each language's morphological and syntactic rules originate 'an endless array of mismatchings' (O'Reilly qtd. in Van Hulle 2004: 386), which significantly complicate the critical apparatus. In this sense, it will be useful if we resort to the notion of non-interchangeable versions, which is suggested by Gérard Genette when he says that a literary work may have plural immanences that are not identical and interchangeable (Genette 1994: 187). That means that the Portuguese versions, on the one hand, and the French versions on the other form two independent blocks within the same textual unit that constitutes a poem.

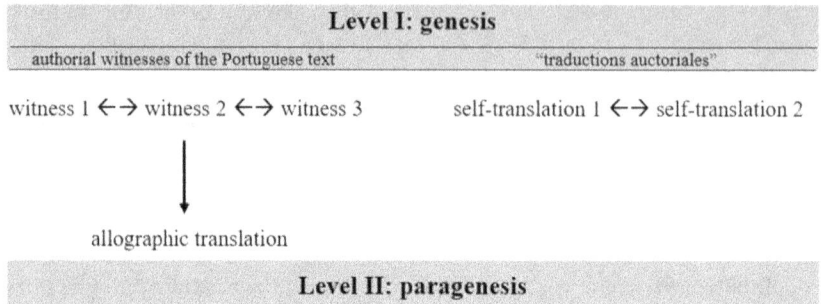

Figure 6.9 Editorial model of the ongoing project.

To put this in visual terms, Figure 6.9 presents the editorial model designed for the project.

At the main level of the edition, there is a chronological and non-hierarchical presentation of all the authorial witnesses, organized into two sections: the Portuguese versions (collated through an apparatus) and the French versions (also compared with each other). At the same time, a paragenesis device, located in marginal notes, will include the respective allographic translations, thus providing a representation of the work's genesis *in extenso*.

A digital editorial approach

Naturally, a multilevel edition such as this would be difficult to achieve in a printed book, due to the material constraints of the page. Only in recent decades has this type of non-linear presentation been fully explored, thanks to the electronic hypertext. Briefly, we may say that the digital paradigm is based on a series of programming languages that process the textual information marked by the editor, enabling different kinds of automatic treatment and display. Therefore, the transcriptions and the apparatus must be represented in a formal semantic language, easily interpretable by computers through existing or bespoke software solutions.

In this project, we will be using TEI-P5 conformant XML for text encoding, and resort to the XSLT, CSS and JavaScript styles that comprise the open-source interface of the Versioning Machine.[16] The software has been adopted by several international projects[17] and is appropriate for displaying multiple versions of text in a flexible and dynamic environment.

In order to illustrate how these functionalities may apply to our editorial model, the chapter will now conclude with a short demonstration, using one poem by Pedro Homem de Mello. It is entitled 'Canção verde' and consists of a cluster of eighteen authorial witnesses, schematically represented in Figure 6.10: sixteen of them written in Portuguese, and two in French. Additionally, there are two allographic translations made by Armand Guibert and Isabel Meyrelles.

Allographic Translation, Self-Translation and Alloglottic Rewriting 99

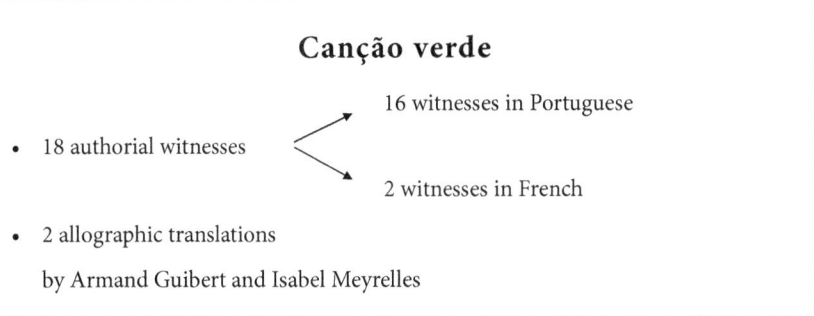

Figure 6.10 Document witnesses of the poem 'Canção verde'.

The first step to be taken is transcribing all the assembled documents in a single XML file. The Portuguese authorial witnesses are encoded with an in-line apparatus, using the TEI-P5 location-referenced method,[18] which associates lines of corresponding text, by specifying a @loc attribute within the <app>s that need to be assembled. Elsewhere in the document, the same procedure is repeated for the French versions, but in this case, a @type='trans' attribute may be added to the <rdg>s (Figure 6.11). Since the location values that associate the French readings are different from those specified in the <app>s of the Portuguese witnesses, two separate collations are generated, giving shape to the above-mentioned concept of non-interchangeable versions.

On the other hand, the allographic translations (made by Armand Guibert and Isabel Meyrelles) may be recorded within <note> elements, with a @type='critical' assigned attribute (Figure 6.12). That will grant them a subordinate position towards the authorial versions, represented in the <body> of <text>.

Once the encoding is complete, a transformation to HTML is executed, applying the Versioning Machine's stylesheet. This will automatically reconstruct eighteen individual version panels and sequentially display them into a horizontal scrolling page, which users may choose to visualize and reorder in multiple possible combinations. For this demonstration, let us focus on the Portuguese witness (N) and the French versions (O and P) that belong to BNP, E14, box 9 (folder 2).

After an introductory *Bibliographic Panel* (where metadata and a synopsis of the poem's compositional history are provided), the user will find a parallel display of individual versions with different layers of critical and genetic information. In the example shown in Figure 6.13, these include transcriptional choices for alternate spelling or regularized forms (represented by the <choice> <sic> <corr> and <choice> <orig> <reg> elements), traces of in-document authorial revisions (encoded with the <del> and <add> elements) and variant readings (encoded with <app> and <rdg>). These variants are highlighted between either the French versions or the Portuguese witnesses because of the separate collation generated by the apparatus.

Furthermore, the allographic translations (encoded within the <note> elements) will appear in the *Notes Panel*, to be accessed through user manipulated pop-up windows (Figure 6.14).

This presentation will provide the user with a heuristic display of the work's genesis, which 'conveys and embodies a pluralistic notion of text', intimately related to the

100   *Genetic Translation Studies*

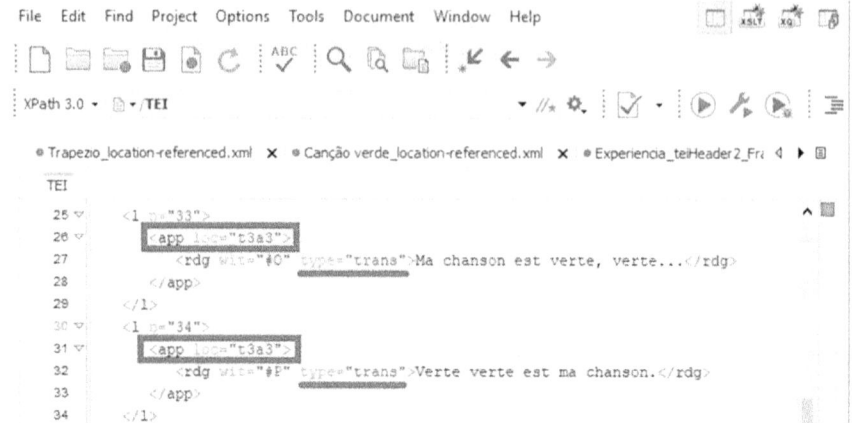

Figure 6.11 Encoded apparatus for line 33 of witness O (French version) and line 34 of witness P (French version), using the location-referenced method. The respective <rdg>s are identified with @type='trans'.

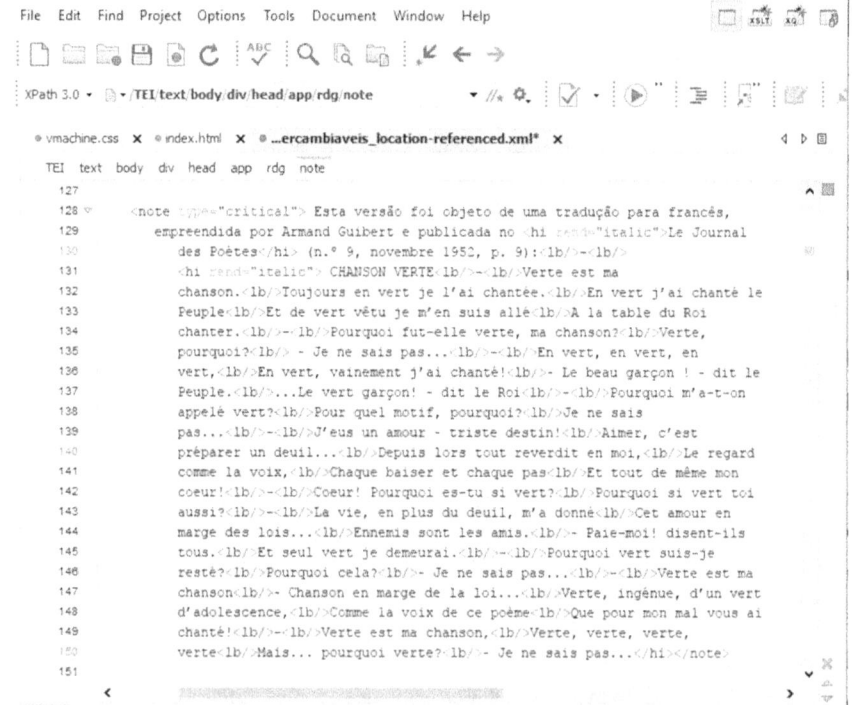

Figure 6.12 Encoding an allographic translation, within the element <note>.

Allographic Translation, Self-Translation and Alloglottic Rewriting   101

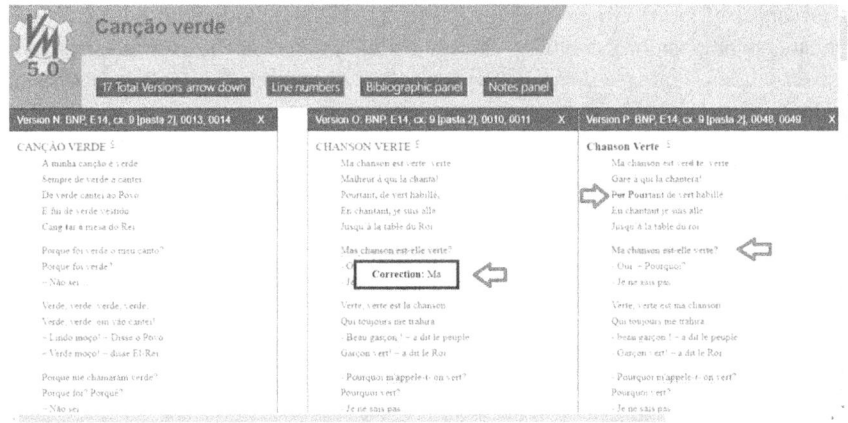

Figure 6.13 Display of witnesses N, O and P in the VM's interface. It includes transcriptional choices ('Correction'), traces of authorial alterations (strikethrough and bold passages) and variant readings (shadow highlight).

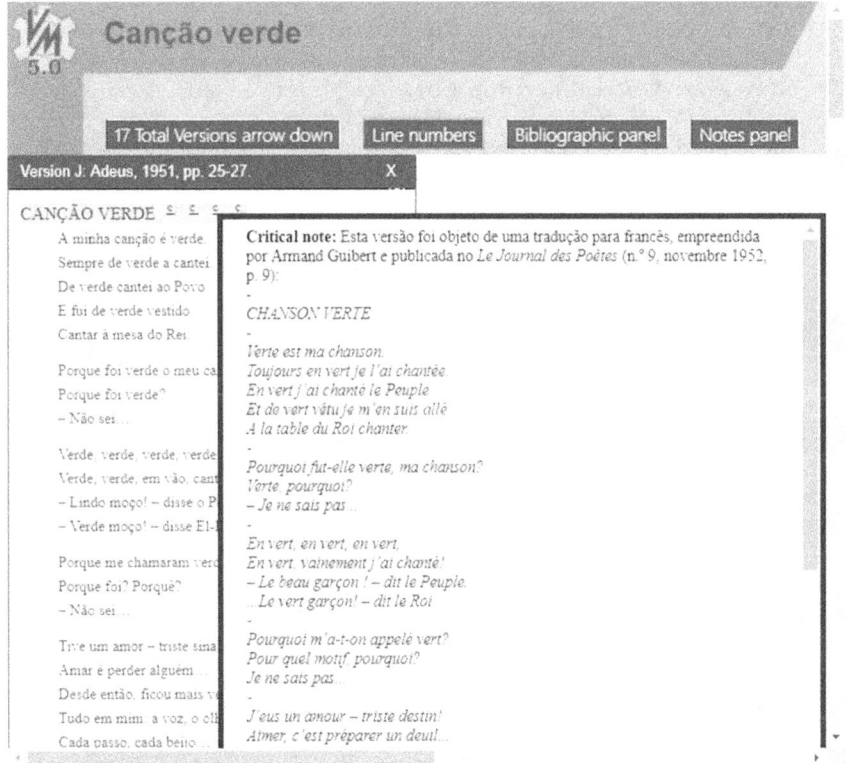

Figure 6.14 Display of an allographic translation (encoded as <note>), in the VM's interface.

affordances of the electronic medium (Sahle 2016: 30–1). An edition in such terms enhances compositional fluidities, favours textual awareness and facilitates research into exo-, endo-, epi- and paragenesis, which – as we have seen – is particularly relevant in Pedro Homem de Mello's bilingual poems. As a consequence, it may be of interest to translation studies, as much as to genetic criticism and scholarly editing, boosting the unexpected intersections between these two fields of study.

Documentation

Biblioteca Nacional de Portugal (BNP), E14, box 9 (folders 2 and 6).
Biblioteca Nacional de Portugal (BNP), E16, box 42/29.
Biblioteca Pública Municipal do Porto (BPMP), ML-P15C-no. inv. 1134C.
Helena Telles da Silva (HTS), private collection.

Notes

1   Umberto Eco (2003: 236) identified three subtypes of intersystemic interpretation with marked variation in the substance: interlinguistic interpretation (translation between natural languages), rewriting (reworked versions of one text by the same author) and translation between non-linguistic systems.
2   The author published some of these books in multilingual editions. *Danças Portuguesas* (Mello 1962) included a French and an English version by Maurice Villemur and Elaine Sanceau, while *Danças de Portugal* (Mello 1966) was translated by Marie Radelet and Elaine Sanceau. In the author's archive, there is yet another text about tourism and landscape, which was translated by Elaine Sanceau ('The Costa Verde' – BPMP, ML-P15C-no. inv. 1134C).
3   This unpublished anthology belongs to the archive of João Gaspar Simões, at the Portuguese National Library (BNP, E16, box 42/29). According to Isabel Meyrelles (private correspondence), the book was commissioned by David Mourão-Ferreira, but was never published. The typescript at BNP is identified as 'Le Deuxième modernisme: la Génération de Presença: 1927–40. Seléction, préface et notes de João Gaspar Simões. Choix de textes et traduction de Isabel Meireles'. In pages 74–83, there is a section dedicated to Pedro Homem de Mello, which includes a brief presentation of the author and the respective translations.
4   Arnold Caesar Hawkins (b. 1909) was born into a Scottish family based in Porto, owner of the Dow's Port wine house. After completing his education at the Trinity College, he founded the English Room at the University of Porto (1940) and the British Institute of Porto (1943), where Pedro Homem de Mello was also a teacher. In the early 1950s he was appointed to a lecturing position at the University of Oxford and later acted as the British Council Representative in Austria.
5   The cover states 'Arnold C. Hawkins | Lusitanian Lyrics', while the title page adds: 'Lusitanian Lyrics: Selections from the Poems of Pedro Homem de Mello Translated by Arnold C. Hawkins'.

6   There is confirmation of their close friendship in two of Mello's books. *Cartas de Inglaterra* (Mello 1973) opens with the poem 'Friendship', offered by 'Bill and Dulci' (Arnold Hawkins and his wife Dulcie Violet Fimister) to 'Pedro and Helena' (Pedro Homem de Mello and his wife Helena de Pamplona). Years later, the poet would dedicate *Carta a Bill* (Mello 1977) to this friend, whose photo is printed on the title page.

7   As noted by Andrea Ceccherelli (2013: 13), between authorized translation and self-translation there is a vast middle ground, occupied by various modes of collaboration. At the one end of the scale, some authors dialogue with their translators, giving their stamp of approval to the translations that are signed by others (i.e. translation in collaboration with the author). At the other extreme of the spectrum, there are also authors who partly or entirely assume the authorship of the translations, even if they are assisted by one or more native speakers (i.e. assisted self-translation).

8   In this regard, let us mention the new subdiscipline of genetic translation studies, which 'analyses the practices of the … translator', through his working documents (Cordingley and Montini 2015: 1).

9   Pedro Homem de Mello published a few French poems, of which there are no Portuguese versions available: 'Mystère', 'Alentejo (Paysage portugais)', 'Félicité', *Prisma*, III (3) (1939a: 143–6). It is possible that they were written directly in that language, since French was his second idiom, similarly to what happened with most European writers until the end of the Second World War (Grutman 2013: 46).

10 BNP, E14, box 9 (folder 6), letter from Alain Bosquet, dated 2 January 1952.

11 We could not find any volume with Pedro Homem de Mello's poems in Pierre Seghers's collection *Autour du Monde*. So far, only one of these French versions from BNP, E14, box 9 (folder 2) was found in the Portuguese magazine *Prisma*, III (3) (1939: 144), although it is not published as a translation of 'Aquarela'. Indeed, it has a very different title: 'Águeda (Paysage portugais)'.

12 John Dryden (1680) identified three different ways of translating: 'First, that of Metaphrase, or turning an Authour word by word, and Line by Line, from one Language into another. … The second way is that of Paraphrase, or Translation with Latitude, where the Authour is kept in view by the Translator, so as never to be lost, but his words are not so strictly follow'd as his sense …. The Third way is that of Imitation, where the Translator (if now he has not lost that Name) assumes the liberty not only to vary from the words and sense, but to forsake them both as he sees occasion.'

13 In his study of three prominent self-translators (Green, Beckett, Nabokov), Michael Oustinoff (2001: 29–34) establishes a first typology of self-translation strategies, comprising: (1) naturalizing self-translation ('auto-traduction naturalisante'); (2) decentred self-translation ('auto-traduction décentrée') and (3) (re)creative self-translation ('auto-traduction [re]créatrice').

14 In 'Beyond Translation: Self-Translation', María Recuenco Peñalver asks: '[W]hat are we talking about when we refer to self-translation? Is it a translation, a new original, a work in progress, a second version, a final version that supplants the first one?' (2011: 200). In the course of her analysis, she identifies five different theoretical positions: self-translation as an intermediate point between creation and translation, self-translation as creation and translation, self-translation as translation, self-translation as recreation (second original or version) and self-translation as a continuation of the original.

15   Bought in 1986 by the Portuguese National Library, BNP E14 corresponds to a part of Pedro Homem de Mello's personal archive, and many folders seem to preserve the author's arrangement of the materials. Although this is a strong argument for the joint editorial handling of the Portuguese and French witnesses in box 9 (folder 2), mention should be made of other types of isoglottic rewriting, which involve scattered documents in the genetic dossier. The theoretical discussion implied in such cases deserves further consideration, but some critics consider that, no matter how different they may seem to be, versions 'can never be revised into a different work' (Bryant 2002: 85) and in no circumstances can be unlinked from one another. Others argue that a work may be regarded as new whenever a certain degree of continuity is not preserved from one version to the next (McLaverty 1991: 137), since authors may quote or recycle verbal material, without this implying the rewrite of an earlier composition. In this case, a systematic scale should be drawn for the continuum of textual fluidities to identify the turning points between a version and what may constitute a different text.

16   The interface was originally conceived in 2000 by Susan Schreibman: http://v-machine.org.

17   A list of projects using the Versioning Machine can be found at http://v-machine.org/vm-in-use/versioning-machine-in-use/.

18   This method is prescribed in the critical apparatus tag-set http://www.tei-c.org/release/doc/tei-p5-doc/en/html/TC.html and is one of the encoding methodologies compatible with the Versioning Machine's interface http://v-machine.org/documentation/#loc-ref.

References

Anonymous (1952a), 'Pedro Homem de Mello', *Le Journal des poètes*, 9: 9.

Anonymous (1952b), 'Pedro Homem de Mello', *Soberania do Povo*, 5682: 1, 4.

Bensimon, Paul (2002), 'Les groupes adjectivaux binaires antéposés', *Palimpsestes*, 14: 131–5. Available online: http://palimpsestes.revues.org/1664 (accessed 15 September 2018).

Bryant, John (2002), *The Fluid Text: A Theory of Revision and Editing for Book and Screen*, Ann Arbor: The University of Michigan Press.

Ceccherelli, Andrea (2013), 'Introduzione', in Andrea Ceccherelli, Gabriella Elina Imposti and Monica Perotto (eds), *Autotraduzione e Riscrittura*, 11–22, Bononia: Bononia University Press.

Cordingley, Anthony and Chiara Montini (2015), 'Genetic Translation Studies: An Emerging Discipline', *Linguistica Antverpiensia: New Series: Themes in Translation Studies*, 14: 1–18.

Dryden, John (n.d.), 'The Preface to Ovid's Epistles (1680)', in Marie-Alice Belle (ed.), *TTT: Textes Théoriques en Traduction*, Paris: Université Sorbonne Nouvelle – Paris 3. Available online: https://ttt.hypotheses.org/159 (accessed 10 March 2018).

Eco, Umberto (2003), *Dire Quasi la Stessa Cosa: Esperienze di Traduzione*, Milano: Tascabili Bompiani.

Fitch, Brian T. (1985), 'The Status of Self-Translation', *Texte*, 4: 111–25.

Genette, Gérard (1994), *L'Œuvre de l'art: immanence et transcendance*, Paris: Seuil.

Grutman, Rainier (2009), 'Self-Translation', in Mona Baker (ed.), *Routledge Encyclopedia of Translation Studies*, 257–60, London and New York: Routledge.
Grutman, Rainier (2013), 'Beckett e oltre: autotraduzioni orizzontali e verticali', in Andrea Ceccherelli, Gabriella Elina Imposti and Monica Perotto (eds), *Autotraduzione e Riscrittura*, 45–61, Bononia: Bononia University Press.
Hawkins, Arnold C. (1941a), *Lusitanian Lyrics*, Porto: Lello & Irmão.
Hawkins, Arnold C. (1941b), 'Lusitanian Lyrics: Selections from the Poems of Pedro Homem de Melo', *The Anglo-Portuguese News*, 118: 9.
McLaverty, James (1991), 'Issues of Identity and Utterance: An Intentionalist Response to "Textual Instability"', in Philip Cohen (ed.), *Devils and Angels: Textual Editing and Literary Theory*, 134–51, Charlottesville and London: University Press of Virginia.
Mello, Pedro Homem de (1934), *Caravela ao Mar*, Lisboa: (n.p.).
Mello, Pedro Homem de (1937), *Jardins Suspensos*, Porto: Marânus.
Mello, Pedro Homem de (1939a), 'Mystère', 'Alentejo (Paysage portugais)', 'Félicité', *Prisma*, III (3): 143–6.
Mello, Pedro Homem de (1939b), *Segrêdo*, Porto: (n.p.).
Mello, Pedro Homem de (1940), *Estrêla Morta*, Porto: (n.p.).
Mello, Pedro Homem de (1941a), 'Dance of the Hours', trans. Arnold C. Hawkins, *The Anglo-Portuguese News*, 95: 4.
Mello, Pedro Homem de (1941b), 'Truth', trans. Arnold C. Hawkins, *The Anglo-Portuguese News*, 98: 6–7.
Mello, Pedro Homem de (1942), *Pecado*, Lisboa: Edições Gama.
Mello, Pedro Homem de (1943), 'Scene', trans. Arnold C. Hawkins, *The Anglo-Portuguese News*, 219: 4.
Mello, Pedro Homem de (1945), *Príncipe Perfeito*, Lisboa: Edições Gama.
Mello, Pedro Homem de (1947), *Bodas Vermelhas*, Porto: Editorial Domingos Barreira.
Mello, Pedro Homem de (1948), *Miserere*, Porto: (n.p.).
Mello, Pedro Homem de (1951), *Adeus*, Porto: (n.p.).
Mello, Pedro Homem de (1954), *O Rapaz da Camisola Verde*, Porto: Saber.
Mello, Pedro Homem de (1955), *Grande, Grande Era a Cidade*, Porto: Lello & Irmão.
Mello, Pedro Homem de (1957), *Poemas Escolhidos e o Livro Inédito Os Poetas Ignorados*, Porto: Lello e Irmãos.
Mello, Pedro Homem de (1962), *Danças Portuguesas*, Porto: Lello & Irmão.
Mello, Pedro Homem de [1966], *Danças de Portugal*, Porto: Livraria Avis.
Mello, Pedro Homem de (1967), *Nós Portugueses Somos Castos*, Lisboa: Ática.
Mello, Pedro Homem de (1973), *Cartas de Inglaterra*, Porto: Lello & Irmão.
Mello, Pedro Homem de (1977), *Carta a Bill*, Porto: (n.p.).
Meyrelles, Isabel (1971), *Anthologie de la poésie portugaise du XIIe au XXe siècle*, Paris: Gallimard.
Oustinoff, Michael (2001), *Bilinguisme d'écriture et auto-traduction: Julien Green, Samuel Beckett, Vladimir Nabokov*, Paris: L'Harmattan.
Pereira, Elsa (2017a), 'Challenges of a Digital Approach: Considerations for an Edition of Pedro Homem de Mello's Poetry', in Peter Boot et al. (eds), *Advances in Digital Scholarly Editing*, 177–81, Leiden: Sidestone Press. Available online: https://www.sidestone.com/books/advances-in-digital-scholarly-editing (accessed January 2018).
Pereira, Elsa (2017b), 'O Exercício da Revisão e seu Tratamento Editorial: para uma edição da poesia de Pedro Homem de Mello', *Revista da ABRALIN*, 16 (1): 139–54.

Perry, M. (1981), 'Thematic and Structural Shifts in Autotranslations by Bilingual Hebrew–Yiddish Writers', *Poetics Today*, 2 (4): 181–92.

Pierazzo, Elena (2015), *Digital Scholarly Editing*, Farnham: Ashgate.

Popovič, Anton (1976), *Dictionary for the Analysis of Literary Translation*, Edmonton: University of Alberta.

Rada, Roy (1991), *Hypertext: From Text to Expertext*, Maidenhead: McGraw-Hill.

Recuenco Peñalver, María (2011), 'Más allá de la traducción: la autotraducción', *Trans*, 15: 193–208.

Reiman, Donald H. (1987), *Romantic Texts and Contexts*, Columbia: University of Missouri Press.

Sahle, Patrick (2016), 'What Is a Scholarly Digital Edition?', in Matthew J. Driscoll and Elena Pierazzo (eds), *Digital Scholarly Editing: Theories and Practices*, 19–39, Cambridge: Open Book Publishers.

Santoyo, Julio-César (2004), 'Self-Translation: Translational Competence Revisited (and Performance as Well)', in Eberhard Fleischmann, Peter A. Schmitt and Gerd Wotjak (eds), *Translationskompetenz*, 223–5, Tübingen: Stauffenburg.

Scheibe, Siegfried (1995), 'Theoretical Problems of the Authorization and Constitution of Texts', in Hans Walter Gabler, George Bornstein and Gillian Borland Pierce (eds), *Contemporary German Editorial Theory*, 171–92, Ann Arbor: University of Michigan Press.

Schreibman, Susan et al. (2016), *Versioning Machine 5.0: A Tool for Displaying & Comparing Different Versions of Literary Texts*. Available online: http://v-machine.org (accessed 9 January 2018).

Shillingsburg, Peter L. (2004), *Scholarly Editing in the Computer Age: Theory and Practice*, Ann Arbor: The University of Michigan Press.

Sullivan, Hannah (2013), *The Work of Revision*, Cambridge, MA: Harvard University Press.

Tanselle, G. Thomas (1990), *Textual Criticism and Editing*, Charlottesville: University Press of Virginia.

Van Hulle, Dirk (2004), 'Samuel Beckett, Comment c'est/How It Is and/et L'Image: A Critical–Genetic Edition/Une Édition critico–génétique, ed. Edouard Magessa O'Reilly. New York and London: Routledge, 2001. 759 p.', *Variants*, 2 (3): 383–6.

Van Hulle, Dirk (2015), 'Translation and Genetic Criticism: Genetic and Editorial Approaches to the "Untranslatable" in Joyce and Beckett', *Linguistica Antverpiensia, New Series: Themes in Translation Studies*, 14: 40–53.

Van Hulle, Dirk (n.d.), 'Electronic Textual Editing: Authorial Translation: The Case of Samuel Beckett's Stirrings Still/Soubresauts', *TEI: Text Encoding Initiative*. Available online: http://www.tei-c.org/About/Archive_new/ETE/Preview/vanhulle.xml (accessed 9 January 2018).

Part Two

Translators' stories and testimonies

7

The body in letters: Peter Handke as translator of René Char

Joana Moura
*Catholic University of Portugal/Centre for Comparative Studies,
University of Lisbon*

Introduction

On the occasion of a translation prize awarded to the French writer and translator Georges-Arthur Goldschmidt, Peter Handke makes a remarkable observation about Goldschmidt's translation practice: 'I have never met a translator who works so much with his body. In that sense, when you translate, you are a laboring body. One can feel the clay in the sentences written by Georges-Arthur Goldschmidt, but only as a trace; we find very subtle traces of the man laboring with his body' (2007: 442).[1] Similarly, in a text dedicated to Fabjan Hafner for his *Petrarca Übersetzerpreis*, Handke describes how at the time of his own first book publication he was struck by the strong physical presence of a translator who challenged his preconceived stereotype of the subservient, invisible translator: 'The *full-bodied man* did not at all correspond to my image of the translator: instead of a merely silent silhouette, he *dominated the scene*; not at all the quietude of a servant, rather the *clangor of a fighter*' (2007: 433; emphases added).

Indeed, Handke's highlighting of the physical attributes of these two translators contrasts with the conventional idealization of the translator as a disembodied figure in the history of translation theory. In fact, the particularity of Handke's manifold depictions of the translator figure lies in his recurring focus on the real-life translator, and more precisely, on the role of the translator's body in the translational experience, a concern that he has explored not only in his translation paratexts (prefaces, essays and correspondence), but also in his extensive translation practice and in his fictionalized translator figures in works like *Die linkshändige Frau* (*The Left-handed Woman*, 1978) or *Bis daß der Tag euch scheidet oder Eine Frage des Lichts* (*Till Day You Do Part Or A Question of Light*, 2010) (see Moura 2017).

Sections of this chapter have been adapted from the author's (unpublished) doctoral dissertation entitled *The Difference That a Body Makes: Figurations of the Translator's Body and Mistranslation in Peter Handke's Translation Narratives*. Please turn to the bibliography for full reference.

Handke's focus on the bodily quality of the translator is not a commonplace approach to the study of translation(s). But while studies underpinning the significance of a specifically corporeal translator remain marginal in translation studies, a few scholars have pursued this line of thinking in the recent past. In 1991, Douglas Robinson was the first to call attention to what he termed the somatic dimension of translation in his groundbreaking *The Translator's Turn* and has since continued to explore the translator's (embodied) subjectivity as a crucial aspect of the translation process.[2] A few years later, Anthony Pym also claimed that translators are 'people with flesh and blood bodies' (1998: 161), insisting that we study the work of translators in the plural rather than limit ourselves to only paying attention to the 'abstract term, the translator, in the singular' (1998: 169). Theo Hermans reinforced Pym's tendency to personalize the translator figure by condemning the fact that translators have been consistently forced to strip themselves of their bodies when they translate; as a result of this, Hermans notes how translators have historically remained 'hidden, out of view, transparent, incorporeal, disembodied and disenfranchised'.[3]

In addition, a number of academic publications have addressed the need to consider the centrality of the translator figure in translation research – a translator-centred theoretical framework that Andrew Chesterman has categorized under the umbrella term of 'TranslaTOR Studies' (2009: 13; emphasis in the original). Exemplary in this regard are three recent collected volumes[4] dedicated to the work of translators as writers, featuring articles by leading scholars in the field, some of which directly address the impact of the translator's body in the construction of the translated text (Maier 2006; Tymoczko 2016). Carol Maier's contribution to this topic needs to be foregrounded here, for her writings on translation have *de facto* recognized the translator's body as integral to the work that translators do. In the words of the editors of *Translators Writing, Writing Translators*, Maier's 'rethinking of the translator's role presents the translator as a co-constructor of meaning, a collaborator, whose body is thoroughly engaged in the process of translation' (2016: 19).

Other translation scholars have focused on developing research methodologies to investigate the intricacies of the translator's creative process by incorporating the translator's biography in the study of translation as a way to humanize the figure of the translator. Anthony Cordingley and Chiara Montini's recent theorization of genetic translation studies offers a valuable framework to examine the 'practices of the working translator and the evolution, or genesis, of the translated text by studying translators' manuscripts, drafts and other working documents' (2015: 1).[5] Focusing on an archive-based approach to translation, Jeremy Munday also recognizes the need to study the translator's drafts as records of his or her creative methods and to privilege the translator's 'personal papers'[6] from the archive, including not only drafts but also personal correspondence and other relevant documentation, as a way to write the 'microhistory of translators' (2014: 64).

It is remarkable that Munday actually speaks about the researcher's work in the translator's archive in terms of a physical sensation by saying that 'it is possible to smell the translator in the archive'.[7] This allusion to the translator's archive as the repository where the traces of the translator's body can be found alludes to the importance of archival materials not only as having the potential to investigate the translator's professional relationship to the other agents involved in the process of translation (source text author, editors, etc.), but also in providing a glimpse into his or her personal networks and thus opening up the possibility of incorporating the affective dimension of the translator's life in the study of translation(s).

Drawing on such theoretical models that privilege the role of the translator's figure and his or her working process through the study of the translator's paratextual materials, this chapter explores Handke's understanding of the translator's body as a creative resource in the translational experience. More specifically, I reflect on the role that the translator's physical and emotional dimensions play in the translation process by studying Handke's translation commentary and the correspondence exchanged between him and René Char at the time of Handke's translation (into German) of a selection of poems from Char's *Le Nu perdu* (The Lost Nude) – a volume published in 1984 entitled *Rückkehr stromauf*. Methodologically, I work within the framework of genetic translation studies to examine the exogenetic materials (letters, postcards and photographs) gathered during my archival research of Handke's literary collection at the Austrian National Library's literary archive in Vienna, which was guided and supplemented by the meticulous analyses available in the online research platform *Handkeonline*.

When I speak of enquiring into the role of the translator's body in Handke's work, I wish to explore how his physical, emotional and phenomenological dimensions influence the translator's working process. This chapter begins by contextualizing Handke's conception of the translator's task as a phenomenology of writing that involves the translator's physical and emotional experience of reading and (re)writing the source text, to then exploring the question of how the correspondence between the translator Peter Handke and the author René Char allowed Handke to materialize their author–translator dialogue and to incorporate it in his working process, thus personalizing his experience as translator of the French poet's work.

The corporeal translator's (moving) desk

It is important to understand Handke's creative process – not only as a translator but also as a writer of original literary works – in the context of a phenomenology of writing. Klaus Kastberger (2012: 3) has referred to a geological turn in Handke's development as an author, noting that after his writing crisis in the late 1970s/early 1980s, Handke adopts a particular creative mode in which the writer's real-life experience of writing becomes central to his work. Georges-Arthur Goldschmidt has defined Handke's writing practice in the 1980s as a 'corporeal exploration' (1985: 75), which insightfully portrays Handke's conception of writing as a process in which the writer constructs his texts through the experience of his or her body's perceptions of the material world – a description that also fittingly characterizes Handke's translation praxis (Moura 2019).

A particular authorial strategy that contributed to Handke's phenomenological writing project is his decision to use only pencils to write. As critics have pointed out, Handke's obsession with the pencil is related to the fact that this practice allows him to write slowly and when travelling, a routine that he developed when he was touring around Europe and the United States (Hansel 2009: 225). In an interview with Elisabeth Schwagerle and Klaus Kastberger, Handke explains how he reinvented himself as a writer at that time, when he did not have a stable desk:

> To me this was, to say the least, the highlight of my writing experience, when I thought: Now I am really present, I am now whole as I write here, and we can see the waves in the water and the water rats coming out of it, and the dragonflies are buzzing, and a robin looks at me funny, and I look back at it funny. (2009: 16)

In the early years of the 1980s, as he was struggling with producing original works, Handke decided to translate a selection of poems from René Char's *Le Nu perdu* into German. Similar to the phenomenological writing mode described above, Handke's translations of Char were also informed by the translator's lived experience of both the geographical and imagined locations that the author, and the translator alike, inhabit during the process of writing and translating, respectively. In *Nager dans la Sorgue* (Swimming in the Sorgue), an article included in a 1986 issue of the journal *Europe* dedicated to René Char, Handke gives an account of his working process when he translated Char that well illustrates his conception of translation as a markedly bodily experience:

> Four years ago I began translating *Le Nu perdu* by René Char. ... My translation work never took place inside the house, at my desk. The solution (yes, it was always a solution, a clarification) always came to me *outdoors*, in front of the house, and always when I was walking, especially when I was doing the hundred steps in the garden; never sitting down, often when I suddenly stopped and laughed, always in broad daylight, *under the sun*. Yes, the most flamboyant translation-helper for the oracles of René Char, so pure and so lucid, was the sun, even the sometimes a little misty Austrian sun ... But my most comprehensive understanding as a reader–translator manifested itself one day in Antibes, by the sea, as I was breathing the words of René Char like a *pneuma*. (qtd. in Goldschmidt 1988: 193–4; emphases in the original)

This reflection encapsulates Handke's experience of translating Char's poetry, which he describes as a process that took place when he was moving around outdoors and that was dependent on the translator materializing a physical and emotional relationship with the source text's author, with the text itself and with the landscape that it inhabits.[8]

Indeed, Handke claimed that he was unable to translate Char's poems when sitting at his desk, at home. Rather, he is convinced that the desk of the literary translator (here Handke) is not to be limited to the space occupied by the material object – a table, presumably – where the translator engages in a mental process of translating between different languages; according to Handke's account above, the work that translators do is also carried out by their bodies through the sensuous experiences to which they are exposed, such as walking in the garden, smelling the air of the sea and feeling the warmth of the sun. As a result, the translator's desk necessarily becomes an unstable, travelling space that allows the translator to move around as he or she tries to decipher the source text and write the translation.

In a radio interview with ORF[9] in January 1985, Handke corroborates the phenomenological impetus of his translation method during this project: 'I always went for walks or travelled to places carrying my French edition ... The translation came about in Salzburg, mostly during the summer. Perhaps this is not that important; it is a small detail, but this translation work was only possible outdoors.'[10] In a letter to his friend Alfred Kolleritsch in February 1984, Handke makes an analogous point, explicitly adding a spiritual dimension to his conception of translation as a phenomenological practice. He describes his translation work as 'a travail, but a luminous one, carried out under the sun (from the sun comes the word = Bible)'.[11] According to Handke, his phenomenological practice as a translator is intimately related to his understanding of translation as an act of searching that is at once mental, physical and spiritual, thus instigating the translator to become a moving body, and making the search itself a somatic endeavour.

Indeed, physical motion was central for Handke during his translations of Char's poetry. In August 1983, Handke paid a visit to Char in his hometown of L'Isle-sur-la-Sorgue, but not because he was interested in asking predictable questions about passages in the source text he might be having trouble translating. Similar to his habit of translating Char's poetry outdoors under the sun in Salzburg, Handke wanted to be exposed to the author's landscape in L'Isle-sur-la-Sorgue; he spent two days walking around the area, observing the surroundings, listening to a local jukebox and swimming in the river Sorgue (Goldschmidt 1988: 194). In this translation project, the translator Peter Handke is thus best defined as a phenomenological explorer whose desk becomes a moving body that travels to the places that the source text inhabits. What also stands out in Handke's understanding of translation is that he actually encourages the translator to actively and productively make use of his or her body's abilities as translational resources.

Peter Handke, René Char: Two bodies walking (and writing letters)

Speaking of his experience as a literary translator, Peter Handke has repeatedly emphasized that it is the act of searching that makes translation so rewarding and challenging for him: 'A lot of translators keep asking the author questions like, what do you mean here? I always try to find answers on my own; translation would otherwise not be exciting for me. Translation would not be a joyful task if I had to write a letter to the author every time I had a question' (qtd. in Schwagerle 2009: 94).[12] His comment might suggest that, as a translator, Handke is not the type to write letters to the author of the work he is translating. While the existing correspondence between Handke and Char disproves such a conjecture, the content of the letters actually confirms Handke's claim that he does not write to the author to ask questions about the source text. Rather, in the specific case of Handke's translations of Char, these letters bear witness to the construction of a significant translator–author dialogue between two literary figures.

I now turn to the discussion of how this epistolary exchange between Peter Handke and René Char relates to Handke's idea of translation as a corporeal exploration. I mainly investigate the possibility that the physical, emotional and phenomenological dimensions of their relationship, particularly as it is expressed in these letters, considerably informed Handke's process of translation, as well as his more general conception of the translator's task. In other words, I analyse the extent to which their correspondence – which is the material evidence of their dialogue during this translation project – can be understood as a translational resource in Handke's translation practice.

According to my research at the literary archive in Vienna, Handke's genetic dossier of his translations from René Char's *Le Nu perdu* includes five letters (accompanied by two Polaroid pictures) and two postcards that Handke sent to Char, as well as two letters and four postcards that Char sent to Handke, all of which were written in French. With the exception of one of the letters, which Handke wrote to Char after the published translation came out, these letters were exchanged between 1983 and 1984. The genetic dossier held in Vienna also includes a letter from Handke to Char's wife Marie-Claude Char, as well as a letter from the publishing house Carl Hanser addressed to Handke. A copy of the notebook dating from the time between March and July 1983 in which Handke keeps a log of his translation activity during this time is also to be found in the archive, as well as Handke's first handwritten draft of his translation and his annotated hard copy of Char's *Le Nu perdu*. As previously mentioned, a transcript of Handke's radio interview with ORF is also held at the archive.

In the earliest of these letters, which Handke wrote to Char on 1 July 1983, the Austrian writer and translator mentions how he was 'happier every day from working on your [Char's] texts'.[13] Handke goes on to describe his intense feeling of joy while working on these translations, mentioning how he learned to read anew by translating Char's poetry. Considering Handke's repeated claim that reading is an integral part of the translation process, this letter serves to reinforce the idea that this experience helped him redefine his attitude towards the practice of translation; in addition, the laudatory tone of the message also exhibits a certain willingness on Handke's part to create an emotional bond with Char, especially considering the spiritual subtext of Handke's comment about discovering a 'universal childhood'.[14]

Regarding this idea of a universal childhood, Elizabeth Schwagerle notes that 'in the translations of René Char, his task becomes a revelation; Handke speaks of oracles, namely of new images that emerge from these translations and that have no relation whatsoever to my own childhood or to my personal memories' (2009: 97–8). What Handke's words imply is that through his experience of translating the poetry of René Char, his consciousness transcends his own collection of childhood memories, reaching what he calls a universal childhood, a kind of collective and unconscious level of imagery that allows him to purportedly get closer to Char's poetic universe; furthermore, Handke's comment suggests that this spiritual experience will help him transform the words of Char's poems into images, so that he can then rewrite these images in German.

According to Handke, the moment in which the translator reaches this transcendental state can be described as being 'beyond words', back in a state of consciousness inhabited by forms, similar to these new images he perceives and cannot identify as his own childhood memories.[15] It is important to emphasize that images – that is, that initial stage of words as idealized by Handke – play a crucial role in all of his translation projects. For Handke, the image works as a medium between the different language systems of the source and target texts, suggesting that one does not translate from one language to another, but rather that the source text is, through the translator's subjective experience of reading the text, transformed back into a prelinguistic state, which is then reimagined in the target language.

In the translations of René Char's poetry, Handke's process of travelling back to the image, that is, to the moment of linguistic creation, is connected to his experience of reading. Referring to the intimate link between reading and the image in Handke's creative process, Schwagerle comments that '[i]n translation, reading does not serve interpretation; rather, it serves to take in and absorb words and images' (2009: 96). In an interview with Herbert Gamper, Handke goes as far as to say that 'the worst that can happen in translation is to interpret instead of transposing (carrying over)' (Handke and Gamper 1987: 219). In refusing to think about reading and translation as mental acts of interpretation, Handke favours a model of translation which rests upon a principle of recreation in which the translator is not to translate his or her *interpretation* of the source text, but rather his bodily *experience* with the text.

Clive Scott's phenomenological approach to translation is useful in understanding Handke's idea of translation; Scott claims that he sees 'the task of the translator as that of translating not *an interpreted text* but the *phenomenology of reading*' (2012: 1; emphases in the original). For Scott, in translation 'the processing of language is … sense-giving rather than sense-recuperating: meaning is a *project* of language. The danger is that translation concentrates on the recuperation of meaning and overlooks its own task of generating sense, of being part of a sense-generative dialogue' (2012: 30; emphasis in the original). Taking into account that Handke places the image at the genesis of any act of translation, it is not surprising that he will consistently draw on images to create a 'sense-generative dialogue' (Scott 2012: 30) with Char during the time of this project.

Indeed, in his letters to René Char, the written message seems to serve as a caption to the image, which always occupies centre stage. Handke privileges photographs over verbal communication as a way to materialize his physical encounters with Char in Austria or France; these images allow him to go back to moments that they spent together walking and observing nature. In a letter from 20 October 1983, Handke includes a Polaroid image of a wooden staff, the meaning of which he explains in the letter's very short verbal message: 'Dear René Char, here it is, your wooden staff; and he plays the role of a neighbour to me. Thank you.'[16] Clearly, in this case, it is Handke's desire to share the image of this object with Char that motivates the writing of this letter, or rather, it is Handke's wish to show his endearment to that material object that seems to represent their friendship. In *Nager dans la Sorgue*, Handke also mentions a wooden staff, explaining that it was a gift he received from Char in L'Isle-sur-la-Sorgue: 'I have this staff right in front of me and see it as *another point of reference*' (qtd. in Goldschmidt 1988: 193; emphasis in the original).

More specifically, the image of the wooden staff likely refers to an instrument that symbolizes the times of bonding between Handke and Char, when they went on their routine walks. By mentioning this staff, Handke is foregrounding the importance of the journey and attaching an affective meaning to this object, which he claims now serves as his companion, his neighbour. The specificity of the Polaroid photograph as a medium that records the immediacy of lived experience emphasizes Handke's aim to materialize their shared moments of companionship. It is important to note that this object was also highly regarded by Char, as his letters and postcards to Handke show. In four different postcards dating from May and August 1984 and February and September 1985 written by Char and addressed to Handke, the French poet also refers to this wooden staff in a very endearing form, disclosing that this staff was actually picked, cut and pruned by Handke – a tailor-made object designed as a sign of their friendship and as a celebration of their journeys walking side by side in Austria and France.[17] Considering the consistent mentioning of this object in their correspondence, it seems fair to say that it metaphorically stands for the construction of their friendship and of a poetic affinity between Handke and Char.

It is important to highlight the phenomenological impetus of their letters, taking into account that, as mentioned before, they invariably harken back to episodes of both of them spending time exploring their surroundings outdoors, not only in the sense of a physical activity but also as a poetic motif that represents their closeness and their sharing of what could be called a 'common poetic path'. In a postcard that Handke sent to Char in 1985, Handke once again mentions how he thought of greeting Char 'while walking on the limestone rocks, once again, from repetition to repetition … I often think of you, as I remember one of your landscapes'.[18] In another letter to René Char dating December 1986, Handke writes about how walking around in snowy Salzburg in the winter reminded him of Char, because, he says, 'I know how you love the winter'.[19] Symbolically, as if trying to send Char a real (material) piece of his experience of walking in the Salzburg landscape, Handke writes this letter in a tree bark: 'I think of you, after I peeled a piece of its skin from a tree (birch?), on which I am writing this somewhat unworthy letter.'[20]

Schwagerle (2009: 95) suggests this gesture might reflect Handke's willingness to respond to Char's habit of writing and painting in pieces of dry bark, and I propose that it also speaks to Handke's method of emphasizing the experiential (material and emotional) processes involved in translating. In this case, it relates specifically to his relationship with the author of the source text and to his poetic *oeuvre*; by sending Char letters that contain images and references that harken back to their physical encounters, Handke is able to create a narrative about this translation experience and to foreground his ongoing dialogue with the poet whose work he is translating.

Concluding remarks: The translator–author dialogue

As we have seen, Handke's letters to Char rarely ever mention the poems that Handke is translating or any translation difficulties he might have during his task as a translator.

Rather, they address moments – usually represented in these letters by images, to be precise – that awaken in Handke the memory of Char and lead him to a friendly relationship with the man and his work. By sending Char letters about moments in his everyday life that relate to Char's creative strategies, Handke is opening up a dialogue between the author's writing process and his own translation work, constructing a narrative about their collaborative work. For even if Handke's letters are invariably short, their messages always express the sense of a profound understanding between Char's poetic sensibilities and his own.[21]

The fact that Handke so consistently nourishes this feeling of friendly intimacy with Char's poetic imagination[22] also suggests that if such an idealized oneness in poetic kinship is at all attainable, at least on some level, it requires the translator to understand the text not only mentally, but also to perceive it physically, that is, through the material experience of text and world. In other words, Handke's approach to Char's poetic universe rests upon creating an affective relationship with the author by bringing together moments of his sensorial experiences of the quotidian as he reads Char on the one hand, and, on the other, by letting his body experience the phenomena that inhabit Char's poetry in order to be able to relive them first hand and then recreate these experiences in his translation work.

Towards the end of his text *Nager dans la Sorgue*, Handke reflects on his impulse to go to L'Isle-sur-la-Sorgue and bathe in the regional river, comparing it to the episodes that involve Franz Grillparzer and Franz Kafka being emotionally moved by respectively materializing a both physical and imaginary interaction with Goethe; according to Handke's account, while Grillparzer was brought to tears when he came to visit Goethe in person and touched his hand, Kafka went to Goethe's house many years after his death just to feel the bricks on the wall of the building during the night. Handke writes: 'My willingness to swim in the Sorgue river in the summer of 1983 probably stems from a similar impulse. – One day, I wrote down in my notebook: Among all the great ones, only Goethe made me feel that moving sensation of fraternity – the others are either fathers or children' (qtd. in Goldschmidt 1988: 194).

Handke's comparison between his wish to experience the spaces inhabited by Char and the episodes involving Grillparzer and Kafka once again draws on the importance of physical presence as a source of inspiration for the writer's and, in the case of Handke here, the translator's creative process. But by referring to the figure of Goethe, as well as by telling the stories of Grillparzer and Kafka's admiration for the German poet, Handke is also addressing the question of belonging to a literary tradition as an important factor in literary creation. He frames the relationship between those who are part of this Goethean literary tradition as being organized according to a principle of fraternity rather than paternity;[23] in this sense, he seems to be suggesting a constellation of influences between writers and translators that does not function hierarchically, as is conventionally the case, but rather horizontally.

This connects to our reading of the Handke–Char correspondence as being part of the construction of a fraternal friendship between two authorial figures involved in a translational liaison. Clearly, in his translations of René Char, Handke wants to emphasize the empathy that exists between author and translator, so that his personalized exchange of letters with Char serves to reinforce his sense of translation as a collaborative effort, as a dialogue between two bodies. Handke's phenomenological understanding of translation urges us to rethink the extent to which, as translators, we can (and should) consider our physical and emotional dimensions as resources for translational practices (Scott 2012). For Handke understands translation as a conversation that involves reading and writing (letters, in this case), in which the translator performs his role as a second writer who collaborates in the renewal of the source text.

Acknowledgements

I would like to thank the staff at the Austrian National Library Literary Archive for their assistance in accessing these archival materials.

Notes

1. Unless noted otherwise, all translations are mine.
2. To give an example from another work by Robinson, he addresses the translator's body as the site of translational subjectivity by asking whether translators, who have bodies, are allowed to have subjectivities or are merely to serve as 'borrowed bodies for the writing of other writers' (2001: 3).
3. This quotation is taken from an amended version of a paper delivered by Theo Hermans at the Chinese University of Hong Kong on 31 March 2000. This version, entitled 'Shall I Apologize Translation', is available online: http://discovery.ucl.ac.uk/516/1/Ep_Apologizetrans.pdf (accessed 14 June 2018).
4. The three works I am thinking of are the 2006 collection edited by Susan Bassnett and Peter Bush *The Translator as Writer*, Esther Allen and Susan Bernofsky's book entitled *In Translation: Translators on their Work and What it Means* and the volume dedicated to Carol Maier published in 2016 under the title *Translators Writing, Writing Translators*, edited by Françoise Massardier-Kenney, Brian James Baer and Maria Tymoczko. Please turn to the bibliography for full references.
5. As Cordingley and Montini explain, this new form of translation research 'explores the foundations of [the genetic] approach in the French school of *critique génétique*, which developed a methodology for studying the drafts, manuscripts and other working documents (*avant-textes*) of modern literary works with the aim of revealing the complexity of the creative process engaged in their production' (2015: 1).
6. Munday referred to the translator's personal papers in his keynote lecture at the academic conference *The Translator Made Corporeal: Translation History in the Archive*, which took place at the British Library in London on 8 May 2017.
7. Munday also made this comment in his keynote lecture at the conference *The Translator Made Corporeal: Translation History in the Archive*.
8. Handke's concept of the 'reader–translator' must be explicated here, as it is crucial for his focus on the translator's body, also in this project. In an entry from his published diaries collection *Am Felsfenster morgens*, Handke writes 'I can best read René Char

when I am translating him' (1998: 80). In the above quotation from *Nager dans la Sorgue* Handke also speaks of his role as a 'reader–translator', foregrounding the importance of the translator's reading experience in terms of how Char's text taught him to read slowly, so as to experience reading itself as translation.
9   ORF stands for *Österreichischer Rundfunk* and refers to the Austrian national radio emission agency.
10 A transcript of this interview is currently held at the Austrian National Library Literary Archive under reference ÖLA SPH/LW. This quotation from the interview is available online: http://handkeonline.onb.ac.at/node/2586 (accessed 21 July 2018).
11 This quotation is available online: http://handkeonline.onb.ac.at/node/2586 (accessed 21 July 2018).
12 This quotation is originally from: Peter Handke and G. A. Goldschmidt (1989), 'Discussion entre Peter Handke, Georges-Arthur Goldschmidt et le public', *Études de lettre*, 4: 36–52.
13 These letters (from Handke to Char) are currently held at the Austrian National Library Literary Archive under reference numbers ÖLA 348/B1-5. They are, for the most part, also available online. This letter is available online: http://handkeonline.onb.ac.at/node/2586 (accessed 26 June 2018).
14 Handke's notion of a 'universal childhood' evokes an ambiguous connection between translation, mystical thinking and the body that must be addressed here in relation to Robinson's work (2001). On the one hand, when translating, Handke claims to give up his agency as a translator, as he enters a terrain that lies beyond his own childhood imagery; on the other hand, Handke emphasizes how he could only achieve this state of spiritual communion with the text through a physical experience, in which his bodily perception of the world plays a decisive role. Handke's use of the term *pneuma* in this context reinforces the ambiguity of the relationship between the translator's bodily experience of the landscape and the spiritual dimension of Handke's translational poetics; the meaning of *pneuma* harkens back to ancient Greek culture and crystallizes this dichotomy between body and soul, for it was used both as a physiological and philosophical term to refer to body and to spirit. Handke's understanding of *pneuma* seems to preserve that duality in his thinking about translation as a corporeal exploration that combines mystical thinking and the physical traversing of space, connected to the purported revelation that occurs when the translator's body is busy deciphering the sensuous world.
15 In an attempt to clarify the inner workings of his mental process of translation, Handke foregrounds the centrality of these mental images he creates: 'This is how translation always worked for me: I was unable to translate a sentence before I managed to see a totally language-free image in place of the foreign tongue. The foreign tongue had to disappear and become a language-free image, and only then would I usually – how should I phrase it – structure this image in German. But to translate from the foreign language into my German language – that never happened; instead, I always waited or wanted to wait until the image of this sentence appeared to me' (qtd. in Schwagerle 2009: 97).
16 This letter and Polaroid (from Handke to Char) are available online: http://handkeonline.onb.ac.at/node/2586 (accessed 26 June 2018).
17 These letters (from Char to Handke) are currently held at the Austrian National Library Literary Archive under reference ÖLA SPH/LW.
18 This letter (from Handke to Char) is available online: http://handkeonline.onb.ac.at/node/2586 (accessed 26 June 2018).

19 Available online: http://handkeonline.onb.ac.at/node/2586 (accessed 26 June 2018).
20 Available online: http://handkeonline.onb.ac.at/node/2586 (accessed 26 June 2018).
21 My reading of their correspondence as weaving a profound kinship between the poetic sensibilities of the two writers during Handke's translations of Char differs from Elisabeth Schwagerle's understanding of this collection of letters. She acknowledges Handke's admiration for Char at this point in his life, but speaks of the 'indeed not … very active correspondence between the two authors … Certainly, there were a few letters … There were also two or three visits that Handke did to Char, otherwise the rather endearing distance from both Handke and Char' (2009: 95).
22 While Handke's remarks about Char's writing during the 1980s, that is, when he translated Char's poetry, unmistakably display Handke's admiration for the French poet, it is important to mention that more recently Handke has been critical of Char's poetry, describing how Char's writing sometimes gets on his nerves. For more on this, see Schwagerle (2009: 95).
23 It must be noted that Handke's words here exclude women from what he calls the great poets in German language literary tradition.

References

Allen, Esther and Susan Bernofsky (eds) (2013), *In Translation: Translators on Their Work and What It Means*, New York: Columbia University Press.
Char, René (1984), *Rückkehr stromauf*, trans. Peter Handke, München and Wien: Carl Hanser Verlag.
Chesterman, Andrew (2009), 'The Name and Nature of Translation Studies', *Hermes – Journal of Language and Communication Studies*, 42: 13–22.
Cordingley, Anthony and Chiara Montini (2015), 'Genetic Translation Studies: An Emerging Discipline', *Linguistica Antverpiensia, New Series: Themes in Translation Studies*, 14: 1–18.
Goldschmidt, Georges-Arthur (1988), *Peter Handke*, Paris: Éditions du Seuil.
Goldschmidt, Georges-Arthur (1985), 'Raumglück', in Gerhard Melzer and Jale Tükel (eds), *Peter Handke: Die Arbeit am Glück*, 75–81, Königstein: Athenäum.
Handke, Peter (1978), *The Left-handed Woman*, trans. Ralph Manheim, New York: Farrar, Straus and Giroux.
Handke, Peter (1998), *Am Felsfenster morgens*, München: Deutscher Taschenbuch Verlag.
Handke, Peter (2007), *Meine Ortstafeln, meine Zeittafeln*, Frankfurt am Main: Suhrkamp.
Handke, Peter (2010), *Till Day You Do Part Or A Question of Light*, trans. Mike Mitchell, London, New York and Calcutta: Seagull Books.
Handke, Peter and Herbert Gamper (1987), *Aber ich lebe nur von den Zwischenräumen – Peter Handke im Gespräch mit Herbert Gamper*, Zürich: Ammann Verlag.
Handke, Peter, Klaus Kastberger and Elisabeth Schwagerle (2009), 'Es gibt die Schrift, es gibt das Schreiben', in Klaus Kastberger (ed.), *Peter Handke. Freiheit des Schreibens – Ordnung der Schrift*, 11–30, Wien: Paul Zsolnay Verlag.
Hansel, Michael (2009), 'Langsam – in Abständen – stetig. Peter Handke und der Bleistift', in Klaus Kastberger (ed.), *Peter Handke. Freiheit des Schreibens – Ordnung der Schrift*, 222–36, Wien: Paul Zsolnay Verlag.
Kastberger, Klaus (2012), 'Bodensatz des Schreibens. Peter Handke und die Geologie'. Available online: http://handkeonline.onb.ac.at/forschung/pdf/kastberger-2012a.pdf (accessed 10 October 2018).

Maier, Carol (2006), 'Translating as a Body: Meditations on Mediation (Excerpts 1994-2004)', in Susan Bassnett and Peter Bush (eds), *The Translator as Writer*, 137-48, London and New York: Continuum.
Massardier-Kenney, Françoise, Brian James Baer and Maria Tymoczko (eds) (2016), *Translators Writing, Writing Translators*, Kent, OH: The Kent State University Press.
Moura, Joana (2017), 'The Difference That a Body Makes: Figurations of the Translator's Body and Mistranslation in Peter Handke's Translation Narratives', PhD thesis in Comparative Literature, SUNY Stony Brook, New York.
Moura, Joana (2019), 'On Translation as a Corporeal Exploration: The Task of the Translator According to Peter Handke', in Fabjan Hafner and Wolfgang Pöckl (eds), '... übersetzt von Peter Handke' – *Philologische und translationswissenschaftliche Analysen*, 221-43, Berlin: Frank & Timme.
Munday, Jeremy (2014), 'Using Primary Sources to Produce a Microhistory of Translation and Translators: Theoretical and Methodological Concerns', *Translator: Studies in Intercultural Communication*, 20 (1): 64-80.
Pym, Anthony (1998), *Method in Translation History*, London and New York: Routledge.
Robinson, Douglas (1991), *The Translator's Turn*, Baltimore and London: The Johns Hopkins University Press.
Robinson, Douglas (2001), *Who Translates? – Translator Subjectivities beyond Reason*, Albany: State University of New York Press.
Schwagerle, Elisabeth (2009), 'Das war eigentlich die schönste Übersetzungserfahrung, die ich je hatte. Peter Handke und René Char', in Klaus Kastberger (ed.), *Peter Handke. Freiheit des Schreibens – Ordnung der Schrift*, 87-108, Wien: Paul Zsolnay Verlag.
Scott, Clive (2012), *Translating the Perception of Text – Literary Translation and Phenomenology*, London: Modern Humanities Research Association and Maney Publishing.
Tymoczko, Maria (2016), 'Victory by Verse', in Françoise Massardier-Kenney, Brian James Baer and Maria Tymoczko (eds), *Translators Writing, Writing Translators*, 131-54, Kent, OH: The Kent State University Press.

8

On the bodily dimension of translators and translating

Barbara Ivančić
University of Bologna
Alexandra L. Zepter
University of Cologne

Introduction

Over the last decades, embodiment theories have been mainly developed in the cognitive sciences as well as in various cultural sciences, in philosophy, psychology and linguistics. The concept of 'embodiment' refers to the notion of a specific relation between the system of human cognition and the human body. Central is the claim that human cognition forms a functional unit together with the entire human body in such a way that the human ability for thinking is tightly connected to the cognition's embedment *in* a human body – a human body which itself is embedded in an environment (see e.g. Tschacher 2006: 15, 132). Zepter (2013) discussed embodiment related to the human (cognitive) faculty of language and has argued that the body, including our perception, our senses, our social-interactive actions and our inner feelings, can be understood as an expansible resource for language production, reception, language understanding and language learning. Since the beginning of the twenty-first century, the notion of embodiment has also had an impact in the field of translation studies. In particular, among primarily cognitive-oriented translation process researchers there have been 'scattered moves to reembed translation process research': 'These moves hint at a need to rethink the theoretical basis of this broad area of study' (Muñoz 2016: 1), which is traditionally mind focused, in line with the body–mind dichotomy that has been shaping the Western thought patterns at least since Descartes.

Our chapter aims to affirm these needs based on the idea of the interdependence of brain, body and environment, and in this context, we argue that genetic translation studies can also help to strengthen this idea. The crucial link of evidence is provided by the fact that recently more and more translators started to produce texts in which they reflect upon the identity of translators by describing themselves, their idea of translation and their translation practices. As we will show, the individual experience and the concept of *body* – with its dimensions of perception, senses, movement and emotion – play a central role in such translator's self-representations.

We start by focusing on this particular and rather new type of material, which represents an example of what Munday (2014: 68) calls 'extra-textual primary sources'. As we sum up in the next section, some translation studies scholars even speak about a specific literary genre. Looking at some significant examples, the third section shows that when translators reflect on themselves and the process of translation, they very often refer to the body in terms of a motional and emotional experience. This suggests that processes of translation become enhanced by involving the whole body, that is, the cognitive, the emotional and the physical dimension of the human being. Not only do translators become 'flesh-and-blood people' in this way, as Anthony Pym (2001) phrased it, but also the translation act itself gets a corporeal dimension and can be understood as embedded in a body. From that point of view, translators endorse (more or less implicitly) the idea of the bodily origins of meaning, thought and language – thus, the idea which has been developed in various sciences under the term 'embodiment' or 'embodied cognition'.

Complementing the correspondent theoretical foundation, the fourth section directs us to the concept of 'embodiment', investigating the relationship between the corporeal dimensions of language, the corporeal dimension of translating that emerges from the translators' self-representations and the fictionalization of the corporeal translator. Summing up our thoughts in the fifth section, we argue that embodiment theories can give several impulses to translation studies which still have to be theoretically and empirically explored. From our point of view, extra-textual material and, more generally, genetic material can provide a rich source for those who want to embark on this research path.

Extra-textual material produced by translators

Over the last years, Italian literary translators have been particularly productive in producing the extra-textual primary sources we are dealing with in this chapter, that is, texts in which translators describe their working practices and their idea of translation.[1] In this context, several terminological proposals have been made in order to designate the corresponding text typology. As a matter of principle, all these terminological proposals reflect a substantial heterogeneity characterizing these texts, in which autobiographical descriptions, critical reflections as well as fictionalization coexist. The term *racconti di traduzione* (stories of translation) proposed by Antonio Lavieri (2007: 18) focuses, for example, on the narrative character of the translators' self-representations, whereas Giulia Baselica (2015) points out their autobiographical dimension, terming them *autobiografia del traduttore* (translator's autobiography).

Even though the biographical component does play an important role in these texts, the focus is not on the course of the author's life, but rather on the process of translating and its role in the translator's and author's life and identity. From that point of view, Ivančić (2016: 26) suggests the term *translation biographies*, recalling in this respect the term *language biography* used in sociolinguistics to designate biographical narrations in which language assumes an existential role in the life of the narrator. Just as language biographies foreground 'the concept of *Spracherleben*, the lived experience of language' (Busch 2015), in the translators' self-representations it is the 'lived experience of translation' that becomes particularly salient. Thus, it is the work of translating or rather the process of translating that assumes an existential role in life stories, and the narration represents more or less explicitly the poetics of translation of the author/translator.

By analogy with the term *language biography* that includes also the text typology of the interview, we extend the term *translation biographies* to interviews in which translators consciously reflect upon translation. In both cases, we deal with 'overtly mediated testimonies', in the terminology of Munday (2014: 68); the grade of mediation is certainly different, but this is not a crucial difference in our context. The most relevant aspect here is the conscious reflection on the working practices and conditions as well as on the own attitudes and personalities, which also includes episodes from everyday life as well as 'fascinating incidental details' (Munday 2014: 77) in the lives of translators. Consequently, what emerges from this type of texts is the idea of translation as a holistic process that involves the whole person and that depends on the interactions between the person and his or her environment.

The corporeal dimension in translation biographies

In order to develop and exemplify our point, we take a closer look at the translation biographies of Swetlana Geier (2008), Susanna Basso (2010), Laura Bocci (2004) and Franco Nasi (2008). In all four cases, we find *corporeal* aspects concerning the dimensions of emotions, senses and/or movement. That is, if we recall the image of Anthony Pym (2001), the translators present themselves as 'flesh-and-blood people' – and they often refer to the translation process itself in terms of body and of 'flesh and blood'. In other words, the translator becomes *corporeal* by describing the translation process; and on this account, translation becomes corporeal too.

An interesting sample for this kind of bodily dimension comes from Swetlana Geier: Geier was the prominent translator of Dostoyevsky's novels into German and is famous in the German world of literary translation as 'the woman with the five elephants', an image created by herself referring to the five major Dostoyevsky's novels she translated in a project that took about twenty years to conclude. In a lengthy book interview with her (cf. Geier 2008) – which can be considered a translation biography – Geier describes herself and her fundamental idea of translation – the quintessence of translation, as she calls it – such that the translation process involves internalizing the text and not sticking to single words. She expresses this idea with the following image:

> I had a wonderful teacher: And when I was translating something, she would say to me in German: 'Nase hoch beim Übersetzen' – Stick your nose up in the air when you are translating. That means: Lift your head while translating, instead of translating from left to right. A translation is not a caterpillar crawling from left to right, a translation always emerges from the whole. That is all … One has to make the text entirely one's own. The Germans say *internalize*, 'verinnerlichen'.[2] (Geier 2008: 62)

The expression 'stick up your nose', which is not to be understood in the sense of 'to be snotty', is a corporeal image that can be read as a metaphor for the idea of internalizing the text, and it also describes a concrete physical posture towards the text. The crucial point of such reference is the following: it is by all means likely that Geier effectively *uses* the concrete physical posture in order to support herself in the process of internalizing the text. But also if she just picks up on the metaphorical status of the expression, the application of this particular bodily metaphor already suggests that for Geier, successful translating goes beyond a pure mental process and is to be grasped holistically involving the person as a whole.

Correspondingly, 'das Ganze', the whole ('a translation always emerges from the whole'), is a central concept in Geier's poetics. It should be related to another central image in her reflections: the one of the so-called 'Gehäuse' (English *shell, housing*). The image refers to the famous painting of Antonello da Messina, *St. Jerome in His Study* (German *Hyeronimus im Gehäuse*), where Hieronymus, the patron saint of the translators, is represented within a kind of shell. Starting from this association, Geier describes the image as follows:

> The translator always translates within his/her *Gehäuse*. One cannot get out of it. I *have to* stay in this space, otherwise I cannot convey anything. ... This gives a personal and unique flavour to my work. ... The *Gehäuse* is certainly not a metaphor for the translation process. It is a very old image for the body as a shell of the soul. ... The *Gehäuse*, the personality of the translator, is as much relevant as the divergence between languages. I translate from German and I feel the German language as a Russian person, and I am never free from that. Messina's painting is so beautiful just because Jerome seems to be within a shell. (Geier 2008: 118, 119, 121; emphasis in the original)

Thus, we have here the *body* as a shell, the housing of the mind and the personality respectively, and this body is always involved in the process of translating since it is the whole, the entire person who *feels the languages* and who does the translation work. In the citation, Geier does not explain how the body is or can be involved in her holistic act of translation. She rather argues on an implicit level which nevertheless recalls the philosophical work of Eugene Gendlin who developed the concept of Felt Sense in order to explain how any human action and in particular any language use and any constitution of meaning is due to an interplay of language, situation *and* body:

> So the body *implies* a next step of speech or action or knowledge or feeling. The word 'implies' is important to me. Suppose though that I didn't say the body *implies* the next step. Suppose I said the body is *pregnant* with the next step. You would say, 'Yes, I understand.' ... Suppose I say the body *cooks* the next step; *bakes* the next step; *lacks* the next step, or *holds its breath longing for* the next step. By this time you would know what I am saying, even if I use no word at all but just write that the body ....s the next step. In that blank, my word 'implying' says *and is* the intricacy which is greater than the schemes that any one of the possible words bring with it. (Gendlin 1992: 193; emphases in the original)

> The body senses the whole situation, and it urges, it implicitly shapes our next action.
> It senses itself living – in its whole context – the situation. (Gendlin 1992: 342)

In the next section, we will see how the theory of embodiment can help us understand more concretely such bodily involvement – a corporeal dimension which quite generally is implied in linguistic activity, but furthermore can be used as an expansible resource in any corresponding processes including, as we argue, the process of translation. First, we want to give a few more examples of the implicit endorsement of this corporeal dimension in translator's reflections upon their own translation practices.

Susanna Basso, who belongs to the most important translators of English narratives into Italian, points out in her book *Sul tradurre. Esperienze e divagazioni di una militante* (On Translation. Experiences and Digressions of a Militant) the great physical effort that translation implies. Therefore, she compares the act of translating to climbing a mountain, as well as swimming or walking on a rope like a tightrope walker (cf. Basso 2010: 97, 25 and 142). For Basso, the physical effort is always intimately connected with the process of breathing: translating means searching for the appropriate rhythm of breathing (Basso 2010: 25) and this search is on its part intimately connected with *slowness* (Basso 2010: 142). Slowness belongs to one of the key words in Basso's translation biographies: it refers to the capacity of *listening* to the text as well as waiting for the (right) words to emerge (Basso 2010: 7). From her point of view, even consulting a dictionary can be compared to a 'physical gesture' (Basso 2010: 6), which offers the translator 'a kind of break, like lighting a cigarette, to distract herself for a moment and then go back to work more focused' (Basso 2010: 6).

In a similar way, Laura Bocci, translator from German into Italian and author of *Di seconda mano. Né un saggio né un racconto sul tradurre letteratura* (At Second Hand. Either a Study or a Story on Translating Literature) grasps translation as 'an experience that offers and at the same time requires the slowest reading possible' (2004: 36). Or take Franco Nasi, translator from English and author of *La malinconia del traduttore* (Nasi 2008; translated into English as *Translator's Blues*, cf. Nasi 2016): for Nasi as well, slowness seems to be essential for the translation practice – a practice which requires respect and care for others' words.

Just as Swetlana Geier, also Basso, Bocci and Nasi refer to specific physical gestures as well as to attitudes that involve the body while reflecting upon the translation practice. Moreover, when Basso describes her experience as the translator of Alice Munro (she is the main translator of Munro's work into Italian), it turns out that, in the specific case of this author, she likes to write by hand instead of using the computer, as she does in other cases. Basso explains this habit as a necessity to feel the text physically.

Curiously, a very similar observation is reported by Munday with regard to Bernard Miall, a 'prolific translator from French who corresponded with his editors and the publisher every two or three days for the 39 years of their collaboration' (Munday 2014: 76). These personal papers reveal many details about the translator and his everyday life, among them also 'his preference for handwriting his translations rather than using his "very old Remington"', as he underlines in a letter from 1918 (see Munday 2014: 76). At first sight, this might seem to be a detail, but on a closer examination, such details reveal the corporeal dimension of the translational act; and at the same time, they refer to a corporeal conception of language.

In linguistics, such a corporeal conception of language is not uncontroversial, but it has been strengthened in the last decades, inter alia in the course of the elaboration of embodiment theories in various disciplines.[3] One of the first German language linguists, who explicitly investigated the connection between body and human communication, was Harald Weinrich. He developed the concept of the 'Leiblichkeit der Sprache', that is, 'language made corporeal' (see Weinrich 2006a and 2006b). And similar to the thoughts of Basso, *the hand* is very present in Weinrich's considerations as he understands the hand as 'an organ of communication' whose function in the written language can be compared to that of the mouth and the ear in orality.

Both the mouth and the ear are indeed often mentioned in the translation biographies as well: the ears referring to the sense of hearing, the mouth referring to the use of the voice in the translational process. A good example is again provided by Swetlana Geier, who assigned a central role to voice and hearing in her working habits. Reviewing the documentary film that Vadim Jendreyko dedicated to Geier, based on the book interview we mentioned above (see Geier 2008), several scenes portray the translator together with an assistant – a professional musician – whom she uses as a kind of ideal reader. The assistant slowly reads aloud her translation to her and she explains some fine points of her translation through this kind of exchange.

Thus, drawing a first conclusion, we can say that the body can play a decisive role in translators' narrations – as a constant term of reference or comparison while reflecting upon translation. Accordingly, we would say that while reflecting consciously upon translation and the translators' identity, upon mental processes, decision making, the impact of emotions and attitudes to norms, the translators more or less implicitly touch upon the idea of 'embodiment' or 'embodied cognition'.

Embodiment

As already pointed to in the first section, embodiment theories have been developed in the last decades in the cognitive sciences as well as in various cultural sciences, in philosophy, psychology and linguistics. In this chapter, we can only sketch the main ideas; for a more elaborate introduction, see, for example, Tschacher (2006) and Zepter (2013: 34ff). Basically, 'embodiment' can be defined as the relation between the system of human cognition and the human body, to such an extent that the cognitive system is understood to always be correlated to a body in which it is embedded. The cognitive system and its organ, the brain, are embedded in a body, and the cognitive system/brain and body are embedded in an environment – and without this twofold embedment, the cognitive system cannot function intelligently. Thus, if our cognitive system was not embodied, we would not have any ability for (abstract) thinking or problem solving and no capability to profit from experiences or to capture relations and contexts between things (Tschacher 2006: 15, 132). Altogether, central to the theory of embodiment is the claim that human cognition forms a functional unit together with the entire human body.

In order to develop in the course of the human existence, the human mind needs a physical organ, the brain, and an environment in which the brain is embedded – an environment which supplies the mind, the brain and the human being with experiences. The crucial assumption in this context is the following: the human body does not only provide – by means of the senses – the 'contact' between the mind and the environment, but rather the body itself forms an essential part of the indispensable environment. Thus, stimuli received through the senses do not simply influence the body and provoke certain thinking processes, a certain behaviour and/or a certain motoric reaction. The idea is instead that cognition is based on a permanent interaction: the mind interacts (1) through the body with the state of the outer environment; and (perhaps even more basic) (2) with the state of the inner environment, that is, the state *of* the body. In these latter interactions, the expression, the posture, the tension of the body and the emotions play a decisive role. Both the wider environment and the body can control and influence the development of cognitive patterns (cf. Tschacher 2006: 15, 31; Lakoff and Johnson 1999: 16ff). Therefore, the body constitutes at the same time (1) a medium for environmental experiences and (2) a source for experience.

Shaun Gallagher, a prominent researcher in embodiment theory, illustrates with various examples how among other things our movements and our body postures can 'inform and form' our thinking (Gallagher 2005: 8ff and 244ff). Visual perception, for example, involves the constant task of holding the perceived world steady, whereas the perceiving body is in constant movement; such a visual stability is necessarily dependent on motoric control. In these processes, we do not only perceive the shape and the size of objects phenomenally; the phenomenal size of an object also depends on the relative distance of the observer to that object. Therefore, we conceive of objects also pragmatically as something that can be grasped and manipulated, and in this pragmatic regard, shape and size remain invariant. Either the perceived object is something that can be grasped and manipulated in certain ways, or it is not.

Generally, the ontogenetic development of perceptual and cognitive faculties enhances in correlation to the infant's expansion of crawling and the increasing of the overall mobility; and in many areas, infants develop specific perceptual strategies depending on certain already available motoric skills (see also Gibson 1988). Now, from an embodiment perspective, language is also a cognitive and at the same time bodily phenomenon. Considering our language production and reception – thus, the actual *acts* in which language is *used* – we have to recognize that we speak language, listen to language, write and read language always as 'whole' people who have a mind and a body. The actual acts of language production and reception always involve not only cognitive but also perceptual, motoric and emotional processes.

To give very simple examples: oral speech originates in a vocal tract; in order to listen, we do not need only ears, but also awareness and attention, the latter are intimately connected with motivation and emotions. Quite generally, speaking and gesturing complement one another. In order to write, we need either hands to do it ourselves or a mouth to dictate to somebody who does the writing for us. In all these situations of language use, the body 'sneaks in' and is involved in the process. Certainly, the distribution and the specific interaction of the cognitive and the corporeal dimensions can differ from act to act, but there does not exist an act of language production or reception without any corporeal dimensions included.

These examples might seem fairly uncontroversial, but the point of embodiment theories is precisely that the corporeal dimensions *exceed* a pure *medial* factor. In other words: where our body constitutes a medium for language use and communication, this medium can also influence the language system as such. In theories of Embodied Cognition, researchers argue that even in the mental processing of linguistic meaning and in the understanding of concepts there are multiple mental domains involved – domains that concern perception, senses, social-interactive actions and/or inner feelings (see among others MacWhinney 1999; Lakoff and Johnson 1999; Barsalou 1999, 2008, 2009; Gallese and Lakoff 2005; Pecher and Zwaan 2005; Johnson 2007).

Brian MacWhinney (1999) shows that in order to understand (in reading or listening) a specific sentence or a specific expression comprehensively, the recipient has to take an appropriate perspective – a perspective from which he or she can interpret the sentence or the expression. MacWhinney distinguishes several possible perspectives, but all are related to (human) perceptual and accordingly bodily experiences. For example, our mental definition and our mental understanding of a concept like 'banana' results from the perspective of 'affordances', that is, the perspectives of our body in contact with individual objects that fall under this concept:

> When we hear the word *banana*, each of these affordances [in vision, smell, taste, touch, skeletal postures, haptic actions, and even locomotion] becomes potentially activated. The visual affordances or images may be the quickest to receive activation. If the sentence requires nothing more, this may be all that we experience. However, just activating the raw visual image is enough to enable embodied processing of the word *banana*. (MacWhinney 1999: 218)

In some cases, the grammar of a language reflects such a perspective which establishes a direct relationship between the object of cognition and the perceiving corporeal subject in the morphological structure of the lexical items: in Navajo, the word for 'chair' is *bikáá'dah'asdáhí*, which means literally translated 'on-it-one-sits'; the word for 'table' is *bikáá'dání*, literally translated 'at-it-one-works' (MacWhinney 1999: 219).[4]

Finally, MacWhinney's previous example of the word *banana* also points to another aspect: given our past experiences and their processing, our actual language reception furthermore is always dependent on the context and on 'us' as recipients. All these factors influence our specific processing of a concept, a sentence or a text:

> In order to understand sentences, we must become actively involved with a starting point or initial perspective. We use this perspective as the foundation for building an embodied understanding of the sentence. For example, when we listen to a sentence such as *The skateboarder vaulted over the railing*, we take the perspective of *the skateboarder* and imagine the process of crouching down onto the skateboard, snapping up the tail, and jumping into the air, as both rider and skateboard fly through the air over a railing and land together on the other side. Identifying with the skateboarder as the agent, we can evaluate the specific bodily

actions involved in crouching, balancing, and jumping. The more we know about skateboarding, the more deeply we understand this utterance. (MacWhinney 1999: 214ff)

Now, MacWhinney's point can also be changed in the following way: if our understanding of concepts and their linguistic expressions gradually deepens with the expansion of our bodily experiences, we can understand the body not only as a necessary condition but also as an expansible resource for the understanding of concepts and their linguistic expressions – and obviously, this should not only be true for the reception/production and the learning of a first language, but for language learning in general. And accepting this interrelation for monolingual reception and production, it is only a small step to recognize the body as a potential resource for the process of *translating* linguistic expressions from one language to another.

Therefore, coming back to the topic of translation: what does embodiment theory provide for the research on translation biographies and on the theory of translation? We argue that on the level of theory building, it can support the development of a conceptually precise description and understanding of how a successful translation process can be constituted and of the translation process by itself. Section 3 presented implicit observations on how the searching for adequate wording and/or for the adequate rhythm in a particular translating context can be fuelled by a holistic process and can activate specific physical gestures as well as attitudes that involve the body. From an embodiment perspective, such an approach corresponds to a procedure in which the translator becomes 'actively involved with a starting point or initial perspective' and 'use[s] this perspective as the foundation for building an embodied understanding of the sentence' (MacWhinney 1999: 214ff) – or, in a broader sense, of the source and the target language. To this effect, the findings of embodiment theories match the implicit insights that we have seen are prominent in the translation biographies and the translators' self-representations. All the mentioned testimonies suggest the idea that body, that is, the lived body and its memory, influence our actual experience and thus also the translation practice.

Conclusions

We have argued that many self-representations of translators and accordingly *translation biographies* show a *corporeal dimension* and implicitly embrace the idea of embodied cognition and embodied language. The findings of embodiment theories imply that the body – understood in a broad sense – is not only a necessary condition but also an expansible *resource* for language reception, production and understanding. Our aim was to show that these findings can support theory building in translation studies and that genetic translation studies can give important impulses in this connection.

Thus, it seems to us that embodiment theory, research on extra-textual material such as translation biographies and translation process research present an entire range of points of intersection which require more attention and open up new fields of research. Furthermore, exploring these intersections can also inspire the teaching of translation.

We just want to point out that the relevance of integrating a didactic perspective is twofold. On the one hand, if professional translators use 'more bodily thinking' (Gendlin 1992: 203) in their translating, we can certainly ask how we can stimulate and support a corresponding approach in teaching translation. That is, how could a corporeal dimension be integrated in the academic education of translators to such an extent that students can learn to use the body as a resource for their translating as well? Significantly, on the other hand, in order to be able to develop correspondent teaching concepts, we have to further elaborate and realize possible ways of building embodied understandings of specific linguistic expressions in the course of a translation process. As a consequence, theoretical and empirical research in the field of didactics can also enhance our (embodied) theory of translation.

Notes

1. Due to our own affiliation in Italian and German translation studies and linguistics, we started our research by focusing on these contexts and met with a prospering discourse. At least, the cases presented in this chapter should be taken as representative examples that, as we argue, reveal the potential of the translator's and translation's bodily dimension.
2. All translations are by Ivančić, unless otherwise noted.
3. See Zepter (2013: 58ff) who discusses in detail the long linguistic tradition of ignoring a bodily dimension in the modelling of language theory, in favour of conceptions that reduce language to an exclusively cognitive/mental phenomenon. This reduction furthermore carries over to the practice in the didactics of translation where it is still common to primarily focus on its cognitive dimensions.
4. For more examples and a more detailed introduction in the theories of Embodied Cognition, see also Zepter (2013: 201ff). The reviewers of the chapter furthermore pointed to puzzling constructions (in English and other languages with prepositions) like 'the book is on the table', but not 'the table is underneath the book'. Such an example likewise highlights that the physical experience of having a body is deeply entrenched in the way we conceive experience and express it in linguistic terms.

References

Barsalou, Lawrence W. (1999), 'Perceptual Symbol Systems', *Behavioral and Brain Sciences*, 22: 577–660.

Barsalou, Lawrence W. (2008), 'Grounded Cognition', *Annual Review of Psychology*, 59: 617–45.

Barsalou, Lawrence W. (2009), 'Simulation, Situated Conceptualization, and Prediction', *Philosophical Transactions of the Royal Society B*, 364: 1281–9.

Baselica, Giulia (2015), 'Un nuovo microgenere', *Tradurre. Pratiche, teorie, strumenti*. Available online: http://rivistatradurre.it (accessed 3 August 2015).

Basso, Susanna (2010), *Sul tradurre. Esperienze e divagazioni militanti*, Milano: Bruno Mondadori.

Bocci, Laura (2004), *Di seconda mano. Né un saggio, né un racconto sul tradurre letteratura*, Milano: Rizzoli.
Busch, Brigitta (2015), 'Expanding the Notion of the Linguistic Repertoire: On the Concept of *Spracherleben* – The Lived Experience of Language', *Applied Linguistics*, 38 (3): 340–58. Available online: https://doi.org/10.1093/applin/amv030 (accessed 13 November 2018).
Documentary on Swetlana Geier (written and directed by Vadim Jendreyko). Available online: https://5elefanten.ch/en/.
Gallagher, Shaun (2005), *How the Body Shapes the Mind*, Oxford: Clarendon Press.
Gallese, Vittorio and George Lakoff (2005), 'The Brain's Concepts: The Role of the Sensory-motor System in Conceptual Knowledge', *Cognitive Neuropsychology*, 22 (3/4): 455–79.
Geier, Swetlana (2008), *Ein Leben zwischen den Sprachen. Russisch-deutsche Erinnerungsbilder. Aufgezeichnet von Taja Gut*, Dornach: Pforte.
Gendlin, Eugene T. (1992), 'The Wider Role of Bodily Sense in Thought and Language', in Maxine Sheets-Johnstone (ed.), *Giving the Body Its Due*, 192–207, Albany: State University of New York (SUNY) Press.
Gibson, Eleanor J. (1988), 'Exploratory Behavior in the Development of Perceiving, Acting and the Acquiring of Knowledge', *Annual Review of Psychology*, 39: 1–41.
Ivančić, Barbara (2016), *Manuale del traduttore*, Milano: Editrice Bibliografica.
Johnson, Mark (2007), *The Meaning of the Body. Aesthetics of Human Understanding*, Chicago and London: The University of Chicago Press.
Lakoff, George and Mark Johnson (1999), *Philosophy in the Flesh. The Embodied Mind and Its Challenge to Western Thought*, New York: Basic Books.
Lavieri, Antonio (2007), *Translatio in fabula: la letteratura come pratica teorica del tradurre. Prefazione di Jean-René Ladmiral*, Roma: Editori riuniti University Press di Gei.
MacWhinney, Brian (1999), 'The Emergence of Language from Embodiment', in Brian MacWhinney (ed.), *The Emergence of Language*, 213–56, Mahwah, NJ: Lawrence Erlbaum Associates Publishers.
Munday, Jeremy (2014), 'Using Primary Sources to Produce a Microhistory of Translation and Translators: Theoretical and Methodological Concerns', *The Translator*, 20 (1): 64–80.
Muñoz Martín, Ricardo (2016), *Reembedding Translation Process Research*, Amsterdam and Philadelphia: John Benjamins.
Nasi, Franco (2008), *La malinconia del traduttore*, Milano: Medusa.
Nasi, Franco (2016), *Translator's Blues*, Lewes: Sylph Editions.
Pecher, Diane and Rolf A. Zwaan (eds) (2005), *Grounding Cognition: The Role of Perception and Action in Memory, Language, and Thinking*, Cambridge: Cambridge University Press.
Pym, Anthony (2001), 'To Localize and Humanize … On Academics and Translation'. Available online: http://usuaris.tinet.cat/apym/on-line/translation/humanize.html (accessed 6 November 2018).
Tschacher, Wolfgang (2006), 'Wie Embodiment zum Thema wurde', in Maja Storch, Benita Cantieni, Gerald Hüther, and Wolfgang Tschacher (eds), *Embodiment. Die Wechselwirkung von Körper und Psyche verstehen und nutzen*, 11–34, Bern: Huber.
Weinrich, Harald (2006a), 'Einige kategoriale Überlegungen zur Leiblichkeit und zur ‚Lage' der Sprache', in Harald Weinrich (ed.), *Sprache, das heißt Sprachen*, 15–26, Tübingen: Narr.

Weinrich, Harald (2006b), 'Kurzer Blick auf die Hand?', in Harald Weinrich (ed.), *Sprache, das heißt Sprachen*, 39–45, Tübingen: Narr.
Zepter, Alexandra L. (2013), *Sprache und Körper. Vom Gewinn der Sinnlichkeit für Sprachdidaktik und Sprachtheorie*, Frankfurt am Main: Peter Lang Verlag.

9

The translator's view of translation: Analysis of testimonies published in the Portuguese journal *Colóquio Letras* (1980–2000)

Dominique Faria
*Centre for Comparative Studies,
University of Lisbon/University of the Azores*

Translation studies have long sought to uncover what goes on in the translator's mind when he or she is working, either through interviews, think-aloud protocols or eye tracking. More recently, genetic studies have been put to the same use, although, unlike the previous methods, they have focused on 'the textual evidence of the activity of translation rather than the translating subject' (Harding and Cortès 2018: 198). This chapter studies this textual evidence of the translators' work, not through what Bellemin-Noël calls an *avant-texte* (1982) – drafts, notes, proof corrections, correspondence – but through the analysis of eight self-reflective articles written by translators and published in the Portuguese literary journal *Colóquio Letras*.

Unlike *avant-textes*, which are generally assumed to be loosely written during the translation process itself, these articles were written once the work was finished, for the purpose of being published and read by others. This type of text is carefully prepared, containing selected information only. It fulfils 'the requirements of printing – it is sanctioned by its own conformity; it has the dignity and imperturbability of the obedient and achieved' (Scott 2006: 112). All the more so since these particular articles are meant to be read mostly by scholars (the direct target reader of *Colóquio Letras*). In this analysis, it will therefore be borne in mind that these articles are a retrospective account of the translation process.

Notwithstanding their differences with regard to *avant-textes*, as Jeremy Munday puts it, '[t]he window these pronouncements provide into the working practice of the translator may be unobtainable through other means' (2015: 128). They are a first-hand account of the whys and hows of translation. This sort of testimony is by no means frequently found, since translators tend to cover their traces, probably due to their lack of authority after centuries of being regarded as simple re-creators (Durand-Bogaert 2014: 9).

Following the principles of descriptive translation studies (Toury 1995), these texts will be read as sources of information about the translator's work and thoughts on translation, but also as providing historical evidence about the way translation was perceived within the Portuguese national context at a specific time. The texts in question were published in the late twentieth century – five during the first half of the 1980s and three between 1994 and 2000. They are the sole testimonies written by translators in this journal during this two-decade period. In Portugal, in the 1980s, translation studies were at an early and decisive stage, as pointed out by Teresa Seruya (2015: 21–2) and Francisco Magalhães (1996: 233–44). Researchwise, translation was for the first time acknowledged as an independent field of study (from comparative studies and linguistics), as shown by the academic conferences held during this period and the books entirely dedicated to the study of translation (Seruya 2015: 22). This had consequences in terms of university courses, since most undergraduate degrees in translation were created in the late 1980s and the early 1990s, in the major Portuguese universities. This seems to suggest that Portuguese researchers were not impermeable to the work that was being done abroad by Susan Bassnett and André Lefevere in shaping what is now known as translation studies.

The journal *Colóquio Letras*

Colóquio Letras played a key role in this context, since it is an academic literary journal, one of the very few existing in Portugal at the time. It was a scholarly publication edited by some of the most notable Portuguese intellectuals, from Jacinto Prado Coelho (1920–84) to David Mourão Ferreira (1927–96). It therefore promoted research and became a means for academics to keep up to date with important academic trends. The journal has been strongly focused on Portuguese literature. A report published in 2007[1] provides statistical data about the contents of the journal from its beginnings to that year, showing that seventy per cent of the studies deal with Portuguese literature, eight per cent relate to literary theory, ten per cent focus on foreign literatures, nine per cent on Brazilian literature and two per cent on African literature written in Portuguese. This report also includes a special reference to translation, presented as an area the journal cherishes. According to the editors of the journal, this is visible through the reviews of translated books and translations of foreign poems into Portuguese. This special focus on translation is probably not unrelated to the fact that the journal is associated with the Calouste Gulbenkian Foundation, which has an international scope.

During the 1980s and 1990s in particular, *Colóquio Letras* contributed to the growth of studies on translation in Portugal, by consistently emphasizing the role of translation and translators in spreading Portuguese literature abroad. Between 1980 and 1985 alone, *Colóquio Letras* published ninety-two texts about translation (Faria 2013). It did so through short articles notifying the reader of new translations of Portuguese literature abroad, but also by providing book reviews of recently published translations (where the name and often a biography of the translator are included), and through testimonies like the ones that will be studied, in which the translators are given an opportunity to write about how they experience and perceive translation.

The general tone used in this journal to refer to translations and, more importantly, to translators shows a clear understanding of their function as cultural agents, and of the complexity and difficulty of the task itself. This is unexpected and somewhat ahead of its time, in the context of Portuguese culture. In a book review for a translation, published in *Colóquio Letras* in 1982, its author states, referring to the translator's work: 'An extremely difficult task, one which in Portugal – unlike other European countries, not to go further afield – stubbornly continues to be underestimated' (Sousa Rebelo 1982: 77).[2] This journal has striven to change this state of affairs. A note published at the end of one of the articles to be studied – Jonathan Griffin's – fully illustrates this:

> This text replicates the talk given in 1981 at the Gulbenkian Foundation by the great translator of Fernando Pessoa into English, and it has the rare value of a reflexive testimony. (Griffin 1982: 27)

The adjectives chosen to refer to the translator – 'great' – and to his text – of 'rare value' – display the journal's respect for the translator figure. This is not exclusive to this particular translator, who is well known for his quality work. If we go through the articles about newly published translations of Portuguese literature, a comment on the role of the translator in spreading Portuguese literature abroad is often present, as in the following examples:

> This is one more relevant service the Portuguese culture owes to Ángel Crespo. (Anonymous 1982: 101)

> Librarian at the Hispanic Society, Jean R. Longland continues to contribute with her English versions to the dissemination of our poetry in the United States. (Anonymous 1980: 103)

The eight texts under study are therefore published in an uncommon context of praise for translation and translators.

The translators

In order to interpret the testimonies, we first have to understand who their authors were and what they are talking about when they speak of translation. Although I will not delve very deeply into this issue, I cannot but stress how urgent it is to gather information on the translator figure, thus contributing to what Chesterman (2009: 13) calls 'TanslaTOR Studies', which focuses 'on the agents involved in translation, for instance on their activities or attitudes, their interaction with their social and technical environment, or their history and influence' (2009: 20).

As for the authors of the texts under scrutiny, they were mostly foreigners: Claire Cayron is French, Boris Schnaiderman is Ukrainian, Inês Oseki-Dépré is Brazilian, Jonathan Griffin is British. In addition, they specialized in translating canonical Portuguese-speaking authors: Fernando Pessoa (1988–35) takes the lead, followed by Miguel Torga (1907–95), Guimarães Rosa (1908–87), Luís Vaz de Camões (c 1525–c 1580), Eugénio de Andrade (1923–2005), Herberto Helder (1930–2015), Raul Brandão (1867–1930) and Fernando Namora (1919–89), to mention but a few. Most of them translate into English or French, with the exception of Carlos Pitta, who translated a philosophical work into Portuguese (the only reference to his translations we could find), and Boris Schnaiderman, who translated from the Russian.

They were all acknowledged for their work, having received prizes and other signs of recognition. Françoise Laye was awarded a translation prize in Portugal and another one in France for her translations of Fernando Pessoa. Jonathan Griffin was made 'Cavaleiro da Ordem de Santiago' (Knight of the Order of Saint James of the Sword) in Portugal and 'Chevalier de l'Ordre des Arts et des Lettres' (Knight of the Order of Arts and Letters) in France, for his translations. Patrick Quillier was invited to oversee the publication of the complete works of Fernando Pessoa at the prestigious French 'Collection Pléiade'.

The short biographical note published in the journal and other external sources provided further information on the translators, who share some traits. Some have a PhD and taught abroad: Alexis Levitin taught at an American university, Inês Oseki-Dépré and Boris Schnaiderman were professors in Brazilian universities, and Patrick Quillier also taught at a French university. Some were published writers themselves. Boris Schnaiderman, Carlos Pitta and Claire Cayron have published essays on literature and other related subjects, whereas Françoise Laye and Jonathan Griffin were fiction writers.

Inês Oseki-Dépré,[3] Carlos Pitta[4] and Patrick Quillier[5] published other articles (besides those under study) in *Colóquio Letras*, which show they were researchers as well as translators. Moreover, some of these translators later wrote essays and other articles on translation. This is the case for Claire Cayron, who, in 1987, published *Sesame, pour la traduction – une nouvelle de Miguel Torga* (Sesame, for Translation – A Short Story by Miguel Torga), or Inês Oseki-Dépré, who published *Théories et pratiques de la traduction littéraire* (Theories and Practices of Literary Translation) in 1999, and *Traduction & Poésie* (Translation and Poetry) in 2000.

These short presentations of the translators show that they are renowned for doing quality work, and also that they generally have a background which enables them to critically reflect on their activity as translators. This could explain why they were given the opportunity to write for the journal. None of them had a university degree in translation (which is not surprising in the 1980s). Rather, most of them studied literature, literary theory or comparative studies. The fact that there are almost no Portuguese translators or texts being translated into Portuguese in this list is disappointing for research purposes, although it could be attributed to the core purpose of the journal, which is to study and promote Portuguese literature (abroad).

The translators' testimonies

The texts we will explore are not homogeneous and call for some differentiation. As mentioned before, five were published in the 1980s, as opposed to three published after 1990. Moreover, the 1980s texts are longer, ranging from seven to twelve pages, whereas the texts published after 1990 have seven, three and two pages, respectively. Despite their differences, this is an impressive sample, given that translators are seldom granted any physical space inside publications to express themselves, be it in prefaces or translator notes. Jorge Almeida e Pinho (2006) analysed nearly 200 preambles of literary texts written by Portuguese translators over several decades and concludes that the few prefaces that do exist were mostly written by famous authors or intellectuals who were allowed to express themselves on their work as translators due to their reputation as writers.

We have no information on what – if any – instructions were given to the translators, nor if writing the article was their own initiative or if they were invited by the journal to do so. Nonetheless, one of the most surprising aspects of these articles is that they tend to refer to theoretical issues. Two of them explicitly mention 'translation theory':

Natural tendency to suspect theories. (Cayron 1985: 34)

So, more than of a translation theory, I prefer talking about the translator's deontology. (Cayron 1985: 40)

Some time ago, I offered to write a formal and academic paper on translation theory. Now, after reading some collected essays ... after carefully examining old issues of *Translation Review* ... I found out, to my surprise, that I cannot adhere to any of it: the fact is I have no theory at all. (Levitin 1994: 22)

The reference to theory can be explained by the translators' academic backgrounds, but also by the scholarly context in which the texts were going to be published. Nonetheless, the two translators mention theory in order to dismiss it, saying they do not fully obey any theory and suggesting that every text demands a slightly different approach. In fact, an idea that arises repeatedly in almost every text is that there is no recipe for translation: 'No theory can, *a priori*, work as a roadmap for the wandering translator. Each poem is a new challenge; each translation may demand its own strategy' (Levitin 1994: 27). Conversely, their discourse shows that they clearly separate (oppose, almost) theory from practice. Griffin effectively summarizes this paradox: 'In theory, translating is impossible – but in practice we do translate. Because we need to' (1982: 21).

There is also some evidence that they are up to date with translation research. Levitin directly states that he did some research prior to writing the article and lists the anthologies and journals he accessed to write the article; Cayron quotes Antoine Berman and George Steiner and repeatedly argues against ethnocentrism. Still, underlying their discourse is the perception of theory as a rigid set of rules and predicaments about translation, stipulating how to translate correctly. According to Susan Bassnett, this was no longer the prevailing view in the 1980s, since scholars were mostly interested in 'seeking not to evaluate but to understand the shifts of emphasis that had taken place during the transfer of texts from one literary system into another' (2002: 7).

These translators also devote much of their time and efforts to discussing the concept of faithfulness. In the earlier texts from 1985, the translators clearly felt the need to justify and explain their standpoint on this concept, the one they most frequently referred to. Associated with it are other well-known notions, typical of the way translation was treated in the early stages of its study. Two of the most commonly evoked are 'betrayal' and 'unfaithfulness'. These point to the pejorative notions of transgression and lack of trust, the implicit value judgements that had pervaded much discourse on translation for centuries, as synthesized in the famous French expression *belles infidèles* (applied to translations), or the Italian dictum *traduttori, traditori* (referring to translators). To these, they oppose 'freedom' and 're-creation', considered main ingredients when translating. Most translators insist on the fact that the translated text is a different text, that the translator replaces a poem with another poem (Griffin 1982: 22), thus clearly challenging the widespread belief that translation is a 'mechanical' rather than a 'creative' process (Bassnett 2002: 13).

The concept of faithfulness is mostly debated through the dichotomy free translation and literal translation:

> I believe very free translations should only be made in exceptional cases. Both resorting to free translation and giving into the lifeless word-for-word are similar kinds of laziness. Equally harmful? I don't think so. ... [A] translator who is enslaved by the 'word-for-word' is a bad translator. (Griffin 1982: 25)

> [I]n practical terms, we don't feel the dilemma of literalness *or* re-creation. In his or her work, each translator coordinates one attitude with the other, any of which is useful in a given step but harmful in another. (Cayron 1985: 40; emphasis in the original)

> [T]he horror of the never-ending sea of *literalness* – translating the letter, that is, letter for letter. (Pitta 1985: 25; emphasis in the original)

> Ideally: some literalness, some projection. (Pitta 1985: 26)

Although they refer to the dual conception of translation – 'free translation', 're-creation', 'projection', on the one side, 'word-for-word', 'literalness' on the other – these translators recommend neither free nor literal translation. Instead, they plead for a balance between the two, with a tendency to endorse free translation and overtly criticize literal translation. This is not a very common standpoint either for translators or for scholars, and even less so in 1980s Portugal. Suffice to say that in his 2005 article on 'free translation' for the *Routledge Encyclopedia of Translation Studies*, Douglas Robinson still refers to '[t]he normative assumption that translation is either faithful or free (and that if it's faithful it translates either individual words or individual sentences)', adding '[s]o deep does the ban on free translation run that it is difficult even to begin to think about it in positive, appreciative ways' (2005: 90–1).

In the texts published in the 1990s the notion of faithfulness is not evoked very often; it does not seem to be very central to the way translators explain their tasks. Significantly, in 1994, Alexis Levitin defines translation as compensation: 'If I had to name what it is I do, I would call it *compensation*' (Levitin 1994: 24; emphasis in the original). In 2000, Françoise Laye resorts to metaphors to explain translation which no longer imply mistrust towards the translated text: 'restoring' (*restituindo*), 'bring to the light' (*trazê-lo à luz*), allow the text to 'emigrate' (*emigrar*) (Laye 2000: 346). The conventional imagery is nevertheless still occasionally present in these later texts, revealing a residual suspicion of translation and translators. Laye mentions the intention to 'be totally faithful to those pages' (2000: 346), and Levitin thinks of the target text as dependent on the source text, claiming its right to be naturally 'inexact' (*inexactas*), 'not a replica' (*não-replicatórias*) (1994: 22), and that of the translator to 'cheat' (*alguma batota*) (Levitin 1994: 26), 'compensate for the loss' (*recompensar ... da perda*), 'be irreverent' (*minha irreverência*), 'counteracting the original' (*contrariando o original*) (1994: 27), in order to translate well.

These articles also show that the translators tend to see themselves as part of a triad, along with the reader and the author/his or her text. The author figure is not mentioned as often as one might expect (let us not forget that these translators work with canonical writers, who are generally treated with extreme deference). Although references to the (author's) text are more recurrent, some translators do mention the author:

> We sometimes have the strange feeling, as a translator, of being in communion with the [the poem's] creator, of sharing with him an act of defiance. (Griffin 1982: 22)
>
> Translating means to fuse ourselves: a question of respect. (Pitta 1985: 20)
>
> The longing for identification ... which allows us to *know the other as other*. (Cayron 1985: 36; emphasis in the original)
>
> [T]he respect for the author's work ['faithfulness', one would say]. (Oseki-Dépré 1985: 48)

Listing the words and expressions used to refer to the translator's rapport with the author shows these range from plain 'respect' to complicity: 'communion', 'sharing', 'fuse', 'identification' (which is not unrelated to the fact these translators view translation as a creative activity).

References to the target reader are more frequent than to the author. Griffin and Oseki-Dépré mention their purpose of allowing the reader to experience aesthetical pleasure while reading: '[Translators have the responsibility of translating well, so they can provide] their readers with the satisfaction which can only come from creation' (Griffin 1982: 25); 'the search for a certain "readability," active as much as gratifying for the French reader' (Oseki-Dépré 1985: 48). Bearing in mind a projection of their readers' needs and expectations while translating seems to be a common trait among most of these translators. In fact, the reader works as a beacon, he or she is the ultimate judge, he or she alone is allowed the privilege of determining whether the text is well translated or not:

> (Don't respect the letter of the text so much!), *but don't distance yourself so much from it* [the reader tells the translator]! (Pitta 1985: 26; emphases in the original)

If I did not go far enough, if I went too far or erred in both directions … it is up to the reader to decide. (Levitin 1994: 27)

If he fails this arduous task, the reader will certainly protest: 'My God, how poorly translated!' (Laye 2000: 346)

The main purpose of the translators as they express it in these texts seems to be to serve the reader and the source text, more than pleasing the publishers, the scholars (who are the target readers of their articles in *Colóquio Letras*), or even, one might venture, respecting the author per se.

The previous excerpts illustrate yet another trait common to all these texts: they emphasize the constant questioning of the chosen solutions and a feeling of dissatisfaction with the final result. The translators overtly accept that other solutions may be possible and equally valid and that others may consider that the translation could be improved. It also becomes obvious, through reading their texts, that they are used to being criticized for their options and accept it as a natural consequence of their trade.

In the eight articles there are very few references to practical aspects of the translators' working conditions, and the information we do have access to is heterogeneous. Even so, Jonathan Griffin, Claire Cayron, Pratick Quillier and Françoise Laye all provide information about the process of selecting the texts to be translated. Quillier and Laye were invited by their publishers to translate Fernando Pessoa, a request they interpreted as a sign of recognition. Griffin reveals that he is also sometimes assigned texts to translate, which he does with pleasure (he calls it 'refreshing'). However, it would seem that most of the poems he translated were those he enjoyed so much that he felt compelled to translate them. For Cayron also, it was her interest in the work of Miguel Torga which led her to translate it. She complains about how difficult it was to convince the French publisher to accept Torga's work for publication, because he was not known in France. She describes herself as a freelance translator, saying it frees her of time constraints; she adds that the publisher makes absolutely no changes to her versions of the texts. This is quite useful information for research in translation studies, since there are not many published works providing information about the role publishers play in the translation process. Despite the fact that it is one single source of information on this subject – no other translators mention such topics – and that the translator chose to deal with it, the issues she selected and the way she treated them reveal her own preconceived ideas about the relationship between translator and publisher. The absence of time constraints and the fact that the publisher does not correct her text are conveyed as positive and exceptional.

Boris Schnaiderman, who translates directly from Russian into Portuguese, reveals other sorts of information about his work. He explains that he prepared the first version of a text in Portuguese and then sent it to the famous Brazilian translator and poet Haroldo de Campos (1929–2003), who adapted it. We can also tell from his article that he has the habit of reading his translations to friends and in public readings. From these experiences he gathers suggestions for improving his versions of the texts.

This is not without importance, since most biographical notes on Schnaiderman emphasize the fact that he was one of the first to translate directly from Russian into Portuguese. Working on a collaborative context seems to have made that possible. He also mentions his work as a literature professor, saying that his experience of analysing poems provides him with the tools to interpret the texts and thus become a better translator.

Claire Cayron is the only translator who describes the stages of her translating work in an effort to systematize the process as she experiences it: she first gathered all the data referred to in the text she was going to translate, then she read the rest of the author's books to identify echoes and to better understand the author's view of the world, and finally she started translating (after having prepared a first draft of the translation, she worked on a second version, then a third version, and the final revision). She estimates the average time it takes her to go through each stage: half the time, twenty months, was dedicated to the first draft, whereas the second version took less than a quarter of the total time and much less time was devoted to the remaining tasks. She discusses her different methods and mentions the states of mind and feelings they entail: the first draft is described as craftwork, the second version is defined as audacious and producing a sense of euphoria, whereas the third revision aims at restoring the balance between source and target languages and cultures. It is an interesting account, for it provides insight into the translation process, but one which finds no echo in the other texts.

It is possible that these translators did not see much interest in speaking of the extratextual aspects of their trade. Françoise Laye mentions that the French publisher invited her to translate Pessoa, but does not want to elaborate on that subject, claiming she does not want to linger over technical details that do not help explain the 'hard fight the translator has to face in any of Pessoa's texts' (Laye 2000: 345).

Instead, large parts of these eight testimonies are dedicated to expressing the translators' feelings towards their work. One of the most striking aspects of the texts is that they resort to a metaphorical discourse that stresses the idea of seduction and pleasure used to explain both their reaction to the source text and their sensations while translating. Some translators mention having felt taken by the texts when they first read them. Claire Cayron characterizes translating as 'desire' and 'passion' (1985: 36). Françoise Laye names it 'seduction' (2000: 347) and describes her reaction to the first time she came in contact with the text she translated: 'I was taken by its reading' (2000: 345). Oseki-Dépré reveals she decided to translate a text because of 'the pleasure experienced during its reading' (1985: 43). Griffin provides us with a more detailed description of a similar situation: '[T]here comes a poem which imprisons me, seduces me and keeps me from reading other poems [or even from reading the rest of the poem] before translating into English what I've just read' (1982: 25). And he adds: 'I feel "subjugated" [and start translating] with delicious excitement' (Griffin 1982: 25).

A comparable tone is used by most of the translators to explain how they feel when translating. Griffin describes it as a 'delightful task' (1982: 25), one which he carries out with 'enthusiasm' (1982: 25). Cayron prefers to depict it as 'euphoria' and 'love' (1985: 39) and Pitta compares his pleasures with those of the author, concluding that 'the writer ... does not know such a joy' (1985: 22). Levitin mentions feeling 'gratified' (1994: 25) and 'happy' (1994: 28), whereas Quillier talks of the 'pleasures' and the 'delight' of translating (1998: 95).

This semantic field of pleasure is nevertheless closely followed by a lexical set referring to hardship and often suffering. Translating is considered 'a hard task' (Oseki 1985: 46; Laye 2000: 346). Carlos Pitta, who writes a less objective text, provides a vivid portrayal of this same idea, comparing the translation process to crucifixion (Pitta 1985: 22), to the pains of giving birth, even likening the translator to a 'leper during labour' (Pitta 1985: 27). Levitin portrays how 'the translator purs[ues] his or her combat, fighting the demons of both languages' (1994: 27), and Quillier considers 'maybe the hardship was not in vain' (1998: 95), if the reader feels pleasure when reading the target text. These are clearly not our average professional translators' comments.

Concluding remarks

By publishing these testimonies, *Colóquio Letras* has willingly contributed to changing the status quo of translation, and to reversing what Lawrence Venuti calls the translator's invisibility. These texts, along with the large number of articles on translation (and their content), published by the journal during the second half of the twentieth century – at a time when translation was hardly considered a research field in itself – show a tendency to value and promote translation and indirectly the emergence of translation studies in Portugal.

Referring to some authors' accounts of their creative processes, Hay stresses the fact that '[t]he writer who speaks of his book today is no longer the same one who was at his table yesterday or two days ago' (2007: 22). The same could be said about the translators who, after having translated different texts, prepared these testimonies for publication, endeavouring to provide the reader with some insight into what it is like to translate. In so doing, they made an effort to reflect critically upon their own work and its flaws, risking criticism.

Despite their differences – they come from different cultural backgrounds, translate into several languages and cultures, live in different countries – common traits were sought when reading their testimonies. In fact, their carefully prepared discourse questions a set of widespread assumptions at the time, namely that translation should be faithful to the source text, that the most faithful way of translating is to keep the target text as close as possible to the source text, that the translated text is a mere copy of the source text. These foreign translators openly oppose and dismiss these prevailing beliefs about translation. In doing so, they seem to think differently from their Portuguese peers. Jorge Almeida e Pinho's study clearly shows that Portuguese translators are more prone to state their 'faithfulness to the original text and the author's supposed intentions' (2006: 176) and to adopt an attitude of invisibility vis-à-vis the author's creativity. Although the ten-year span that separates the two sets of articles is not enough to detect a change in the translators' discourse on translation, the truth is that those who wrote in the 1990s no longer felt the need to justify their position on faithfulness, which might suggest a slight change in focus amongst the translator community.

The fact that these translators seldom refer to the external aspects of their trade is also noteworthy. Instead, they opted for an explanation about the way they perceive translation. Their descriptions show a tendency to think of the translation process as a triangular relationship involving mostly translator, text and reader. A relationship which brings them much pleasure, but also much pain.

Notes

1   See http://coloquio.gulbenkian.pt/historia/relatcoloquio_letras.pdf.
2   Unless otherwise noted, all translations are mine.
3   Inês Oseki-Dépré (1977), 'Leitura Finita dum Texto Infinito: "Galáxias" de Haroldo de Campos', *Revista Colóquio Letras*, 37: 24–33.
4   Carlos Pitta wrote three other texts for the journal, all of which were book reviews: (1986), 'Recensão Crítica a "Ficção", de António Ramos Rosa', *Revista Colóquio Letras*, 94: 120–1; (1987), 'Recensão Crítica a "Tronos e Dominações", de João Miguel Fernandes Jorge', *Revista Colóquio Letras*, 96: 109–11; (1987), 'Recensão Crítica a "Para Não Falar", de Helder Moura Pereira', *Revista Colóquio Letras*, 98: 117.
5   Patrick Quillier (1990), 'Os Címbalos de Pessoa', *Revista Colóquio Letras*, 117/118: 120–8; (1999), 'Fictions du postlude. Poèmes im-possibles en hommage à José Saramago, à propos de son livre *L'Année de la morte de Ricardo Reis*', *Revista Colóquio Letras*, 151/152: 293–7; (2009), 'Hétérodoxie, hétérophonie, hétéronymie', *Revista Colóquio Letras*, 171: 133–41.

References

Almeida e Pinho, Jorge (2006), *O Escritor Invisível. A Tradução tal como É Vista pelos Tradutores Portugueses*, Lisboa: Quidnovi.
Anonymous (1980), 'Jean R. Longland e a Poesia Portuguesa', *Revista Colóquio Letras*, 57: 103.
Anonymous (1982), 'Poetas Traduzidos: Eugénio, Cesariny e Outros', *Revista Colóquio Letras*, 65: 101.
Bassnett, Susan (2002), *Translation Studies*, London and New York: Routledge.
Bassnett, Susan and André Lefevere (eds) (1990), *Translation, History, Culture*, London: Pinter.
Bellemin-Noël, Jean (1982), 'Avant-texte et lecture pyschanalytique', in Louis Hay and Péter Nagy (eds), *Avant-texte, texte, après-texte. Actes du colloque international de textologie à Mátrafüred (Hongrie), 13–16 octobre 1978*, 161–5, Budapest: Akadémiai Kiadó.
Cayron, Claire (1985), 'Itinerário duma Tradução. A Edição Francesa da Obra de Miguel Torga', *Revista Colóquio Letras*, 87: 33–42.
Chesterman, Andrew (2009), 'The Name and Nature of Translator Studies', *Hermes – Journal of Language and Communication Studies*, 42: 13–22.
Durand-Bogaert, Fabienne (2014), 'Ce que la génétique dit, la traduction le fait', *GENESIS. Revue internationale de critique génétique*, 38: 7–10.
Faria, Dominique (2013), 'La revue *Colóquio Letras* et la mise en valeur de la traduction au Portugal', *Atelier de traduction. Dossier: la critique des traductions II*, 20: 95–108.

Griffin, Jonathan (1982), 'Reflexões dum Tradutor sobre os Problemas da Versão Literária', *Revista Colóquio Letras*, 66: 21–7.
Harding, Sue-Ann and Ovidi Carbonell Cortès (eds) (2018), *The Routledge Handbook of Translation and Culture*, New York: Routledge.
Hay, Louis (2007), 'Critique génétique et théorie littéraire: quelques remarques', in Paul Grifford and Marion Schmid (eds), *La Création en acte. Devenir de la critique génétique*, 13–28, Amsterdam and New York: Rodopi.
Laye, Françoise (2000), 'O "Livro do as" de Fernando Pessoa … ou o Desassossego do Tradutor', *Revista Colóquio Letras*, 155/156: 345–7.
Levitin, Alexis (1994), 'O Trabalho do Tradutor: Apologia de um Pragmatista', *Revista Colóquio Letras*, 132/133: 21–8.
Magalhães, Francisco José (1996), *Da Tradução Profissional em Portugal*, Lisboa: Edições Colibri.
Munday, Jeremy (2015), 'The Role of Archival and Manuscript Research in the Investigation of Translator Decision-Making', in Maureen Ehrensberger-Dow, Susanne Göpferich and Sharon O'Brien (eds), *Interdisciplinarity in Translation and Interpreting Process Research*, 127–40, Amsterdam and Philadelphia: John Benjamins.
Oseki-Dépré, Inês (1985), 'A Tradução Francesa das "Primeiras Estórias" de João Guimarães Rosa', *Revista Colóquio Letras*, 87: 43–50.
Pitta, Carlos (1985), '"Traductio": Questões de Vivência', *Revista Colóquio Letras*, 87: 20–31.
Quillier, Patrick (1998), 'Douze poèmes de Fernando Pessoa, dont quelques inédits, destinés à la collection Pléiade', *Revista Colóquio Letras*, 147/148: 94–5.
Robinson, Douglas (2005), 'Free Translation', in Mona Baker (ed.), *Routledge Encyclopedia of Translation Studies*, 87–90, London and New York: Routledge.
Schnaiderman, Boris (1980), '"Hybris" da Tradução, "Hybris" da Análise', *Revista Colóquio Letras*, 57: 5–12.
Scott, Clive (2006), 'Translating the Literary: Genetic Criticism, Text Theory and Poetry', in Susan Bassnett and Peter Bush (eds), *The Translator as Writer*, 106–18, London and New York: Continuum.
Seruya, Teresa (2015), 'The Project of a Critical Bibliography of Translated Literature and Its Relevance for Translation Studies in Portugal', in Rita Bueno Maia, Marta Pacheco Pinto and Sara Ramos Pinto (eds), *How Peripheral Is the Periphery? Translating Portugal Back and Forth*, 21–30, Newcastle upon Tyne: Cambridge Scholars Publishing.
Sousa Rebelo, Luís (1982), 'João Almeida Flor, Monólogos Dramáticos por Robert Browning', *Revista Colóquio Letras*, 70: 76–8.
Toury, Guideon (1995), *Descriptive Translation Studies and Beyond*, Amsterdam and Philadelphia: John Benjamins.

10

Mapping context through epitext: Gregory Rabassa's writings and his translations of Lobo Antunes's works

Marisa Mourinha
Center for Comparative Studies, University of Lisbon

Introduction

The aim of this chapter is to illustrate in what way translators' epitexts (Genette 1997: 3)[1] can be useful to understand the context in which translations are made: in this case, we focus on one specific translator, Gregory Rabassa, paying particular attention to his translations of the Portuguese-language author António Lobo Antunes.

Our theoretical apparatus stems from translation theories which fall into the framework of what came to be known as 'the sociological turn': these are theories which build on Bourdieu's approaches to art[2] and that adopt a sociological view of culture (e.g. Casanova 2004). By doing so, they counter the tendency to see literature as a fundamentally isolated phenomenon, with its own set of rules, which differs from the rest of human activities, and places it in its context, where implications and constraints are not only of cultural but also anthropological, sociological and economic nature. In this regard, their views converge with fundamental points of the Polysystem Theory, to whose proponent the '"text" is no longer the only, and not necessarily for all purposes the most important, facet, or even product, of this system' (Even-Zohar 1990: 33).

This chapter originated in a wider study of the English translations of António Lobo Antunes. While examining the translations of this Portuguese author, one name stood out, in spite of the proverbial invisibility of translators: that of Gregory Rabassa, teacher, scholar and celebrated translator. Our research here rests mostly on the academic papers written by or on Rabassa, and is complemented by interviews, press reviews, his own memoir and other writings that mention his work as a translator. What we hope to illustrate with this chapter is in what way those documents help to contextualize Rabassa's translations of António Lobo Antunes.

This chapter has been written within the context of an ongoing research as a PhD candidate, with the FCT grant PD/BD/135207/2017.

The translator: Gregory Rabassa

Born in 1922, Rabassa had a first-hand experience of the evolution of the profession of literary translation throughout the second half of the twentieth century. He not only was a part of it, but is considered to have had great responsibility in what came to be known as the Latin-American boom (Guzmán 2010: 142). One of the most influential cultural agents in the field of translation in the twentieth century, he would not begin to translate professionally until the mid-1960s – and 'by chance' (Guzmán 2010: 144).

He was a full-time instructor at Columbia College when he was invited to collaborate in *Odyssey*, a literary review a few colleagues were putting together, 'as the editor in search of new writing in Spanish and Portuguese … I found a lot of things and, of course, they had to be translated. That was where it all started' (Rabassa 2005: 24). This experience paved the way, in this translator's life, for the next life-changing moment or, as he puts it, for serendipity to strike again, in the shape of a phone call from Sara Blackburn at Pantheon Books, inviting him to translate a book by a (then) young Argentinian writer. It was Julio Cortázar's *Rayuela*. Without having read the whole book, he submitted the first chapters to the publisher:

> Both Sara and Julio liked my version so I signed a contract to do my first translation of a long work for a commercial publisher. It was the start of a career I hadn't sought after and the beginning of a beautiful friendship with the incomparable Julio. True to my original instincts (or perhaps my inherent laziness and impatience) and to the subsequent amazement of those to whom I confessed my hubristic ploy, I translated the book as I read it for the first time. (Rabassa 2005: 27)

Still, with that very first work, he won the first National Book Award for Translation. This was the first but by no means the last prize of Rabassa's career. But much of his success as a translator is due to his rendition of a significant work by an author who achieved iconic status within the context of Spanish-American literature: Gabriel García Márquez's *Cien años de soledad*.[3] The book's success and the continuous praise of Rabassa's translation – among them, the author's, who declared to prefer, on several passages, Rabassa's version to his own (García Márquez 1982) – greatly contributed to establish his reputation as a literary translator.

This is what can be considered a consecrated translator,[4] whose choices are respected enough to influence reception. As 'one of the world's greatest translators' (Bassnett 2011: 18), it should come as no surprise that his work became, in turn, an object of academic studies. The most relevant of them is María Constanza Guzmán's work, which includes her doctoral thesis of 2006, later published in book form (2010), not without originating several articles, focusing mostly on Rabassa's role in the building of the Latin-American canon. Also noteworthy is an article by Bolaños Cuéllar (2011), in which he condenses Rabassa's views on translation, and applies them to the analysis of several translations of *Cien años de soledad*, including Rabassa's rendition.

Rabassa in context

Clifford E. Landers, once a professor of Political Science at the New Jersey City University, is himself the author of a large number of translations from the Portuguese, having rendered into English works by names such as Lobo Antunes, Jorge Amado or Rubem Fonseca. In 2001, he published a work of his own, in which he reflects on his career as a literary translator, sharing strategies and advice with those who are interested in following the same path. In it, he mentions Rabassa repeatedly (pages ix, 7, 14, 25, etc.). But one reference in particular is of interest to our present purpose: a passage in which Landers describes literary translation as a labour of love, specifically because it is either underpaid or not paid at all. After listing a series of reasons why one might undertake this occupation, he writes:

> There are many reasons for doing literary translation, but ultimately only you can decide which ones impel you. As for money, it has been omitted from these deliberations because if it's your primary motivation for doing literary translation, you should choose another field. … While it's a cliché that literary translation is a labour of love, basically it is. … (At this writing, even the most prolific of living translators of Spanish- and Portuguese-language literature, Gregory Rabassa, … has not given up his university day job.) (Landers 2001: 6)

This is relevant as it provides insider information on what it is to be a literary translator in the United States. It is quite telling that Landers's comment from 2001 corroborates what Rabassa himself had let us know back in 1974 when, in his paper 'If This Be Treason: Translation and Its Possibilities', after a series of cautious remarks, he finally decrees: 'It is time for at least one definitive statement about translation: it is impossible to make a handsome living from it' (Rabassa 1974: 37–8). That no significant improvement has been reached in this respect can be inferred from his account of the evolution that took place, during his lifetime, in the world of literary translation, from the times he got paid a flat fee to those in which he got his share of the royalties when sales were high – too late for him, though, as his bestselling works were those he translated at the very beginning of his career (cf. Rabassa 2005: 93–4).

As Rabassa puts it in the interview he gave Guzmán: 'Even though the situation is getting a little better, I don't think translation is lucrative here in the States either' (Guzmán 2010: 144). Landers's testimony may also be useful in helping us understand why, as he points out, 'college faculties tend to be over-represented among literary translators' (Landers 2001: 166). Reading about both these translators' experiences, we come to the realization that it is unlikely that one with the necessary skills to be a literary translator will be found – or sought – outside academia; because even if the world is not devoid of curious, cultivated people with a personal taste for literature, publishers are likely to turn to academia when in search of a translator.

Since translators' prefaces are a rarity (McRae 2012), the advantages of having access to this kind of peritext are substantial, as they make explicit underlying factors which end up having decisive results in the translation process. Rabassa's writings not only clearly tell us how he worked, they also provide an array of valuable information, most of which can be obtained by reading between the lines: Rabassa's Pantheon story, for instance, may be read as an example of how translators were drafted. Both his memoir and Landers's practical guide supply first-hand testimonials regarding the translators' working conditions. What for them may be but a casual remark is likely to provide translation researchers with the very answers they were chasing after, or at least to prod them onto the right direction. This was the case with the examples above, in which Rabassa explains how he was drafted as an translator, what his qualifications were, how much experience he had until then and how he was financially compensated for translating books that ended up being bestsellers, or by authors who went on to win a Nobel Prize.[5]

Rabassa's views on translation

As a teacher and scholar, Rabassa was also in a position to express his own ideas about translation, which he did, in texts ranging from the strictly academic to the autobiographical: in the early 1970s, he participated in a collective volume published by the P.E.N. American Center, with an article named 'The Ear in Translation'; 'If This Be Treason: Translation and Its Possibilities' came out in *American Scholar* in 1974, and was later republished, along with two other papers, in a volume edited by William Frawley (1984). His 1989 paper 'No Two Snowflakes Are Alike: Translator as Metaphor' served as the basis for Lawrence Venuti's criticism of the self-effacing he considered recurrent among literary translators, using Rabassa as an example for his thesis and accusing Rabassa of having that romantic conception of authorship Venuti seeks to denounce (Venuti 1992: 3).

If Venuti's inferences can rightly be drawn from that 1989 article, they are not entirely fair: while not his first, this paper was also not his last; Rabassa (deceased in 2016) continued to translate, to give interviews and to write on translation-related issues. It would be inaccurate to say that Rabassa's views on translation have drastically changed throughout his life and career; but they have been finely tuned. In the only book he ever authored, *If This Be Treason: Translation and Its Dyscontents* (2005),[6] Rabassa takes up many of the arguments, metaphors and even examples of his previous writings, and illustrates them with real-life stories of his relationships with the authors and works he has translated. Dubbed by the publisher *A Memoir*, it consists of a summary of Rabassa's reflections on the subject of translation, and it provides extensive and otherwise unavailable insights into his lifelong career, be it as a translator or as an academic. In it, the author narrates his experience with every author he had translated so far.

If there is a common ground, a note which can be found throughout Rabassa's production on the subject, it is that of 'impossibility': in his 1989 paper 'No Two Snowflakes Are Alike', he begins by challenging the concept of equivalence, or at least its applicability to the field of translation. This paper has as a subtitle, 'Translation as Metaphor', and in it the author argues that not only translation proper but also any operation in which language is involved is necessarily, and by its very nature, inexact: 'A word is nothing but a metaphor for an object or, in some cases, for another word' (Rabassa 1989: 1).

Later, in his work from 2005 *If This Be Treason: Translation and Its Dyscontents*, that very conception would be formulated in more radical terms: translation is impossible. The keywords of his theoretical itinerary range from the more consensual terms of those first articles published or re-published during the 1980s, such as *transformation* or *adaptation* (Rabassa 1989: 2), or even *transposition* (Rabassa 1984: 22), to the final provocation, patent in the very title of his 2005 retrospective work, *If This Be Treason*.[7] As he stated in an interview to *The New York Times*: 'My thesis in the book is that translation is impossible ... People expect reproduction, but you can't turn a baby chick into a duckling. The best you can do is get close to it' (Bast 2004).

From this point of view, the keyword would be *approximate*, but the fact is that every critical writing by Rabassa challenges classical and quaint notions such as *correspondence* and *fidelity*. As far as the accusation of treason goes, rather than contesting it, what Rabassa does is to reduce it to absurdity, by putting translation in a context of cultural operations in which every element is anything but univocal: 'Words are treacherous things, much more than any translator could ever be' (Rabassa 2005: 4).

Another very strong position of his is the insistence on the fact that translation is a collaborative work. To some extent, this can be considered a corollary to his *impossibility* axiom: insofar as translation as imitation is impossible, the task at hand will necessarily involve mediation between the two terms; in a more simplistic analysis, the translator must connect two languages, but the truth of the matter is, and this is what turns it from tricky into impossible, the translator must establish contact between two worlds of meaning – and, in literary expression, because of its very nature, meaning is everything but univocal. 'This means that the translator must be close in one way or another to the writer' (Rabassa 1974: 31).

While in 1974 Rabassa mused on the notions of reading and writing, in 2005 he described his task as one that had everything to gain from actual interaction with the author. In his case, since he translated almost exclusively contemporary authors (the only exception is Machado de Assis), this was indeed an option.[8] It often came with a bonus: translators who, like Rabassa, translate into a central language have, on occasion, the possibility of actually discussing translation choices with the author, because chances are they have some knowledge of the target language, making their collaborative efforts even more productive. His exchange with Julio Cortázar was particularly rich, partly because of the author's proficiency in the target language.[9] In any case, Rabassa made it a point to consult with the author in matters concerning the understanding of the source text, whenever he considered it necessary.

Rabassa's translations of António Lobo Antunes

The case of the Portuguese author Lobo Antunes emerges as an exception to the rule: even though he personally met Rabassa, he had little interest in discussing translation (Rabassa 2005: 144). This should come as no surprise for anyone who has read the testimony left by French translator Carlos Battista (Cabral 2003: 382), in which the same idea is conveyed: Lobo Antunes seems to be hard to involve in the translation process.

Rabassa made a habit of having a close working relationship with the authors he translated, whenever possible – even if it means getting creative, as was the case with the Cuban writer José Lezama Lima, with whom Rabassa managed to put together an intricate epistolary network, going through Paris and using his good friend Cortázar as a middleman (Rabassa 2005: 109). And yet, this same individual, having translated three books by Lobo Antunes and having met him in person on more than one occasion, casually remarks in his 2005 memoir that he had no saying in the choice of the title for the English version (*The Return of the Caravels*), and goes on to comment on the choice as it had been made by the publisher, for practical, editorial reasons. Rabassa seems to ignore the scandal which surrounded the Portuguese title *As Naus*.

The Portuguese novel which came out in 1988 was to be called *O Regresso das Caravelas* (*The Return of the Caravels*); however, due to a copyright mishap, its title had to be changed at the last minute – after the last minute, to be precise, since book covers had already been printed. The publication had to be postponed, because someone else had, meanwhile, registered that name, and the novel was hastily renamed *As Naus* (literally, *The Carracks*) (Pedrosa 1988). And this is the reason why so many foreign translations (it happens in English, but also in French, German and other languages) bear the name that the original Portuguese novel could not have. The fact that Rabassa seems to be unaware of this makes us think that the author–translator relationship did not go as far as it did with some other authors: it seems as though they never even discussed the title.

Rabassa's account of how he came into contact with Lobo Antunes's prose discloses the story of how his works entered the United States. As the translator reports, he had first heard of the Portuguese author through a former student of his – Elisabeth Lowe, who is responsible for the very first translation of Lobo Antunes.[10] Years later, he was approached by Thomas Colchie, Antunes's agent at the time, who invited Rabassa to translate one of his works, leaving the choice up to him: 'I looked over the ones in question and settled on *Fado Alexandrino*' (Rabassa 2005: 143).

The longest book in Lobo Antunes's production so far,[11] *Fado Alexandrino* depicts a detailed fresco of the Portuguese society in the years before, during and after the revolution of 1974. Published by Grove Press in 1990, it was met with praising reviews. Ariel Dorfman, an authoritative critic who wrote for *The New York Times*, not only showed knowledge of Lobo Antunes's previous translated work but wrote laudably of this one. Referring only fleetly to 'Gregory Rabassa's splendid translation', he praises intensely both of the author's translated novels, but insists that *Fado Alexandrino* is 'more difficult' (Dorfman 1990).

This kind of review may not be the most effective way to help sell a translated work in a context that is knowingly hostile to translation as such. Dorfman's stand, though, is not an uncommon one: Chad Post, in an extremely complimentary piece in which he is 'trying to convince an imaginary reader why he/she should invest his/her mental energy and time into this particular quasi-obscure, complicated novelist', mentions the 'strange stream-of-consciousness style', of 'a "difficult" Portuguese author whose books probably don't sell all that well' (Post 2011). Even Rabassa admits: 'Lobo Antunes belongs to that large array of writers I have done who can be called "difficult"' (2005: 143).

In his memoir, he recalls the collaboration with the writer's wife: 'With the translation of *Fado Alexandrino* I was aided enormously by Maria João who went over it checking every dot and title since António had had done with it and told me to do it in any way I saw fit' (Rabassa 2005: 144). The translation's frontispiece would acknowledge this, stating the translator's 'heartfelt thanks'. What Rabassa's book does not tell us is whose decision it was to publish the novels, and more specifically those by Lobo Antunes, with no paratext whatsoever. *Fado Alexandrino* includes, at the end, two short sentences 'About the author': 'António Lobo Antunes is the author of seven novels. He currently lives in Lisbon' (Antunes 1990: 499). Since the whole novel revolves around a period of recent Portuguese history, unknown to the average reader, providing a little more context could have been an asset.

The same problem presents itself even more severely in the second work[12] Rabassa translated by this author, *The Return of the Caravels*, an allegory which juxtaposes two time frames and two sets of historical events which are even more obscure to the general public: the golden age of the overseas expansion from the sixteenth century and the collapse of the colonial empire in the 1970s. The book challenges much of Portugal's historical mythology and becomes utterly hermetical without any paratext. And yet, that is precisely what the English translation offers. This lack of paratextual elements is noticeable enough for one reviewer to take a stand.

If translations are seldom assessed by reviewers, this is partly due to one rather obvious limitation: the average critic neither knows the source language nor has had access to the original. Michael Pye from *The New York Times* is an exception – actually, the only one we came across:[13] he not only knew Portuguese, but was at least to some extent learned on Portuguese history and culture; enough to claim that Lobo Antunes, who is 'profoundly Portuguese', 'has a particular place and a history':

> It is so particular that if you're not Portuguese you may need a little help – for example, to recognize the Luis who's lumbered with his father's body, sitting at a cafe table writing his 'octaves', as Camões, poet of the 16th century, composer of eight-verse stanzas that tell of storms and jousts and a distant Isle of Love. In Gregory Rabassa's translation, the help never comes. Antunes makes the reader work at the text, a hard but pleasurable business, and Rabassa actually makes things more difficult. (Pye 2002)

If the reader of *Fado Alexandrino* might need supporting information on a regime and a revolution little known outside the Portuguese-speaking world, the reader of *The Return of the Caravels* even more so: 'Here he has boldly blended the homecoming of veterans and colonists from Africa with the return leg of Vasco da Gama's voyage to India. Cervantes and Camões both appear out of the past in a modern setting' (Rabassa 2005: 143). Pye is Portuguese-savvy enough to discuss both the novel and the translation on an even footing with Rabassa – which, as far as we know, he never did. But he left very harsh remarks in his 7 April 2002 piece:[14]

154 *Genetic Translation Studies*

> An odd selection of ordinary Portuguese words goes untranslated – for lobster, clothespin, buffalo. And a selection of odd words goes unexplained. Does everyone else know that a vernier has to do with an astronomical instrument? That an aphtha is a cold sore? There's an impossible pun when congers (as in conger eels) pluck 'sardine flowers from balconies with their teeth', since 'sardine flowers' could have to do with fishing for sardines; but English speakers might not guess that *sardinheiras da varanda* are less surreal than they seem. They can only be balcony geraniums.
>
> The effect is of a translation in which you are never quite sure if you are concentrating furiously on Antunes's genius or Rabassa's problems. (Pye 2002)

His list goes on, and it includes at least two different sets of problems.[15] One corresponds to what Guzmán will identify as criticism for being 'too foreign' or 'not smooth enough' (2010: 83) that some impute to Rabassa's renditions. But there is more to it, in this particular case: the 'odd selection' of untranslated 'ordinary Portuguese words' (Pye 2002) is indeed puzzling. On the other hand, the 'odd words' that Pye complains about 'go[ing] unexplained' are English words, that he reckons too high-brow for the average reader – and, more importantly, introducing an asymmetry in relation to the source text. This would converge with the results of Bolaños Cuéllar's analysis of *One Hundred Years of Solitude*.

According to Bolaños Cuéllar, Rabassa's translation of García Márquez (that had caused such a positive impression on the Colombian author) is *better* than the original – if by *better* we mean 'of a higher register of language'. Rabassa's style is such that, when translating García Márquez's relatively plain prose, he tends to use calques, falling back into a Latin-rooted vocabulary, instead of a more current lexicon of Anglo-Saxon origin.[16] This kind of behaviour that could be disastrous if undertook by an unexperienced translator may be what earned Rabassa his fame. As he knows only too well, a translator is also a writer.

Considering Bolaños Cuéllar's study and Pye's review, one could extrapolate that Rabassa would have behaved in relation to Lobo Antunes's Portuguese prose as he had done with that of García Márquez. The accusation does not stand completely, since Lobo Antunes's style is far from *plain* – certainly a lot less straightforward than García Márquez's. His vocabulary ranges from the popular, on the verge of dialect, at times, to the highly educated, or erudite, depending on the narrative voice in question. But what does happen in *The Return of the Caravels* is that Rabassa's by then distinctive style shows through Lobo Antunes's narrative. Whether both are compatible or not, may be up for discussion, but this would account for the 'odd words' that Pye says lack explanation.

The other set of issues he mentions, though, are of a different nature: foreign words that are left untranslated could be in fact the symptom of a foreignization strategy. But what we are faced with is, indeed, an odd selection of words. Toponyms are mostly left untouched, as they should, since there is no translation for nearly all of them; but for Lisbon, the existing English word is used,[17] as is the case with Tagus (the *Tejo* river, in Portuguese). On page 87 of the translation, Vasco da Gama produces a 'poker deck', instead of the original 'baralho da sueca', since 'sueca' is a popular Portuguese card game unknown to the rest of the world (and, incidentally, by no means similar to poker). But on pages 7 and 8 of the translated text, an indeed 'odd selection of ordinary Portuguese words goes untranslated' (Pye 2002): on page 7, '*agora veja là*'[18] (in italic, unlike the original, and with the wrong accent; every one of the following instances reproduces the use of italics in the English translation, none of which are present in the Portuguese edition), a line of direct speech woven into a torrent of several simultaneous streams of consciousness, but translatable as something that in the context appears to be between a warning and a threat, loosely ranging from 'don't screw up' to 'it's up to you', or more simply from 'don't you forget' to 'mind you'; the next page features the unexplainable 'with the clothes basket *das molas*', corresponding to 'cesta das molas da roupa' in the original, which is a prosaic 'basket of clothespins' and, a little further down the same page, another italic stating '*à torreira*', an idiom that conveys the idea of being 'under the very warm sun'. It is rather hard to explain why an experienced translator would leave in the original language expressions such as these. But it looks more like insufficient proofreading than like controversial translation choices. Michael Pye may have had the same impression, since he concludes: 'The rockiness is shameful, since one more draft could have cured it' (2002).

Rabassa's memoir was published in 2005, as he was beginning to translate the third book by Lobo Antunes. We have no information whether or not he read or was in any way informed by book reviews; one can only speculate that he did, even though he does not seem to reply directly either to critics or to potential readers of Lobo Antunes. When commenting on the difficulty of the author's prose, he states:

> [M]y advice to the readers is simply to read, approach him once again as though he were Góngora or as though they were listening to one of Beethoven's late quartets through sheer hearing. These problems or difficulties (I'm not sure which they are, and there is a difference) show up in an even more severe form in the second novel of his that I did, *The Return of the Caravels*. (Rabassa 2005: 143)

If it is unlikely that he is answering to Pye's remarks (opposing Antunes's genius and Rabassa's problems), the way Rabassa refers to his performance echoes Christiane Nord's model of text analysis in translation (Nord 1991), in which she distinguishes translation problems (that are objective, pertaining to the text) and difficulties (subjective, dwelling in the translator). He chooses, though, not to decide whether the fault is his or the text's. One recurring note in this book is his leaving the verdict up to the reader. The accusation of treason that is formulated on the very title (*If This Be Treason*) will never be entirely dealt with. It is, at first, met with the defying mockery of Patrick Henry's quote: 'If this be treason, make the most of it' (Rabassa 2005: 3); and later, on the very last chapter, the author dissolves the knot of the imputation of treason by proposing a 'Scots verdict: not proven' (Rabassa 2005: 189), leaving it up to the reader to judge.

To sum up, we can say that Rabassa's experience of translating the Portuguese author António Lobo Antunes did not quite follow the script which the translator states he was likely to adopt. Concerning the first book, *Fado Alexandrino*, we know that all the help he had was provided by the then wife of the writer. In his memoir,

Rabassa comments on the style and the plot of the second book he translated, *The Return of the Caravels*, but does not mention any exchange between him and the writer. And, concerning the third (and last) translation by Rabassa of Lobo Antunes, *What Can I Do When Everything's On Fire?*, we know from an interview the author gave to Alessandro Cassin that 'Rabassa did not ask a single question' (2008). One can only speculate that the translator, after the initial resistance he felt on the part of the writer, simply decided to do without his assistance.

It seems likely that some event or chain of events hindered the end result of *The Return of the Caravels* during the publishing process (maybe not the translation itself, but the proofreading), the shortest of the books Lobo Antunes ever wrote – but also a very peculiar one, with its strong allegorical dimension, an experiment the author was never to repeat.

In *Fado Alexandrino*, the reader may stumble, on occasion, upon an (oddly) untranslated word, like the *snook* served for dinner, mysteriously left in Portuguese ('robalo', 292), giving the impression that the menu is more exotic than it actually was; but it is a rather isolated instance in a very long book, in which the biggest difficulty would be to render the language of war veterans – not much of a challenge for Rabassa.

What Can I Do When Everything's On Fire?, which was praised by the translator's 'pitch-perfect ear for colloquial speech' (Manrique 2008), belongs to a later phase of the author's career in which his works become, somewhat paradoxically, harder to read but easier to translate: while the characters become less clear to discern, their voices intertwined without warning (granting the author the epithet of 'polyphonic'), the speech itself is often of a lower register. Hence, there is no longer the temptation to use high-brow words which are obscure to the average English-speaking reader, and the translator is faced with the main challenge of rendering different voices with adequate register and vocabulary. And Rabassa does this, all in all, successfully: the translation does a good job at conveying the various intertwining threads of stream-of-consciousness monologues. For instance, 'aventesma'[19] (292) becomes 'spook' (264); 'saudoso pai, saudoso esposo'[20] (213) gives way to 'beloved father, beloved husband' (190); 'já se sabe'[21] (233) is successfully translated with 'of course' (199); and, just to mention one more out of the many possible examples, the doctor's question 'Que raio de árvore é isto?' (212) becomes 'What the hell kind of tree is that?'[22] (189).

Closing remarks

As a conclusion, we may say that having access to Rabassa's writings, and to others' studies on his activity, has contributed significantly not only to better understand his work but also to define the context in which he developed it. Rabassa's work as a translator is thus complemented by his reflections on the matter, and this kind of epitext ends up providing very useful information, if not directly on the translation under analysis, undoubtedly on the translator himself and his methods and circumstances, in a way that mere analysis of translations could never do.

From Rabassa's epitexts, much can be discovered about his training as well – way beyond what his resumé would tell: for instance, his discussion of the translation of the *Aeneid* (Rabassa 1989: 6) gives us an idea of the weight of classical culture in his education; we know from an interview how he was always able to speak five of the many languages he had learned in his lifetime (Bast 2004). From his interviews, his memoir and his academic papers, what stands out is an erudition, a preparation and a resourcefulness that may help understand his success as a translator – even because, as Rabassa (1974: 35) himself would tell us, most opinions issued on the quality of translations judge the writing rather than the translating skills.

Notes

1   Genette's concept of 'paratext' can be divided into two sub-categories, in which peritext is a part of the book itself (including the cover and its design), and epitext includes everything else around but outside the book – from press reviews to interviews with the author (or anyone involved in the creative process, for that matter), as well as letters, diaries and, as in the case at hand, academic papers as well.
2   Seminal, in this case, are the works *Les Règles de l'art: genèse et structure du champ littéraire* (1992) and *Les Structures sociales de l'économie* (2000).
3   *One Hundred Years of Solitude* (Harper & Row, 1970). Advised by Cortázar, García Márquez waited for three years for a break in Rabassa's already full schedule, as he absolutely wanted him to translate his novel (Rabassa 2005: 94).
4   As Casanova (2004: 135) puts it.
5   Miguel Ángel Asturias was awarded the Nobel Prize for literature shortly after the publication of Rabassa's first translation of *Mulata de tal* (1967); other laureates include Gabriel Márquez in 1982 and Mario Vargas Llosa in 2010.
6   Guzmán (2010) will argue that Venuti is not entirely right, building greatly on material from this memoir that came out in 2005.
7   The book's title is borrowed from Rabassa's 1974 *American Scholar*'s article (both have the same title and different subtitles).
8   Incidentally, Clifford Landers concurs with Rabassa, regarding the importance of the contact with the author (cf. Landers 2001: 86).
9   An Argentinian born in Brussels, Cortázar (1914–84) lived in Switzerland, Spain and France, besides Argentina. Famous for his novels and short stories, he started out as a translator, having translated from the English and French languages, authors such as Allan Poe, Defoe, Chesterton, Yourcenar or Gide.
10 António Lobo Antunes (1979), *Os Cus de Judas*, Lisboa: Vega. Translated by Elisabeth Lowe as *South of Nowhere* (New York: Random House, 1983), and subsequently translated by Margaret Jull Costa as *The Land at the End of the World* (New York: W. W. Norton, 2011).
11 The standard size for this series, 14 cm × 21 cm, had to be extended into 15.5 cm × 23.5 cm, so as to make the novel fit in the 500 pages of this edition.
12 *As Naus*, from 1988, came out in 2002 under the title *The Return of the Caravels*, as mentioned above.
13 Pye's article was the only case in which the translation as such is discussed; there are countless instances mentioning Rabassa's name in celebratory terms, without specifying translation choices. Jaime Manrique, in a *Washington Post* piece on *What Can I Do When Everything's On Fire?*, goes as far as to say '[h]is latest novel, *What*

Can I Do When Everything's on Fire?, translated into English with a pitch-perfect ear for colloquial speech by the legendary Gregory Rabassa, is another dissection of Portugal's sick soul' (Manrique 2008).

14 This review brings inevitably to mind Rabassa's recurrent reference to Sara Blackburn's character 'Professor Horrendo', dreaded and unpopular, however often right in his claims (Rabassa 1974: 36).
15 Actually, one could consider three sets of problems, the third being translation errors in a strict sense.
16 'In fact, Rabassa did "enhance" the Spanish original by using an overall stylistic strategy. Whenever it was possible to render a Spanish word by two choices, either a word of Anglo-Saxon origin or another one from a Latin root, Rabassa tended to choose always the lexical entry from Latin origin, and in case there is another choice also from Latin origin that is not similar to the Spanish original, he would generally prefer the similar one. The immediate effect of these lexical choices by Rabassa is that the English text reads with a higher stylistic register when compared with the original Spanish' (Bolaños Cuéllar 2011: 122).
17 The English word is used, but subject to an adaptation: *Lixbon*, in order to mimic the original's *Lixboa*, a quaint orthography of the word that the author uses as an archaization strategy.
18 Literally, 'now see here'.
19 Literally 'ghost', it is used as an insult; the implied meaning is that someone's physical appearance is enough to cause fear.
20 While 'pai' and 'esposo' are indeed 'Father' and 'husband', 'saudoso' is the adjective for 'saudade', the Portuguese word which won the fame of being untranslatable; 'saudade' is a single word to convey the meaning, common to most languages, of 'missing someone'; hence, 'saudoso' would be the one who is 'missed'; in this context, though, Rabassa's solution is more adequate.
21 An idiom, which literally means 'one already knows'.
22 While the rest of the sentence is translated quite literally, the adaptation required here had to do with 'raio', 'lightning', a quaint and rather mild imprecation which we would agree that functionally corresponds to the English use of 'hell' in this context.

References

Antunes, António Lobo (1983), *Fado Alexandrino*, Lisboa: Dom Quixote.
Antunes, António Lobo (1988), *As Naus*, Lisboa: Dom Quixote.
Antunes, António Lobo (1990), *Fado Alexandrino*, trans. Gregory Rabassa, New York: Grove Press.
Antunes, António Lobo (2001), *Que Farei Quando Tudo Arde?* Lisboa: Dom Quixote.
Antunes, António Lobo (2002), *The Return of the Caravels*, trans. Gregory Rabassa, New York: Grove Press.
Antunes, António Lobo (2008), *What Can I Do When Everything Is On Fire?*, trans. Gregory Rabassa, New York and London: W. W. Norton.
Asturias, Miguel Angel (1967), *The Mulatta and Mr. Fly*, trans. Gregory Rabassa, London: Peter Owen.
Bassnett, Susan (2011), *Reflections on Translation*, Bristol: Multilingual Matters.

Bast, Andrew (2004), 'A Translator's Long Journey, Page by Page', *The New York Times*, 25 May.
Blanco, María Luisa (2002), *Conversas com António Lobo Antunes*, Lisboa: Dom Quixote.
Bolaños Cuéllar, Sergio (2011), 'Gregory Rabassa's Views on Translation', *Forma y Función*, 24 (1): 107–29.
Bourdieu, Pierre (1992), *Les Règles de l'art: genèse et structure du champ littéraire*, Paris: Seuil.
Bourdieu, Pierre (2000), *Les Structures sociales de l'économie*, Paris: Seuil.
Cabral, Eunice et al. (eds) (2003), *A Escrita e o Mundo em António Lobo Antunes. Actas do Colóquio Internacional António Lobo Antunes da Universidade de Évora*, Lisboa: Dom Quixote.
Casanova, Pascale (2004), *The World Republic of Letters*, trans. M. B. DeBevoise, Cambridge and London: Harvard University Press.
Cassin, Alessandro (2008), 'Geography? It Doesn't Exist: Antonio Lobo Antunes with Alessandro Cassin', *The Brooklyn Rail*, 10 November. Available online: https://brooklynrail.org/2008/11/books/geography-it-doesnt-exist-antonio-lobo-antunes-with-alessandro-cassin (accessed 5 May 2018).
Dorfman, Ariel (1990), 'Secretly Linked to the Same Woman', *The New York Times*, 29 July.
Even-Zohar, Itamar (1990), *Polysystem Studies, Poetics Today 11:1*, Durham: Duke University Press.
Frawley, William (1984), *Translation: Literary, Linguistic, and Philosophical Perspectives*, Newark: University of Delaware Press.
García Marquez, Gabriel (1970), *One Hundred Years of Solitude*, trans. Gregory Rabassa, New York: Harper & Row.
García Márquez, Gabriel (1982), 'Los pobres traductores buenos', *El País*, 21 July.
Genette, Gérard (1997), *Palimpsests: Literature in the Second Degree*, Lincoln: University of Nebraska.
Guzmán, María Constanza (2010), *Gregory Rabassa's Latin American Literature: A Translator's Visible Legacy*, Lewisburg: Bucknell University Press.
Landers, Clifford E. (2001), *Literary Translation: A Practical Guide*, Clevedon: Multilingual Matters.
Manrique, Jaime (2008), 'Fragmented, yet Lyrical and Entrancing', *Washington Post*, 5 November. Available online: http://www.washingtonpost.com/wp-dyn/content/article/2008/11/04/AR2008110403218.html??noredirect=on (accessed 5 May 2018).
McRae, Ellen (2012), 'The Role of Translators' Prefaces to Contemporary Literary Translations into English: An Empirical Study', in Anna Gil-Bardají, Pilar Orero and Sara Rovira-Esteva (eds), *Translation Peripheries. Paratextual Elements in Translation*, 63–82, Bern: Peter Lang.
Nord, Christiane (1991), *Text Analysis in Translation: Theory, Methodology, and Didactic Application of a Model for Translation-Oriented Text Analysis*, Amsterdam and Atlanta: Rodopi.
Pedrosa, Inês (1988), 'O Regresso das Caravelas', *Revista Ler* (Spring): 8–11.
Post, Chad (2011), 'Why Read António Lobo Antunes', *The Quarterly Conversation*, 6 September. Available online: http://quarterlyconversation.com/why-read-antonio-lobo-antunes (accessed 5 May 2018).
Pye, Michael (2002), 'Afloat on the Seas of the Past', *The New York Times*, 7 April.
Rabassa, Gregory (1974–5), 'If This Be Treason: Translation and Its Possibilities', *The American Scholar*, 44 (1): 29–39.

Rabassa, Gregory (1984), 'If This Be Treason: Translation and Its Possibilities', in William Frawley (ed.), *Translation: Literary, Linguistic, and Philosophical Perspectives*, 21–9, Newark: University of Delaware Press.
Rabassa, Gregory (1989), 'No Two Snowflakes Are Alike: Translation as Metaphor', in John Biguenet and Rainer Schulte (eds), *The Craft of Translation*, 1–12, Chicago: The University of Chicago Press.
Rabassa, Gregory (2005), *If This Be Treason: Translation and Its Dyscontents, a Memoir*, New York: New Directions Publishing.
Venuti, Lawrence (1992), *Rethinking Translation: Discourse, Subjectivity, Ideology*, London and New York: Routledge.

Part Three

Translators at work

11

The Coindreau archives: A translator at work

Patrick Hersant
University of Paris 8/Institut des textes et manuscrits modernes – ITEM/CNRS, Paris

Though it is not entirely new, interest in genetic criticism is still too recent within translation studies to have inspired more than specialized and fragmentary work. The field is almost entirely devoted to poetry translation, and, if the rough drafts of poet–translators like Saint-John Perse, Paul Celan or Philippe Jaccottet have recently been the subject of critical studies, these primarily undertake a comparison between the translator's process and the poet's work.[1] Only in 2014 did a special issue of the journal *GENESIS* allow us to celebrate the marriage of genetic criticism and translation studies without restrictions or exclusions, and in a way that involved translators who are not poets and even translators who are not writers – non-literary translators, whose drafts the journal reproduced in number, and in colour. Even more recently, the journal *Transalpina* dedicated an issue to the genesis of translations in the field of Italian literature (Agostini-Ouafi and Lavieri 2015), and the journal *Linguistica Antverpiensia* sketched the outline of 'genetic translation studies' (Cordingley and Montini 2015: 1–18). In theory, this new subject seems inexhaustible to a scholar of translation studies; in practice, alas, translators' drafts remain rare and limited, for the most part, to the twentieth century. In fact, we can lament with Fabienne Durand-Bogaert that most translators 'do not bother to preserve the traces of different angles of approach that led them to adopt a particular lexical or syntactic choice' (Durand-Bogaert 2014: 8). Certain specialized archives nonetheless offer researchers a vast terrain to explore – the Lilly Library at Indiana University, the Literary Translation Archive at the University of East Anglia, the Beinecke Library at Yale University, the Harry Ransom Centre at the University of Texas at Austin and the Institut mémoires de l'édition contemporaine (Institute for Contemporary Publishing Archives [IMEC]) near Caen, which has collected an archive of translators' manuscripts over the years. The addition of this kind of material to the scattered archives of poet–translators immediately proves its value, even in the sheer abundance of manuscripts. Instead of (or in addition to) examining and commenting on the hazards of poetry translation, which are fascinating but highly specific, we can observe a long-distance effort, following the translator at work through dozens of years and comparing his methods with those of his contemporaries.

On the topic of English to French literary translation, the dossiers archived at IMEC are at once copious and disappointing; their contents are often limited to press packets, correspondence between editors and translators that privileges legal or financial questions over literary ones, non-annotated galleys and other printed versions. But the IMEC archives also contain several notable, and even remarkable, exceptions, which are undoubtedly best illustrated by the Coindreau papers. Over several examples, taken almost at random from the profusion of the archive, it becomes apparent that Coindreau's drafts can lead to many forms of work – from the most particular to the highly systematic. They permit a great diversity of approaches, whether the goal is to illustrate this or that hypothesis suggested by a comparison between the original and the published translation or to shed light on his method of working. Lastly, they allow us to see the translative process at the very moment it is taking place, and not as translators describe it in retrospect, with more or less objectivity and sincerity, when they are questioned after the fact.

Born in 1892, Maurice Coindreau taught French at Princeton University from the 1920s to the 1960s, and to avoid getting bored, 'he translated' (cited by Gresset 1992: ii).[2] Over the course of his career, he translated some fifty novels, including thirteen from the Spanish – Goytisolo, Sánchez Ferlosio and Quiroga – and the rest from American English, with a marked preference for novelists from the Southern United States like Faulkner, Dos Passos, Capote, Styron, Steinbeck, Hemingway and many others he introduced in France. As a faithful, regular translator for Éditions Gallimard, he was both a prospector and an unparalleled scout, a true ambassador of transatlantic literature – so much so that Sartre could say, 'American literature – that's the literature of Coindreau' (Gresset 1992: xv).

The source–draft–target sequence

The Maurice Coindreau archives preserved at IMEC include (in the realm of English) the drafts of a dozen novels and short stories, representing, in many forms, up to four or five successive states of a translation, with a first attempt in a notebook with paper and pencil, corrected in red, then typed and corrected once or twice more before establishing the definitive version. By itself, studying these successive states has much to teach us about Coindreau's translative method; however, the 'compulsion for comparison' (Berman 2009: 65) that drives all translation studies scholars encourages us to add two more documents called the 'source' and the 'target'. The source is the original edition Coindreau used, which in most cases is the first American edition. The target is the first published edition of the French translation, before any subsequent revisions.[3] This way, each text presents itself in three successive versions; for William Goyen, whose novel will be our first example, we have *The House of Breath* (first American edition, in italics), 'La Maison d'haleine' (translator's draft, in quotations) and *La Maison d'haleine* (first French edition, in italics). Where the traditional comparative approach only examines the original text and the published translation, we propose to introduce the translator's drafts between them. In the source–draft–target sequence, the translative process occupies, for once, the central position – in terms of chronology, certainly, but also in the text's genetics, because Goyen's original is as definitive as Coindreau's published version.[4] Here, only the operation of translating is fluctuating and temporary – alive, in effect, as witnessed by the many states of its perpetual metamorphosis.

The House of Breath, William Goyen's first novel, is at once the portrait of a 'fallen splendid house', of a small, Southern town, and of the author himself. In poetic, sometimes hallucinatory prose, Goyen constructs a complex narrative whose mystical element is apparent from the opening lines:

> [A]nd then I walked and walked in the rain that turned half into snow and I was drenched and frozen; and walked upon a park that seemed like the very pasture of Hell where there were couples whispering in the shadows ... Yet on the walls of my brain, frescoes: the kneeling balletic Angel holding a wand of vineleaves, announcing; the agony in the garden; two naked lovers turned out ... (1950: 1)

> Alors je marchai, je marchai sous la pluie qui tournait à la neige, et j'étais morfondu, transi; et j'arrivai dans un parc, fidèle image des prairies de l'Enfer. Des couples y chuchotaient dans l'ombre ... Et cependant, sur les parois de mon cerveau, des fresques: l'Ange danseur, agenouillé, un thyrse à la main, annonciateur; l'agonie dans le jardin; deux amants nus, chassés ... (1954: 21)

A classic comparison of these two published versions, the original and its translation, already reveals a number of interesting points which might help to outline Coindreau's translative poetics – on the condition, of course, that these elements prove to be recurring, which is to say distinguishable in the whole of the book and not just in this one passage. One can see here, for example, that Coindreau opts for the *passé simple* and the imperfect at the expense of the *passé composé*; avoids the calque 'je marchai et marchai';[5] omits 'half'; prefers, over the adjective 'trempé', the rather outdated 'morfondu'[6] of a more formal register; creates two sentences where the English only has one; substitutes a simple apposition after a comma for the explicit comparison 'that seemed like'; recovers an 'and' by adding it later; respects the elision of the verb in the phrase 'on the walls of my brain [there were] frescoes'; shortens 'wand of vineleaves' into 'thyrse'; follows the word order of the English whenever possible; and so on. This type of survey, based on a rapid examination of the source–target sequence, makes up the usual material for translation studies scholars. Yet, between the English original and its French translation, we can benefit from inserting Coindreau's typed manuscript. Here (Figure 11.1) is how the second part of the passage above appears:

> Et cependant, sur les parois de mon cerveau, des fresques: l'Ange danseur, agenouillé un~~e baguette de pompras~~ *thyrse* à la main, annonciateur; l'agonie dans le jardin; deux amants nus chassés;

Figure 11.1 IMEC, Michel Gresset collection, Maurice-Edgar Coindreau subcollection (hereafter cited as CND), box 3, Translations 1952-57, 'La Maison d'haleine' by William Goyen, typescript, fol. 1.

Transcription:[7] Et cependant sur les parois de mon cerveau, des fresques: l'Ange danseur, agenouillé, une baguette de pampre <thyrse>[8] à la main, annonciateur; l'agonie dans le jardin; deux amants nus chassés ...

Not only does this typed account carry the traces of adjustments, corrections and even typographic indications ('font size 14' '12 Garamond'), as much as signs of the imagined page it will one day moult into, but it is also preceded by an earlier version (Figure 11.2), handwritten in this case, which has also been corrected several times:

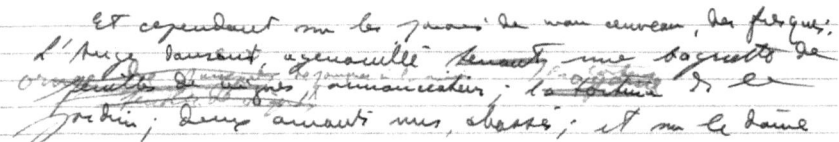

Figure 11.2 IMEC, CND 3, Translations 1952–57, 'La Maison d'haleine' by William Goyen, manuscript, fol. 1.

Transcription: Et cependant sur les parois de mon cerveau, des fresques: l'Ange dansant eur, agenouillé, tenant une baguette ornée de pampres feuilles de vigne<de pampres à la main>feuilles de vigne, annonciateur; la torture <l'agonie> <la torture> dans le jardin; deux amants nus, chassés ...

So we find ourselves in the presence of a diverse succession of states, with some fixed and some still unstable, revealing with singular clarity something that is ordinarily left unseen – the passage of one language into another, but also of one text into another. In these first lines, one drawn-out example will allow us to observe the methods through which 'holding a wand of vineleaves' is transformed into 'un thyrse à la main'. There are four sets of successive corrections on the manuscript, plus one last, decisive correction on the typescript. A diachronic, linear transcription makes apparent, in italics, the modifications made in five successive states of the adjective 'balletic' and the phrase 'holding a wand of vineleaves':

V1. Et cependant sur les parois de mon cerveau, des fresques: l'Ange *danseur*, agenouillé, *tenant une baguette de feuilles de vigne*, annonciateur; la torture dans le jardin; deux amants nus, chassés ...

V2. Et cependant sur les parois de mon cerveau, des fresques: l'Ange *dansant*, agenouillé, une baguette *ornée de pampre à la main*, annonciateur; la torture dans le jardin; deux amants nus, chassés ...

V3. Et cependant sur les parois de mon cerveau, des fresques: l'Ange dansant, agenouillé, une baguette *ornée de feuilles de vigne* à la main, annonciateur; la torture dans le jardin; deux amants nus, chassés ...

V4. Et cependant sur les parois de mon cerveau, des fresques: l'Ange dansant, agenouillé, une baguette *de pampre* à la main, annonciateur; la torture dans le jardin; deux amants nus, chassés ...

V5. Et cependant sur les parois de mon cerveau, des fresques: l'Ange dansant, agenouillé, *un thyrse* à la main, annonciateur; la torture dans le jardin; deux amants nus, chassés ...⁹

The progression of these five versions reveals two modifications. The first, 'l'Ange danseur'/'l'Ange dansant', consists of replacing a substantive adjective with a verbal adjective. In grammatical terms, the two versions are as close (or as far) from the original, the qualitative adjective 'balletic'; in semantic terms, both deviate similarly from the original, which has no exact equivalent, and which could be translated by a paraphrase like 'propre à un danseur de ballet';¹⁰ it is therefore in phonetic terms that the difference between versions unfolds. It is quite remarkable that the 'danseur' of the first attempt (V1) is changed to 'dansant' in the first round of revisions (V2), then stays that way through the three rounds of edits which follow (V3–V5), only to be restored to 'danseur' in the published version, no doubt through a final correction in the proofs. The reasons which led to these variations, then to the final choice, are drawn from conjecture (was Coindreau aiming to avoid the three nasal vowels in '*a*nge d*a*ns*a*nt'? Or the homophones 'dansant'/'d'encens'? Or to reproduce the echo of the English suffix 'kneel*ing* ... announc*ing*' with 'dans*eur* ... annonciat*eur*'?), but they are almost certainly dictated by phonetic, and not grammatical or semantic, concerns.

The second modification, regarding the translation of 'holding a wand of vineleaves', consists of a series of variations that are both more numerous and more radical: 'tenant une baguette ornée de feuilles de vigne', 'une baguette ornée de pampre à la main', 'une baguette ornée de feuilles de vigne à la main', 'une baguette de pampre à la main', 'un thyrse à la main'. The first attempt offers an almost exact grammatical copy, with each English word translated, in the order of the original, by a French word of the same type: present participle + article + substantive + preposition + substantive. Then the present participle *tenant* is replaced by the adverbial phrase *à la main*, and moved to the end of the phrase (from V2 through V5, and in the published version); the *feuilles de vigne* evolve into *pampre* (V2), become *feuilles de vigne* again (V3), then *pampre* once more (V4) and finally *thyrse* (V5 and the published version). None of these versions is an error: a *pampre* is a branch of vine, while the *thyrse* is a staff wrapped in a vine branch (characteristic of Bacchus). It is tempting to imagine the mechanisms at work in Coindreau's mind. From one version to another, through each reading and rereading, the process could have unfolded like this:

I first translated word for word, in a literal way; as I reread my work, I found that *baguette de feuilles* to be a rather ungainly formulation – we would say that the baguette is *faite de* feuilles; perhaps it would be better to specify that it is *ornée* de feuilles; no, that's a bit too long, too explicit – better to get rid of *ornée* and return to *pampre*; but there's an even better word, *thyrse*, which translates three words in one.

We could lose ourselves in conjectures here (it would be an understatement to say the Coindreau archives invite them), asking ourselves why and how the exact word finally emerged after so many hesitations (a tardy reminder? a conversation with some Hellenist? consulting a thesaurus?), or concluding that the choice is too elevated when compared with the original (after all, 'thyrsus' exists in English). But this essay is not the place for it – with these few lines taken from *The House of Breath*, we simply wanted to demonstrate how much richer and more informative the source–draft–target sequence is for the scholar of translation studies than solely examining the source and the target. A direct comparison between the first lines of *The House of Breath* and *La Maison d'haleine* would allow some to take note of the transformation from 'a wand of vineleaves' into 'un thyrse', but it does not tell us anything about the process which precipitated this choice. On the contrary, the drafts of 'La Maison d'haleine' constitute a sort of supplementary genetic mediation, encouraging in what it reveals (or at least suggests) – an attentive ear for sound, a high standard for vocabulary, a taste for refined language, etc. The translation process at work, with its hesitations, its temporary corrections and restorations, is visible on every page of Coindreau's drafts. Just as these written traces let us imagine the writer at work, so too do the translator's additions and misgivings permit us to see him at work, to watch over his shoulder as he considers and implements the solutions, the variations, the choices that finally sketch out a plan of translation, a developing method.

The Coindreau method: A survey

One cannot draw the contours of a method or test its effectiveness by looking at a few lines. A more thorough analysis, largely outside of the purview of this study, seems necessary and desirable; for now, we will content ourselves with more precisely determining Coindreau's method by analysing several significant passages. The following excerpt (Figure 11.3) is from *Wise Blood* (1952) by Flannery O'Connor, translated as *La Sagesse dans le sang*:

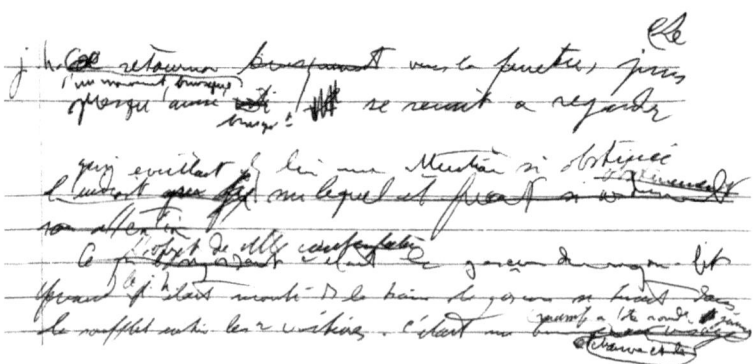

Figure 11.3 IMEC, CND 4, Translations 1959–67, 'La Sagesse dans le sang' by Flannery O'Connor, manuscript, fols. 2–3.

Transcription: Il <Le j. h.> <d'un mouvement brusque> se retourna ~~brusquement~~ vers la fenêtre, puis, presque aussi ~~vite~~ <brusqut>, ~~il~~ se remit à regarder l'endroit <qui éveillait en lui> ~~sur lequel il fixait si ardemment son attention~~ <une attention si obstinée.>
~~Ce qu'il regardait c'~~ <L'objet de cette contemplation> était le garçon du wagon-lit. Quand ~~il~~ <le j. h.> était monté ds le train le garçon se tenait dans le soufflet entre les 2 voitures. C'était un homme <massif> ~~au visage lourd, dont la tête~~ <à tête ronde, chauve et jaune.>

What does this short passage from Coindreau's drafts have to teach us? The transcription reveals an extensively reworked text, following a logic which becomes increasingly apparent when we compare the English original, the first attempt and finally the corrected version in its final state:

Source	He turned toward the window suddenly
1st Draft	Il se retourna brusquement vers la fenêtre
Final	Le jeune homme, d'un mouvement brusque, se retourna vers la fenêtre[11]

The correction here seems motivated by a concern for clarification: two male characters are evoked in this paragraph, and 'le jeune homme' in the final version removes an ambiguity. It is possible to reconstruct the translator's reasoning here: compared to a simple *il*, the choice of *le jeune homme* is certainly more explicit, but also substantially longer. 'Le jeune homme se retourna brusquement vers la fenêtre' would form a long phrase, which is also unbroken, creating a flagrant dissonance with the meaning of the sentence and the liveliness of the gesture it describes.

The following example is harder to interpret with certainty. We can observe a definite tactical change along the way:

Source	a thick-figured man with a round yellow bald head
1st Draft	C'était un homme au visage lourd, dont la tête
Final	C'était un homme massif, à tête ronde, jaune et chauve[12]

The sentence breaks off after 'dont la tête' in the first attempt, as if the translator understood that a sentence begun like this could only end in a rather ungainly way, by placing an excessive stress on the adjectives qualifying the character's head: 'C'était un homme au visage lourd, dont la tête était ronde, jaune, et chauve.' Another hypothesis: Coindreau is correcting an initial confusion, a mistake well known to English learners – 'thick-figured' does not mean 'au visage épais' or 'à la figure épaisse' but 'à la *silhouette* épaisse'.[13] For this reason, then, 'un homme au visage lourd' becomes 'un homme massif'.

The same excerpt displays one of the translator's most frequent and most significant solutions for avoiding a calque:

Source	What he was looking at was the porter
1st Draft	Ce qu'il regardait, c'était le garçon du wagon-lit
Final	L'objet de cette contemplation était le portier[14]

The drafts reveal that for Coindreau, the first attempt almost always copies the unfolding of the original English syntax. Only in a second phase does the classic syntax or rhythm of French substitute for the initial Anglicism, either in the first typewritten sheets (where we can see redactions followed by a correction on the same line), or, more often, in a subsequent round of corrections (where the correction is between lines, sometimes in different coloured ink). Every translator has had the experience, after several straight hours of working on a text, of transposing some formulation or other (lexical or syntactic) from the foreign language. Here, the calque from English must have seemed unacceptable after reading it with fresh eyes, what could be called (to borrow a phrase from Antoine Berman) a 'conversion of perspective'.[15] The author of the first attempt is handling linguistic matter so malleable that everything in it is still possible; the re-reader he becomes later, or immediately after, no longer sees a translation in progress but a foreign book in French.

The Coindreau method: A breakdown

The richness of the archives permits (and even demands) a more in-depth analysis – a patient assessment of the erasures which reveal, if not a system, then at least a method of translation and revision. An exhaustive assessment of the translator's process will eventually add to the survey we have just undertaken of these few salient examples which Berman calls 'signifying zones'.[16] This categorization, once established, reveals three specific concerns: lexical precision, the restructuring of syntagms in the sentence and regard for the register of language.

Lexical precision

The drive for semantic accuracy is reflected by a great number of revised words and expressions; here are several examples taken from translations of different authors, showing first the original English (A), followed by our transcription of Coindreau's draft (B) and finally the version published in French (C). The first excerpt (Figure 11.4) is from a translation of John Steinbeck:

Ils avaient descendu le sentier à la file indienne, et, même en terrain découvert, ils restaient l'un derrière l'autre. Ils étaient vêtus tous les deux des pantalons et des vestes de coton bleu à boutons de cuivre.

Figure 11.4 IMEC, CND 2, Translations 1927–48, 'Des Souris et des hommes' by John Steinbeck, typescript, fol. 2.

A. Both were dressed in denim trousers and in denim coats with brass buttons. (Steinbeck 1937: 9)
B. Partial transcription: Ils ~~portaient~~ <étaient vêtus> tous les deux de s̶ pantalons et de s̶ vestes ~~de toile~~ en <serge de coton bleue> à boutons de cuivre.
C. Ils étaient vêtus tous les deux de pantalons et de vestes en serge de coton bleue à boutons de cuivre. (Steinbeck 1939: 7)[17]

In a time when the terms 'denim' and 'jeans' were not as universally known as they are now, Coindreau begins by undertranslating 'denim' with 'toile' before opting for the explication 'en serge de coton bleue'.

Here (Figure 11.5) is another lexical fine-tuning in a different passage from Steinbeck:

Figure 11.5 IMEC, CND 2, Translations 1927–48, 'Des Souris et des hommes' by John Steinbeck, typescript, fol. 1.

A. and sycamores with mottled, white, recumbent limbs and branches that arch over the pool. (Steinbeck 1937: 7)
B. Transcription: des sycomores aussi <,> dont * <et> les branches <marbrées> e̶t̶ *le s̶ feuillage ~~tachetés et blancs forment retombent~~ <s'allongent> et forment voûte au dessus de l'eau dormante.
C. des sycomores aussi, dont le feuillage et les branches marbrées s'allongent et forment voûte au-dessus de l'eau dormante. (Steinbeck 1939: 5)[18]

By revising 'les branches et le feuillage tachetés et blancs retombent' to 'le feuillage et les branches marbrées s'allongent', Coindreau manages several improvements in one stroke: the initial inversion of two substantives gets rid of an ungainly liaison, the logical pacing is quicker, the rhythm less heavy; he removes the unwelcome repetition of 'et', since the first unit of the sentence is two nominal syntagms and the second is two adjectives; finally, 'marbré' translates, with one word, the white undertone and the striped shadows covering the branches.

The following excerpt (Figure 11.6) is from a novel by Truman Capote:

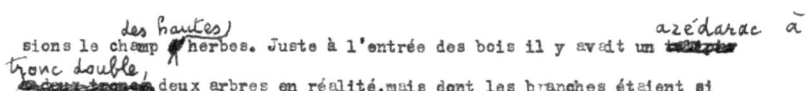

Figure 11.6 IMEC, CND 3, Translation 1952–57, 'La Harpe d'herbes' by Truman Capote, typescript, fol. 12.

A. Just entering the woods there was a double-trunked China tree, really two trees. (Capote 1951: 14)
B. Partial transcription: Juste à l'entrée des bois il y avait un ~~tulipier à deux troncs~~ <azédarac à tronc double>, deux arbres en réalité …
C. Juste à l'entrée des bois il y avait un azédarac à tronc double, deux arbres en réalité … (Capote 1952: 23)[19]

Thanks to a revision of the typescript, the 'tulipier à deux troncs' becomes an 'azédarac à tronc double'. This kind of lexical refinement is common for Coindreau: here, we have provided three examples lifted from hundreds of possibilities. As in the case of 'thyrse' cited above, one can deduce (or at least hypothesize) that Coindreau did not consult a dictionary as he worked, probably to preserve the flow of the first attempt, but later he was careful to find the most rigorous translation of ornithological, botanical or other specialized vocabulary.

The restructuring of syntagms

On almost every page, and sometimes several times per page, Coindreau reorganizes the syntagms that first mimicked the English. This type of adjustment seems to confirm that his initial translation follows the English sentences as much as possible, without altering the arrangement, but he later revisits this first draft to invert words or groups of words. We see this method, for example, in an excerpt from Erskine Caldwell (Figure 11.7):

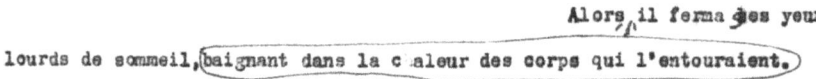

Figure 11.7 IMEC, CND 2, Translations 1927–48, 'Terre tragique' by Erskine Caldwell, typescript, fol. 202.

A Then his eyes closed drowsily while he soaked up the warmth of the bodies beside him. (Caldwell 1944: 227–8)
B. Transcription: Alors, * il ferma ses yeux lourds de sommeil, *baignant dans la chaleur des corps qui l'entouraient.
C. Alors, baignant dans la chaleur des corps qui l'entouraient, il ferma ses yeux alourdis de sommeil. (Caldwell 1948: 204)[20]

A segment of the phrase, in opposition to the present participle, moves from the end to the beginning of the sentence; the final result is both more natural and lighter in French. Here (Figure 11.8) is another example of this process, which Coindreau repeats, also from a novel by Erskine Caldwell:

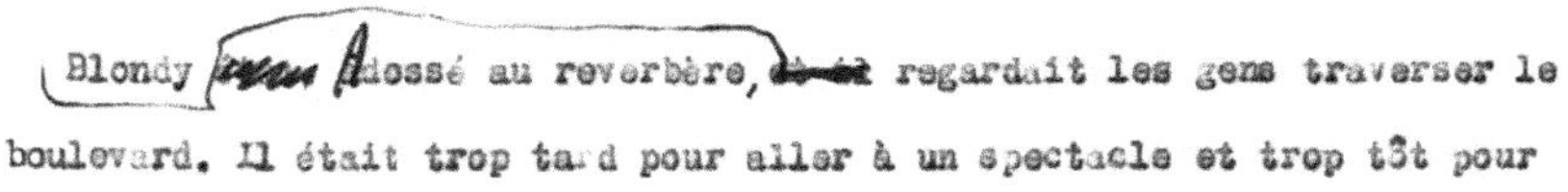

> Blondy ~~preax~~ Adossé au reverbère, ~~le-et~~ regardait les gens traverser le boulevard. Il était trop tard pour aller à un spectacle et trop tôt pour

Figure 11.8 IMEC, CND 2, Translations 1927–48, 'Un Pauvre type' by Erskine Caldwell, typescript, fol. 55.

A. Blondy leaned against the lamp post and watched some people crossing the Boulevard. (Caldwell 1930: 67)
B. Transcription: *Blondy était A/adossé au réverbère, * et il regardait les gens traverser le boulevard.
C. Adossé au réverbère, Blondy regardait les gens traverser le boulevard. (Caldwell 1945: 56)[21]

Notice a slightly more complex restructuring in another excerpt (Figure 11.9), taken, in this case, from a novel by Truman Capote:

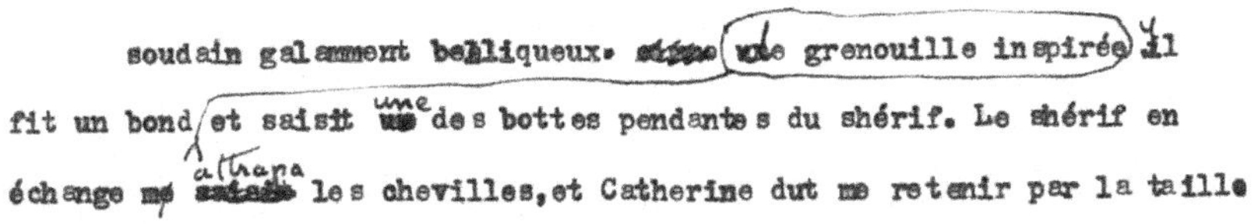

> soudain galamment belliqueux. ~~sispe~~ (une grenouille inspirée) il fit un bond et saisit une des bottes pendantes du shérif. Le shérif en échange me ~~saisit~~ attrapa les chevilles, et Catherine dut me retenir par la taille

Figure 11.9 IMEC, CND 3, Translations 1952–57, 'La Harpe d'herbes' by Truman Capote, typescript, fol. 41.

A. Like an inspired frog he hopped and caught hold to one of the Sheriff's dangling boots. (Capote 1951: 38)
B. Transcription: ~~comme~~ *de une grenouille inspirée I/il fit un bond * et saisit un <une> des bottes pendantes du shérif.
C. Il fit un bond de grenouille inspirée et saisit une des bottes pendantes du shérif. (Capote 1952: 64)[22]

Coindreau seems to have been motivated by rhythmic considerations here; 'Comme une grenouille inspirée, il fit un bond' is corrected to 'Il fit un bond de grenouille inspirée': thanks to this rearrangement, the sentence can do without the comma, reproducing the cadence of the original, which compresses three movement verbs into one line without interruption.

The register of language

A third possible category groups numerous variations and hesitations concerning the register of language. One example (Figure 11.10) is this sentence from William Styron:

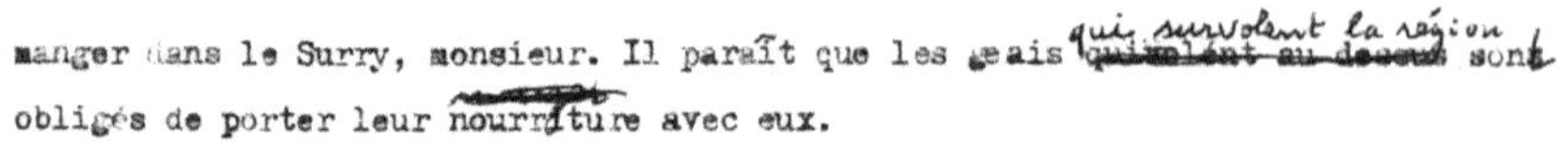

manger dans le Surry, monsieur. Il paraît que les geais qui survolent la région ~~qui volent au-dessus~~ sont obligés de porter leur nourriture avec eux.

Figure 11.10 IMEC, CND 5, Translations 1969–78, 'Les Confessions de Nat Turner' by William Styron, typescript, fol. 177.

A. They says a bluejay flyin' over has to tote his own food. (Styron 1967: 198)
B. Partial transcription: Il paraît que les geais qui ~~volent au-dessus~~ <survolent la région> sont obligés de porter leur <~~manger~~> nourriture avec eux.
C. Il paraît que les geais qui survolent la région sont obligés de porter leur nourriture avec eux. (Styron 1969: 202)[23]

Coindreau has sometimes been criticized for not translating the black American sociolect, and making a Black nanny sound rather like a servant from Vendée. Here, we can see his hesitations over the register of language: the first attempt tries to translate the sociolect of the original with a slightly looser French or one with more populist connotations ('volent au-dessus', 'porter leur manger'). Between the lines, the two modifications reveal an impulse to correct that is quite far from the original. Coindreau the editor is therefore less audacious than Coindreau the primal translator: with 'survolent la région' and 'nourriture', he returns to elevated language and puts it in the most populist mouths.

Our next example, taken from an unpublished translation of Dos Passos (and so lacking the final version 'C'), illustrates the many strategies he uses to transpose and compensate for a more vulgar tone:

A. But what the hell, they can't arrest a guy for a deserter on British soil. (Dos Passos 1932: 20)
B. <J'm'en fous après tout> On n'peut ~~foutre~~ pas arrêter un déserteur en territoire anglais.[24]

The American expression 'what the hell' becomes the adverb 'foutre pas', then the conjugated verb 'j'm'en fous' created by an elision of *je* to *j'*, which is undeniably more natural. The creation and suppression of elisions in rendering common speech is one of the most prevalent revisions in many of these drafts. For example, another from Dos Passos:

> J'ai laissé le<'> mec faire c'qu'i<l> voulait pour dix billets de cinq!
> Vous <n'> sauriez pas les résultats du baseball par hasard.
> Merde, pas moyen de<'> se baigner… et nous ne<'> verrons plus de singes non plus.
> Je <'> voudrais bien savoir c'qu'ils sont ve <'>nus foutre ici, dit Joe.[25]

Note that his concern for the register of language, which is apparent in these drafts, does not always amount to a convincing translation of spoken language. Besides, it is possible to critique Coindreau for re-transcribing common speech by erasing the sociolinguistic origins of the characters concerned. Jean-Marc Gouanvic raises this point about Coindreau's translation (with Georges Duhamel) of Steinbeck's *Grapes of Wrath*: '[I]t appears that, throughout the work, the solution he used was to respect the rules of grammar, giving way to the "familiar" system. The consequence of choosing this option is that the resulting text is characterized by a flattening of sociolectal speech' (Gouanvic 1999: 276–7). This, of course, can be established by a simple comparison between the source and the target – between the published original and its published translation. But we hope this chapter demonstrates that a detailed genetic analysis, made possible by numerous and much-revised drafts, not only corroborates this assertion but also permits us to distinguish between a first attempt that is occasionally loose, concerned with orality, and the changes that transform certain speech into impeccable French.

Examining these drafts eventually confirms the importance Coindreau 'accorded to the notion of correctness – what in English is called "propriety" – the fact that he was never tempted to coin a new word, even by assimilation, or to "strangle" the syntax' (Gresset 1992: viii–ix). Coindreau's literary style has been the subject of several commentaries and critical studies, regarding both his taste for classical high language and his dated, if not questionable, manner of translating orality.[26] Because they did not have access to these manuscripts, the authors of these studies have contented themselves with observing and analysing the translation in its published form, or its revised form on the occasion of a new edition, without seeking to understand Coindreau's translation strategies, which are apparent from a single look at his drafts. Furthermore, the genetic approach brings to light the daily reality of Coindreau's work, the evolution of his techniques over the years, from one novel to the next, and his place in the translation landscape of his contemporaries in the first half of the twentieth century. Last, and perhaps most importantly, his drafts give us a precious glimpse of that grey zone where Durand-Bogaert sees a 'possible world [chosen] at the expense of other worlds which, at a given moment, were equally possible' (2014: 30). As the drafts of translators make up that interface which is ordinarily invisible, they offer the moving image of that '*no man's langue*' (Ladmiral 2005: 474) where the text develops and the language is transformed – through bursts of discovery, temporary approximations and perpetual adjustments.

Translated by Laura Marris

Notes

1 See, for example, Hartmann (2007: 230–62); Dueck (2014); Weissmann (2016: 129–44); Hersant (2018).
2 Michel Gresset (1991: 42–52) is the author of a biographical and critical article on Coindreau, accompanied by a complete bibliography of his published translations.
3 Many of Coindreau's translations were revised for new editions, mainly by Michel Gresset. On this topic, see Pitavy (2004: 153–67).

4   This assertion only applies to the frame of our source–draft–target device: naturally, Goyen's manuscripts (preserved at the University of Texas's Harry Ransom Centre) and those of Coindreau's other authors contain variations, and the text of the novel is not considered 'definitive' except in its published version, our source. As for Coindreau's French version, it is important to specify that this text is only 'definitive' in a relative way, since Coindreau often revised his own translations (with rare and minor corrections) many years after the original publication. See Gresset (2002: 389–92).
5   Literal translation: 'I walked and walked.'
6   Literal translation: 'soaked' or 'drenched' vs. 'morfondu' which means 'chilled' but also 'dejected', 'moping'.
7   This example and all others in French are the author's own transcriptions.
8   < > are used to indicate additions *(Editors' note)*.
9   Literal translations of these versions: V1. 'dancer', 'holding a wand of leaves from the vine'; V2. 'dancing', 'decorated with vine in his hand'; V3. 'decorated with leaves of the vine'; V4. 'of the vine'; V5. 'thyrsus'.
10 Literal translation: 'characteristic of a ballet dancer'.
11 Literal translation: 1st draft, 'He turned himself sharply toward the window'; final, 'The young man, in a sharp movement, turned toward the window'.
12 Literal translation: 1st draft, 'He was a man with a heavy face, whose head'; final, 'He was a heavy-set man, with a round head, yellow and bald'.
13 Translator's note: 'figure' in French does not mean 'figure' – it means 'face'. 'Silhouette' is French for 'figure'.
14 Literal translation: 1st draft, 'What he was looking at, it was the boy from the sleeper-car'; final, 'The object of this contemplation was the porter'.
15 'The first reading still remains, inevitably, that of a foreign work in French. The second reading reads the translation as a translation, which implies a *conversion* of perspective. For, as I have already stated, one is not born a reader of translations, but made one' (Berman 2009: 49).
16 'This pre-analysis and the readings that accompany it will lead to a patient labor consisting of selecting pertinent and significant stylistic examples (broadly speaking) in the original. … What is selected … are those passages of the original that are, so to speak, the places where the work condenses, represents, signifies, or symbolizes itself. These passages are signifying zones where a literary work reaches its own purpose (not necessarily that of the author) and its own center of gravity' (Berman 2009: 54).
17 Literal translation of transcriptions: B. 'they wore <were clothed> both of them in pants and vests of cloth in <blue serge cotton> with brass buttons'; C. 'They were clothed both of them in pants and vests of blue cotton serge with brass buttons.'
18 Literal translation of transcription: B. 'the sycamores too <,> whose * <and> the branches <marbled> and *the foliage mottled and white formed falling back <stretch out> and form an arch over the dormant water'; C. 'the sycamores too, whose foliage and marbled branches stretch out and form an arch over the dormant water.'
19 Literal translation of partial transcription: B. 'Just at the entrance of the woods there was a tulip tree with two trunks<Chinaberry with a double trunk>, two trees in reality'; C. 'Just at the entrance of the woods there was a chinaberry tree with a double trunk, two trees in reality.'
20 Literal translation of transcription: B. 'So * he closed his eyes heavy with sleep, *bathing in the warmth of the bodies that surrounded him'; C. 'So, bathing in the warmth of the bodies that surrounded him, he closed his eyes weighted with sleep.'

21 Literal translation of transcription: B. '*Blondy ~~was~~ L/leaning against the lamp post, *~~and he~~ watched people crossing the boulevard'; C. 'Leaning against the lamp post, Blondy watched people crossing the boulevard.'
22 Literal translation of transcription: B. '~~Like~~ *of ~~an~~ inspired frog H/he makes a leap * and grabs <one> of the sheriff's dangling boots'; C. 'He leaps like an inspired frog and grabs one of the sheriff's dangling boots.'
23 Literal translation of partial transcription: B. 'It seems the jays that ~~fly above~~ <fly over the region> are obliged to bring their <~~eats~~> food with them'; C. 'It seems the jays that fly over the region must carry their own food with them.'
24 IMEC, CND 2, Translations 1927–1948, subcollection 'L'homme qui disait s'appeler Jones', excerpt from *1919* by John Dos Passos, 1931, fol. 4 (unpublished translation). Literal translation: '<I don' give a damn after all> They can't ~~damn well~~ arrest a deserter in English territory.'
25 Ibid., fols. 13, 4 and 7.
26 See Vidal (1991: 151–88).

References

Agostini-Ouafi, Viviana and Antonio Lavieri (eds) (2015), *Transalpina. Poétiques des archives: genèse des traductions et communautés de pratique*, 18.
Berman, Antoine (2009), *Toward a Translation Criticism: John Donne*, trans. Françoise Massardier-Kenney, Kent, OH: Kent State University Press.
Caldwell, Erskine (1930), *Poor Fool*, New York: Rariora Press.
Caldwell, Erskine (1944), *Tragic Ground*, New York: Duell, Sloan and Pearce.
Caldwell, Erskine (1945), *Un Pauvre type*, trans. Maurice-Edgar Coindreau, Paris: Gallimard.
Caldwell, Erskine (1948), *Terre tragique*, trans. Maurice-Edgar Coindreau, Paris: Gallimard.
Capote, Truman (1951), *The Grass Harp*, New York: Random House.
Capote, Truman (1952), *La Harpe d'herbes*, trans. Maurice-Edgar Coindreau, Paris: Gallimard.
Coindreau, Maurice-Edgar (1992), *Mémoires d'un traducteur: entretiens avec Christian Giudicelli*, Paris: Gallimard.
Cordingley, Anthony and Chiara Montini (eds) (2015), *Linguistica Antverpiensia, New Series: Themes in Translation* Studies. *Towards a Genetics of Translation*, 14.
Dos Passos, John (1932), *1919*, New York: Harcourt Brace.
Dueck, Evelyn (2014), *L'Étranger intime: les traductions françaises de l'œuvre de Paul Celan*, Berlin and Boston: De Gruyter.
Durand-Bogaert, Fabienne (2014), 'Ce que la génétique dit, la traduction le fait', *GENESIS. Revue internationale de critique génétique*, 38: 7–10.
Gouanvic, Jean-Marc (1999), '*Polemos* et la traduction: la traduction de *The Grapes of Wrath* de John Steinbeck', *Athanor*, 10 (2): 268–79.
Gouanvic, Jean-Marc (2002), 'John Steinbeck et la censure', *TTR: traduction, terminologie, rédaction*, 15 (2): 191–202.
Goyen, William (1950), *The House of Breath*, New York: Random House.
Goyen, William (1954), *La Maison d'haleine*, trans. Maurice-Edgar Coindreau, Paris: Gallimard.

Gresset, Michel (1991), 'Coup de phare: Maurice Edgar Coindreau, 1892–1990', *Translittérature*, 2: 42–52.
Gresset, Michel (1992), 'Il miglior fabbro', in Maurice-Edgar Coindreau, *Mémoires d'un traducteur: entretiens avec Christian Giudicelli*, i–xvi, Paris: Gallimard.
Gresset, Michel (2002), 'Maurice Edgar Coindreau, traducteur ou "passeur"?', in Paul Carmigiani (ed.), *Figures du passeur*, 385–92, Perpignan: Presses Universitaires de Perpignan.
Hartmann, Esa Christine (2007), *Les Manuscrits de Saint-John Perse: pour une poétique vivante*, Paris: L'Harmattan.
Hersant, Patrick (2018), 'On n'est jamais tout seul: étude génétique d'une collaboration Ungaretti-Jaccottet', *Carnets, revue électronique d'études françaises*, 14. Available online: http://journals.openedition.org/carnets/8795 (accessed 10 November 2018).
Ladmiral, Jean-René (2005), 'Le *salto mortale* de la déverbalisation', *Meta: journal des traducteurs*, 50 (2): 473–87.
Pitavy, François (2004), 'De *The Wild Palms* à *Si je t'oublie, Jérusalem*: quelques réflexions sur la retraduction du Faulkner', *Palimpsestes*, 15: 153–67.
Steinbeck, John (1937), *Of Mice and Men*, New York: Covici Friede.
Steinbeck, John (1939), *Des Souris et des hommes*, trans. Maurice-Edgar Coindreau, Paris: Gallimard.
Styron, William (1967), *The Confessions of Nat Turner*, New York: Random House.
Styron, William (1969), *Les Confessions de Nat Turner*, trans. Maurice-Edgar Coindreau, Paris: Gallimard.
Vidal, Bertrand (1991), 'Plurilinguisme et traduction – Le vernaculaire noir américain: enjeux, réalité, réception à propos de *The Sound and the Fury*', *TTR: traduction, terminologie, rédaction*, 4 (2): 151–88.
Weissmann, Dirk (2016), 'Entre contrôle et confiance: Paul Celan traducteur de ses traductions françaises', in Chiara Montini (ed.), *Traduire: genèse du choix*, 129–44, Paris: Éditions Archives Contemporaines.

12

Authorship and (self-)translation in academic writing: Towards a genetic approach

Karen Bennett
*Centre for English, Translation and Anglo-Portuguese Studies,
Nova University of Lisbon*

Introduction

Few people working in the academic profession would deny the importance of the concept of authorship. Individual career advancement depends increasingly upon a track record of papers published in respected journals, while the financial health of our research centres and university departments in turn relies on the output of identified staff. Hence, there is tremendous pressure to clock up publications bearing our name.

Not unexpectedly, this pressure has led to abuses of the system. There is evidence, for example, that in the sciences the practice of multiple authorship has facilitated the exchange of favours through the acknowledgement of co-authors whose contribution may have been minimal in reality (Carneiro et al. 2007; Desai 2012; Macfarlane 2017). In the humanities the problem is the reverse. As authorship in this domain is still endowed with the aura of 'genius', it is mostly expected to be singular, meaning that second- or third-party interventions in texts are rarely acknowledged at all. Thus, translation, when it occurs, tends to be 'covert',[1] while paratranslational activities such as editing, proofreading or linguistic revision routinely go unattributed.

Nevertheless, the concept of academic authorship has been under scrutiny since the late 1970s and early 1980s, when a spate of high-profile ethnographic studies first drew attention to the messiness of knowledge production. For example, Bruno Latour and Steven Woolgar (1979), in their influential work *Laboratory Life: The Social Construction of Scientific Facts*, described how scientific facts are manufactured with a view to producing influential publications and maximizing individual and group 'credibility capital', while G. Nigel Gilbert and Michael Mulkay's *Opening Pandora's Box: A Sociological Analysis of Scientific Discourse* (1984) deconstructed the 'empiricist repertoire' with which scientists discursively produce and sustain accounts of their theories. Particularly significant in the context of the present volume is Karin Knorr-Cetina's *The Manufacture of Knowledge* (1981), which in Chapter 5 (94–135) traces the process of scientific text production from rough notes to final research paper, making it effectively an exercise in genetic criticism.

A similar dynamic has been followed in more recent studies of academic writing processes that have taken place in the domain of applied linguistics. Perhaps the most famous of these is the longitudinal project entitled *Professional Academic Writing in the Global Context* undertaken by Theresa Lillis and Mary Jane Curry, which tracked the textual production of fifty scholars from four non-Anglophone contexts (Hungary, Slovakia, Spain and Portugal) in two disciplinary fields (education and psychology) over the course of eight years. Using a text-oriented ethnographic approach, Lillis and Curry attempted to capture traces of the history of text production by documenting the various revisions and rewritings needed to put these scholars' academic papers into publishable form. Although the resulting book, *Academic Writing in a Global Context: The Politics and Practices of Publishing in English* (2010), focuses primarily on texts that were written directly in English rather than translated,[2] it nevertheless provides interesting evidence about the way the rhetoric of these authors is successively honed through the intervention of various 'literacy brokers' – a useful category that includes both 'language brokers' (translators, authors' editors, proofreaders, etc.) and 'academic brokers' (supervisors, colleagues, peer reviewers, journal editors), operating on a formal (professional or paid) or informal (amateur or friendly) basis.

In the same year, I myself published the results of a study (Bennett 2010a)[3] that had been undertaken in a similar spirit, though in this case the main focus was on the role played by translation and paratranslational activities in international research publication. Based on a questionnaire rather than on text histories, it sought to uncover the strategies used by Portuguese social science and humanities scholars to get their work published in English. The results revealed a whole spectrum of methods, including: writing the text directly in English; writing it in English with revision by a native speaker; writing in Portuguese and then translating it into English oneself; writing in Portuguese and having it translated by a non-native-speaker colleague or acquaintance, perhaps with revision by a native speaker; writing in Portuguese and having it translated by a native-speaker colleague or acquaintance, having it translated by a professional translator or submitting the text in Portuguese to the publisher, who then has the text translated by 'their' translator (Bennett 2010a: 206).[4] Thus, like Lillis and Curry (2010), this study makes it clear that third-party intervention in scholarly texts is the norm rather than the exception.

In addition, the study also shows that translation in the academic context is emphatically *not* a binary activity involving two people (author and translator) and two texts (source text/target text or original/translation), as the dominant model has tended to assert. Instead, what we are faced with is a series of drafts which progressively adapts the text to the demands of the new language system by means of a complex series of negotiations in which suggestions are proffered, adapted and incorporated over a period of time.

Although none of the above studies has been specifically labelled as genetic criticism, it is clear that they have much in common with that approach, as described by Deppman et al. (2004) and applied to translation studies by Munday (2014) and Cordingley and Montini (2015).[5] All of them are attempting to 'restore a temporal dimension to texts', which they do 'not only by looking for the influence of external social, economic, and cultural circumstances on the text, but also by reading the text's own history, a history that takes into account those external forces and the way they interact ... with the text's development' (Deppman et al. 2004: 5). Some (i.e. Knorr Cetina 1981, Chapter 5; Lillis and Curry 2010) focus specifically on the working documents produced during the preparation of the academic article (i.e. the various manuscripts, drafts and plans known in genetic criticism as *avant-textes*), often complemented with other data sources. And although my own study (Bennett 2010a) was based on a survey rather than on textual scholarship, it nevertheless opens up avenues of enquiry that would be highly susceptible to a genetic approach, as I outline further.

This chapter, then, revisits that earlier study in the light of new questions raised by genetic translation studies, in order to assess its potential to contribute to ongoing debates about authorship and translation in the academic context. To what extent is single authorship a fiction in this domain and why is that fiction so carefully maintained? In a context still dominated by the English language, what is the role played by translation, who is responsible for it and at what point does it actually occur? Finally, what does the entire operation tell us about the way languages and epistemologies interact in the process of global knowledge production?

A crucial node in this investigation will be the concept of self-translation, an area that has begun to attract attention within the context of genetic translation studies. By exploring the various kinds of self-translation manifested in the 2010 survey in the light of new scholarship on the subject, I hope to further complicate the notion of academic authorship and raise new questions about the (social, cognitive and epistemological) processes involved in academic text production.

The chapter begins with a review of the literature about self-translation in general and in the academic domain in particular. It then returns to the 2010 study to gauge the prevalence of this practice among the Portuguese scholars questioned and the place of self-translation within the broader process of second-language academic text production. Finally, the chapter concludes with a discussion of the notions of *intertext* and *interculture*, as raised by Jung (2002: 19, 29–37) and Pym (1998: 177–92), respectively, offering some suggestions for how genetic translation studies might further elucidate these issues.

Self-translation: The literature

After years of neglect,[6] there has recently been an upsurge of interest in self-translation among translation scholars. Monographs and edited volumes have appeared on the subject by Hokenson and Munson (2007), Anselmi (2012), Cordingley (2013a) and Castro et al. (2017), as well as special issues of journals (e.g. Hopkinson 2005; Antunes and Grutman 2014), entries in encyclopaedias and handbooks (Grutman 1998 and 2009; Montini 2010; Grutman and Van Bolderen 2014) and at least one online bibliography (Gentes and Van Bolderen 2010). There have been conferences and workshops, most notably in Italy,[7] and of course various articles dealing with case studies in different languages and contexts.

In most of these works, self-translation is understood in the narrow sense as 'the translation of an original work into another language by the author himself' (Popovič [1976: 19] qtd. in Montini 2010: 306 and Grutman and Van Bolderen 2014: 323) and is carefully distinguished from 'standard', 'ordinary' or 'allograph' translation by the greater *authority* it is felt to exert[8] and the enhanced *agency* of the individual undertaking it.[9] Other distinguishing features that have been identified include a tendency for *bidirectionality* (unlike standard translators, self-translators do not seem to feel constrained to work exclusively into their mother tongue, if indeed they recognize such a thing), *simultaneity* (in that it sometimes occurs before the 'original' text is complete) and *covertness* (in that the work's translated status is often denied or occulted by self-translators and their publishers [Grutman and Van Bolderen 2014: 327–9]).

Elsewhere, though, self-translation is interpreted in a broader, more metaphorical sense, according to which *second-language writing* is understood to be a form of mental self-translation. Instances of this can be found 'in analyses of gender-bending writers (from Oscar Wilde to Manuel Puig) who reinvent themselves sexually and artistically when changing countries and/or languages, either with or without translating their own work' (Grutman and Van Bolderen 2014: 323) and also 'in migration studies … in which writers' identities, their "selves", are remolded by the move to a new country and the integration into a new language-culture' (Grutman and Van Bolderen 2014: 323).[10] A similar understanding of the term is found in the context of postcolonial intercultural writing to describe the 'representation of the Self in the language of the Other' (Bandia 2008: 163–4). In these contexts, the notion is often endowed with a negative charge, suggesting loss of identity and the imposition of alien values by a dominating power.

Despite the fact that Grutman (1998: 17 qtd. in Montini 2010 and Jung 2002: 15) considers self-translation a 'fairly common practice in scholarly publishing',[11] there are actually very few studies of the phenomenon in the academic domain. In fact, I have only found three that explicitly use 'self-translation' in their title (Jung 2002; Chan 2016; Pisanski 2018),[12] though some contrastive studies of academic rhetoric have used self-translations as sources of data (e.g. Van Bonn and Swales 2007; Perales-Escudero and Swales 2011; Alharbi and Swales 2011), while others acknowledge self-translation as a significant strategy in the dissemination process (Montgomery 2009; Morley and Kerans 2013).

The three works that explore academic self-translation explicitly are quite different from each other in the way that they approach the phenomenon. Let us begin by looking at the most recent of these, Agnes Pisanski Peterlin's 2018 article 'Self-Translation of Academic Discourse: The Attitudes and Experiences of Authors–Translators', as it is in many respects the most straightforward of the three.

This is a survey of non-native English-speaking (NNES) authors who publish in English, which focuses on the practice of self-translation in the narrow sense. Nine Slovene scholars from different disciplines were interviewed about their experiences with and attitudes towards academic self-translation, revealing that many of them drafted their papers and research proposals in English and then translated some parts into Slovene to comply with the demands of the national language policy. These self-translations were therefore predominantly from the foreign language into the mother tongue.

The reasons for this practice seem to be related to the relative underdevelopment of the academic register in Slovene and the corresponding existence of state-imposed language-protection policies obliging scholars to present certain texts (predominantly research proposals and abstracts of written and orally delivered papers) bilingually. Many respondents claimed to have learned their subject through English-language textbooks and therefore found it easier to draft their papers directly in that language, and some mentioned explicitly that the specialized terminology in their field had not yet been established in Slovene, forcing them to coin new words whenever they wrote or translated in that language. As regards their attitudes to the activity, these self-translators typically felt themselves to be at liberty to substantially alter the text in relation to the preceding version, in some cases going beyond mere linguistic adaptation to implement major changes of content.[13] This accords with the increased agency reported by other studies (Markkanen and Schröder 1989; Jung 2002; Perales-Escudero and Swales 2011).

Leo Chan's (2016) article on academic production in the Chinese context could not be more different from Pisanski Peterlin's as regards its approach and analysis. He presents the options facing NNES scholars as a stark choice between *non-translation* (understood as an act of resistance to the hegemony of English, inevitably leading to the author's exclusion from the global stage), *translation* (undertaken by a third party or by oneself and resulting in the production of a bilingual text) and *self-translation* (which he ostentatiously places in inverted commas to indicate that he is actually referring to writing directly in the foreign language, with or without a 'collaborator'). Hence, 'self-translation' is here conceptualized in the broader sense as an entirely internal or mental process (Chan 2016: 153, 166),[14] distinguishable from translation proper by its absence of a source text. The fact that Chan presents it as occurring in an ideologically charged environment where English is viewed as an epistemological colonizer brings it closer to the understanding of 'self-translation' that predominates in postcolonial and diaspora contexts.

Verena Jung's book-length work *English–German Self-Translation of Academic Texts and Its Relevance for Translation Theory and Practice* (2002) is by far and away the most complex study of the three, and sheds a lot of light upon these issues. Aiming to 'understand the nature of self-translation and to view it as a means of approaching the question of translation and the problem of equivalence … from a new perspective' (Jung 2002: 13), it takes a text-linguistic approach to a corpus of eight academic self-translations of different lengths and disciplines, which are systematically compared with a control group of 'ordinary' translations of the same texts undertaken by trainees. Self-translation itself is not formally defined at the beginning of the book, but the examples show that she is using it, like Pisanski Peterlin (2018) and most of the other authors reviewed in this section, in the narrow sense of 'the translation of an original work into another language by the author himself' (Popovič 1976: 19).

This unproblematic understanding of self-translation begins to unravel right away in the first chapter with the announcement of several internal distinctions, which are initially presented as binaries: translation into the mother tongue versus translation into the foreign language; unaided versus co-authored translation; homoskopic versus heteroskopic; and simultaneous versus delayed (Popovič 1976: 22–9). However, when Jung applies these categories to her corpus (Popovič 1976: 36–41), it transpires that none of them actually operate as simple binaries in practice, and she finds it necessary to present her results graphically by the use of continuums (Table 2, page 37). These cases, then, all serve to complicate the notion of self-translation in a fruitful way.

In short, then, we have various understandings of self-translation in the academic sphere. The narrow definition, used by Pisanski Peterlin and Jung, draws, of course, upon the conventional distinction between author and translator (in which the former produces an 'original'[15] text and the latter a derivative), implying that, in self-translation, there is a merging or centralization of functions. Used thus, the term 'self-translation' also has connotations of independence and autonomy (in the sense that doing something 'by oneself' essentially means doing it alone). However, in the academic sphere, this is clearly not borne out in practice, for, like the scholars studied by Lillis and Curry (2010), Jung's self-translators admitted receiving (often unacknowledged) help from author's editors and other literacy brokers (2002: 24–5, 37). This suggests that there is work to be done on the concept of 'collaborative self-translation' (Manterola Agirrezabalaga 2017) or 'semiautotraducción' (Dasilva 2016) in the academic context.

The broader understanding of self-translation is also visible in the literature about academic writing. Chan uses the term pointedly, as we have seen, to refer to the process of second-language writing, in which translation is understood to take place internally, in the mind of the author (2016: 153, 166). What is more, the process does not remain in the domain of the cognitive. Chan inflects the term to activate the ideological sense prevalent in postcolonial studies, justifying it with a critique of the hegemony of English in the academic sphere, which he views as a kind of internalized colonialism. However, it is clear from Chan's analysis that there is an important epistemological dimension to this kind of translation, over and above the identity concerns. Invoking my own work on epistemicide (Bennett 2012, also 2007 and 2015), he refers to 'the loss of valuable local knowledge and styles of representation' that is now occurring in Chinese academic publishing due to the 'pressure of "Englishization" in academia and the imposition of Anglo-American discursive practices' (Chan 2016: 160–1).

Self-translation in research publication: The practice

The survey that has served as the springboard for this study (Bennett 2010a) was carried out within the ambit of a much larger project that sought to first chart the divergences between Portuguese and English academic discourses in the humanities and social sciences, and then to explore what happens to Portuguese scholarship in these fields when it is rewritten or translated for international publication. Aiming primarily to gauge the attitude of Portuguese social science and humanities researchers towards academic discourse in both languages, and to find out something about their habits as regards the production of academic texts in English, it was carried out by means of a questionnaire, sent out by e-mail to Portuguese researchers listed on the site of the Portuguese research funding body (the Foundation for Science and Technology) in 2002 and again in 2008.

The questionnaire broached issues such as: the perceived differences between Portuguese and English discourse in the respondent's discipline; the perceived advantages/disadvantages of English academic discourse in relation to Portuguese; attitudes towards the hegemony of English in academic publishing; experience of publishing in English; and, crucially, the methods that scholars used to produce the English text. Amongst these, self-translation, in both senses of the term, clearly played a role in the process of preparing research undertaken in Portuguese for publication in English.

Unfortunately, as self-translation was not a priority of that original study, no further data was gathered on the subject, nor was there any chance of contacting the original respondents a decade later to procure more. Hence, we do not know exactly which fields those researchers came from, whether these were simultaneous or delayed self-translations or whether the Portuguese versions were published before the English ones. What we do know, though, from responses given to the more open questions is that self-translation into English was undertaken fairly routinely alongside other strategies, and that the English texts thus produced were often revised by a language broker afterwards, usually a native speaker. We can conclude that it was, at that time, a common stage in the process of adapting research undertaken in Portuguese for international publication.

In 2018, an attempt was made to compensate for the deficits in the 2010 study by launching a new one that would focus exclusively on self-translation (in the narrow sense). However, disappointingly, only three responses were received, and none of them referred to self-translation as a routine stage in the process of preparing texts for publication in English.[16] Indeed, the marked absence of such 'classic' cases suggests that the scenario may have changed since 2010 and that more Portuguese researchers are now producing their research articles directly in English.[17] When self-translation occurs, it now seems to be on an occasional basis, in response to specific demands or in order to artificially boost a researcher's publication record.

Given this lack of data, it is probably more fruitful to look instead at the (much more prevalent) phenomenon of second-language writing, considered by many, as we have seen, as another form of self-translation. One of the more interesting findings from the 2010 survey was that Portuguese researchers perceived a marked difference between English and Portuguese academic discourse in all disciplines and consciously adapted their style to suit Anglophone expectations. In fact, there was an amazing consistency among the respondents as to what this entailed. They inevitably claimed that they were more precise, succinct or economical when writing in English, and that they used shorter sentences with less subordination, were more pragmatic and factual (less flowery or poetic) and adopted a plainer more straightforward style, with less overt rhetorical manoeuvring. This was consistent with their perceptions of the differences between English and Portuguese academic discourse in their disciplines (expressed in response to an earlier question).[18]

Particularly significant for the present study is that this process of stylistic adaptation was not exclusive to texts written directly in English. Crucially, many of those respondents also said that they would *make similar changes to their Portuguese texts when they knew that they were going to be translated by a third party* (2010a: 206). That is to say, texts that had been written first in Portuguese often underwent a process of adaptation *prior to translation* in order to bring them closer to what their authors perceived the English style to be. What is more, these adjustments were not just cosmetic. Like Chan (2016), these respondents were also very conscious of the structuring effects of discourse and of the epistemological consequences of writing up their research in a hegemonic language. In response to a question about the advantages and disadvantages of English within their area of study, several researchers described English academic discourse as impoverished and reductive compared to Portuguese. For example, one literary scholar claimed that his ideas were 'limited by the conceptual structure of the English language', while a sociologist complained of feeling 'enclosed in Anglo-American concerns and preoccupations (or worldview)' due to 'the ethnocentricity of perceptual and conceptual categories, transmitted by the linguistic tools of an imperial power that is unused and often averse to understanding the place and worldview of the Other' (qtd. in Bennett 2011a: 99; 2010a: 197). In the light of this, then, there seems to be some justification for introducing a new category – that of *epistemological translation*[19] – in order to account for the (often distressing) experience of having to reformulate scholarship that has been prepared in one epistemological paradigm in terms acceptable to another.

What is clear, then, is that the process of preparing research done in one language for publication in another is much more complex than has hitherto been assumed, involving multiple transformations of a linguistic, stylistic and epistemological nature. A genetic approach may thus have an important role to play in clarifying the mechanisms and agents involved.

Towards a genetic approach: Intertexts and intercultures

As we have seen, various agents typically intervene in the production of an academic text, complicating the notion of authorship. Even when the text has been labelled a self-translation (in the narrow or broader senses), we can expect some degree of participation from literacy brokers of both the formal and informal varieties. This suggests that there exists a continuum of coauthorship, which, at the far end, might actually disqualify the term 'self-translation' altogether. Determining just who intervenes and at what point during the process is essential to acquiring a fuller understanding of how academic authorship operates in the global context.

An even more pressing question for translation scholars is of knowing exactly when the crossing of the language barrier actually occurs and who is/are responsible for it. As we have seen, there is evidence that academic texts may be epistemologically adapted prior to actual translation, undermining the conventional understanding of languages as structurally bounded entities. To what extent are languages actually separate in this domain? Is it possible to identify the precise moment when a text written in one language passes into another? And in a world where scholars, teachers, editors and peer reviewers are routinely expected to operate in various languages, is it realistic to assume that one person is single-handedly responsible for that border crossing?

Genetic translation criticism might make a significant contribution to both of these concerns. For example, examination of self-translators' correspondence and the minutes of their meetings should shed light on their conversations with mentors and other colleagues, while a study of the plans, drafts and notes used in the preparation of academic articles would reveal not only the textual consequences of such (tacit) collaborations, but also what language(s) these authors are thinking in during the project design, literature review, data-collection and planning. It could confirm if code-switching and hybridity are present in the pretextual stage, as the disciplinary discourse is negotiated and terminological equivalences are sought. In cases where the knowledge being created is of the local culturally embedded variety, the *avant-textes* may reveal rudimentary attempts to express in English concepts that are particular to the local context. Conversely, they may show the importation into the home language of terms circulating in the international lingua franca, phrase-length structures encountered during reading and/or discussions, or even paragraph or text patterns inculcated in academic writing classes.

At this point, it might be useful to examine the concept of *intertext*, which Jung (2002: 19, 29–37) introduces in the context of a discussion about whether a self-translation may truly be considered a 'second original'. Following Fitch (1985: 116), she argues that, although this might be true in simultaneous self-translation (when the two versions are produced more or less concurrently), the notion works less well in the case of delayed self-translation as 'the self-translator has to read his own text again just as any translator would' (Jung 2002: 29) in order to produce the new work. It is at this point that Jung stumbles upon what is probably the most significant distinction between self- and 'ordinary' translation, an observation that has since been reproduced by Grutman and Van Bolderen (2014: 329):

> The main difference between self-translators and ordinary translators ... is that self-translators can access their original *intention* ... better than ordinary translators and the original cultural context or literary *intertext* of their original work. Although it can be argued that even self-translators cannot completely access their original intention or inner text, I would at least postulate that they can access the *memory of an intention* better than ordinary translators. (Jung 2002: 30; emphases added)

Accessing the intention is, she goes on, essentially a process of *interpreting* that first intention, a notion she explores using Quasthoff's (1980: 48) concept of cognitive memory structure. According to this, there exists in the mind a cognitive version of the text that is accessed whenever one wishes to reproduce the work, though the 'pre-verbal message' is never retold in exactly the same way: rather, the account will be shaped by the new situation and the author's understanding of his or her listeners' or readers' expectations (i.e. the new Skopos).

As for the intertext, Jung is not entirely consistent as to what this entails. When the term is first mentioned, she defines it as 'what knowing the academic language means':

> This is not just a question of terminology ... but also of knowing from extensive reading in that subject the way sentences are conventionally formed and the way everyday words are normally conceptualised in the specific context in question. Thus the *literature in that field* is the intertext that is at the disposal of the writer and the readers. Intertext is used here in accordance with Bakhtin's concept of dialogicity ... not in the sense of one particular text that is quoted by the author, but *a collective knowledge distilled from a multiplicity of texts read by the authors* or even *language usage that they have absorbed*. (Jung 2002: 19; emphases added)

This suggests that the intertext is a set of social practices, akin to what academic writing expert John Swales (1990: 6) calls 'genre conventions'[20] and which others have called 'discourse'.[21] Later, however, Jung's understanding of intertext becomes something altogether more mental, when she redefines it as the 'non-verbalized background structure that cannot be accessed by anyone but the author' (2002: 30). This then becomes the basis for her claim that 'intertext and original intention ... are included in the *pre-stage of the original* that can be accessed by the self-translator, but not by an ordinary translator' (2002: 30; emphasis added).

Elsewhere, though, Jung includes under intertext both *physical documents* ('written sources, texts they [the self-translators] had read and which have influenced their thought') and *mental operations* ('language use and memories of the writing process or of the inner process before the writing process'), claiming that this is material 'that ordinary translators cannot access' (Jung 2002: 29). Today, we might dispute the latter claim: the written sources she lists have of course become objects of study for practitioners of genetic translation studies, while cognitive processes are now routinely investigated using techniques such as speak-aloud protocols and eye tracking.

What Jung *is* clear about, however, is that the intertext forms part of the '*pre-stage* of the original' (2002: 30; emphasis added). This means that she is not using the term in quite the same way as Genette, who defines it as 'a relationship of co-presence between two texts' manifested through mechanisms of quotation, plagiarism or allusion (Genette 1997: 1–2); nor is she using it like Michael Riffaterre, for whom it is 'the perception, by the reader, of the relationship between a work and others that have either preceded or followed it' (qtd. in Genette 1997: 2). For Jung, the intertext seems instead to be something more like a nebulous or foetal phase in a text's formation in which the work is not yet fully individuated from the broader discourse in which it participates. As such it may encompass all the various textual and conversational interactions that the author has engaged in prior to its conception (and indeed those he or she has not participated in directly but which have left traces in the verbal environment), as well as all the preliminary stages of the writing process from brainstorming and planning through to drafting and revising.

Given the multilingual nature of the environments in which such processes typically take place (and here I am thinking not only of the composition of university departments, research teams and conferences but also of online textual environments and data sources), it seems highly probable that the intertexts, thus defined, will bear traces of the various languages and discourses that have contributed to the author's personal evolution. English will play an important role from the outset, it is assumed, given its unrivalled position as the international lingua franca of academic thought. But we are likely to also see traces of the language in which the data has been collected and in which conversations have occurred, the languages of theorists discussed and read (even when they have been read in translation) and those of the various literacy brokers that intervene. Therefore, even when a paper has been apparently drafted in one language and translated, conventionally, into another, we can assume that there will have been other translational acts upstream (of concepts, phrases or larger structures), as the author sought to incorporate insights that arose during reading or discussion.[22] All of these will leave marks in the *avant-textes*, and thus be susceptible to investigation by genetic translation scholars.

At this point, it is useful to recall Anthony Pym's notion of the *interculture*, as described in his book *Method in Translation History* (1998: 177–92) and which is neatly summed up by Hokenson and Munson:

> Pym observes that real translators live and work not in a hypothetical gap between languages, between source and target cultures, but in the midst of them; they combine several languages and cultural competencies at once, and constitute a mid-zone of overlaps and intersections, being actively engaged in several cultures simultaneously. (2007: 4)

Modern academia is such an interculture, I would argue, in that all players – researchers, teachers, authors, literacy brokers – routinely operate in a space that contains elements of at least two linguistic and epistemological cultures: their own, and the dominant one, as represented by English. More complex intercultures may be found in specific situations, such as when Portuguese researchers who publish in English have German philosophy as their object of study or use heuristic tools borrowed from French post-structuralism (both real-life scenarios alluded to in my survey [Bennett 2010a]).

This model of academic production suggests that it may no longer be feasible to view the influences between languages and cultures as unidirectional, flowing from a dominant centre to a purported periphery, as was so frequently argued in the first decade of the twenty-first century (Swales 1997; Canagarajah 2002a, 2002b; Bennett 2007). Instead, the picture now seems more to be one of mutual contaminations and enrichments[23] within a variegated interculture that scholars draw upon at will. Determining the way particular texts gradually take shape within this fecund matrix through the authorial–translatorial actions of multilingual scholars will be a very worthwhile goal for genetic translation studies.

Finally, we should not overlook the processes of rewriting that occur after the academic article has been completed. We know, for example, that the finished text will usually need to be summarized in the form of abstract for publication (which may differ substantially from the prospective abstract prepared to secure funding or a publication contract); that it may be rewritten for oral presentation at a conference or for use in a lesson; and that, further down the line, it might be repackaged in a literature review or as a starting point for a new research proposal. The tools developed within genetic translation studies should also help us understand how these *post-textes* evolve, autonomize and then gradually re-enter the linguistic flux to become part of the intertext that nurtures the scholarship of future generations.

Notes

1. That is, 'a translation which enjoys the status of an original text in the receiving lingua-culture' and which 'is not marked pragmatically as a translation at all, but may, conceivably, have been created in its own right' (House 2010: 245).
2. The authors explain why translation is scarcely represented in their corpus: 'Scholars are overwhelmingly dissatisfied and suspicious of using translation; of course cost is one key issue, with many scholars not able to pay the fees that might secure a high quality translation, a point recognized by professional translators. Scholars do not blame translators per se, but rather the fact that it is very difficult to find a translator who is sufficiently familiar with their subfield specialism to produce meaningful texts' (Lillis and Curry 2010: 95).
3. A longer version of this paper, including extensive quotations from respondents, is available in the book *Academic Writing in Portugal: Discourses in Conflict* (Bennett 2011a: 75–116).
4. Montgomery (2009) offers a similar list of 'forms of translation' used in the academic domain, based on his 'own past work and on observations and discussions involving other translators'.
5. Genetic translation studies analyses 'the practice of the working translator and the evolution, or genesis, of the translated text by studying translators' manuscripts, drafts and other working documents … its object is the textual evidence of the activity of translation' (Cordingley and Montini 2015: 1).
6. A number of reasons have been put forward for this lack of interest in self-translation within translation studies. These include the perception that self-translation is 'more akin to bilingualism than to translation proper' (Grutman 1997: 17 qtd. in Montini 2010: 306); the persistence of the notions of 'author' and 'original' deriving from theories of nationalistic monolingualism (Hokenson and Munson 2007: 2); and the intractable conceptual problems that arise when the bilingual text is approached using conventional text theory (Hokenson and Munson 2007: 2).
7. For example, conferences in Udine (2010 and 2012), Pescara (2010), Bologna (2011) and Florence (2015). See also the conference on *Self-Translation in the Iberian Peninsula* held in Cork in 2013 and another on *Collaborative Translation and Self-Translation* in Birmingham (2016).
8. '[T]he author's authority is transferred metonymically to the final product, which thus becomes a second original' (Grutman and Van Bolderen 2014: 324); 'the self-translated text *is* a second original, rendered into a second language with all the liberty an author always enjoys (but never a translator); an original that has the benefit of *authorial intentionality* …' (Santoyo 2013: 28–9; emphases in the original).
9. Grutman and van Bolderen (2014: 324) claim that 'self-translators are routinely given poetic license to rewrite "their" originals', a claim supported by most other authors such as Cordingley (2013b: 2), Montini (2010: 306) and Grutman (2009: 259).

10   The most famous manifestation of this idea is probably in Salman Rushdie's claim 'we are translated men' ([1982] 1992). Paul Bandia (2008: 163–4) describes self-translation in the context of postcolonial intercultural writing as 'displacement or movement from one's context of origin into an alien, imposed sphere'.
11   This claim is supported by other accounts of academic practices, such as Pérez-Llantada et al. (2011) and Montgomery (2009).
12   There was also a conference on *Self-Translation as Transfer of Knowledge* in Berlin in 2014 (www.zfl-berlin.org/event/selbstuebersetzung-als-wissenstransfer.html), the proceedings of which are forthcoming.
13   Two respondents claimed that the process of self-translation actually helped them revise and develop 'the text', with one specifying that the 'source text' was also altered during self-translation.
14   Chan (2016: 163) bases this argument on Chovanec's claim (2012: 5) that a translatological approach is required for the study of non-native speaker academic writing in English, given the 'transference or "translation" of generic features from first-language writing' which marks such production.
15   The concept of 'originality' is problematized by Hokenson and Munson (2007: 158) and Cordingley (2013a) in the context of the bilingual text.
16   One, by a senior Portuguese academic, had been originally written (and published) in English and was self-translated into Portuguese to be delivered as a keynote lecture at a Portuguese conference; the second, by an English native speaker resident in Portugal, had been written in Portuguese for publication in a national journal, and was self-translated into English to be published for a second time in an international one; the third had been written in Spanish by a Portuguese Hispanist and published in that language, before being self-translated into Portuguese for republication in a Portuguese-language journal. All were in the area of literary studies.
17   If this is the case, it is almost certainly due to the fact that Portuguese universities have in recent years invested heavily in providing courses of English for Academic Purposes and English for Research Publication Purposes, with the result that the current generation of researchers is much more comfortable writing directly in English.
18   This perception largely coincided with the findings of a corpus study designed to identify the main differences between English and Portuguese academic writing in different disciplines (Bennett 2010b, 2011). However, there is evidence that, since then, Portuguese academic discourse in the humanities has changed to become much more like English (Bennett 2014).
19   This is not necessarily restricted to second-language writing. It is clearly present in conventional translation, as I pointed out in my works on epistemicide (Bennett 2007, 2012, 2015).
20   Jung actively assimilates 'intertext' to 'genre conventions' on pages 30 and 35 when she sets about creating a model of the self-translation process.
21   Kress defines discourse as 'a set of possible statements about a given area', which 'organises and gives structure to the manner in which a particular topic, object, process is to be talked about' (1985: 7). The extensive bibliography that now exists about academic discourse generally subscribes to this definition.
22   Montgomery supports this perception by providing a long list of forms of translation commonly used in academia, including 'the writing/reading of emails, letters and other communications in a non-native language, requiring mental translation during the process' and 'discussion among colleagues (in the mother tongue) of an article or talk written/presented in English' (2009: 9–10).

23 While there is clear evidence that Portuguese history discourse is changing to become more like English (Bennett 2014), there are also signs that English academic discourse has incorporated terms and concepts, and even modes of textual organization, from other academic cultures. Indeed, scholars working in the domain of English as a Lingua Franca argue that academic English is no longer the property of native speakers, and the grammatical and lexical features that it has absorbed from other languages mark it out as a specific variety (Mauranen, Hynninen and Ranta 2010; Mauranen 2012).

References

Alharbi, Lafi M. and John M. Swales (2011), 'Arabic and English Abstracts in Bilingual Education Science Journals: Same or Different?', *Languages in Contrast*, 11 (1): 70–86.

Anselmi, Simona (2012), *On Self-Translation: An Exploration in Self-Translators' Teloi and Strategies*, Milano: LED.

Antunes, Maria Alice and Rainier Grutman (eds) (2014), *Auto-Tradução/Self-Translation*, special issue of *Tradução em Revista*, 16 (1).

Bandia, Paul F. (2008), *Translation as Reparation: Writing and Translation in Postcolonial Africa*, Manchester, UK, and Kinderhook, NY: St. Jerome Publishing.

Bennett, Karen (2007), 'Epistemicide! The Tale of a Predatory Discourse', *Translation and Ideology: Cultures and Clashes*, special issue of *The Translator*, 13 (2): 151–69.

Bennett, Karen (2010a), 'Academic Writing Practices in Portugal: Survey of Humanities and Social Science Researchers', *Diacrítica – Série Ciências da Linguagem*, 24 (1): 193–209.

Bennett, Karen (2010b), 'Academic Discourse in Portugal: A Whole Different Ballgame', *Journal of English for Academic Purposes*, 9 (1): 21–32.

Bennett, Karen (2011), *Academic Writing in Portugal I. Discourses in Conflict*, Coimbra: Coimbra University Press.

Bennett, Karen (2012), *English Academic Discourse: Its Hegemonic Status and Implications for Translation (with Particular Reference to Portuguese)*, Saarbrucken: Lambert Academic Publishing.

Bennett, Karen (2014), 'The Erosion of Portuguese Historiographic Discourse', in Karen Bennett (ed.), *The Semiperiphery of Academic Writing: Discourses, Communities, Practices*, 13–38, London: Palgrave Macmillan.

Bennett, Karen (2015), 'Towards an Epistemological Monoculture: Mechanisms of Epistemicide in European Research Publication', in Ramón Plo Alastrué and Carmen Pérez-Llantada (eds), *English as an Academic and Research Language*, 9–35, Berlin: De Gruyter Mouton.

Blommaert, Jan (2010), *The Sociolinguistics of Globalization*, Cambridge, UK, and New York: Cambridge University Press.

Canagarajah, A. Suresh (2002a), *A Geopolitics of Academic Writing*, Pittsburgh: University of Pittsburgh Press.

Canagarajah, A. Suresh (2002b), *Critical Academic Writing and Multilingual Students*, Ann Arbor: University of Michigan Press.

Canagarajah, A. Suresh (2013), *Translingual Practice: Global Englishes and Cosmopolitan Relations*, London and New York: Routledge.

Carneiro, Marco A., Silvia Cangussú and G. Wilson Fernandes (2007), 'Ethical Abuses in the Authorship of Scientific Papers', *Revista Brasileira de Entomologia*, 51 (1): 1–5.

Castro, Olga, Sergi Mainer and Svetlana Page (eds) (2017), *Self-Translation and Power: Negotiating Identities in European Multilingual Contexts*, London: Palgrave Macmillan.
Chan, Leo Tak-hung (2016), 'Beyond Non-Translation and "Self-Translation": English as Lingua Academica in China', *Translation and Interpreting Studies*, 11 (2): 152–76.
Chovanec, Jan (2012), 'Written Academic Discourse in English: From Local Traditions to Global Outreach', *Brno Studies in English*, 38 (2): 5–16.
Cordingley, Anthony (ed.) (2013a), *Self-Translation: Brokering Originality in Hybrid Culture*, London and New York: Bloomsbury.
Cordingley, Anthony (2013b), 'Introduction: Self-Translation, Going Global', in Anthony Cordingley (ed.), *Self-Translation: Brokering Originality in Hybrid Culture*, 1–10, London and New York: Bloomsbury.
Cordingley, Anthony and Chiara Montini (2015), 'Genetic Translation Studies: An Emerging Discipline', *Linguistica Anverpiensia, New Series: Themes in Translation Studies*, 14: 1–18.
Dasilva, Xosé Manuel (2016), 'En torno al concepto de semiautotraducción', *Quaderns: Revista de Traducció*, 23: 15–35.
Deppman, Jed, Daniel Ferrer and Michael Groden (eds) (2004), *Genetic Criticism: Texts and Avant-Textes*, Philadelphia: University of Pennsylvania Press.
Desai, Chetna (2012), 'Authorship Issues', *Indian Journal of Pharmacology*, 44 (4): 433–4.
Fitch, Brian T. (1985), 'The Status of Self-Translation', *Texte*, 4: 111–25.
Genette, Gerard (1997), *Paratexts: Thresholds of Interpretation*, Cambridge: Cambridge University Press.
Gentes, Eva and Trish Van Bolderen (2010), 'Self-Translation', in *Oxford Bibliographies*. Available online: http://www.oxfordbibliographies.com/view/document/obo-9780199913701/obo-9780199913701-0104.xml (accessed 4 March 2019).
Gilbert, G. Nigel and Michael Mulkay (1984), *Opening Pandora's Box: A Sociological Analysis of Scientific Discourse*, Cambridge: Cambridge University Press.
Grutman, Rainier (1997), *Des Langues qui résonnent. L'Hétérolinguisme au XIXe siècle québécois*, Montréal: Fides.
Grutman, Rainier (1998), 'Auto-Translation', in Mona Baker and Kirsten Malmkjaer (eds), *Routledge Encyclopedia of Translation Studies*, 1st edn, 17–21, London and New York: Routledge.
Grutman, Rainier (2009), 'Self-Translation', in Mona Baker and Gabriela Saldanha (eds), *Routledge Encyclopedia of Translation Studies*, 2nd edn, 257–60, London and New York: Routledge.
Grutman, Rainier and Trish Van Bolderen (2014), 'Self-Translation', in Sandra Bermann and Catherine Porter (eds), *A Companion to Translation Studies*, 323–30, Chichester, UK: Wiley-Blackwell.
Hokenson, Jan W. and Marcella Munson (2007), *The Bilingual Text: History and Theory of Literary Self-Translation*, Manchester: St. Jerome Publishing.
Hopkinson, Amanda (ed.) (2005), *Self-Translation*, special issue of *In Other Words*, 25.
House, Juliane (2010), 'Overt and Covert Translation', in Yves Gambier and Luc van Doorslaer (eds), *Handbook of Translation Studies*, vol. 1, 245–6, Amsterdam and Philadelphia: John Benjamins.
Jung, Verena (2002), *English–German Self-Translation of Academic Texts and Its Relevance for Translation Theory and Practice*, Frankfurt am Main: Peter Lang.
Knorr-Cetina, Karin (1981), *The Manufacture of Knowledge*, Oxford: Pergamon.
Kress, Gunther (1985), *Linguistic Processes in Sociocultural Practice*, Victoria: Deakin University Press.

Latour, Bruno and Stephen Woolgar (1979), *Laboratory Life: The Social Construction of Scientific Facts*, Beverly Hills, CA: Sage.

Lillis, Teresa and Mary Jane Curry (2010), *Academic Writing in a Global Context: The Politics and Practices of Publishing in English*, London and New York: Routledge.

Macfarlane, Bruce (2017), 'The Ethics of Multiple Authorship: Power, Performativity and the Gift Economy', *Studies in Higher Education*, 42 (7): 1194–210.

Manterola Agirrezabalaga, Elizabete (2017), 'Collaborative Self-Translation in a Minority Language: Power Implications in the Process, the Actors and the Literary Systems Involved', in Olga Castro, Sergi Mainer and Svetlana Page (eds), *Self-Translation and Power: Negotiating Identities in European Multilingual Contexts*, 191–216, London: Palgrave.

Markkanen, Raija and Hartcnut Schröder (1989), 'Hedging as a Translation Problem in Scientific Texts', in Christer Laurén and Marianne Nordman (eds), *Special Languages: From Human Thinking to Thinking Machines*, 171–9, Clarendon: Multilingual Matters.

Mauranen, Anna (2012), *Exploring ELF: Academic English Shaped by Non-Native Speakers*, Cambridge: Cambridge University Press.

Mauranen, Anna, Niina Hynninen and Elina Ranta (2010), 'English as an Academic Lingua Franca: The ELFA Project', *English for Specific Purposes*, 29 (3): 183–90.

Montgomery, Scott L. (2009), 'English and Science: Realities and Issues for Translation in the Age of an Expanding Lingua Franca', *Journal of Specialised Translation*, 11: 6–16.

Montini, Chiara (2010), 'Self-Translation', in Yves Gambier and Luc van Doorslaer (eds), *Handbook of Translation Studies*, vol. 1, 306–8, Amsterdam and Philadelphia: John Benjamins.

Morley, Greg and Mary Ellen Kerans (2013), 'Bilingual Publication in Academic Journals: Motivations and Practicalities', in Valerie Matarese (ed.), *Supporting Research Writing. Roles and Challenges in Multilingual Settings*, Oxford: Chandos.

Munday, Jeremy (2014), 'Using Primary Sources to Produce a Microhistory of Translation and Translators: Theoretical and Methodological Concerns', *Translator: Studies in Intercultural Communication*, 20 (1): 64–80.

Pennycook, Alastair (2007), *Global Englishes and Transcultural Flows*, London and New York: Routledge.

Perales-Escudero, Moisés and John Swales (2011), 'Tracing Convergence and Divergence in Pairs of Spanish and English Research Article Abstracts: The Case of Ibérica', *Ibérica*, 21: 49–70.

Pérez-Llantada, Cármen, Ramón Plo and Gibson R. Ferguson (2011), '"You Don't Say What You Know, only What You Can": The Perceptions and Practices of Senior Spanish Academics Regarding Research Dissemination in English', *English for Specific Purposes*, 30: 18–30.

Pisanski Peterlin, Agnes (2018), 'Self-Translation of Academic Discourse: The Attitudes and Experiences of Authors–Translators', *Perspectives – Studies in Translation Theory and Practice*. Available online: https://doi.org/10.1080/0907676X.2018.1538255 (accessed 16 January 2019).

Popovič, Anton (1976), *Dictionary for the Analysis of Literature Translation*, Edmonton: Department of Comparative Literature/The University of Alberta.

Pym, Anthony (1998), *Method in Translation History*, London and New York: Routledge.

Quasthoff, Uta (1980), *Erzählen in Gesprächen*, Tübingen: Narr.

Rushdie, Salman ([1982] 1992), 'Imaginary Homelands', in *Imaginary Homelands: Essays and Criticism 1981-1991*, 9–21, London and New York: Granta Books in association with Penguin.

Santoyo, Julio-César (2013), 'On Mirrors, Dynamics and Self-Translations', in Anthony Cordingley (ed.), *Self-Translation: Brokering Originality in Hybrid Culture*, 27–38, London and New York: Bloomsbury.
Swales, John (1990), *Genre Analysis: English in Academic and Research Settings*, Cambridge: Cambridge University Press.
Swales, John (1997), 'English as Tyrannosaurus Rex', *World Englishes*, 16 (3): 373–82.
Van Bonn, Sarah and John M. Swales (2007), 'English and French Journal Abstracts in the Language Sciences: Three Exploratory Studies', *Journal of English for Academic Purposes*, 6: 93–108.

13

Camilo Castelo Branco, author and translator

Carlota Pimenta
Centre of Linguistics, University of Lisbon

Introduction

To illustrate the writer's creative process, Luiz Fagundes Duarte (2007) suggests the image of a war with various battles, or that of a game, fought between the writer and his or her manuscripts. Within this logic, autographic manuscripts are the battlefield and the successive corrections made by the author the spoils of war. Genetic criticism is the subject which turns its gaze from the text as a product to the text as a process and studies the vestiges of that struggle in order to understand the conditions of its emergence and the processes involved in the formation of a literary work.

Marie-Hélène Passos (2008) argues that the writing of original texts and translation are analogous processes, because both transmit a primordial effect to writing. In the case of original texts, this effect originates in the mind of the writer, and in the case of translation, this primordial effect is inscribed in the original text and is rescued and recreated by the translator. That is, through two movements that constitute the process of translation (the reading of the text in the source language and its writing in another language), the translator seeks to understand and recreate the meaning of the original text, in a creative movement opposing the work of translation to that of the work of transcription.

With Passos, we learn that the intersection between writing and translation is invention. Passos argues that the translated text itself is an original (new form), a stage for literary creation. Although it is based on a pre-existing document, the resulting translation is another text, identical in content but different in form from the original. Based on the inspiration that triggers the writing process and the uncertainty that leads to successive rewrites, the emergence and creation process of a translation is, according to Passos, similar to that of the literary text and can also be dealt with by genetic analysis.

As a result, the same modes and phases of writing will be found in the genesis of original literary texts and of literary translations. Of the two modes of literary writing described by Almuth Grésillon (1994), *écriture à processus* (writing in process) and *écriture à programme* (planned writing),[1] the former is the type of writing without a preparatory phase, which takes on its form throughout the actual process of textualization, and the latter is the type of writing that is based on a pre-existing programme which is constructed through various genetic states.

According to Grésillon (1994), the complete genesis of a text goes through three distinct stages, whether documented or not: a pre-drafting phase, which includes preparatory documents such as plans, scripts, scenarios and sketches; a drafting phase, which contains the different stages of drafting construction; and, finally, a *mise au point* (development) phase, covering fully textualized manuscripts and typescripts, making a clean copy, final copies and correction of proofs or editing.[2]

Pierre-Marc de Biasi (2011) clarifies how the two modes of writing condition the genetic profile and types of manuscripts of a work: in writing in process, the pre-drafting phase is mental and, most of the time, does not leave physical traces, while in planned writing, the pre-drafting phase translates into scripts and plans, reading notes, notes and documental research. As for the drafting phase, a writer who uses writing in process usually works on a single manuscript, which is enriched as the draft develops, becoming increasingly complex, while a writer who writes within a programmed manner works with various supports, successively making the various versions of his or her text clean, thus giving rise to more and more simplified documents.

The practices of direct reading–translation and pre-translation attested by Passos (2008) correspond to two distinct translation procedures: the former is the practice of immediate translation in which the translator spontaneously translates as he or she reads, while the latter is the practice of making reading notes before starting to translate. If, with de Biasi (2011), we assume that what distinguishes the two modes of process and programmed writing is, on the one hand, the fact that the pre-drafting phase is or is not documented and, on the other hand, the type of existing documents in the drafting phase, then we can establish a correspondence between these two modes of writing and those two translation practices. The practice of immediate translation, which does not present traces of the pre-translational phase, but begins directly in the textualization phase, working on a manuscript which becomes increasingly complex, is close to the writing in process mode; the practice of pre-translation, characterized by previous annotations in different formats and the cleaned versions of the translation, resembles the programmed writing mode.

It could thus be questioned whether the base text can be considered the programmed writing of the translation, since it presents a general structure, with categories of time, space, characters and action defined *a priori*. It follows that the mode of writing *par excellence* of the translation would be the programmed writing mode, since all translations are based on a pre-existing text which challenges the creative freedom of the translator. However, as stated above, what determines planned writing in a translation is not the inevitable existence of a base text, but rather the existence of notes made by translators themselves in preparation for their work, prior to the textualization phase of translation.

Durand-Bogaert (2014) establishes a relationship between the three genetic phases proposed by Grésillon and the stages of the translation process, namely the pre-translation, drafting and pre-editorial phases. The author advocates a degree of correspondence between the pre-drafting phase of a writer and the pre-translational phase of a translator, stressing, however, that it is difficult to find elaborate plans or general outlines in the genesis of translations. In fact, if, on the one hand, there are translators who, like writers, prepare their work in a structured way, gathering documentation and making notes before beginning to write, on the other hand, it is natural that the level of creative freedom of writers and translators constrains the type of existing materials. In practice, the translation process depends on the base text, which conditions the two movements that characterize the translation process: the reading of the original text and the writing phase.

If the creative freedom of the writer is determined by various factors, such as the linguistic system, literary and cultural history and the audience for whom he or she writes, the creative freedom of the translator is influenced, beyond these, by the very text he or she is translating, which functions as the frame for the translation. However, this dependence on the base text does not nullify the translator's creative freedom. For Samoyault (2014), this is determined by the vulnerability of the source text, which allows for a plurality of readings, as is evident in the multiplicity of translations that can emerge from that particular source text within the same language or in different languages. This idea is also shared by Montini (2014), who underlines the ambiguity of the base text, and by Durand-Bogaert (2014), who describes the source text as the translation hypertext, insofar as it is susceptible to multiple readings. Thus, if in the creative process of original texts the plans and sketches reflect the freedom of the writer in determining the form and content of his or her text, in the creative process of a translation the genetic materials testify to the freedom of the translator in the recreation of that form and of that content in another language, history and culture, in a movement of constant return to the original text where these elements are previously defined.

Thus, if, on the one hand, as Passos (2008) suggests, the process of literary translation can, in its genesis, be equated to the process of literary writing, insofar as both are based on the invention of discourse; on the other hand, it is important to take into account the particularity of the process of translation which lies on a base text, which necessarily conditions the creative freedom of the translator. It will then be appropriate to question whether a writer who is simultaneously the author of original texts and the author of translations follows the same procedures when writing original texts and when translating. Within the theoretical framework of genetic criticism, the present chapter seeks to explore this issue through the study of the writing processes of Camilo Castelo Branco as an author of both original texts and translations.

The Camilian translation *História de Gabriel Malagrida*

Camilo Castelo Branco (1825–90), the great nineteenth-century novelist, was one of Portuguese literature's most outstanding and prolific authors. However, from his extensive literary production, only nineteen autograph manuscripts have survived.[3] These manuscripts have been edited and studied by the team that conducted the research project *Critical and Genetic Edition of Camilo Castelo Branco* at the Centre of Linguistics of the University of Lisbon, leading to important conclusions about the author's writing practices and creative process.[4]

In addition to his extensive original literary work, Camilo was the author of eighteen translations (Cabral 2003: 779–80), of which the only surviving autograph manuscript is *História de Gabriel Malagrida*. Camilo translated it from the original French, *Histoire de Gabriel Malagrida de la Compagnie de Jésus, l'apôtre du Brésil au XVIIIe siècle*, by the Jesuit priest Paul Mury, and wrote its preface. The French edition was issued in 1865 by Charles Douniol publishing house (Paris) and Camilo's translation was published ten years later by Matos Moreira publisher (Lisbon).

The book is a biography of the Italian Jesuit priest Gabriel Malagrida (1689–1761), a missionary in Brazil, who was persecuted by Sebastião José de Carvalho e Melo, the king's minister, and condemned for his involvement in the Távora affair.[5] According to Jessica Firmino (2013), author of a master's dissertation about the genesis of this work, it is likely that Camilo chose to translate this text due to his well-known ideological affinity with the Society of Jesus and the Jesuits, particularly with Father Malagrida.[6] Firmino states that, in addition to supporting Malagrida's memoir and the Jesuits in general, this historical text would add greater substance and seriousness to Camilo's body of work.

In his preface, Camilo presents the pamphlet written by Father Malagrida, which led to his condemnation (*Judgement of the True Cause of the Earthquake That Befell the Court of Lisbon on 1 November 1755*), and also the observations and permission to print the text granted by those responsible for censorship in 1756. The autograph manuscript is presently located at the Sintra Municipal Library (49.HIS.1). This was the only manuscript to be used as the original print template, as evidenced by the notes written for the typographer and by the fingerprints in black ink that he left on various folios. In 1939, the manuscript was donated to the Sintra Municipal Library by Rodrigo Simões Costa (1874–1947), along with other contemporary manuscripts by Camilo Castelo Branco.[7] Besides the autograph manuscript, the first edition, published during Camilo's lifetime, still exists along with the original French book that Camilo annotated himself. This latter book can be currently consulted at the National Library of Portugal (RES 5589 P).

If we recall the two modes of writing described above (writing in process and programmed writing), the genetic dossier of *História de Gabriel Malagrida* mirrors the typical scenario of writing in process. On the one hand, the pre-drafting phase is not significant to the genesis of the translation. In fact, the annotations of the translator regarding the original French book are scarce and the information contained in them does not seem to have had an important influence on the genesis of the translation. There are, moreover, no other traces of a possible pre-translation phase; the first ink writing in the manuscript shows this was the first writing in the work. On the other hand, the drafting phase is mirrored in a single manuscript that is further complicated by successive deletions and rewritings, thus supporting the hypothesis of direct reading–translation. Despite this, the manuscript has not been cleanly rewritten, and serves as the press original, so it also provides witness to the *mise au point* (development) phase theorized by Grésillon (1994) or the *pre-éditoriale* phase proposed by de Biasi (2011).

The genetic dossier of *História de Gabriel Malagrida* is therefore similar to the genetic dossier of two original works of Camilo Castelo Branco, *Amor de Perdição* (Castro 2007: 12–17) and *Novelas do Minho* (Pimenta 2017: 369), but different from the genetic dossier of *A Espada de Alexandre*, since the autograph of this last Camilian work documents the pre-drafting and drafting phases (Sonsino 2015: 87).

As mentioned, the genetic materials of this translation were studied by Firmino (2013). Firmino's work includes the critical and genetic edition of *História de Gabriel Malagrida*, a list of the author's corrections, and their classification according to Ivo Castro's analytical model, which was applied for the first time in his genetic study of Camilo's *Amor de Perdição* (Castro 2007). This model categorizes the corrections based on their chronology, direction of meaning and writing operations in order to clarify Camilo's writing practices.

This chapter proposes a different perspective on the genesis of *História de Gabriel Malagrida*, based on the analytical model developed in the genetic study of Camilo's *Novelas do Minho* (Pimenta 2017). This model revises the categories proposed by Castro (2007), while integrating that of amplitude – a concept that clarifies textual construction and opens up new ways of analysing writing practices. Some conclusions are now presented resulting from this analysis, which contribute to fostering research about the writing process of Camilo as a translator.

Chronology of corrections

According to the chronological criterion, as typified in Castro's model, corrections can be classified as immediate or non-immediate (Castro 2007: 73). What distinguishes them is the correction's relationship with the continuous writing or reading also known as, respectively, *variante d'écriture* and *variante de lecture* (Grésillon 1994: 246). An immediate correction consists in the amendment of the latest form to be written, before any further text is added to the right or below. In contrast, a non-immediate correction is made at a later time, after revision, inserted in spare spaces left by the continuous writing.

For some writers, differentiating between non-immediate and immediate corrections can be determined by the topography of the correction. If a correction is written on the line, it is immediate. If, however, it is introduced in another empty space on the page, it is non-immediate (Grésillon 1994: 246; de Biasi 2011: 76). But in the Camilian case, the classification of corrections in terms of topography has shown a less common authorial specificity with respect to writing practices, which includes inserting the immediate corrections between rows, when the line ahead is still empty (Castro 2007: 78–9; Pimenta 2009: 40). As predicted in an earlier work (Pimenta 2009: 40), it is possible that this procedure is a means for the writer to calculate the length of his text more accurately, in order to comply with the spatial limits required by the publications.

Other differentiation criteria between non-immediate and immediate corrections are the writing and the ink used, the cancellation processes and the most subjective criterion which is the influence that the correction does or does not have on the evolution of the meaning of the sentence. However, there are cases in which none of these criteria are valid:[8]

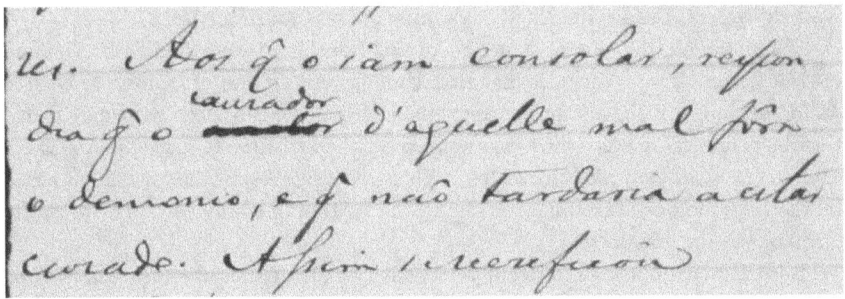

Figure 13.1 Correction in the upper interlinear space.

Example 1. ... To those who were going to comfort him, he answered that the <author>[↑ **perpetrator**] of that evil had been the devil, and that he would soon be healed. ...

(*História de Gabriel Malagrida*: 35)

In the example shown (Figure 13.1), the substitution of 'author' by 'perpetrator' does not substantially alter the meaning of the sentences. The ink and the writing of the correction are identical. Nothing can be concluded from the substitute word's position in relation to other existing words, for it fits perfectly on the top line spacing. One cannot count on the shape of the deletion trace either, for it is not sufficiently studied in the Camilian case, neither on the correction topography, which is not always a differentiating criterion, due to the aforementioned Camilian specificity. It is, therefore, crucial but sometimes impossible to know the chronological status of all the corrections. This situation also occurs in some overlapping corrections, transposition or deletion of elements.

The type of genetic editing carried out by Team Camilo and followed by Firmino adopts a symbolic differentiation of the non-immediate or immediate character of the correction in the case of substitutions, by using square brackets to represent the non-immediate corrections. However, there is no symbology addressing the doubtful substitution we have just mentioned. It is, by default, represented as a non-immediate correction, since the correction does not substantially affect the logical follow-up of the sentence. In interpreting the genesis of the text based on this genetic edition, all these cases were classified as non-immediate corrections, leading to the conclusion that there are more immediate corrections with little contrastive difference between the two groups.

However, this conclusion does not strictly reflect the genesis of *História de Gabriel Malagrida* since there were corrections classified as non-immediate that, strictly speaking, could belong to both chronological groups. An interpretation of the genesis based on the genetic editions has to take into account the limits of the graphical representations, also basing its conclusions on those cases of corrections that cannot be the object of chronological analysis. Thus, within the category of chronology, the present study creates a third group bringing together all the corrections whose chronology cannot be distinguished.

According to these categories, the classification of the handwritten corrections to *História de Gabriel Malagrida* shows that sixty-one per cent of the totality of the translation corrections were made at the time of writing and fifteen per cent were made at the time of revision; however, we cannot know when the remaining twenty-four per cent were made. The contrast between the two non-immediate and immediate categories is therefore much greater than that recorded by Firmino (Figure 13.2).

On the one hand, this novelty emphasizes the spontaneity and speed of the Camilian translation. When comparing the translation corrections with the corrections to the original works by Camilo, it is clear that the process of writing the translation comes even closer to the writing process of *Amor de Perdição*. It is very fast yet hesitant, characterized by spontaneous correction, contiguous to the moment of writing. It is, however, quite distant from the *Novelas do Minho* writing process, a work marked by more lenient correction, mediated by the revision.

This aspect, on the other hand, shows an apparently curious situation which is that a translation, conditioned by the narrative structure of the base text, presents a significant predominance of immediate corrections, as is the case in an original text, in which the narrative is not outlined at the outset. In fact, one could expect that the existence of an *a priori* delineated narrative structure would condition the types of corrections in a text. That is, a writer of original texts could be expected to hesitate more in the process of writing, in his or her quest to build the foundations of the narrative,

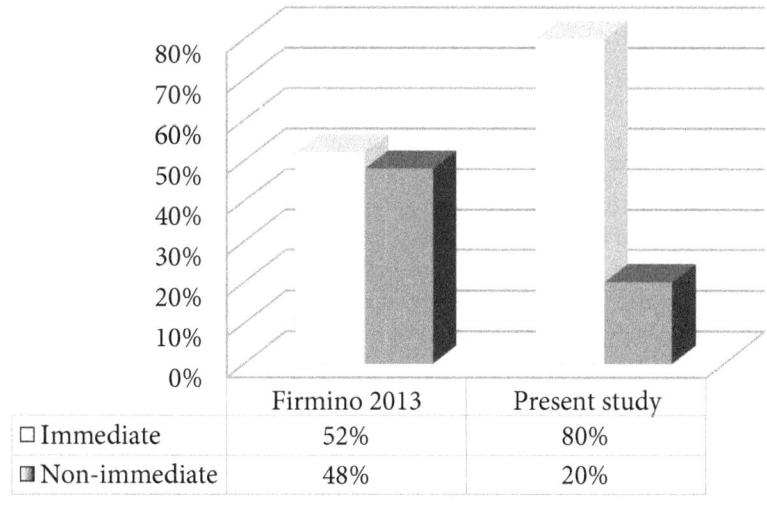

Figure 13.2 Analytical difference.

the action and the profile of the characters, but that translators would show more conviction in writing, since those categories are already predefined in the base text.

However, the marked predominance of immediate corrections in *História de Gabriel Malagrida* shows that the author predominantly amends during the process of writing, although the narrative structure is already mapped out. That proves that the immediate corrections reflect, in this case, authorial hesitations regarding the form and not the diegetic content, that is, the level of the lexical calculation and the discursive formulation.[9] In fact, the predominance of immediate corrections is a natural consequence of writing in process, which, as we have seen, defines this Camilian translation. The immediacy of writing and the corrections mirror the hesitations proper to the practice of direct reading–translation, during which the text is gaining form throughout the process of textualization.

In addition, it should be taken into account that most of the immediate corrections correspond to writing hesitations and unintentional translation errors. Although these corrections are not significant for the genesis of the text in terms of their meaning, they are of great importance for reflecting on Camilo's translation speed, reinforcing Camilo's mastery of French and the ease with which he translated from it (in fact, one should remember that most of Camilo's translations were from French). It proves that the nervous and speedy writing witnessed in *Amor de Perdição* (Castro 2007) is not exclusive to Camilo as the author of an original text, but also characterizes Camilo as a translator, which is in line with the reality of a writer that published a lot of work in a very short time.

The speed of writing and the creative freedom

In this section, translation's dependence on a base text will be verified in the case of the translation *História de Gabriel Malagrida* through two distinct aspects: the number of corrections and the speed of writing.

The comparative study between the total number of corrections of original Camilian texts and the total number of corrections of the *História de Gabriel Malagrida* translation shows that the latter was less amended than texts with greater creative freedom. *História de Gabriel Malagrida* presents an average of three corrections per page, less than the average of four corrections per page in *Amor de Perdição* and the average of nineteen corrections per page in *Novelas do Minho*. Although the contrast between the total number of corrections of the two original works mentioned is very accentuated, which can be explained by the fact that the manuscript of *Novelas do Minho* was the object of a mediated revision that *Amor de Perdição* did not undergo, there seems to be a relationship between the number of corrections and the level of creative freedom in a work. In fact, if we concentrate our attention only on the immediate corrections of the three texts, in order to eliminate this discrepancy between the two original works, we find that *História de Gabriel Malagrida* continues to present a lower average than the original texts, with a value of two immediate corrections per page, less than the average of four immediate corrections per page in *Amor de Perdição* and the average of seven immediate corrections per page in *Novelas do Minho*. It is possible, therefore, to conclude that, in the Camilian case, creative freedom influences the number of corrections to a text, with the translation being amended to a lesser extent than the original texts. This conclusion reveals Camilo's greater confidence in writing as a translator, when he had a pre-existing text as his working base, and a greater degree of uncertainty for Camilo as a writer, when he invented his original texts from scratch.

The second aspect I would like to address is based on the study of the number of writing stages of a text as a way of determining the writing speed of a work. The number of writing stages is defined by the number of times the handwriting, and sometimes the ink of a text, changes indicating the end and the beginning of a new work session. In the manuscript of *História de Gabriel Malagrida*, Firmino concluded that there are at least twenty-five writing stages, which correspond to an average of 10.2 pages per work session. In the genetic study of another Camilian work, *A Espada de Alexandre*, which parodies a book by Alexandre Dumas, Ana Sonsino (2015) observed 6.25 pages per session, having concluded that the writing speed of this booklet was close to the writing speed of the translation of *História de Gabriel Malagrida*. In both cases, the texts are conditioned, respectively, by the base text and by the parodied text.

According to Sonsino's hypothesis, the speed of writing a text is proportional to the work's creative freedom, so it would be expected that the speed of writing a translation was greater than that of composing a completely new text. The study of *Novelas do Minho* confirms this assumption, demonstrating that the writing speed of this original text was slower than the two works mentioned, since it presents an average of 4.5 folios per writing session. Such a conclusion, therefore, fully attests to the speed of Camilian translation, as a consequence of greater writing confidence.

The direction of meaning

The three types of textual direction identified by Castro (2007) are return, projection and redirection, to which we can add a fourth, namely synonymy, already considered by the philologist in another work (Castro 2005). In the case of advancement and retreat of meaning, projection happens when the direction of the text is moved to another place, more or less distant from the original one. The meaning of the text is never lost, only transferred. Return is reversion to an original meaning that was initially rejected. In *História de Gabriel Malagrida*, returns are rare and usually take place without any other meaning having been considered in the meantime, not unlike small hesitations in writing.

In addition to being moved or continued, the text's direction can be retained, despite being rewritten, or changed. In the first case, there is synonymy, that is, a lexical substitution that does not alter the meaning of the text. In the second case, there is a redirection, which implies a change in the meaning of the text, resulting from a hesitation of the author as to how to proceed with the narrative. This phenomenon occurs when a sentence is interrupted, cancelled and restarted in a direction divergent from that which followed before. When taken to an extreme, redirection may include the adoption of the opposite direction (antonym).

In the study of *Novelas do Minho*, only 38 per cent of the corrections were found to fall within these four categories of textual meaning direction, whereas the remaining 62 per cent were not included in any of these four categories, but were found to correspond to (i) minimal changes in the meaning of the text, situated in a wide and ambiguous area of meaning between synonymy and antonymy; (ii) discursive reformulations or transposition of text, in which the meaning of the text does not really change, it only gains a new form; and (iii) corrections in which it is not possible to define the meaning of the text, either because it is impossible to know what was written there, or because they are simply writing lapses, grammatical adjustments, changes in punctuation or spelling corrections.

In the case of the *História de Gabriel Malagrida*, we can also verify that these four typified phenomena do not cover all the translation corrections. However, it has proved very difficult to distinguish between the synonymic and the other lexical exchanges which, while not strictly synonymic, do not imply a substantial change to the meaning of the text; the same holds true for the redirects and discursive reformulations, since, in a translation, the changes of meaning in the sentence naturally relate more to form than to diegetic content. This last difficulty proved to be useful for reflecting on the phenomenon of redirection in a translation.

To sum up, in a translation, diegetic aspects such as characters, time and space, as well as the narrative itself, are already previously defined in the original text. Although the translator's freedom translates into approximation or distance from literality, the original meaning of the text conditions the existence of creative areas marked by diegetic redirection. Thus, passages that could be identified as redirects, due to the fact that they include a deletion followed by a new version with apparently distinct semantics, are, in fact, simple discursive reformulations of an idea previously produced in the original text. See the example below, followed by the original text that served as the basis for its translation:

> **Example 2.** <The pages that you are about to read> Our intention in writing this book is to avenge, by simply exposing the facts, the long-denied memory of a man so dear to Portugal and the Church. (*História de Gabriel Malagrida*: 9)
>
> **Original text.** Dans les pages qui suivent, nous avons eu le dessein de venger, par le simple exposé des faits, la mémoire si longtemps flétrie d'un homme, qui a rendu tant de services au Portugal et à l'Église.
>
> (In the following pages, our purpose was to avenge, by simply exposing the facts, the long-withered memory of a man who has rendered so many services to Portugal and to the Church.) (*Histoire de Gabriel Malagrida*: ii)

By cancelling the expression 'The pages that you are about to read' and restarting the sentence with a different syntax 'Our intention in writing this book …', Camilo moves away from interlinear translation, but does not change the final semantics; that is, the original meaning of the text remains, despite the syntactic reformulation. The writing phenomenon in this correction is not, therefore, a redirection, since, in the latter, the meaning of a new version differs from that of a cancelled version, mirroring significant diegetic changes.

The deviations and approximations to literalness made through syntactic reformulations can, alternatively, be understood as the discursive reformulations of an original idea, whose semantic content is maintained, although it may gain a new form.

However, in the translation *História de Gabriel Malagrida*, we can detect situations where the original meaning of the text was actually changed. As a general rule, these deviations were detected and corrected by Camilo, as shown in the following step, in which the correction makes the text return to the original meaning 'neuf' ('nine'):

Example 3. He had already sailed for <**eight**>[↑ **nine**] days, without finding the savages committed to lead him … (*História de Gabriel Malagrida*: 47)

There is, however, a minority of cases where the original meaning has not been restored and was lost, as the following example illustrates:

Example 4. They did not get tired of contemplating the face of that extraordinary man, whose **white hair and** <**blond**>[↑ **red**] **beard** gave him a certain sense of majesty that commanded respect and veneration. (*História de Gabriel Malagrida*: 95)

Here, Camilo is not faithful to the description of the character made in the original – 'cheveux blonds et sa barbe blanche' (blond hair and his white beard) – ultimately introducing a divergent meaning in the text. This illustrates a redirection phenomenon.

Amplitude of the corrections

The last conclusion stems from the inclusion of a new category of analysis in Castro's 2007 model: the scope of the corrections. The aim here is to explore the issue of the time lag between writing and rewriting and it is thus presented as an alternative to the impossibility of determining the real time of the corrections.

The amplitude of the rewriting is the textual distance between two corrections, or between a correction and another place in the text, which are some way inter-related. In the immediate corrections, the scope is minimal because there is no text between the last written word and the correction. In contrast, in the non-immediate corrections, the amplitude is very flexible: in fact, when a writer suspends his or her writing and goes back to the text to amend it, the amount of text that exists between the pause and the correction can oscillate between a single word and many paragraphs. Most of the time, the amount of text cannot be determined, so it is impossible to know how early the revision corrections actually happened in regard to the moment of writing. However, in the genetic study of *Novelas do Minho*, some cases were detected that allowed the amount of text to be known and led to the conclusion that the predominant corrections in this work were carried out at a moment very close to that of writing, before the conclusion of the sentence in which they were inserted.

The *História de Gabriel Malagrida* manuscript also presents such cases. These are revision corrections conditioning the logical continuation of the sentence, and it is therefore possible to define the point from which it is not feasible to have continued the writing without the correction. In the following example, we see how the substitution 'had/fought' occurred before the 'with' preposition was fixed, since the phrase 'had only with the arms' is non-grammatical.

> **Example 5.** ... disrupted by austerities and tiredness of thirty-three years of the apostolate, in the American forests, he <**had**>[↑ **fought**] only **with** the inflexible arms of virtue and patience. (*História de Gabriel Malagrida*: 180)

In this correction, whose topography proves to be non-immediate, the amplitude does not exceed the level of the sentence, with few words separating the place where the writing was interrupted and the correction. From this analysis, we conclude that there are few such corrections, representing only six per cent of the work's total corrections.

Nevertheless, this study of amplitude can be complemented with the study of the handwriting of the corrections, which often helps to identify the textual moment in which they were performed. The analysis of *Novelas do Minho* showed that a large number of the non-immediate corrections were made in a handwriting similar to the text around them, suggesting that they were made before the end of a given writing stage and a change of handwriting. This information led us to the conclusion that the revision corrections here did not come from a final revision of the text, but rather from fairly frequent partial re-readings in the process of writing the text.

These cases also exist in the translation *História de Gabriel Malagrida*. In the following image (Figure 13.3/Example 6), we can distinguish two types of handwriting: the first accounts for the initial six lines of text and the second for the following eight lines (beginning with 'Malagrida').

> **Example 6.** Near the promontory of St. Agost., in the village of Nossa Senhora do Lago, the sky looked like brass, and the dryness <**desolated**>[↑ **sterilized**] the whole land. The peasants trembled to see <die><disappeared>[↑ lost] the fruit of their labours. **Malagrida**, compassionate, like an angel of peace, rose to the pulpit, and, in the name of the Blessed Virgin, announced that the scourge would be appeased within three days. ...(*História de Gabriel Malagrida*: 131)

Here (Figure 13.3/Example 6), the 'desolated/sterilized' correction was made with the same handwriting as the text around it, different from the more inclined letter initiated in 'Malagrida'. This correction is non-immediate, because the substitute word 'sterilized' overlays the word 'the whole', already existing in the line at the time of the correction. The exact moment in which the writing was interrupted to make the correction is not known, but it is very likely that the correction was carried out, at most, before the new writing stage began.

The present study verifies that these cases of non-immediate corrections made in the same handwriting as that of the text around it represent seventy-five per cent of

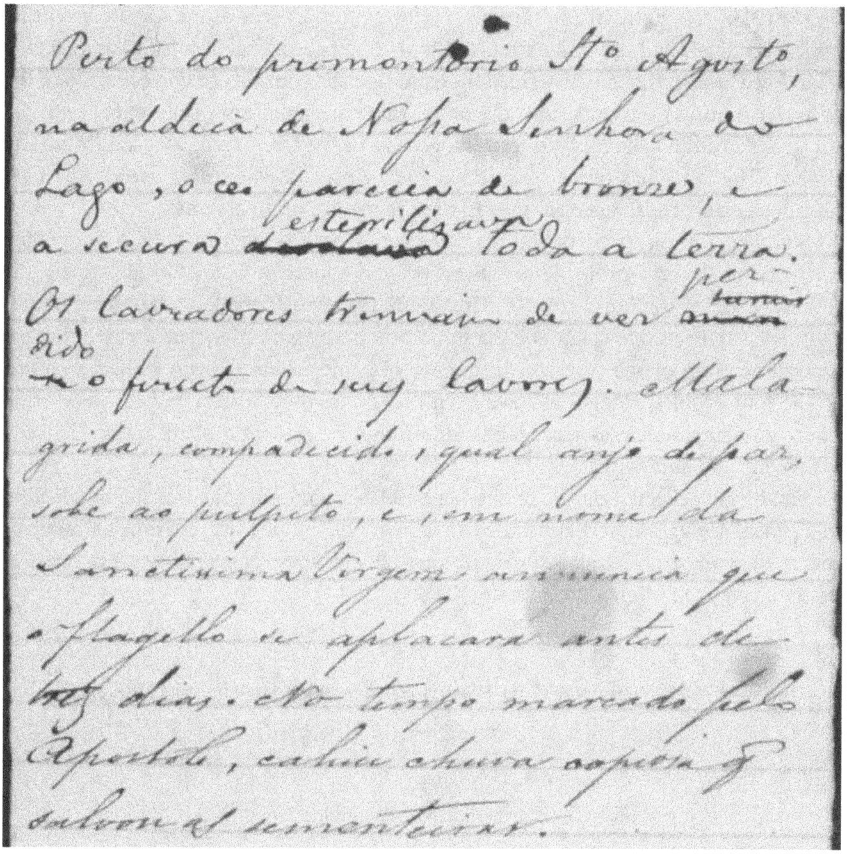
Porto do promontorio Sto Agosto, na aldeia de Nossa Senhora do Lago, o céu parecia de bronze, e a secura esterilizava toda a terra. Os lavradores tremiam de ver perdido o fructo de seus lavores. Malagrida, compadecido, qual anjo de paz, sobe ao pulpito, e, em nome da Sanctissima Virgem annuncia que o flagello se aplacará antes de tres dias. No tempo marcado pelo Apostolo, cahiu chuva copiosa que salvou as sementeiras.

Figure 13.3 Correction made before the beginning of the next writing stage.

the non-immediate correction to the work. By adding these values to those resulting from the amplitude measurement, one can conclude that eighty-one per cent of the non-immediate corrections were made at a time very close to the writing in progress. This conclusion reinforces, on the one hand, the spontaneity with which this work was written and, on the other hand, the idea of writing in blocks, often interrupted for constant returns to the already written text.

Conclusion

The reflections on the chronology of the corrections and their scope strongly suggest that the Camilian translation was mainly amended at the time of writing, in a rapid and spontaneous manner; and that most of the revision corrections were made at a time not long after the time of writing. These conclusions underscore the proximity of the writing and translation processes of Camilo Castelo Branco, based on a common denominator which is the speed of writing.

However, the study of the number of corrections to a text and Camilo's writing stages has illustrated the uniqueness of his writing procedures as a translator. In fact, it has been shown that creative freedom conditions the number of corrections and the speed of writing of a work and, therefore, there are significant differences between the genesis of the original texts and the genesis of the translation by Camilo Castelo Branco. The latter has fewer corrections and evinces faster writing speed, revealing Camilo's greater confidence with translation than with original texts.

Studying the direction of the textual meaning has proved that the four typified phenomena (return, projection, redirection and synonymy) do not encompass the totality of the translation corrections. In addition to a considerable set of indecipherable writing hesitations that cannot be the subject of this classification, substantive changes in the meaning of the text and discursive reformulations that do not fit into any of the four typified categories have been observed. They correspond to a wide and often ambiguous zone as regards distinguishing the direction of meanings between synonymy and antonymy.

Finally, we reflected on the phenomenon of redirection in the translation *História de Gabriel Malagrida* and concluded that many of the departures from literality by means of syntactic reconstructions are, after all, discursive reformulations in order to better convey the original meaning of the text.

Annex. Symbols used in the manuscript genetic transcription

< ... >	Deletion
< ... >[↑ ...]	deletion and substitution above the line

Notes

1. These two modes of writing were proposed by Louis Hay (1984: 307–23). Pierre-Marc de Biasi renames these two types of writing as, respectively, *écriture à structuration rédactionnelle* and *écriture à programmation scénarique* (de Biasi 2011: 74–5).
2. Pierre-Marc de Biasi (2011) subdivides this last phase in two parts: the pre-editorial phase and the editorial phase.
3. The manuscripts of *O Romance de um Homem Rico* and *Amor de Salvação* are missing from the list of manuscripts compiled by Alexandre Cabral (2003: 477–8).
4. See the following works on the genesis of *Amor de Perdição* (Castro 2007), *A Morgada de Romariz* (Pimenta 2009), *O Regicida* (Correia 2013), *História de Gabriel Malagrida* (Firmino 2013), *O Demónio do Ouro* (Sobral 2014), *A Espada de Alexandre* (Sonsino 2015), *Novelas do Minho* (Pimenta 2017) and *A Caveira da Mártir* (Sobral 2018).
5. The Távora affair was a judicial proceeding which consisted in the condemnation and death of the noble Távora family for their alleged involvement in an assassination

attempt against King José I. These proceedings were led by the king's minister, Sebastião José de Carvalho e Melo (the future Marquis de Pombal), known for his contempt for the traditional nobility. Gabriel Malagrida, confessor of the *Marquesa* Leonor of Távora, was hanged and burned on 21 September 1761. On the Távora affair, see Azevedo (1921).

6   On Camilo's relationship with the Jesuits, see Simões (1993).
7   The history of the Camilian manuscripts of the Municipal Library of Sintra can be consulted in Pimenta (2009).
8   The symbols used in the genetic transcription of the manuscript can be consulted in the Annex.
9   See the section 'The direction of meaning'.

References

Azevedo, Pedro de (1921), *O Processo dos Távora*, Lisboa: Biblioteca Nacional.
Branco, Camilo Castelo (n.d.), *Historia de Gabriel Malagrida*'s manuscript, Sintra Municipal Library (49.HIS.1).
Branco, Camilo Castelo (2007), *Amor de Perdição*, ed. Ivo Castro, Lisboa: IN–CM.
Branco, Camilo Castelo (2013), *O Regicida*, ed. Ângela Correia, Lisboa: IN–CM.
Branco, Camilo Castelo (2014), *O Demónio do Ouro*, ed. Cristina Sobral, Lisboa: IN–CM.
Cabral, Alexandre (2003), *Dicionário de Camilo Castelo Branco*, Lisboa: Caminho.
Castro, Ivo (2005), 'O Manuscrito do *Amor de Perdição* e a Edição do Romance', unpublished paper to the 2nd Camilian Congress, 1 June, S. Miguel de Seide.
Castro, Ivo (ed.) (2007), 'Introdução', in Camilo Castelo Branco, *Amor de Perdição*, 9–121, Lisboa: IN–CM.
Correia, Ângela (2013), 'Nota sobre a Edição de *O Regicida*', in Camilo Castelo Branco, *O Regicida*, 198–203, Lisboa: IN–CM.
De Biasi, Pierre-Marc (2011), *Génétique des textes*, Paris: CNRS.
Duarte, Luiz Fagundes (2007), 'Tempo de Perguntar', *Veredas. Revista da Associação Internacional de Lusitanistas*, 8: 11–29.
Durand-Bogaert, Fabienne (2014), 'Les deux corps du texte', *GENESIS. Revue internationale de critique génétique*, 38: 11–33.
Firmino, Jessica Fontes (2013), 'A Génese de uma Tradução de Camilo Castelo Branco: História de Gabriel Malagrida', MA diss., School of Arts and Humanities of the University of Lisbon, Lisboa. Available online: http://repositorio.ul.pt/bitstream/10451/10142/1/ulfl148004_tm.pdf (accessed 3 October 2018).
Grésillon, Almuth (1994), *Éléments de critique génétique. Lire les manuscrits modernes*, Paris: PUF.
Hay, Louis (1984), 'Die dritte Dimension der Literatur', *Poetica*, 16 (3–4): 307–23.
Laviosa-Braithwaite, Sara (2001), 'Universals of Translation', in Mona Baker (ed.), *Routledge Encyclopedia of Translation Studies*, 288–91, London and New York: Routledge.
Montini, Chiara (2014), '*Écrire et décrire la genèse de la traduction. Le Désert mauve et Mercier et Camier*', *GENESIS. Revue internationale de critique génétique*, 38: 85–98.
Mury, Paul (1865), *Histoire de Gabriel Malagrida de la Compagnie de Jésus, l'apôtre du Brésil au XVIIIe siècle étranglé et brulé sur la place publique de Lisbonne le 21 Septembre 1761*, Paris: Charles Douniol.

Passos, Marie-Hélène Paret (2008), 'Da Crítica Genética à Tradução Literária: o Caminho da (Re)Criação e da (Re)Escritura. *Anotações para uma Estória de Amor* de Caio Fernando Abreu', PhD thesis in Brazilian, Portuguese and Luso-African Literature, Federal University of Rio Grande do Sul, Porto Alegre.

Pimenta, Carlota (2009), 'Edições Crítica e Genética de *A Morgada de Romariz* de Camilo Castelo Branco', MA diss. in Romance Studies, Portuguese Literature, School of Arts and Humanities of the University of Lisbon, Lisboa.

Pimenta, Carlota (2017), 'O Processo de Escrita Camiliano em Novelas do Minho. Análise Genética', PhD thesis in Textual Criticism, School of Arts and Humanities of the University of Lisbon, Lisboa.

Samoyault, Tiphaine (2014), '*Vulnérabilité de l'oeuvre en traduction*', GENESIS. *Revue internationale de critique génétique*, 38: 57–68.

Simões, Manuel (1993), 'Camilo Apologista dos Jesuítas', *Lusitana Sacra. Revista do Centro de Estudos de História Religiosa*, 5 (2nd series): 299–317.

Sobral, Cristina (2018), '*A Caveira da Mártir*: um Romance que Camilo Não Escreveu em Duas Semanas', in Elsa Pereira and Francisco Topa (eds), *João Penha (1839–1919) e o seu Tempo*, Porto: School of Arts and Humanities of the University of Porto/ Afrontamento.

Sonsino, Ana Luísa (2015), 'A Espada de Alexandre, de Camilo Castelo Branco: Polémica Origem e Invulgar Génese de um Texto Polémico e Invulgar', MA diss. in Textual Criticism, School of Arts and Humanities of the University of Lisbon, Lisboa.

14

Vasconcelos Abreu's *O Panchatantra*: An unpublished and unfinished translation

Marta Pacheco Pinto
Centre for Comparative Studies, University of Lisbon
Ariadne Nunes
Institute of Literature and Tradition Studies, Nova University of Lisbon

Introduction

The research conducted under the aegis of the project *Texts and Contexts of Portuguese Orientalism: The International Congresses of Orientalists (1873–1973)* has led to the identification of orientalists whose body of work has given visibility to various branches of Oriental studies in Portugal.[1]

Guilherme de Vasconcelos Abreu (1842–1907) is one such orientalist who distinguished himself in the field of Sanskrit studies and comparative religions, mythologies and literatures. Although he was well reputed in nineteenth-century Portugal and in the international community of orientalists, up to now this figure and his work have attracted little interest from scholars. One reason for this might be the short-term success of Sanskrit studies in Portugal.

The inception of these studies in this country dates from around 1870, that is, three centuries after the foundation of the Portuguese State of India (Goa) in 1505 and when it was already a discipline in its own right in most Europe: 'By about 1860, Indology as a discipline was firmly established: Sanskrit manuscripts had found their way into European university collections, chairs were established, and grammars and lexicons were made available' (Figueira 1991: 24). Portuguese Sanskrit scholarship was not built on a sustained body of translations and even less on intense production of manuscript editions of Indian literature unlike in England or Germany, for instance, as opposed to what was happening in other fields of knowledge in Portugal, such as Ethiopian studies under the pioneering lead of Esteves Pereira (1854–1924). Translations of Indian literature in Portugal were reduced to the occasional activity of a handful of philologists translating mostly directly from Sanskrit sources. Vasconcelos Abreu (e.g. 1878a), Sebastião Dalgado (1897, 1916), Esteves Pereira (e.g. 1917, 1921, 1924) and Bernardino Gracias (e.g. 1925) were the most prolific translators. In 1873 the poet Cândido de Figueiredo (1846–1925) authored the first verse translation of an episode of the epic *Rāmāyana*, the death of Yajnadatta, yet he covertly used Hippolyte Fauche's French translation (published in 1864) as source text and was severely criticized and discredited by Vasconcelos Abreu (1873) for what the latter viewed as unethical behaviour. Portuguese Sanskrit studies were particularly associated with the publication of lexicographical resources, grammar books with exercises using translation as a learning/teaching method, monographs and textbooks (with translated fragments from Indian classics). Vasconcelos Abreu greatly contributed to each of these segments, in addition to playing an active role in learned societies and networks for the dissemination of scientific knowledge, such as the Lisbon Geographical Society or the International Congresses of Orientalists, with which his name was regularly associated from 1873 to 1892.

Vasconcelos Abreu taught Classical and Vedic Sanskrit language and literature within the *Curso Superior de Letras* (The Higher School of Letters), forerunner of the current School of Arts and Humanities at the University of Lisbon. Shortly after his death in 1907, part of Vasconcelos Abreu's private library was acquired between 1911 and 1912 by the same school (Santos 2010: 71), where it is presently located. So far around five hundred books have been identified as belonging to the Vasconcelos Abreu collection. Among these books, two are part of a three-volume manuscript that reveals the genesis of a translation project, that of *Panchatantra*, the oldest known collection of Indian tales. The present study will focus on this translation project that was however left unfinished and unpublished.

Based on the analysis of the handwritten drafts contained in the two existing volumes, it is our purpose in this chapter to shed light on Vasconcelos Abreu's translation methodology in order to (1) interrogate the reasons for his abandoning of the project and (2) draw conclusions about the more general role played by translation not only in his work as a Sanskritist but also in the state of the discipline of Sanskrit studies in Portugal. To this end, the chapter is structured in three parts. First, we make a brief socio-biographical survey of Vasconcelos Abreu's profound knowledge of Sanskrit philology to elucidate on the genetic environment behind the production of the *Panchatantra*'s unfinished translation. The second part examines the extant volumes and analyses the handwritten drafts following a comparative genetic perspective. The third part discusses translation within Vasconcelos Abreu's written production against other contemporary translators' discourses about translating Sanskrit literature and comments on Portuguese Sanskrit studies, thereby addressing a specific chapter of the Portuguese history of translation.

Vasconcelos Abreu: The orientalist and his library

Guilherme de Vasconcelos Abreu began as a man of science, a mathematician (studied 1860–64) and naval engineer (studied 1865–69) and then became a Sanskritist, first by avocation and later by training and profession. Two life events were pivotal in Vasconcelos Abreu's trajectory as an orientalist. Firstly, the invitation addressed to him by the royal architect Possidónio Narciso da Silva (1806–96) to join the Portuguese delegation to the first International Congress of Orientalists (Paris, 1873). Secondly, his appointment in 1877–78 to the *Curso Superior de Letras* to teach Classical and Vedic Sanskrit language and literature, a position he would hold until shortly before his death.

Vasconcelos Abreu was the first professor of Sanskrit in Portugal. His appointment followed his return to Portugal after a two-year period of study abroad. From 1875 to 1877, he was granted a scholarship by the Portuguese government to acquire philological knowledge in important European hubs of Oriental studies, namely Paris (at the École des Hautes Études and Collège de France in 1875 and 1876–77) and Munich (at the University of Munich in 1875–76), which stand, respectively, for two countries that were disputing leadership in Sanskrit scholarship in the second half of nineteenth century (McGetchin 2003: 580).

The Portuguese Ministry of Foreign Affairs, and also the Ministry of Public Instruction, encouraged the growth of Oriental studies in Portugal, but neglected to provide the necessary resources and facilities, as Vasconcelos Abreu constantly complained, especially in the forewords to his works. The Sanskritist attributed the government's lack of strategic engagement with Oriental studies and failure to tackle these questions to indifference and even a disregard for national history (Vasconcelos Abreu 1892: iii–v). This did not, however, prevent him from contributing to the field with pedagogical and scientific works that he claimed would be of value to Portuguese missionaries and colonial officials stationed in India (Vasconcelos Abreu 1890; Vasconcelos Abreu 1892: iv). On several occasions he described the studies he carried out as substantiating 'the science of language' (e.g. Vasconcelos Abreu 1874: 13), then a new research area establishing itself under the label of philology.

The collection of books at the library of the School of Arts and Humanities of Lisbon is just a part of the Sanskritist's personal library. The whereabouts of the remaining holdings are unknown. The archive is not digitized, so it is only accessible locally. The items it contains can be grouped and described as follows:

(i) texts produced by Vasconcelos Abreu himself about the symbolic value and importance of Sanskrit as well as didactic exercises for learning the language;
(ii) grammars and other instruments for studying Sanskrit written in different European languages (especially French, German and English), which were most probably used to prepare his lessons and produce his own teaching materials;
(iii) other books about Sanskrit literature and recensions of Sanskrit works; and
(iv) books and journals on Oriental studies in general.

Some of these items abound with handwritten marginal notes by the author or dedications by those people who offered him the specimens. The marginalia of his book collection have already been examined as a case study in a master's dissertation (Santos 2010) that helped inform the present chapter.

Within Vasconcelos Abreu's personal library,[2] two parchment-bound books were found providing handwritten drafts of a translation project, initiated but not completed: the Portuguese translation of the *Panchatantra*.

The *Panchatantra*: A failed attempt or a postponed project?

The *Panchatantra*, an Indian frame narrative combining verse and prose that belongs to the literary tradition of tales, fables and allegories, is generally accepted as dating back to the third century BC. Its compilation in both Sanskrit (Hindu) and Pali (Buddhist) is attributed to Vishnu Sharma. Together with the fourteenth-century *Hitopadeśa* it is part of the so-called Nitishastra genre, which concerns man's life relationships addressed particularly from an ethical and political viewpoint (Dalgado 1897: vii). The original tales of the *Panchatantra* have been lost, and only testimonies and recensions are available. In his published work, Vasconcelos Abreu sometimes quotes this narrative poem to illustrate the use of Sanskrit grammar, to discuss literary genres or Indian literature overall, or to provide examples for his studies of comparative philology or mythology.[3]

The volumes in Vasconcelos Abreu's personal library belonging to the *Panchatantra* translation project were organized and bound similarly, with blank pages intended for annotations deliberately interleaved with the printed source edition used. All the handwritten annotations are by Vasconcelos Abreu himself.

One volume, here referred to as volume A, corresponds to Vasconcelos Abreu's study and annotations of the Sanskrit text concerning vocabulary, grammar and prosody. The other volume, here volume B, is the proper translation. The handwritten drafts of both volumes dialogue with one another by presenting both the introduction to *Panchatantra* and part of its first tantra (book). Neither of the volumes is dated, yet one can easily assert the precedence of volume A, which is clearly a work tool, over volume B. The orthographic differences between both volumes emphasize this precedence.

Volume A serves as a study notebook. Indeed, the spine of the volume provides the handwritten indication that the volume is about 'my study of classical Sanskrit'. It includes grammatical or formal descriptions of passages of the Sanskrit text, lists of word-for-word, or phrase-for-phrase, translation possibilities, in addition to sometimes collating Western editions of the *Panchatantra* and suggesting further reading. Vasconcelos Abreu puts numbers on certain words and phrases in the Sanskrit text and then provides their literal translation, offers a supply of synonyms, and/or explains their meaning or grammatical function. The cover and the title page of volume A confirm this grammar-oriented exercise that the handwritten subtitle makes explicit (Figure 14.1): 'Vishnu Sharma's *The Panhtchatantra* annotated according to the works of Benfey, Lancereau, Kielhorn and Bühler and in part *analysed grammatically* and *translated for study* [purposes] by G. de Vasconcelos Abreu' (Emphases added).[4]

The most important translations, editions and studies of Sanskrit available at the time had been made by the authors that Vasconcelos Abreu cites here: Benfey, Lancereau, Kielhorn and Bühler, whose annotations the Portuguese Sanskritist intended to cross-reference to produce his own translation.

The handwritten drafts in volume B are on the whole quite legible and reveal minor corrections. According to the handwritten title page, it contains 'The Panchatantra//"The Five Books" of tales, fables and apologues by Vishnu Sharma.//

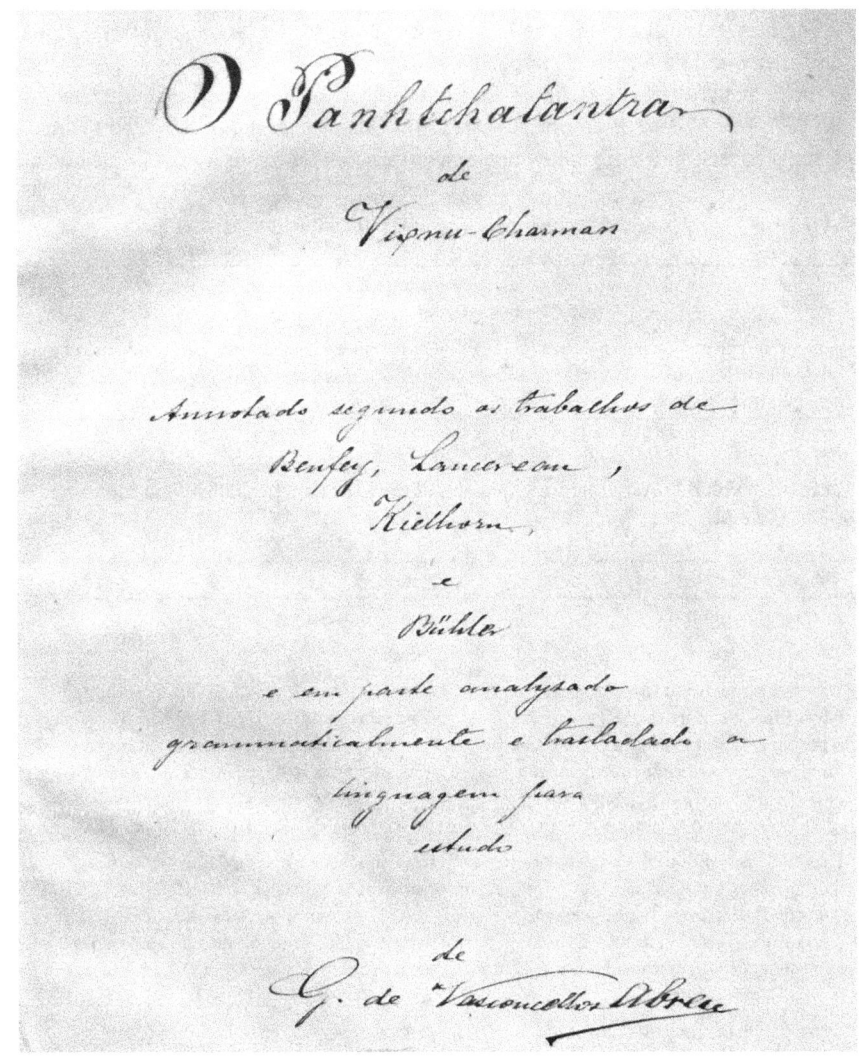

Figure 14.1 The title page of Vasconcelos Abreu's *Panchatantra* (volume A).

Sanskrit text edited and annotated by//Kielhorn and Bühler//and translated// into Portuguese language//and added with notes//by G. de Vasconcelos Abreu'.[5] No actual notes are found in the volume, just the translation of the introduction to the *Panchatantra* and part of its first tantra, the so-called 'The Estrangement between Friends'. Contrary to A, B offers a clean, fixed translation of the text, as the short passage below shows:

Volumes A and B can thus be said to correspond to the orientalist's translational competence and performance, respectively (Toury 1995).

Incidentally, the back cover of Leopold von Schroeder's book *Indiens Literatur und Cultur in Historischer Entwicklung* (1887), which is part of Vasconcelos Abreu's personal library, bears the following handwritten note: 'I might translate this book. I

Table 14.1 Volumes A and B: the translation of the Introduction's last sentence.

Volume A	Volume B
Quem recitar ou ~~quem~~ ouvir [↑ constantemente] êste livro da níti (da sabedoria do Mundo), jamais será humildado nem mesmo por Xacra	Quem êste livro da níti aprender, q.^{m} o ouvir ler constantemente, jamais será humilhado nem mesmo por Xacra.

Table 14.2 Volumes A and B: A comparison of the handwritten drafts of the Introduction to *Panchatantra*.

Volume A	Volume B
extraord.^{te} **estúpidos**	sumamente **estúpidos**
eles sentiram **aversão** pe'los livros	**avessos** ao estudo
Das (três causas): **não (nos) nascer filho, haver (nos) êle morrido**, ou **(termos)** um tolo, o melhor (é) **filho** morto ou não ter nascido filho, porque para bem pequena **mágoa (são)** os dois emq.^{to} q. o tolo **consome a vida**.	A escolher-se vale mais **não nos ter nascido filho** ou **ter-nos morrido** o que nasceu, do que **termos um filho** estúpido; passa ao cabo de pouco tempo a **mágoa** de se perder um filho ou de o não ter e **consome**-nos toda **a vida** o filho parvo
É certam^{te}. **interminável o estudo** das palavras; emq^{to}. que **a vida** é breve e m^{tas}. as **contrariedades**; tome-se **pois a esséncia** e **deixe**-se o que é insignificante, como da **agua** com que está **mixturado** os **cisnes** (do paraíso) tiram o **leite**	**Interminável** é **o estudo** da gramática e muito curta **a vida** e cheia de **contrariedades**, é bem certo! Tomemos, **pois, o essencial** e **deixe**mos de parte as minundéncias, como aqueles **cisnes** que separam o **leite** da **água** que se lhe **mistura**.
de **proficiencia** inexcedivel em tudo a **sabedoria**	**proficiente** em todo o **saber**
compondo cinco livros	e **compôs** os **cinco** tantras
'A desunião dos amigos', 'A aquisição dos amigos', 'A inimizade dos corvos e das corujas', 'A perda dos bens adquiridos', 'O procedimento inconsiderado'	A desunião dos amigos, A aquisição dos amigos, A inimizade dos corvos e das corujas, A perda dos bens adquiridos, O procedimento inconsiderado

Our highlights mark the lexical coincidences between volumes A and B.

will first translate it by writing directly in the book the meanings as I think I ought to provide them. It is a trial; then I will see what to do; in any case it is easier.' This note can be easily transposed and applied to the *Panchatantra* translation project. Accordingly, it would be just a trial.

The handwritten drafts in both volumes are interrupted after around twenty pages at the same point in the text. The introduction to *Panchatantra* in volume B, though it is a more fluid text, is close to that of volume A (Table 14.2). More significantly, the title page of each manuscript provides clues as to the genesis of this translation project. The title page of volume B provides an explanatory note declaring that:

> Together with this volume there are two other parchment-bound volumes*, and these are the MS in which I provide the grammatical analysis and *the literal translation of the whole Panchatantra, which I wrote for the use of my students.*
> * The volumes are in folio. I don't *have them today; I gave them away.* (Emphases added)

First, this note reports the existence of a third volume with the complete literal translation of the *Panchatantra*. This third volume, designated volume C, has not yet been found. It would be either (1) prior to the two existing (incomplete) manuscripts or (2) an intermediate text between volumes A and B. This way, volume B can be hypothesized to be a revised copy of C, the literal translation. The inclusion in volume B of an explanation for the symbols and red colour employed in the handwritten draft suggests the existence of a target readership for this translation, and that it was being prepared for publication, the symbols being intended for the typographer.

Second, the literal translation – that is, the missing volume C – was made to be used in the classroom to teach, guide and assess students. The weight of didactic materials in Vasconcelos Abreu's published work corroborates the pedagogical intention he outlined.

Third, the note emphasizes that Vasconcelos Abreu made a literal translation of the whole *Panchatantra*. Should this be true, and only the missing volume would allow us to confirm it, then volume C would be a full previous translation of the Indian classic likely from a different source text or edition. Alternatively, the translator would have carried out, simultaneously with volume A, the literal translation (volume C) as informed by the grammatical analysis, which did not however seek from the outset to be comprehensive – let us not forget the descriptive subtitle of volume A, 'in part analysed grammatically'. In any case, volume B would have been initiated thereafter.

The idea of a complete literal translation could explain the existence of at least two translated tales from *Panchatantra* that cannot be found in either volume A or B and were included in other works by Vasconcelos Abreu, namely:

(i) the tale 'O Burro Vestido com a Pelle do Tigre' (The Donkey Dressed in the Tiger's Skin), which is included in an anthological work of Indian literary genres that started being printed in 1883 but was only issued in 1891 as *Manual para o Estudo do Sãoskrito Classico* (Manual for the Study of Classical Sanskrit)

(1891: 237). As stated by the orientalist–translator, this rendition follows the Sanskrit text that complies with Kielhorn and Bühler's 1868 edition of the *Panchatantra*, revised in 1873;

(ii) a parable that was eventually published in 1902[6] in a study of the influence of Indian literature on Portuguese sixteenth-century playwright Gil Vicente (1902: 71–6), in particular, his play *Auto da Mofina Mendes* (1534). A previous version

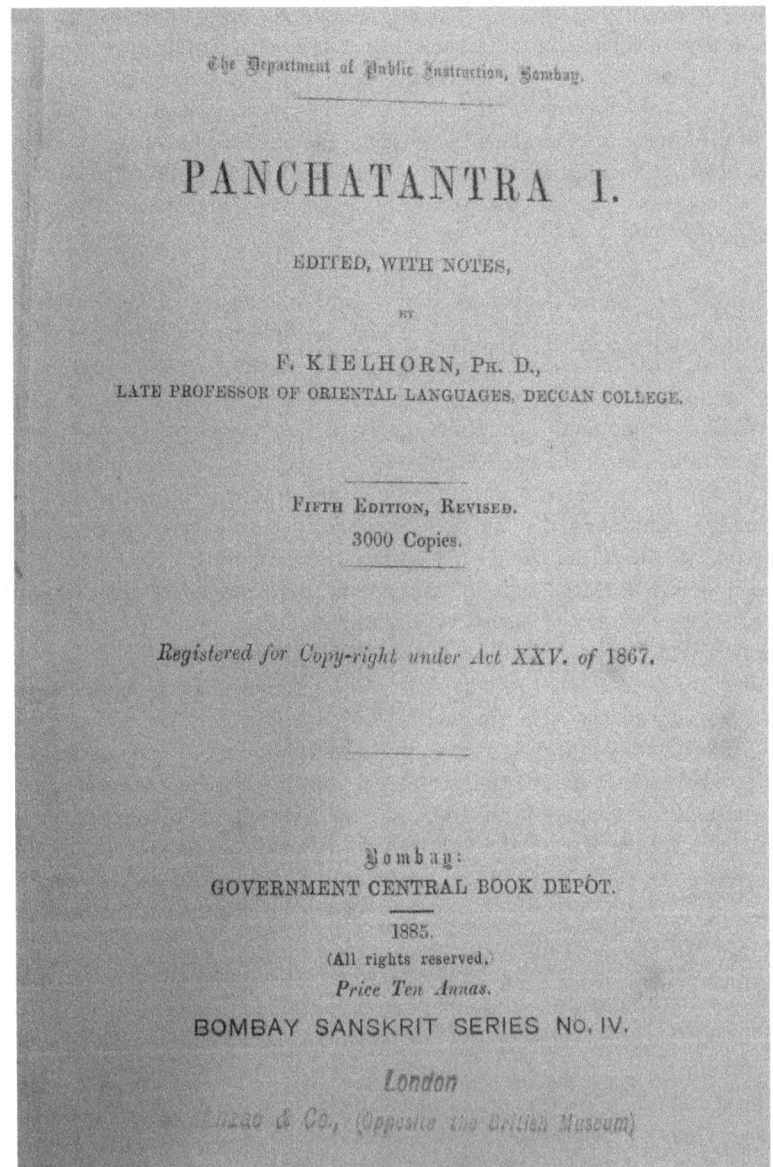

Figure 14.2 The title page of the source edition used in volume B.

with some lexical differences, titled 'O Mofino Brâmane e Escudela de Farinha' (this tale is commonly rendered in English as 'The Brahmin's Dream'), was published in *Exercicios e Primeiras Leituras de Sámscrito* (1889: 131–3).

On the verso of the title page of volume A, a handwritten note provides another clue: 'I did not make the annotations indicated above because shortly after this volume was prepared for the work, I purchased the oeuvre of Benfey, Bühler and Kielhorn.' This note informs us that during the course of his study Vasconcelos Abreu purchased new recensions of *Panchatantra* by Benfey and by Bühler and Kielhorn. In 1885, a three-volume revised edition of *Panchatantra* by Georg Bühler and Franz Kielhorn was published within the Bombay Sanskrit Series. This 1885 fifth edition consists of the source text that in volume B is interleaved with blank pages for translation (Figure 14.2). However, this is not the edition on which volume A relies; the source edition of volume A was published previously in 1872 in Calcutta by Shri Jivananda Vidyasagar Bhattacharya[7] (Figure 14.3). How Vasconcelos Abreu obtained this edition is unknown, but it is likely that Reinhold Rost (1822–96), chief librarian of the India Office in London, sent it to him as apparently he used to get him the latest works printed in India (e.g. Santos 2010: 79 n. 128).

Based on Vasconcelos Abreu's annotations, we can therefore conjecture that:

(i) volumes A and B were not produced simultaneously, though both were interrupted at the same point in the text;
(ii) the work on volume A began in, or shortly after, 1872 and was interrupted once Vasconcelos Abreu had purchased Kielhorn and Bühler's fifth edition of the *Panchatantra*, at the very least in 1885–86;
(iii) the work on volume B began after 1885–86;
(iv) the literal translation contained in a supposed volume C can be assumed to have been produced either before 1872 as part of a previous translation stage, or after 1872 and before the acquisition of Kielhorn and Bühler's fifth edition. This way, the orientalist–translator might have used the same source edition as in volume A, or instead the edition followed for producing the previously mentioned tale 'O Burro Vestido com a Pelle do Tigre'.

Portuguese philologist Adolfo Coelho's statement in his introductory book to Portuguese literature via ancient and medieval literature, *Noções de Litteratura Antiga e Medieval como Introduccção á Litteratura Portugueza*, is enlightening and actually clarifies the *terminus ad quem* of volume C. Coelho, a close friend of Vasconcelos Abreu and himself a professor at the *Curso Superior de Letras*, clearly stated in 1881 that '*Panchatantra* was translated into all the main literary languages of the universe' (1881: 8–9). Assuming that the Portuguese scholar does not exclude his native language from the 'main literary languages of the universe', it is fair to presume that Vasconcelos Abreu's volume C would have been included in this state of the art and, therefore, completed at least by 1881, that is, four years before initiating volume B.

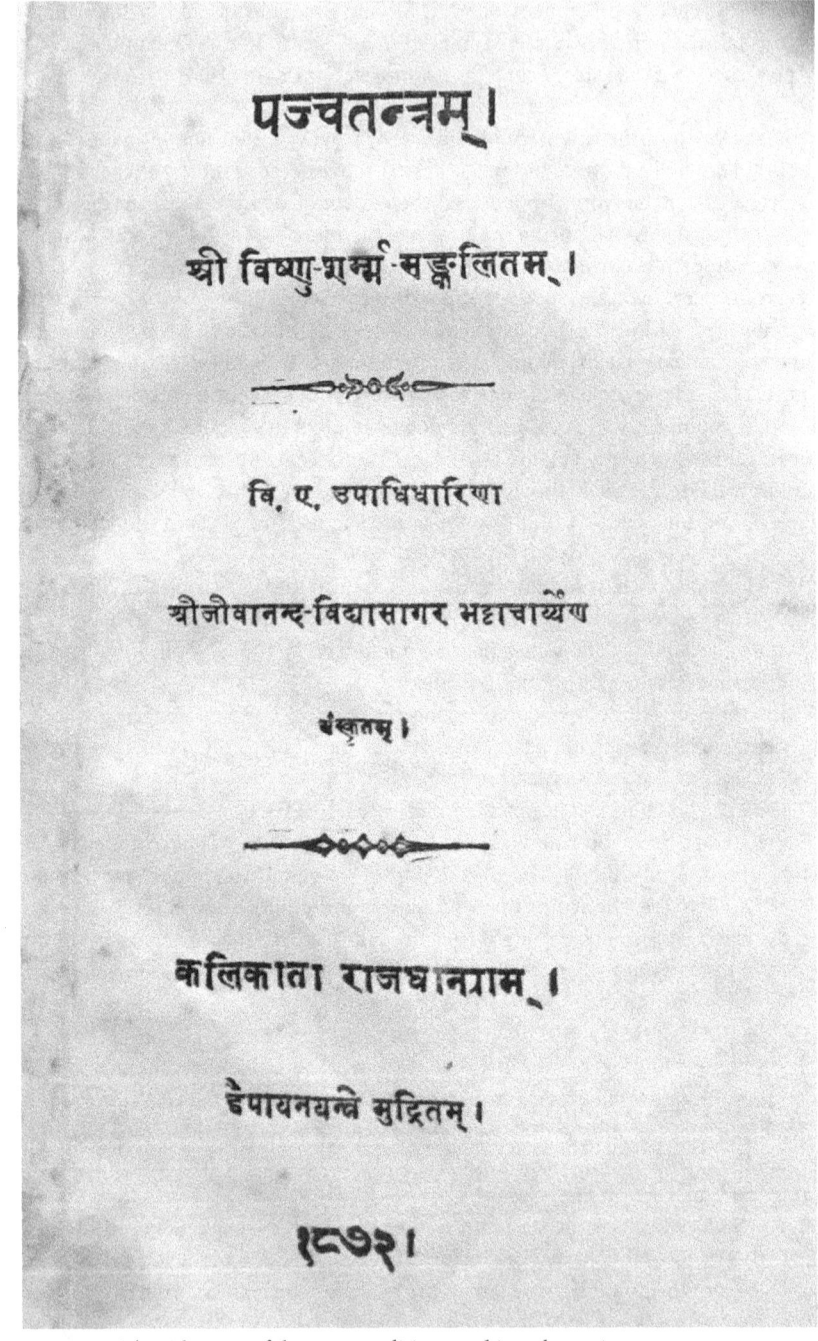

Figure 14.3 The title page of the source edition used in volume A.

The handwritten note provided in volume A explains in part why Vasconcelos Abreu interrupted the annotation work. It does not however explain why he completely dropped out of the translation project. In addition to hypothetical feelings of discouragement due to the magnitude of the task of grammatically annotating the work,[8] the new recension of the *Panchatantra* by Kielhorn and Bühler with updated and revised notes could risk making the study and translation carried out up to that moment obsolete. Here one should point out that Benfey's translation and study, also mentioned in the handwritten note to volume A, dates from 1859 and does not use the same base text as Kielhorn and Bühler's edition (Vasconcelos Abreu 1889: 25 and 27).

The analysis of the handwritten drafts of volumes A and B shows that Vasconcelos Abreu is meticulous in opting for a two-stage work methodology, first the linguistic analysis and translation afterwards. He does not assume translation light-heartedly; his methodological procedure requires time, dedication and ultimately pleasure against the backdrop of a national context lacking in financial support to Oriental studies and against his personal and professional obligations, which he often gives as an excuse either for the delay in publishing a new study or for the quality of the work delivered. The *Panchatantra* translation project could therefore have been abandoned because it was too time-consuming. Moreover, the instability of the source text, constantly undergoing new interpretations, selection and emendation, was certainly a drawback to any attempt at translating a classic.

From Vasconcelos Abreu's written production, it is noteworthy that he never published a complete translation of an Indian literary text and never commented on his unfinished attempt at translating the *Panchatantra*. The orientalist–translator simply abandoned the project and never spoke of it again.

The first published partial and complete Portuguese translations of Sanskrit

In 1869, Vasconcelos Abreu authored a prose translation of the 'Daçâratha e Yadjnhadatta' (Dasaratha and Yajnadatta) episode of the *Rāmāyana* in a Portuguese literary journal, *Jornal Litterario*. Not only was this the earliest work he ever published, but it is also the first published translation of a Sanskrit literary text directly into Portuguese.

Almost ten years later, in 1878, Vasconcelos Abreu published his literal translation of the first act of the classic drama *Śākuntala* in a deluxe bilingual edition.[9] As is the case with the unfinished *Panchatantra*, no extratextual statement by Vasconcelos Abreu can be found on this rendition. The orientalist–translator seems to refrain from commenting on his translational performance in contrast to his essay and didactical publications that he tends to quote from work to work. The only exception to this silence is the footnote describing the translation method adopted for his first published translation 'Daçâratha e Yadjnhadatta':

> This translation is almost *ad verbum*. In this study I had always in mind three things: – 1st faithfulness to the idea; 2nd faithfulness to meaning; 3rd faithfulness to the words. And I am convinced that my translation cannot be accused of jeopardizing faithfulness.
> After translating word for word, I would be struck by the idea, would analyse the feeling and in keeping with the two grammars I would then translate. First, a whole stanza ... Afterwards I would separate the two verses, and only then would I serve the Portuguese language without committing the crime of being unfaithful. (Vasconcelos Abreu 1869: 13)

Vasconcelos Abreu's advocacy of literalness is hardly surprising, as it would be expected from a young practitioner with little translation experience, not to mention the symbolic status of the Sanskrit language with a centuries-old history, or the novelty of the task Vasconcelos Abreu had in hand. Already during his study period in Paris, Vasconcelos Abreu says, in his report, that he had shared with Abel Bergaigne (1838–88), Professor at the École Pratique des Hautes Études:

> [E]xcerpts from the *Rāmāyana* and chapters of the Nala episode;[10] the translation of the first kathānaka by Vetála carried out in Paris, as well as the translation of the introduction to the *Hitopadeśa* and part of the mitra-lābha. (1878b: 6)

Significantly, with regard to the fourteenth-century *Hitopadeśa*, which appropriates and rewrites apologues from the *Panchatantra*, Vasconcelos Abreu selected the same formal segments for translation as the ones featured in volumes A and B for the *Panchatantra*, that is, the introduction and part of the first section of the book (in this case, the *mitra-lābha*).[11] The unfinished and unpublished translations of the *Hitopadeśa* and *Panchatantra* seem to be nothing more than a translation trial that was suspended or hypothetically postponed, since neither was ever published in translation by Vasconcelos Abreu.

The first complete Portuguese translation of a Sanskrit text was not published until 1897 and was the work of Vasconcelos Abreu's successor at the *Curso Superior de Letras*, Sebastião Rodolfo Dalgado (1855–1922). This Goa-born orientalist translated the *Hitopadeśa*,[12] and the introduction to the work is authored by Vasconcelos Abreu, who congratulates Dalgado on his pioneering endeavour:

> The book ... is translated from the Sanskrit original. And because this is the first complete translation of a Sanskrit work to come to light in Portuguese, the work is in itself an event that will have to be remembered later in the history of our literature. (1897: xv)

> Of these (literary) products (in Sanskrit) the most well-known, because it is the closest to the original source through which the Indian influence on literature reached the West and in the Middle Ages, Europe, is the classical work entitled the *Panchatantra*, that is: 'The five books (of apologues, fables and tales)'. (1897: xviii)

On the one hand, Vasconcelos Abreu highlights Dalgado's translation as a landmark in the history of Portuguese literature and, we add, of the Portuguese translation history. On the other hand, the *Panchatantra* is considered to be the classic that most obviously displays the influence of Indian literature on the European literary system. Again, no mention is made of the orientalist–translator's own attempt at translating the collection.

The circulation of Sanskrit language and literature in nineteenth-century Portugal relied more on the production of language manuals and essay writing about Sanskrit than on the importation of knowledge through translation or critical editions of texts originally written in Sanskrit, although the existing body of works on Sanskrit encompasses dispersed fragments of translated Indian literature.

From the 1870s until the 1920s, Sanskrit studies were visibly alive in Portugal, but with the death of Vasconcelos Abreu's successor in 1922 they began to decline. Can the lack of a sustained body of translations of canonical Indian literature be deemed a symptom, or even a cause, of Portuguese Sanskrit studies failing to persist?

One question that arises here is linked to the fact that the majority of the texts translated from Sanskrit, a classical language, and published in Portuguese, a modern European language making use of a different script, are presented as literal translations. Dalgado's statements on a 1918 version of *Śākuntala* by a fellow Goan are as representative as any, and eventually echo his foreword to his own translation of the *Hitopadeśa* twenty years earlier, which in turn sheds light on Vasconcelos Abreu's translation project (Table 14.3).

In line with Dalgado's testimony, when translating classic and canonical texts into vernacular (the so-called act of 'vulgarization'), literalness would help preserve toponyms and anthroponyms, deities, folklore – in a word, the text's Oriental otherness

Table 14.3 Sebastião Rodolfo Dalgado's statements on translation.

In this translation I set out to render the original as closely *de verbo ad verbum* as possible …. It is true that a freer translation providing only the interpretation of the spirit of the work would be more attractive and perhaps more appealing to the general public. But it would lose much of its Oriental originality. And I am very much engaged in making known how the ancient Aryans from Bharatvarsha used not only to think but also to express themselves. (Dalgado 1897: xii–xiii)	My ideal for classical Sanskrit productions is as literal a translation as possible, as is the case with the Bible, preserving the Oriental flavour and scent in terms of both form and content …. I know from experience that the Portuguese translation of Sanskrit books, however interesting these might be and please other European peoples, should not target the vulgarization of Indian literature but solely aim at providing the few existing amateurs in Sanskritology with a glimpse of what they cannot read or understand in their source language. I think this is why my learned predecessor in the chair, Vasconcelos Abreu, did not make any complete translation of any Sanskrit work, except for a few excerpts as samples for specific purposes. (Dalgado 1918: 2048 and 2051)

by virtue of its Oriental flavour or local colour.[13] For instance, in both volumes A and B Vasconcelos Abreu opts for using the Sanskrit word 'niti' (see previous example in Table 14.1), whereas Benfey (1859: 3) paraphrases the term with 'Lebensweisheit' (the wisdom of life). Significantly, in volume A the Sanskrit word is followed by an explanation between parentheses, 'da sabedoria do Mundo' (the World's wisdom), which is in line with Benfey's paraphrase. In volume B, the explanation is deleted, thus emphasizing the text's local colour, or, put differently, rendering it more foreign. Lancereau in turn domesticates the term by embedding it in a political note: 'The one who ... reads or continually hears *this political treatise* will never be defeated, not even by Śakra' (1871: 5; emphasis added).

Back in 1873, when Vasconcelos Abreu condemned Cândido de Figueiredo's indirect translation of the Yajnadatta episode of the *Rāmāyana*,[14] he put forward three main arguments: errors in the transliteration of names; the non-identification of the source text; and the lack of local colour, an argument which is not however unpacked (Vasconcelos Abreu 1873: n.p.).[15] Forty years later, Portuguese orientalist discourse on translating Indian literature would reproduce the same tropes and advocacy of fidelity to the original.

These issues certainly echo the controversy that overtook the Société Asiatique in the 1820s, setting Florists against anti-Florists, that is, 'those who liked to exoticize and romanticize Asian cultures (the Florists) and those who wanted a stricter and rigorous reliance on direct translation (the anti-Florists)' (McGetchin 2003: 572–3). The German scholar Friedrich Schultz (1799–1829) was one of the main representatives of the anti-Florists; in 1825 he argued for 'an alternative method, less literary and more scientifically precise' and 'criticized "philologer–poets" and their loose, poetic, literary approach to studying and translating Oriental texts' (McGetchin 2003: 570). Guilherme de Vasconcelos Abreu along with Sebastião Dalgado aligned themselves with the anti-Florist side. By contrast, Cândido de Figueiredo stood at the opposite extreme with his rendition in Portuguese decasyllables. This attitude exemplifies compliance with the formal conventions of the target culture, which clearly conflicts with anti-Florist concerns.

Around 1820, as Douglas McGetchin points out, 'the Florist literary methods were discredited, at least in academic circles', this heated debate being 'an early example of the nineteenth-century shift from romantic literary enthusiasm to empirical positivism' (2003: 570). For what is worth, Vasconcelos Abreu was a supporter of positivism, which he enthusiastically advertised among Portuguese intellectuals (Littré 1874: 149). This philosophical system was grounded in an objective and neutral observation and depiction of reality (the facts), in order to eliminate any subjectivity. Philology developed simultaneously in the second half of the nineteenth century as a science to which, as noted, Vasconcelos Abreu claimed he was contributing. As a discipline, philology came to focus on the writing and restoring of national literary histories and traditions, in which the preservation of the original meaning is central. The aim of critical editions, the main production of philologists, then, was to establish the text as written by its author. Texts had to preserve their original meaning, something that would only be achieved by erasing any changes introduced in the course of time[16] (or by distance in space, as in the case of Oriental literature). Philology was thus seen as having 'the capacity to retrieve the experiences of the past, of lost cultures, through close study of the written record' (Simon 1990: 19). The written record is the literal one, which would correspond to the objective truth about language and literature. The anti-Florist stance resonates with this philological framework: the only way to learn about distant, Oriental civilizations would be to read, and hence to translate, literally what their authors have written.

It is under this positivist philological approach to Oriental literature, to which translation belongs, that Vasconcelos Abreu reconciled literalness with the preservation of Oriental flavour. As Dorothy Figueira however remarked, 'even philology ... did not necessarily allow the translator to succeed where the dilettante failed. Both the philologist and the dilettante fell prey to their prejudices; the former's derived from knowledge, the latter's from ignorance' (1991: 195). In the case of Vasconcelos Abreu, it is knowledge that drives his translation rationale.

Concluding remarks

The missing volume C of Vasconcelos Abreu's *Panchatantra* project is labelled as a 'literal translation'. If C is a literal translation, what kind of translation is volume B? By holding an ontological status different from C, would it be a translation intended to please general readers that was however interrupted, or hypothetically postponed, given the prevalence of the scholarly norm of foreignization that is entailed in literalness? Or, to finish this speculative exercise, could an ethical and pedagogical commitment towards science, as flagged up by the Florist controversy, have something to do with the discontinuation of the translation project?

Richard Jacquemond has convincingly shown that 'since Orientalism is first and foremost an area of scholarship, it is no wonder that the criterion of good translation in the Orientalist paradigm is one of "scientific accuracy". The translation is not meant to be read by a nonprofessional reader' (1992: 149). Following Jacquemond's footsteps, Phrae Chittiphalangsri emphasizes that

> [t]he preference for science-related methodology in the translation of Oriental literature continued in European scholarship for most of the nineteenth century. The more Orientalist scholarship develops, the more translation becomes associated with scientific accuracy. (2009: 15)

To orientalist scholars, scientific accuracy tended to be more important than aesthetics, literariness, high style or readers taking comfort in reading; scientific accuracy became a translation ethos to anti-Florist orientalist–translators. The fact is, Vasconcelos Abreu envisaged his task as an orientalist as one of making science and as contributing to the creation of a scientific milieu in Portugal that in his eyes was still non-existent by the 1890s. As a result, he would have developed a pedagogical view of translation; by complying with a scientific paradigm for translating, he would envisage translation as an empirical instrument for accessing Oriental literary, cultural, mythological knowledge. In his introduction to Dalgado's *Hitopadeśa*, Vasconcelos Abreu clearly states:

> Monsignor Dalgado did not intend to be literate; he sought instead to be exact. His language resents the fact that he did not live in Portugal; it holds the Indian flavour. This holds philological interest which should not be undervalued. (1897, xvi)

Corroborating our analysis, would only the translations that preserve the Indian flavour be worth completing and publishing? If the hypothetical volume C containing 'the literal translation of the whole *Panchatantra*' was written 'for the use of my students' (explanatory note to volume B), maybe volume B was targeted at a different, more general audience. In such case, perhaps Vasconcelos Abreu did not feel up to, or was sceptical about, translating the *Panchatantra* to please readers outside academic circles, that is, non-specialists of Sanskritology, because this simply was not the target audience of orientalist scholarship. Volume B in particular seems to have been a testing tool in a two-stage translation project left unfinished by someone whose self-imposed scientific mission was to produce specialized knowledge for the instruction of prospective orientalists, either scholars or agents at the service of a colonial enterprise.[17]

Notes

1. This project and therefore the present work are supported by the Portuguese Foundation for Science and Technology, I.P., within the framework of 'Projeto 3599 – Promover a Produção Científica, o Desenvolvimento Tecnológico e a Inovação – Não Cofinanciada' (PTDC/CPC-CMP/0398/2014). We thank Patricia Odber de Baubeta for revising this chapter.
2. We thank the director of the library of the School of Arts and Humanities of Lisbon, Pedro Estácio, and his team for granting us full access to the archive.
3. This is particularly the case when Vasconcelos Abreu discusses the animal imagery patent in the Portuguese sixteenth-century epic *The Lusiads* and its echoing of Buddhist legends in *Passos dos Lusíadas* (1892: 64).
4. Unless otherwise noted, all translations are ours.
5. Theodor Benfey's two-volume German translation came out in 1859, *Pantschatantra: Fünf Bücher indischer Fabeln, Märchen und Erzählungen*. The first volume consists of the introduction and study of the text, whereas the second is the German translation. In 1871, a French translation by Édouard Lancereau was published under the title *Pantchatantra, ou, Les cinq livres: recueil d'apologues et de contes*. A copy of this translation can be found in the private library of Sebastião Dalgado located at the Lisbon Academy of Sciences. Both editions are recommended by Vasconcelos Abreu to learners of Sanskrit (e.g. 1891). A retranslation followed in 1872 with Jean A. Dubois's *Le Pantcha-tantra ou les cinq ruses* (A. Barraud). Kielhorn and Bühler authored a five-volume edition of *Panchatantra* in Sanskrit with grammatical and semantic annotations in English. The first edition was issued in 1868, and it was

constantly revised until 1885 (second edition in 1873, third edition in 1879, fourth edition in 1882).

6   The orientalist–translator seems to suggest that the translation results from collating Kielhorn and Bühler's 1885 and 1879 editions (the fifth and the third editions, respectively).

7   We thank Shiv Kumar Singh for helping us deciphering this information.

8   According to Jackson (2001: 34), note-takers would often leave unfinished the task of filling in the blank pages; they would enthusiastically start this task, but over time they would give up discouraged by its size unless it was of course absolutely crucial.

9   The source text used was most probably the 1859 edition found in his private library by Prem Chunder Tarkabágish (Premachandra Tarkavagisa), who follows the Bengalī recension. At the time the Bengalī recension was discredited by the Devanāgarī recension that was proven to be the most ancient: 'Jones's use of the Bengalī recension is followed by Chézy and Fauche, while the Devanāgarī recension is popular among later translators namely Monier-Williams, Foucaux and Bergaigne'; 'some of these translators denounce the Bengalī recension used by Jones and his successors as corrupted and impure, and instead recommend the Devanāgarī recension as a master script of *Śakuntalā*' (Chittiphalangsri 2009: 123 and 132). Surprisingly or not, Vasconcelos Abreu does not use the edition followed by Abel Bergaigne, his master in Paris.

10 Nalopākhyānam is an especially popular episode of the *Mahābhārata* among foreign learners of Sanskrit.

11 The first known manuscript of the *Hitopadeśa* dates from 1373 (Dalgado 1897: x). The first part of the *Hitopadeśa*, *mitra-lābha*, is about gaining friends, which corresponds to the second book of the *Panchatantra*. Its first tantra, *mitra-bheda*, the one that is studied and partially translated in volumes A and B, is contrariwise about the loss of friendship, or estrangement between friends.

12 Exactly one hundred and twelve years after an Indian text was first translated directly from Sanskrit not only into English but into a European and modern language (with Sir Charles Wilkins's translation of the *Bhagavad Gītā* from Sanskrit in 1785).

13 The risk with the concept of 'local colour' as it is often used is that it can easily be taken as synonymous with exoticism, or exoticizing. Vladimir Kapor has shown that as a literary practice exoticism is a derivation of the Romantic local colour (see particularly his chapter 'L'Exotisme et l'imaginaire social', 2007: 131–80).

14 Cândido de Figueiredo being a poet, and not, in Vasconcelos Abreu's words, 'an orientalist, neither an Indianist, nor a dilettante, not even a curious in love for the Sanskrit originals' (1873), is expressly condemned by the Sanskritist.

15 Although Vasconcelos Abreu does not expand on his idea of 'local colour', his concern would be to realistically retrieve via translation one's experiences of the distant Oriental culture, as the *niti* example illustrates. For that, it would be important to describe and render the distant Orient exactly as it is presented in its proper context, that is, literally.

16 Scribes are often presented as sources of variation in medieval literature; philologists have tended to erase the scribes' textual presence from copies in an attempt to reconstruct authors' original words, which was the goal of classic philology.

17 As an orientalist Vasconcelos Abreu overtly positioned his work in a specialized field of production, one that in the 1980s Bourdieu described as the field of restricted production: 'The field of production *per se* owes its own structure to the opposition

between the *field of restricted production* as a system producing cultural goods (and the instruments for appropriating these goods) objectively destined for a public of producers of cultural goods, and the *field of large-scale cultural production*, specifically organized with a view to the production of cultural goods destined for non-producers of cultural goods, "the public at large"' (1993: 115; emphases in the original). Each field of cultural production would have its own translational norms. To the orientalist community, translating would be a statement of scholarship, and translation would be a space for stating orientalist expertise; translational norms would thus help distinguish specialists from non-specialists.

References

Benfey, Theodor (1859), *Pantschatantra: Fünf Bücher indischer Fabeln, Märchen und Erzählungen*, vol. 2, Leipzig: F. A. Brockhaus.

Bourdieu, Pierre (1993), 'The Market of Symbolic Goods', in Randal Johnson (ed.), *The Field of Cultural Production: Essays on Art and Literature*, 112–41, Cambridge: Polity Press.

Chittiphalangsri, Phrae (2009), 'Translation, Orientalism and Virtuality: English and French Translations of the *Bhagavad Gītā* and *Śakuntalā* 1784–1884', PhD thesis, University College London, London.

Coelho, F. Adolpho (1881), *Noções de Litteratura Antiga e Medieval como Introducção á Litteratura Portugueza*, Porto: Magalhães & Moniz.

Dalgado, Sebastião Rodolfo, (trans.) (1897), *Hitopadexa ou Instrucção Util. Versão Portugueza Feita Directamente do Original Sanskrito*, Lisboa: Antiga Casa Bertrand.

Dalgado, Sebastião Rodolfo (trans.) (1916), *História de Nala e Damayanti: Episódio do Mahabhárata*, Coimbra: Imprensa da Universidade.

Dalgado, Sebastião Rodolfo (1918), 'Xacuntalá. Drama Sânscrito de Calidaça Traduzido do Original por Bernardino Gracias' [introduction], *Boletim da Segunda Classe*, XI (3) [1916–17]: 2037–53.

Figueira, Dorothy (1991), *Translating the Orient: The Reception of Śākuntala in Nineteenth-Century Europe*, Albany: State University of New York Press.

Figueiredo, Cândido de, trans. (1873), *Morte de Yaginadatta: Episodio do Poema Epico – o Ramayana: versos portuguezes*, Coimbra: Imprensa da Universidade.

Gracias, Bernardino (trans.) (1925), *A Nuvem Mensageira* by Kālidāsa, annotated and with a preface by Bernardino Gracias, Lisboa: Imp. Lucas.

Jackson, H. J. (2001), *Marginalia: Readers Writing in Books*, New Haven: Yale University Press.

Jacquemond, Richard (1992), 'Translation and Cultural Hegemony: The Case Study of French-Arabic Translation', in Lawrence Venuti (ed.), *Rethinking Translation: Discourse, Subjectivity, Ideology*, 139–58, London and New York: Routledge.

Kapor, Vladimir (2007), *Pour une poétique de l'écriture exotique*, Paris: L'Harmattan.

Lancereau, Édouard (1871), *Pantchatantra, ou, Les cinq livres: recueil d'apologues et de contes*, Paris: Imprimerie Nationale.

Littré, Émile (1874), 'La Philosophie positive en Portugal', *La Philosophie positive*, XIII (July–December): 149–50. Available at http://gallica.bnf.fr/ark:/12148/bpt6k778845 (accessed 14 January 2018).

McGetchin, Douglas T. (2003), 'Wilting Florists: The Turbulent Early Decades of the Société Asiatique, 1822–1860', *Journal of the History of Ideas*, 64 (4): 565–80.
Pereira, Francisco Maria Esteves (1917), 'O Canto Terceiro do Buddhacarita. Poema de Açvaghosa. Estudo litterario', *Boletim da Segunda Classe da Academia das Sciências de Lisboa*, XI (2, March–July): 845–59.
Pereira, Francisco Maria Esteves (1921), 'A *Bhagavad-Gîtâ*. Tradução Sumária em Português por um Autor Anónimo do século XVII', *Boletim da Classe de Letras*, XV (1, November–March): 78–110.
Pereira, Francisco Maria Esteves (1924), 'Viçvántara. IX Játaka do Jatakamala por Ayra Sura, sôbre a Prática da Virtude da Beneficência', *Boletim da Segunda Classe da Academia das Sciências de Lisboa*, XVIII: 125–51.
Santos, Fernanda (2010), 'Marginália nas Colecções das Bibliotecas: o Fundo Guilherme de Vasconcelos Abreu na Biblioteca da Faculdade de Letras da Universidade de Lisboa', MA diss., School of Arts and Humanities, University of Lisbon, Lisboa.
Simon, Eckehard (1990), 'The Case for Medieval Philology', in Jan Ziolkowski (ed.), *On Philology*, 16–19, University Park: The Pennsylvania State University.
Toury, Gideon (1995), *Descriptive Translation Studies and Beyond*, Amsterdam and Philadelphia: John Benjamins.
Vasconcelos Abreu, Guilherme de (1869), 'Om! – Adoracao a Ganeca. (Episodio do Poema Oriental – Ramayana)', *Jornal litterario*, 2–3–4 (1st year, February): 13–15, 21–2, 28–9. Available at https://digitalis-dsp.uc.pt/html/10316.2/35541/item1_index.html (accessed 10 April 2018).
Vasconcelos Abreu, Guilherme de (1873), 'Folhetim. O Sr. Cândido de Figueiredo e o seu Folheto. Litteratura indiana', *Jornal do Commercio*, 5 December, n.p.
Vasconcelos Abreu, Guilherme de (1874), *Exposição Feita perante os Membros da Commissão Nacional Portugueza do Congresso Internacional dos Orientalistas Convocados para Constituirem uma Associação Promotora dos Estudos Orientaes e Glotticos em Portugal*, Lisboa: Typographia Luso-Britannica de W. T. Wood.
Vasconcelos Abreu, Guilherme de (1878a), *O Reconhecimento de Chakuntala. Impressao Specimen do Acto I do Celebre Drama de Kalidasa. Trasladado Litteralmente do Saoskrito segundo a Recensao Bengali*, Lisboa: Imprensa Nacional.
Vasconcelos Abreu, Guilherme de (1878b), *Investigações sobre o Caracter da Civilisação Árya-Hindu*, Lisboa: Imprensa Nacional.
Vasconcelos Abreu, Guilherme de (1889), *Exercicios e Primeiras Leituras de Sámscrito (Apéndice ao Manual). Tômo I. Gramática e antolojía*, Lisboa: Imprensa Nacional.
Vasconcelos Abreu, Guilherme de (1890), 'O Instituto Oriental e Ultramarino Português. Idéas Succintas àcêrca da sua Criação', *Boletim da Sociedade de Geografia de Lisboa*, 9: 521–45.
Vasconcelos Abreu, Guilherme de (1891), *Manual para o Estudo do Sãoskrito Classico. Tomo II: Chrestomathia*, Lisboa: Imprensa Nacional.
Vasconcelos Abreu, Guilherme de (1892), *Passos dos Lusíadas*, Lisboa: Imprensa Nacional.
Vasconcelos Abreu, Guilherme de (1897), 'Introdução', in *Hitopadexa ou Instrucção Util*, xv–xxii, Lisboa: Antiga Casa Bertrand.
Vasconcelos Abreu, Guilherme de (1902), *Os Contos, Apólogos e Fábulas da Índia: Influéncia Indirecta no Auto da Mofina Méndez, de Gil Vicente*, Lisboa: Imprensa Nacional.
Vasconcelos Abreu, Guilherme (trans.) (n.d.), Ms. *Panchatantra*, by Vishnu Sharma, 2 vols., Library of the School of Arts and Humanities of the University of Lisbon, ULFL 085615.

15

Coda

Genetic Translation Studies: Conflict and Collaboration in Liminal Spaces is the first book published in English language specifically on genetic translation studies (GTS) and claiming to situate itself in the emerging field of GTS.

The thirteen chapters gathered here draw on a geographically and historically diverse body of case studies, exhibit an acute awareness of the hermeneutical importance of marginalia and certainly view translators as creative agents. Interestingly, a significant number of the chapters bear in their titles the name of the translator whose genetic dossier and/or creative process is under scrutiny, a fact which underpins that the new field of GTS does indeed give visibility to the translator figure. Apart from shedding light on methodological research tools and exploring the kinds of data one can expect from applying a genetic approach to translation, the chapters present the outcomes of current individual projects highlighting the joys and hardships of archival research, while emphasizing the need for a comparative frame of mind relating the various textual materials so as to access translational agents' 'black box' and working conditions, decision-making and performance. In their empirical coverage of a wide range of topics pertaining to GTS, many contributors bring to light unexploited archival material, show different ways of combining close and distant reading, destabilize the notions of original, source text and translation, in addition to drawing a picture of the translation praxis as an open, endless rewriting process.

The Portuguese literary scene stands out as a privileged focus of study, although it has been traditionally neglected within Western translation studies and genetic scholarship overall. For this reason, we believe this book is quite promising for engaging with GTS as it is shaped by the Portuguese scholarship and for making known across borders research activities in Portugal, besides offering itself as a case study for comparison with other less visible Western translation traditions.

The five chapters of the opening section contribute to conceptualizing the emerging field of GTS. They provide 'hands-on' studies that exemplify how the intersection of genetic criticism with translation studies can productively happen, therefore demonstrating the research possibilities and added value of exploring GTS. This intersection is fruitful when it comes to identifying the various agents involved in a translation event, especially when collaborative practices are often occluded, misconstruing translation as a solitary affair. The chapters in this section deconstruct this idea, describing the agency of the actors implied in translation processes as revealed by genetic documentation.

The second section of the volume explores four cases of 'Translators' Stories and Testimonies' by presenting voices and bodies of literary translation practitioners, who tend to be positively portrayed and appear in both direct and indirect speech. The introductory chapter prepares the ground for the following contributions, which expand the focus of GTS from a text-centred to an agent-centred methodology and show in different ways how to access the translation process from the outside to within. All these chapters examine specific exogenetic tools as a way of gaining insight into the translator's competence and performance.

The third and last part of the volume expands the positive interaction between translation and genetic criticism by addressing individual processes of literary translation from different periods and geographies, that is, microhistories of translators and their translations under the overarching theme of 'Translators at Work'. It collects four case studies that enquire into prose translators' performances, working practices and textual strategies, as well as their contextual significance and impact. All the case studies bring in archival material (mostly translation drafts, both manuscripts and typescripts), and ultimately exemplify how the genetic dossier of a translator can be established and how a genetic comparative approach to translation contributes to clarifying translational performance and writing processes.

To sum up, GTS proposes a disciplinary and epistemological intersection that goes beyond the binary logic of source and target text, of author versus translator; instead of oppositions, GTS proposes a creative continuum in which source and target texts are explored as working phases. It is our conviction that as a whole the volume will be useful to researchers and scholars in search of new ways of working with archival material, interrogating textual processes and engaging with conflicts and collaborations between translational agents.

TO BE CONTINUED ...

Index

academic discourse 18, 184–5, 191 n.18, n.21
  English 184–6, 192 n.23
addition 7, 31, 78, 82, 168, 176 n.8
African American culture 15, 55–7, 60
African Americans 57–9
agency 4, 6, 9, 11, 13, 15–16, 18, 28, 39, 65, 83, 119 n.14, 182–3, 233
alliteration 44, 49–51
amendment 7, 18–19, 66, 76, 78, 80–1, 201
amplitude 19, 201, 207–9
anthology 32, 34, 37, 60, 62–3, 68 n.4, 94, 102 n.3, 139
antonymy 206, 210 (*see also* synonymy)
Antunes, António Lobo 17, 147, 149, 151–6, 157 n.10
  Return of the Caravels, The 152–6, 157 n.12
archival 13, 39, 61–2, 67
  material 6, 15, 71, 75–8, 82–4, 110, 233–4
  research 2, 12, 111, 233
archive 7, 13, 18, 35–6, 61, 93, 102 n.2, n.3, 104 n.15, 110, 114, 163–4, 167, 170, 215, 228 n.2 (*see also* translator's archive)
  Austrian National Library Literary 16, 111, 119 n.10, n.13, n.17
  digital 2, 11, 13–14, 89
  Kyllikki Villa 85 n.9, n.14, n.15, n.18, n.19, n.20, 86 n.22
assonance 44, 51
auctoritas 5, 8
audiovisual 13
Austin, Alfred 32, 34–5
author 1–5, 8–11, 13–19, 27–32, 35–8, 43–4, 46–7, 49, 51, 52 n.7, 57–8, 61–2, 76, 78, 89–91, 93–7, 102 n.1, n.2, n.3, 103 n.7, 104 n.15, 111–13, 116–17, 120 n.21, 124–5, 127, 137, 139, 141–4, 147–56, 157 n.1,

n.8, n.9, 158 n.17, 165, 170, 175, 175 n.2, 176 n.4, n.16, 179–80, 182–4, 186–9, 190 n.2, n.6, n.8, n.9, 197–202, 204–5, 215, 216, 226–7, 229 n.16, 234
Authorial and Editorial Voices in Translation (Hanne Jansen and Anna Wegener) 10, 35
authority 5, 51, 75, 135, 182, 190 n.8
authorship 5, 12, 39, 51, 92, 103 n.7, 150, 179, 181, 186
  coauthorship 186
autobiography 2, 36, 38, 124
autograph 1, 31, 93, 199–201
autographic 29–31, 35, 39, 197
avant-texte 2, 7, 9, 12, 30, 118 n.5, 135, 181, 187, 189 (*see also* post-texte)

base text 74, 97, 198–9, 203–5, 223
Bassnett, Susan 118 n.4, 136, 139–40, 148
Basso, Susanna 16, 125, 127–8
Beckett, Samuel 3–4, 8–11, 103 n.13
Bellemin-Noël, Jean 68 n.5, 135
best-text 15, 71, 74–8, 80, 82–3, 85 n.7
Bible 5, 29, 50, 113, 225
Bilingual Text, The (Jan W. Hokenson and Marcella Munson) 11, 181, 189, 190 n.6, 191 n.15
bilingual 11, 20 n.11, 93, 102, 223
  writers 9
  text 183, 190 n.6, 191 n.15
bilingualism 11, 31, 190 n.6
biography 2, 7, 16, 110, 124–5, 136, 200 (*see also* translation biographies)
black box 17, 233
Bocci, Laura 16, 125, 127
Book of Disquiet digital archive 14
Branco, Camilo Castelo 18–19, 199–201, 203–7, 209–10, 211 n.6
  História de Gabriel Malagrida 18, 199–208, 210, 210 n.4

Cabrera Infante, Guillermo 52 n.7
Caeiro, Alberto 20 n.5, 31–5, 39 n.3
cancellation 201
Capote, Truman 18, 164, 171–3
Casanova, Pascale 147, 157 n.4
Cayron, Claire 137–43
censorship 7, 200
    censorship translation studies 7
    self-censorship 59
Char, René 16, 111–18, 118–19 n.8, 119 n.13, n.16, n.17, n.18, 120 n.21, n.22
Chesterman, Andrew 6–7, 110, 137
chronology 96, 164, 201, 203, 209
close reading 12, 15–16, 55, 233
closelaboration 15, 51–2, 52 n.7
Coindreau, Maurice 18, 164–5, 167–75, 175 n.2, n.3, 176 n.4
cognitive sciences 123, 128
collaboration 3, 7, 9–10, 15–16, 39, 40 n.4, 84, 103 n.7, 127, 153, 187, 234
collaborative 3, 10–12, 15, 17, 78, 117–18, 143, 151, 184, 233
    editions 14
    translation 10, 15, 20 n.9, 28, 43–5, 49, 51–2
Collaborative Translation: From the Renaissance to the Digital Age (Anthony Cordingley and Céline Frigau Manning) 3, 10, 84
collation 1, 74–5, 83, 92, 99
collating 72, 74–5, 83, 85 n.4, n.7, 216, 229 n.6
Colóquio Letras 17, 135–8, 142, 144
Communism 55, 66
competence 11, 17–18, 67, 218, 234
compilative translation 15, 71–5, 77, 82, 84, 85 n.4 (*see also* eclectic translation)
conflict 9–10, 19, 57, 234
constraints 1, 15, 29, 35, 40 n.4, 98, 142, 147
copy 1, 5, 13, 30–2, 45, 74, 85 n.12, 95, 114, 144, 167, 219, 228 n.5
    clean 198
    editors 10
copy-text method 85 n.7
Cordingley, Anthony 2–4, 8, 10–11, 27–8, 30, 35–6, 38–9, 43, 65, 74–5, 83–4, 103 n.8, 110, 118 n.5, 163, 180–1, 190 n.5, n.9, 191 n.15
corporeal 16, 110–11, 114, 119 n.14, 124–32
corporeality 16 (*see also* translator's body)
correction 10, 15, 19, 35, 43–6, 48–50, 52 n.4, n.6, 62, 101, 135, 166–70, 176 n.4, 197–8, 201–10, 216
    immediate 201–4, 207 (*see also variante d'écriture*)
    non-immediate 201–3, 207–9 (*see also variante de lecture*)
    topography 201–2, 208
correspondence 7, 10, 15–16, 43, 47, 65, 72, 75, 78, 91–2, 102 n.3, 109–11, 113–14, 116–17, 120 n.21, 135, 164, 187
creative 6, 13, 19, 46, 48, 63, 95, 103 n.13, 110–11, 117, 141, 152, 197–9, 204–6, 210, 233–4
    process 7, 15, 17–18, 43, 51, 55, 63, 96, 110–11, 115, 117, 118 n.5, 140, 144, 157 n.1, 197, 199–200, 233
    translation 51
creativity 5, 7, 17, 65, 144
critical 6, 30–2, 47, 75, 99, 120 n.22, 124, 151, 163, 175, 175 n.2 (*see also* edition)
    apparatus 97, 104 n.18
    text 14
critique génétique 35, 39, 40 n.4, 118 n.5 (*see also* genetic criticism)

de Biasi, Pierre-Marc 2, 4–6, 20 n.7, 29–30, 34, 62, 68, 198, 200–1, 210 n.1, n.2
deletion 37, 200, 202, 206, 210
Deppman, Jed 6, 68 n.5, 180–1
descriptive translation studies (DTS) 1, 4, 8, 136
dialogue 5, 7, 13, 16, 47, 49, 51, 59, 111, 113–18
diaspora 183
digital scholarly editing 16
discipline 5, 9, 17, 19, 27, 39, 74, 128, 182–3, 185, 191 n.18, 213–14, 226
Dollerup, Cay 73, 83, 84 n.2, 85 n.4
domestication 63

Dos Passos, John 18, 164, 174, 177 n.24
draft 2–4, 10, 18, 29, 62, 91–2, 110, 118 n.5, 135, 155, 163–4, 168–70, 174–5, 176 n.4, 180–1, 187, 198, 234
  first 1, 9, 45, 143, 169–70, 172, 176 n.11, n.12, n.14
  handwritten 15, 19, 114, 214–19, 223
  manuscript 55, 62, 67, 76
  of translator 2, 7, 43, 110, 163–4, 190 n.5
drafting phase 198, 200–1
  pre- 198–201
drawriting 15, 55, 62
Duarte, King of Portugal 14, 30–2, 35

eclectic translation 72 (*see also* compilative translation)
Eco, Umberto 89, 102 n.1
écriture à processus 197 (*see also* writing in process)
écriture à programme 197 (*see also* planned writing, programmed writing)
edition 5, 8, 13–14, 20 n.11, 32, 38, 45, 59, 74–5, 85 n.6, n.7, n.8, n.12, 92–3, 96–8, 102, 102 n.2, 113, 155, 157 n.11, 164, 175, 175 n.3, 200, 213, 216–17, 219–23, 228–9 n.5, 229 n.6, n.9
  critical 5, 27, 75, 85 n.6, 201, 225–6
  critical-genetic 91
  digital 13, 89
  diplomatic 85 n.6
  documentary 85 n.6
  genetic 14, 16, 27, 91, 201–2
  genetic-critical 16, 89
  multilevel 98
editor 2–4, 9–10, 14–15, 36–9, 60, 63, 75, 98, 110–11, 127, 136, 148, 164, 174, 180, 184, 187
editorial model 16, 98
embodied cognition 124, 128, 130–1, 132 n.4
embodiment 7, 16, 123–4, 128–9, 131
  theory 16, 123–4, 127–31
emend 73, 83
emendation 83, 223
empirical dossier 15, 55, 67
endogenesis 4, 20 n.1, 102

endogenetic 2, 34
epigenesis 4, 14, 102
epistemological 8, 18–19, 181, 183–4, 186, 234
  culture 18, 189
  translation 18, 186
epitext 9, 17, 147, 156, 157 n.1
Erasmus 5
error 36, 167, 226
  translation 73, 76–9, 82–3, 158 n.15, 204
ethics 61
exile 36, 44, 56
exogenesis 2, 20 n.1, 102
exogenetic 2, 4, 16–17, 19, 57, 111, 234
extratextual 12, 17, 124, 131, 143, 223

facsimile 11, 85 n.6
faithful 57, 65, 140–1, 144, 164, 207
faithfulness 139–41, 144, 224
Ferrer, Daniel 6, 68 n.5, 180–1
fidelity 67, 151, 226
Fitch, Brian 96–7, 187
Fitzgerald, Robert 15, 43–52, 52 n.6
foreignization 154, 227
foreignizing strategy 17
Fowlie, Wallace 44–5, 52 n.4

Gabler, Walter 14
Gallimard 18, 45, 164
Geier, Swetlana 16, 125–8
genesis 3–4, 7, 10–12, 14–19, 28–9, 43–4, 51, 72, 75, 83–4, 92–3, 97–9, 110, 115, 163, 190 n.5, 197–202, 204, 210, 210 n.4, 214, 219
GENESIS. Revue internationale de critique génétique 8–9, 29, 163
genetic 2–3, 6–8, 11, 13–15, 17–19, 20 n.8, n.11, 27–9, 31, 35, 38, 43–4, 51, 62, 66, 75, 92, 99, 118 n.5, 124, 135, 168, 175, 181, 186–7, 189, 197–9, 201–2, 205, 207, 210, 211 n.8, 214, 233–4 (*see also* edition)
  criticism 1–9, 11–14, 16–19, 20 n.7, 28–9, 39, 40 n.4, 74, 92, 102, 163, 179–81, 197, 199, 233–4 (*see also* critique génétique)
  dossier 2–4, 6, 11–12, 14–16, 55, 60, 62, 65, 67–8, 89, 104 n.15, 114, 200–1, 233–4

translation studies (GTS) 1, 3–4, 8–16, 19, 27–8, 30, 38, 43, 52 n.2, 103 n.8, 110–11, 123, 131, 163, 181, 188–90, 190 n.5, 233–4
geneticist 1, 3–5, 18, 30
genetics 40 n.4, 164 (*see also* manuscript genetics, textual genetics, translation genetics)
Genette, Gérard 93, 97, 147, 157 n.1, 188
genius 5–6, 154–5, 179
genre 12–13, 20 n.8, 124, 188, 191 n.20, 216, 219
Goldschmidt, Georges-Arthur 109, 111–13, 115, 117, 119 n.12
Greetham, David C. 74–5
Grésillon, Almuth 2, 6, 35, 40 n.4, 62, 197–8, 200–1
Griffin, Jonathan 137–43
Groden, Michael 6, 68 n.5, 180–1
Grutman, Rainier 11, 96–7, 103 n.9, 181–2, 187, 190 n.6, n.8, n.9
Guzmán, María Constanza 148–9, 154, 157 n.6

Handke, Peter 8, 13, 16, 109–18, 118–19 n.8, 119 n.12, n.13, n.14, n.15, n.16, n.17, n.18, 120 n.21, n.22, n.23
Handkeonline 20 n.12, 111, 119 n.10, n.11, n.13, n.16, n.18, 120 n.19, n.20
Hay, Louis 5–6, 144, 210 n.1
Heine, Heinrich 5
Hermans, Theo 5, 110, 118 n.3
Huss, Joanna Trzeciak 10
hypertext 13, 97–8, 199
hypertextual 14

Iaroslavskaïa, Evgenéa 14, 36–9
Indian literature 213, 216, 220, 225–6
indirect translation 11–12, 15, 72–3, 77, 82–4, 226
inference 7, 14, 28, 30–1, 35, 150
Institut mémoires de l'édition contemporaine (IMEC) 18, 163–6, 168, 170–4, 177 n.24
intention 37, 55, 61, 65–6, 75, 141, 144, 187, 206, 219
  authorial 5–6
  original 61, 187–8
interaction 4–5, 9, 14, 18, 35, 67, 117, 125, 129, 137, 151, 188, 234

interculture 18, 181, 186, 189 (*see also* Anthony Pym)
interlingual 16, 89, 96
interlinguistic materials 2
interpretation 5, 30, 37, 45, 115, 202, 223, 225
  authorial 51
  interlinguistic 89, 102 n.1
  intersystemic 89, 102 n.1
intertext 18, 181, 186–90, 191 n.20
intertextuality 3
interview 2, 83, 112–15, 119 n.10, 125, 128, 135, 147, 149–51, 156–7, 157 n.1
invisibility 6, 144, 147

journalism 57, 59, 66
Joyce, James 4, 31
Jung, Verena 18, 181–4, 187–8, 191 n.20

Kazantzakis, Nikos 15, 71, 75, 78

language broker 180, 185
latency 14, 28
Laye, Françoise 138, 140–4
Lefevere, André 136
Levitin, Alexis 138–42, 144
liminal space 9
literacy brokers 180, 184, 186, 189
literary history 10–12, 226
literary style 18, 94, 175
literalness 5, 19, 140, 207, 224–5, 227
Lopes, Alexandra 9

Maia, Rita Bueno 12, 72–3, 76, 82, 84 n.1
Maier, Carol 110, 118 n.4
Manning, Céline Frigau 3, 10, 84
manuscript 1–2, 5–6, 11–15, 19, 29–30, 36, 38, 43, 45–51, 52 n.3, n.6, 61–6, 92–3, 118 n.5, 163, 166, 168, 175, 176 n.4, 181, 197–200, 204–5, 208, 210, 210 n.3, 211 n.7, n.8, 213–14, 219, 229 n.11, 234 (*see also* draft)
  genetics 4 (*see also* genetics)
  translation 15, 18, 63
  translators' 4, 43, 110, 163, 190 n.5
  typed 165

marginalia 2, 215, 233
market 11, 36
materiality 7, 9, 13
McGann, Jerome 40 n.4, 75
McKenzie, D. F. 40 n.4
mediating 84
    language 72
    text 72–3, 76, 82
medieval literature 221, 229 n.16
Mello, Pedro Homem de 16, 89–94, 97–8, 102, 102 n.2, n.3, n.4, n.5, 103 n.6, n.9, n.11, 104 n.15
memoir 2, 17, 147, 150, 152–3, 155, 157, 157 n.6, 200
memory 13, 48, 114–15, 117, 131, 187–8, 206
mental 16, 113, 119 n.15, 130, 132 n.3, 152, 188, 198
    act 115
    process 112, 119 n.15, 126, 128, 183
    project 35
    self-translation 182
    translation 191 n.22
    work 15, 63
metaphor 5, 7, 9, 44, 47, 49, 51, 61, 63, 78, 83, 126, 140, 150–1
microhistory 7, 15, 67, 110, 234
migration 182
Miłosz, Czesław 15, 55–67
    'Negro spirituals' 15, 55, 57, 60–3, 66–7, 68 n.4
Montini, Chiara 2–4, 8, 10, 27–8, 30, 35–6, 38–9, 43, 65, 74–5, 83, 103 n.8, 110, 118 n.5, 163, 180–2, 190 n.5, n.6, n.9, 199
multi-translators 9
multiple texts 13, 75, 97
Munday, Jeremy 7, 10, 20 n.8, 67, 75, 83, 110, 118 n.6, n.7, 124–5, 127, 135, 180

Nasi, Franco 16, 125, 127
ne varietur 6
non-translation 17, 183

omission 64, 76, 78–80, 82–3
orientalism 227
orientalist-translator 19, 220–1, 223, 225, 227, 229 n.6
original 6, 8, 10–11, 13, 15, 19, 65, 71–2, 77–8, 84, 90, 93, 95–7, 103 n.14, 141, 153–5, 158 n.16, n.17, 164–5, 167–9, 173–5, 176 n.16, 180, 187–8, 190 n.6, n.8, n.9, 197, 200, 207, 224–6, 229 n.14, 233
    pseudo- 11–12, 20 n.11
original meaning 6, 205–7, 210, 226
original text 5, 43, 72, 83, 96, 144, 164, 182, 184, 190 n.1, 197, 199, 203–6, 210
originality 5, 191 n.15, 225
    pseudo- 12
Oseki-Dépré, Inês 137–8, 141, 143–4
    Théories et pratiques de la traduction littéraire 138
    Traduction & Poésie 138
Oustinoff, Michael 95, 103 n.13

Paloposki, Outi 12, 72, 77, 83, 85 n.5
Panchatantra (Vishnu Sharma) 19, 214–21, 223–5, 227–8, 228 n.5, 229 n.11
paratext 109, 153, 157 n.1
paratranslational 179–80
Passos, Marie-Hélène Paret 43, 52 n.2, 197–9
performance 11, 17–18, 155, 218, 223, 233–4
peritext 9, 17, 149, 157 n.1
Perse, Saint-John 15, 43–52, 52 n.3, n.4, n.6, 163
    Amers 45, 52 n.4
    Chronicle 15, 44–6, 49–51, 52 n.6
    Chronique 43–4, 47–51
    Seamarks 52 n.4
personal 16–17, 61, 104 n.15, 110–11, 114, 126, 149, 189, 223
    collections 5
    library 5, 215–16, 218 (*see also* private library)
    papers 2, 7, 110, 118 n.6, 127
Pessoa, Fernando 6, 8, 14, 20 n.5, 31–5, 39, 39 n.3, 137–8, 142–3
phenomenological 16, 111–16, 118
phenomenology 111, 115
philology 214–16, 226–7, 229 n.16
Pięta, Hanna 12, 72–3, 76, 82, 84 n.1
Pitta, Carlos 138, 140–1, 143–4, 145 n.4
poet-translator 11, 52, 163
poetics 15, 44, 49, 51, 52 n.3, 119 n.14, 125–6
    translative 18, 165

poetry 16, 20 n.8, n.11, 44, 59–60, 63, 66, 68 n.4, 89–91, 94, 97, 112–15, 117, 120 n.22, 137 (*see also* translation)
polyglotism 11
Polysystem Theory 147
Popovič, Anton 72, 96, 182–3
Portuguese literature 17, 136–8, 199, 221, 225
post-publication 74
post-texte 2–3, 7, 9, 17, 190 (*see also avant-texte*)
post-textual 2, 4, 17
post-war 55–6, 58–9, 67
pre-editorial 198, 210 n.2
pre-publication 74
printing 2, 85 n.12, 135
private library 2, 60, 214, 228 n.5, 229 n.9 (*see also* personal library)
prize 109, 138, 148
    Nobel Prize 52 n.3, 56, 150, 157 n.5
product 3–6, 11, 28, 67, 85 n.4, 147, 190 n.8, 197, 224
projection 140–1, 205, 210
proofs 2, 62, 167, 198
proofreading 155–6, 179
published text 2, 6, 29, 62, 72
published version 15, 35, 67, 91, 164–5, 167, 176 n.4
publisher 4, 9, 17, 36, 39, 127, 142–3, 148–50, 152, 180, 182, 200
    records 3
publishing contracts 3
publishing house 2–3, 10, 18, 28, 35–8, 85 n.14, n.19, 114, 200
Pym, Anthony 8, 18, 110, 124–5, 181, 189 (*see also* interculture)

Quillier, Patrick 138, 142, 144

Rabassa, Gregory 17, 147–57, 157 n.3, n.5, n.7, n.8, 157–8 n.13, 158 n.14, n.16, n.20
    If This Be Treason: Translation and Its Dyscontents 150–1, 155
racism 55, 57–9, 66–7
redirection 205–7, 210
retranslation 3, 11, 74, 84 n.2, 85 n.5, 228 n.5
return 199, 205, 209–10

review 2–3, 17, 45, 51, 59, 136–7, 145 n.4, 147–8, 152, 154–5, 157 n.1, 158 n.14, 181, 187, 190
Partisan Review 56
Translation Review 139
reviewer 153, 180, 187
reviser 2–3, 9–10, 18
revision 1, 6, 15, 45, 47–51, 93–4, 99, 143, 164, 167, 170, 172, 174, 179–80, 201, 203–4, 207–9
rewriting 6, 11, 13, 16, 19, 55, 63–4, 94, 102 n.1, 111, 180, 189, 200, 207, 233
    alloglottic 89, 93–4
    isoglottic 104 n.15
rhythm 15, 44–6, 50–1, 95, 127, 131, 170–1
Robinson, Douglas 110, 118 n.2, 119 n.14, 140
Robinson, Peter 5, 14
Romanelli, Sergio 7, 11, 52 n.2, 76
Rosa, Alexandra Assis 12, 28, 72–3, 76, 82, 84 n.1, n.2
Routledge Encyclopedia of Translation Studies 8, 140

Samuel Beckett Digital Manuscript Project 11
Sanskrit 19, 213–21, 223–6, 228 n.5, 229 n.10, n.12, n.14
Saramago, José 8, 27
Schnaiderman, Boris 137–8, 142–3
Scott, Clive 115, 118, 135
Second World War 15, 56, 58, 103 n.9
self-translation 2, 8, 11–12, 14, 16, 18, 20 n.11, 44, 89, 93–6, 103 n.7, n.13, n.14, 181–7, 190 n.6, 191 n.13, n.20
self-translator 4, 103 n.13, 182–4, 187–8, 190 n.9
Seruya, Teresa 136
Shillingsburg, Peter L. 85 n.3, 97
song 13, 55, 60–1, 63–4, 66, 68 n.4, 90
source language 17, 96, 143, 153, 197, 225
    ultimate 72–3
source text 2–4, 10, 12, 15–16, 30–1, 55, 62, 64–7, 71–4, 76, 81–4, 84 n.2, 85 n.4, n.5, 86 n.24, 92, 96, 111–13, 115–16, 118, 141–4, 151, 154, 180, 183, 191 n.13, 199, 214, 219, 221, 223, 226, 229 n.9, 233–4
    de facto 15, 71–2, 74–6, 78–9, 82–4

ultimate 72–3, 82, 84, 86 n.23
Steinbeck, John 18, 164, 170–1, 175
Styron, William 18, 164, 173–4
subjectivity 110, 118 n.2, 226
synonymy 205–6, 210 (*see also* antonymy)

Tanselle, Thomas G. 71, 75, 85 n.6, n.7, 94
target 3, 18, 74, 164–5, 168, 175, 176 n.4, 189, 219, 226
   audience 37, 228
   reader 135, 141–2
   text 71, 73–4, 84, 95–6, 115, 141, 144, 180, 234
target language 17, 36, 60, 72–3, 84 n.2, 85 n.5, 96, 115, 131, 143, 151
   ultimate 72
testimony 7, 14, 16–17, 125, 131, 135–8, 143–4, 149, 152, 216, 225
Text Encoding Initiative (TEI) 16, 98–9
textual 1–8, 11–12, 14–15, 17, 19, 27–31, 34–5, 39 n.2, 43, 67–8, 73–6, 78, 89, 95, 97–8, 102, 104 n.15, 135, 180, 187–8, 190 n.5, 192 n.23, 201, 205–8, 210, 229 n.16, 233–4
   critic 15, 74, 91
   criticism 4, 15, 71, 74–5
   genetics 3, 10 (*see also* genetics)
   scholarship 5, 8–9, 28, 40 n.4, 71, 74, 76, 181
Toury, Gideon 1–3, 19, 35, 71–2, 74, 136, 218
traces 8–9, 16, 27, 43, 72, 75, 99, 101, 109–10, 135, 163, 166, 168, 180, 188–9, 198, 200
transcription 5, 11, 14, 30–1, 34, 52 n.5, 98, 166, 169–70, 197, 210, 211 n.8
translation
   allographic 2, 89–93, 96–101
   biography 124–5, 127–8, 131 (*see also* biography)
   contract 76–7, 82, 85 n.14, n.19
   event 6, 11, 233
   free 140
   genetics 28, 35, 39 (*see also* genetics)
   literal 17, 30, 47, 140, 216, 219, 221, 223, 225, 227–8
   literary 2, 5, 9–10, 13, 43, 46, 58, 125, 148–9, 163, 197, 199, 234
   papers 28

poetry 56, 62–3, 65, 68 n.4, 163 (*see also* poetry)
process 1, 3, 6–7, 10–12, 16–18, 28, 35–6, 43–4, 51, 55, 60, 62, 67, 71, 73, 75–6, 83, 110–11, 114, 123–7, 131–2, 135, 142–5, 149, 152, 168, 197–9, 209, 233–4
pseudo- 11–12
sociology 6
studies 1–9, 11, 14, 17, 19, 27, 35, 39, 74, 84, 102, 110, 123–4, 131, 132 n.1, 135–6, 142, 144, 163–5, 168, 180, 190 n.6, 233
support 73, 82
theory 109, 131–2, 139, 147
translational norms 11, 230 n.17
translator 1–2, 4–12, 15–19, 20 n.9, 27–8, 35–9, 43–4, 46–7, 49, 51, 52 n.7, 55, 61, 63–8, 71–8, 83–4, 90–1, 103 n.7, n.8, n.12, 109–18, 118 n.2, 118–19 n.8, 119 n.14, 123–8, 131–2, 135–45, 147–52, 154–7, 157 n.9, 163–4, 169–70, 174–5, 180, 182, 184, 187–89, 190 n.2, n.4, n.5, n.8, 197–201, 204–5, 210, 213, 219, 227, 229 n.9, 233–4
   literary 112–13, 124, 148–50
translator's
   archive 12–13, 75, 83, 110 (*see also* archive)
   body 109–11, 118 n.2, n.8, 119 n.14 (*see also* corporeality)
   creative process 7, 110, 117
   dictionary 60
   encyclopaedia 60, 67
   papers 15, 71–2
   strategy 16, 82
   workshop 2–3, 11
Translators Writing, Writing Translators (Françoise Massardier-Kenney, Brian James Baer and Maria Tymoczko) 110, 118 n.4
translatorship 11, 18
typescript 1–2, 13, 15, 55, 61–7, 93, 95–6, 102 n.3, 165–6, 170–4, 198, 234

unfaithful 224
unfaithfulness 140
untranslatable 4, 92, 158 n.20
untranslatability 4–5

Van Hulle, Dirk 2–5, 8, 11, 28, 31, 72, 74, 83, 92, 97
  Manuscript Genetics: Joyce's Know-how, Beckett's Nohow 11
variant 5, 27, 43–5, 47–51, 61, 91–2, 96–7, 99
variante d'écriture 201 (*see also* immediate correction)
variante de lecture 201 (*see also* non-immediate correction)
variation 2, 20 n.7, 37, 89, 94, 97, 102 n.1, 167–8, 173, 176 n.4, 229 n.16
  rhythmic 94
Vasconcelos Abreu, Guilherme de 19, 213–19, 221, 223–8, 228 n.3, n.5, 229 n.9, n.14, n.15, n.17
Venuti, Lawrence 6, 144, 150, 157 n.6
  Translator's Invisibility, The 6, 144
version 1, 3–4, 6, 11, 14–16, 20 n.7, 29–30, 35–6, 38, 43, 45, 49–50, 52, 61, 66–7, 71–2, 74–83, 85 n.7, n.12, 86 n.23, 91, 93–100, 102 n.1, n.2, 103 n.9, n.11, n.14, 104 n.15, 118 n.3, 137, 142–3, 148, 152, 164–7, 169–70, 174, 176 n.4, n.9, 183, 185, 187, 198, 206–7, 220, 225
Versioning Machine 16, 98–9, 104 n.17, n.18

Villa, Kyllikki 15, 71, 75–83, 85 n.13, n.14, n.15, n.16, n.18, n.19, n.21, 86 n.22
witness 7, 14, 31, 35, 93, 96, 99–101, 104 n.15
  authorial 2, 89, 97–9
writing 5–6, 10–11, 14, 17, 19, 29, 31, 35–7, 39, 55, 62–3, 68, 76, 94, 96, 110–12, 115, 118, 118 n.2, 120 n.22, 129, 147–51, 156–7, 182, 191 n.10, n.14, n.22, 197–210, 210 n.1, 225–6
  academic 11, 18, 180, 184, 187–8, 191 n.14, n.18
  authorial 4
  planned 197–8 (*see also écriture à programme*)
  praxis 11
  process 1–2, 5–6, 11, 13–14, 18, 31, 45, 96, 112, 117, 180, 188, 197, 199, 201, 203–4, 208, 234
  in process 197–8, 200, 204 (*see also écriture à processus*)
  programmed 198, 200
  second-language 182, 184–5, 191 n.19
  speed 19, 204–5, 209–10
  stage 32, 93, 205, 208–10
  translatorial 4, 18